11

S0-ABD-058

GETBACKERS

GETBACKERS

Volume 11

Art by Rando Ayamine
Story by Yuya Aoki

TOKYOPOP®

HAMBURG // LONDON // LOS ANGELES // TOKYO

GetBackers Vol. 11
Written by Yuya Aoki
Illustrated by Rando Ayamine

Translation - Alexis Kirsch
English Adaptation - Ryan Shankel
Associate Editor - Peter Ahlstrom
Retouch and Lettering - Derron Bennett
Production Artist - Jose Macasocol, Jr.
Cover Artist - Kyle Plummer

Editor - Aaron Suhr
Digital Imaging Manager - Chris Buford
Production Managers - Jennifer Miller and Mutsumi Miyazaki
Managing Editor - Jill Freshney
VP of Production - Ron Klamert
Publisher and E.I.C. - Mike Kiley
President and C.O.O. - John Parker
C.E.O. - Stuart Levy

 A TOKYOPOP® Manga

TOKYOPOP Inc.
5900 Wilshire Blvd. Suite 2000
Los Angeles, CA 90036

E-mail: info@TOKYOPOP.com
Come visit us online at www.TOKYOPOP.com

ISBN: 1-59182-973-9

First TOKYOPOP printing: August 2005
10 9 8 7 6 5 4 3 2 1
Printed in Canada

Story Thus Far:

Ginji Amano can amplify and control electromagnetic waves. Ban Mido has the power to create illusions in people's minds for one minute. Together they are the GetBackers, a retrieval agency whose motto is "We get back what shouldn't be gone." For the right price, they'll recover anything that's been taken.

Thanks to a faked Evil Eye by Ban, the GetBackers and their friends have defeated boy genius MakubeX and his plan to use a nuclear bomb to convince the "God" of Infinity Fortress to reset the system. They've also discovered one of the secrets behind the Fortress' strange world—that a large number of its inhabitants are actually virtual creations that seem real due to the Fortress' electromagnetic waves interfacing directly with everyone else's brains!

Metaphysical considerations aside, all that's left now for the GetBackers is to retrieve the item they were hired for in the first place, "I.L.," MakubeX's implosion lens atomic bomb component. Though MakubeX seems to be cooperating, will he have any more tricks up his sleeves before handing it over? And is the injury Ban got while faking the Evil Eye bothering him more than he lets on?

Ya caught up? Then here we go.

Table of Contents

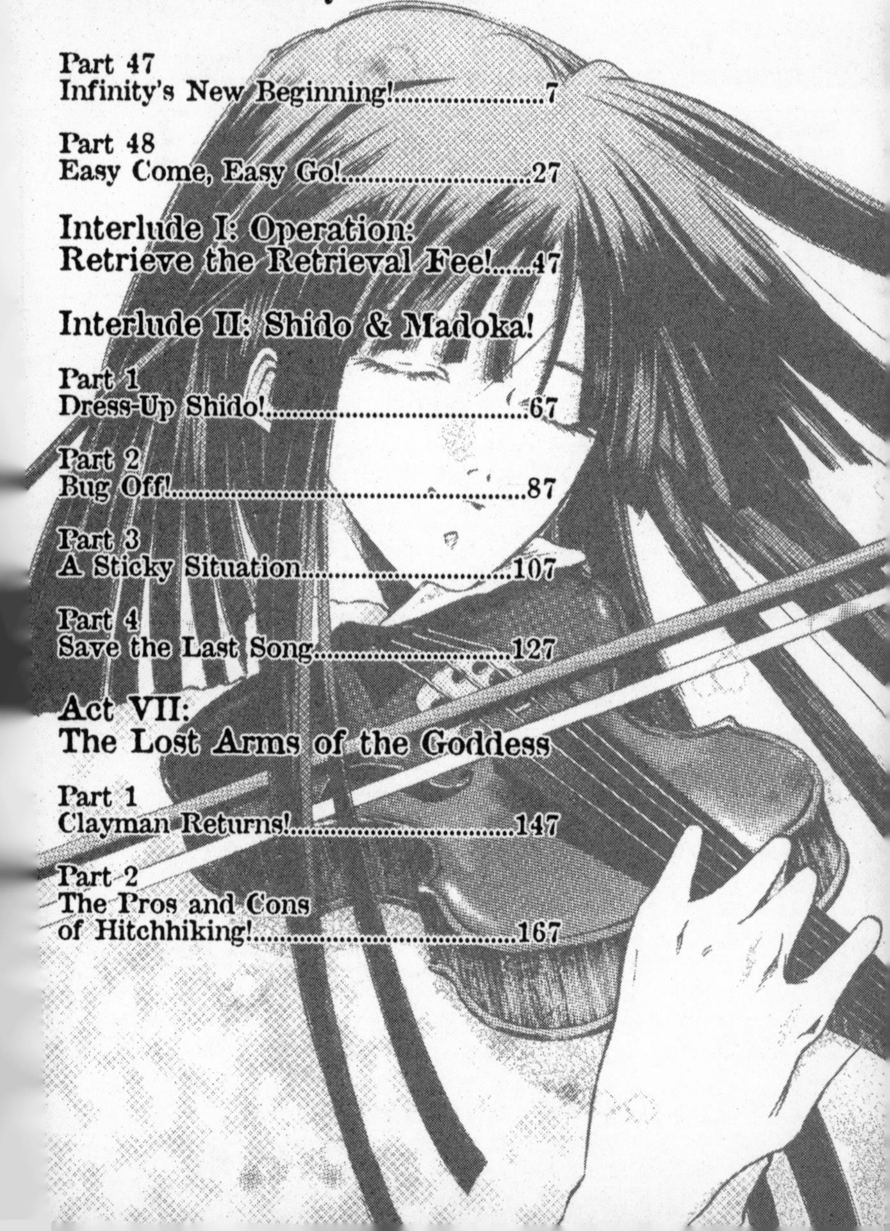

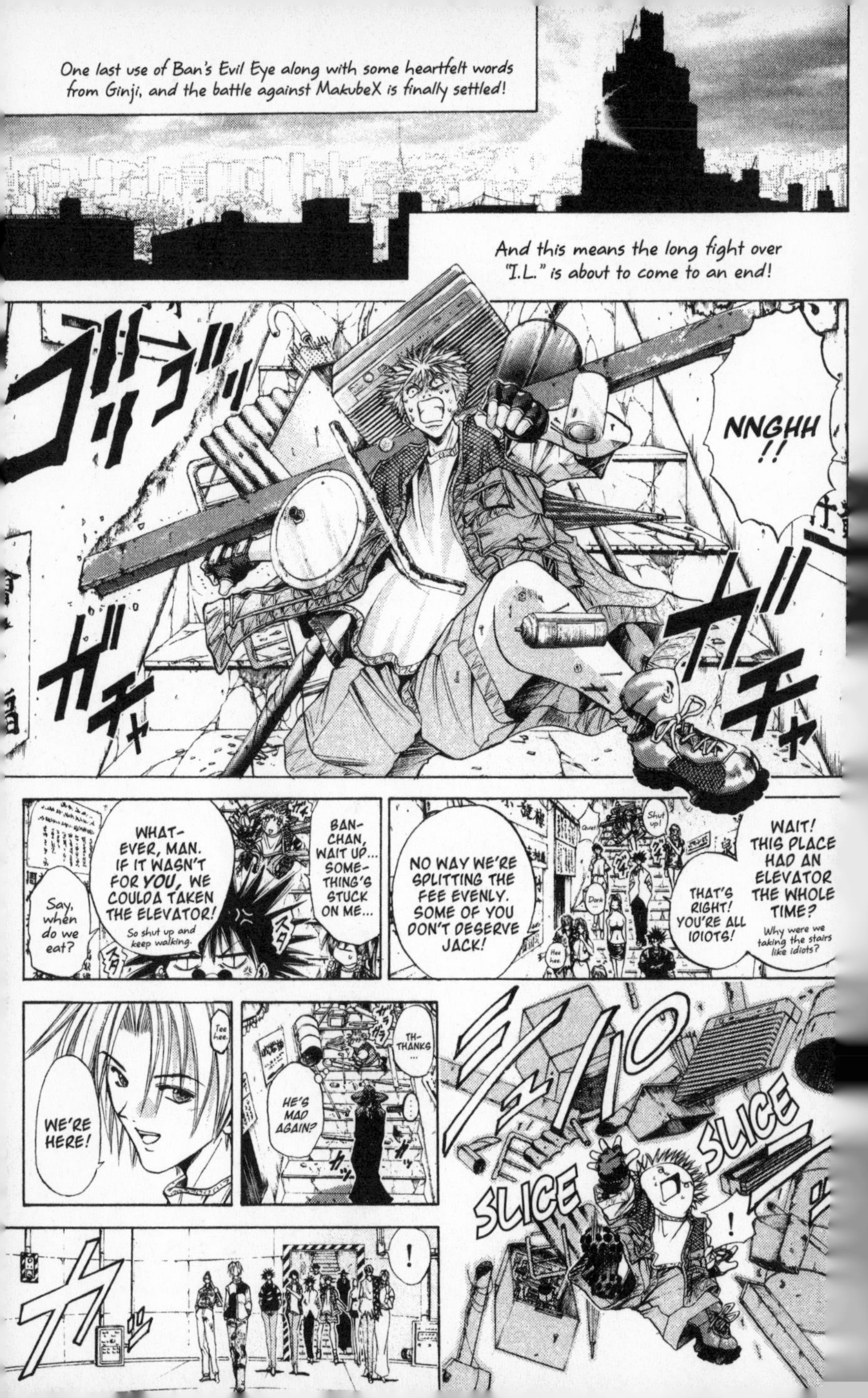
One last use of Ban's Evil Eye along with some heartfelt words from Ginji, and the battle against MakubeX is finally settled!
And this means the long fight over "I.L." is about to come to an end!
NNGHH !!
WAIT! THIS PLACE HAD AN ELEVATOR THE WHOLE TIME?
Why were we taking the stairs like idiots?
Shut up!
THAT'S RIGHT! YOU'RE ALL IDIOTS!
Dork...
Hee hee.
NO WAY WE'RE SPLITTING THE FEE EVENLY. SOME OF YOU DON'T DESERVE JACK!
BAN-CHAN, WAIT UP... SOME-THING'S STUCK ON ME...
WHAT-EVER, MAN. IF IT WASN'T FOR YOU, WE COULDA TAKEN THE ELEVATOR!
So shut up and keep walking.
Say, when do we eat?
SLICE
SLICE
!
TH-THANKS...
HE'S MAD AGAIN?
...
Tee hee.
WE'RE HERE!
!

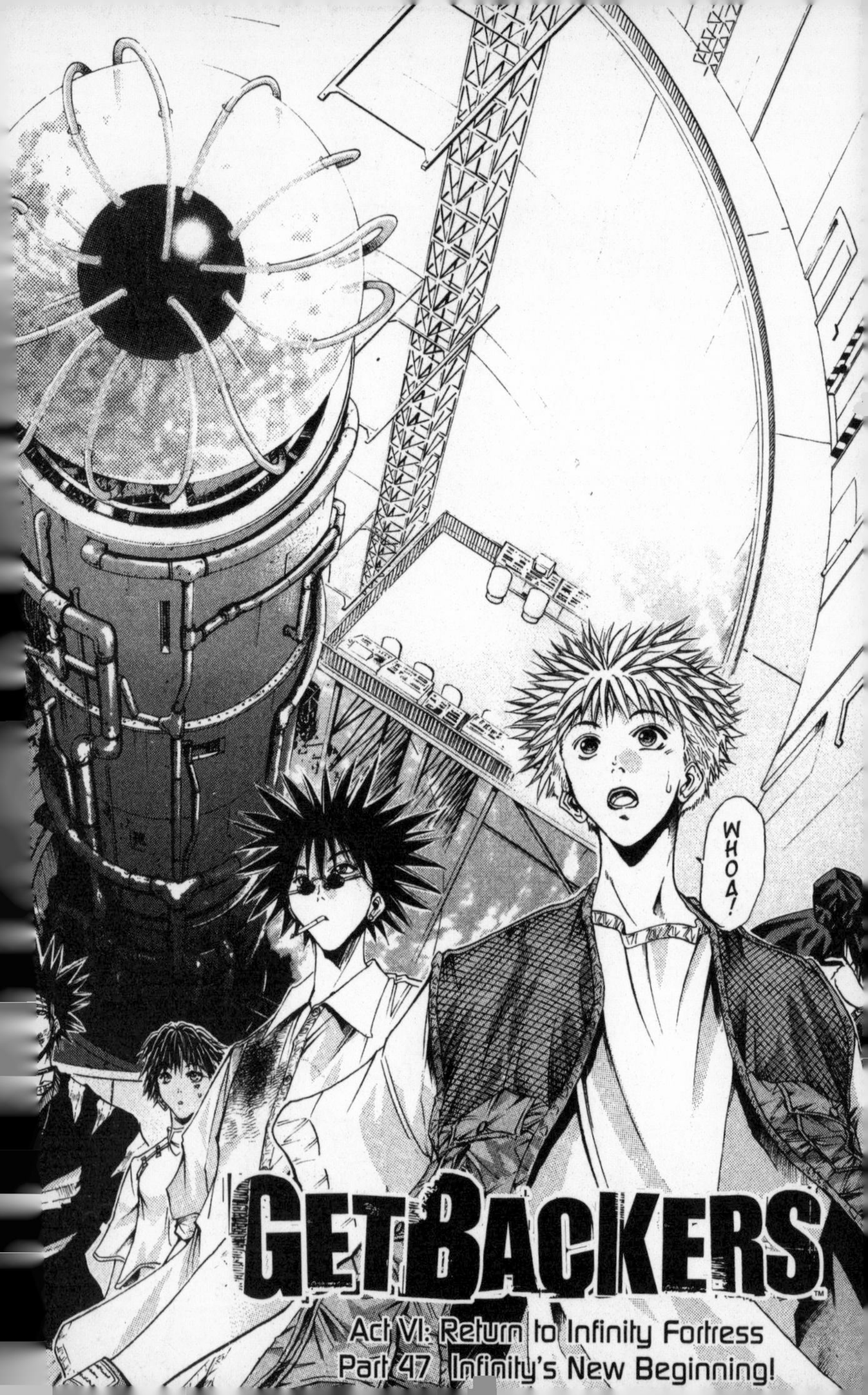
WHOA!
GETBACKERS™
Act VI: Return to Infinity Fortress
Part 47 Infinity's New Beginning!

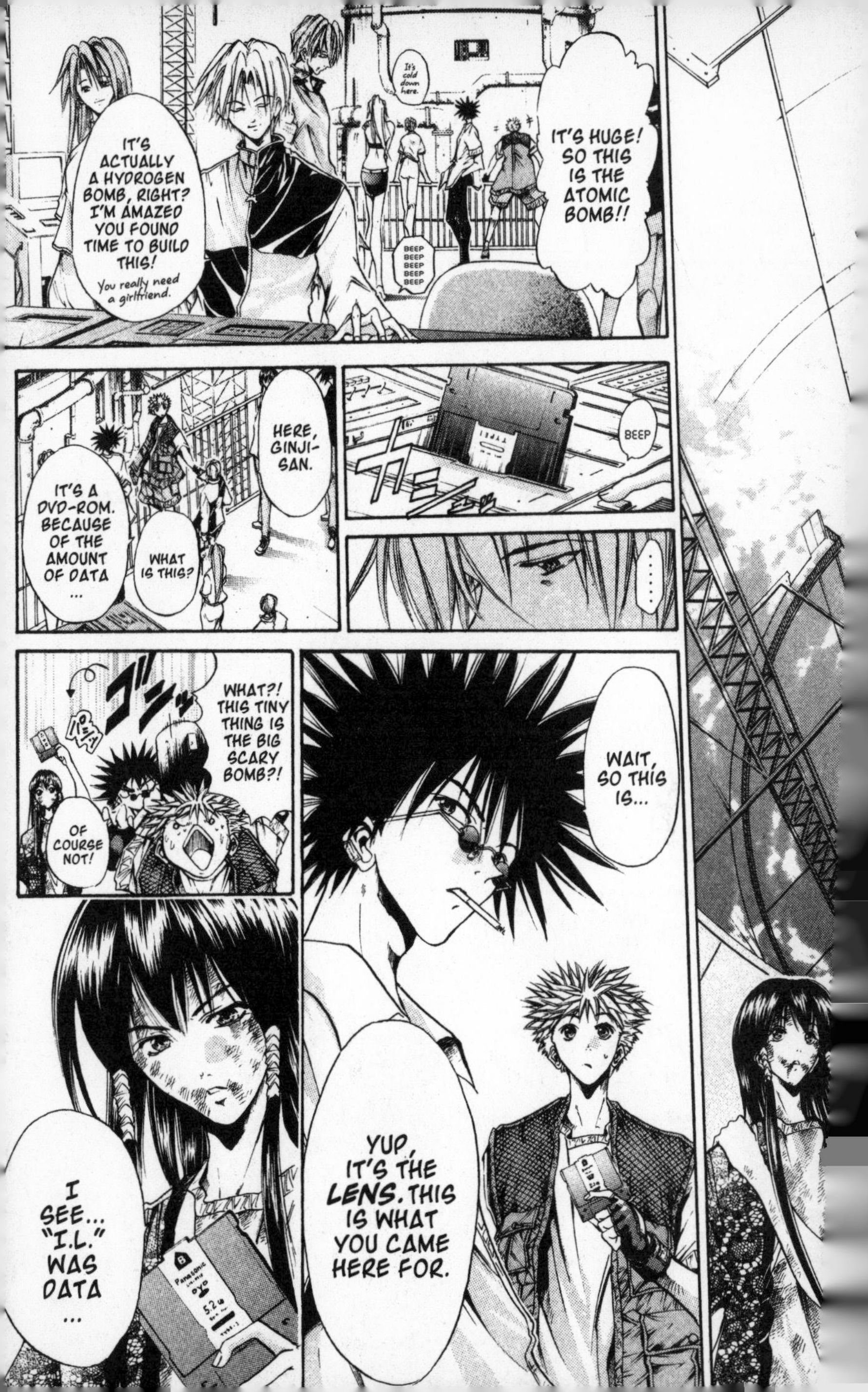
IT'S HUGE! SO THIS IS THE ATOMIC BOMB!!
It's cold down here.
BEEP BEEP BEEP BEEP BEEP
IT'S ACTUALLY A HYDROGEN BOMB, RIGHT? I'M AMAZED YOU FOUND TIME TO BUILD THIS!
You really need a girlfriend.
BEEP
......
HERE, GINJI-SAN.
WHAT IS THIS?
IT'S A DVD-ROM. BECAUSE OF THE AMOUNT OF DATA ...
WAIT, SO THIS IS...
YUP, IT'S THE LENS. THIS IS WHAT YOU CAME HERE FOR.
WHAT?! THIS TINY THING IS THE BIG SCARY BOMB?!
OF COURSE NOT!
I SEE... "I.L." WAS DATA ...

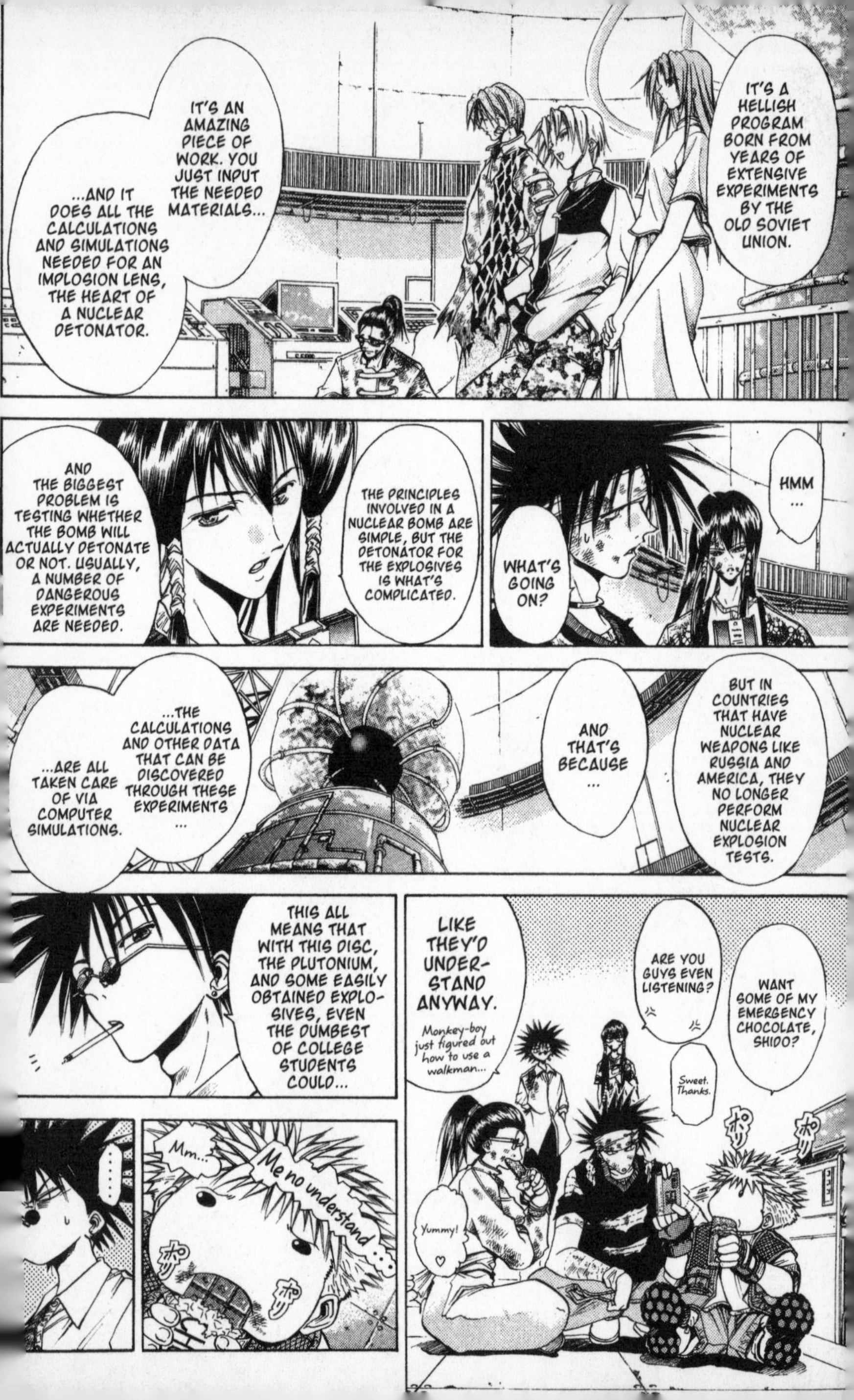

IT'S A HELLISH PROGRAM BORN FROM YEARS OF EXTENSIVE EXPERIMENTS BY THE OLD SOVIET UNION.
IT'S AN AMAZING PIECE OF WORK. YOU JUST INPUT THE NEEDED MATERIALS...
...AND IT DOES ALL THE CALCULATIONS AND SIMULATIONS NEEDED FOR AN IMPLOSION LENS, THE HEART OF A NUCLEAR DETONATOR.
HMM ...
WHAT'S GOING ON?
THE PRINCIPLES INVOLVED IN A NUCLEAR BOMB ARE SIMPLE, BUT THE DETONATOR FOR THE EXPLOSIVES IS WHAT'S COMPLICATED.
AND THE BIGGEST PROBLEM IS TESTING WHETHER THE BOMB WILL ACTUALLY DETONATE OR NOT. USUALLY, A NUMBER OF DANGEROUS EXPERIMENTS ARE NEEDED.
BUT IN COUNTRIES THAT HAVE NUCLEAR WEAPONS LIKE RUSSIA AND AMERICA, THEY NO LONGER PERFORM NUCLEAR EXPLOSION TESTS.
AND THAT'S BECAUSE ...
...THE CALCULATIONS AND OTHER DATA THAT CAN BE DISCOVERED THROUGH THESE EXPERIMENTS ...
...ARE ALL TAKEN CARE OF VIA COMPUTER SIMULATIONS.
WANT SOME OF MY EMERGENCY CHOCOLATE, SHIDO?
ポリ ポリ
ARE YOU GUYS EVEN LISTENING?
Sweet. Thanks.
LIKE THEY'D UNDER-STAND ANYWAY.
Monkey-boy just figured out how to use a walkman...
Yummy!
THIS ALL MEANS THAT WITH THIS DISC, THE PLUTONIUM, AND SOME EASILY OBTAINED EXPLO-SIVES, EVEN THE DUMBEST OF COLLEGE STUDENTS COULD...
Mm...
Me no understand...
ポリ ポリ
......

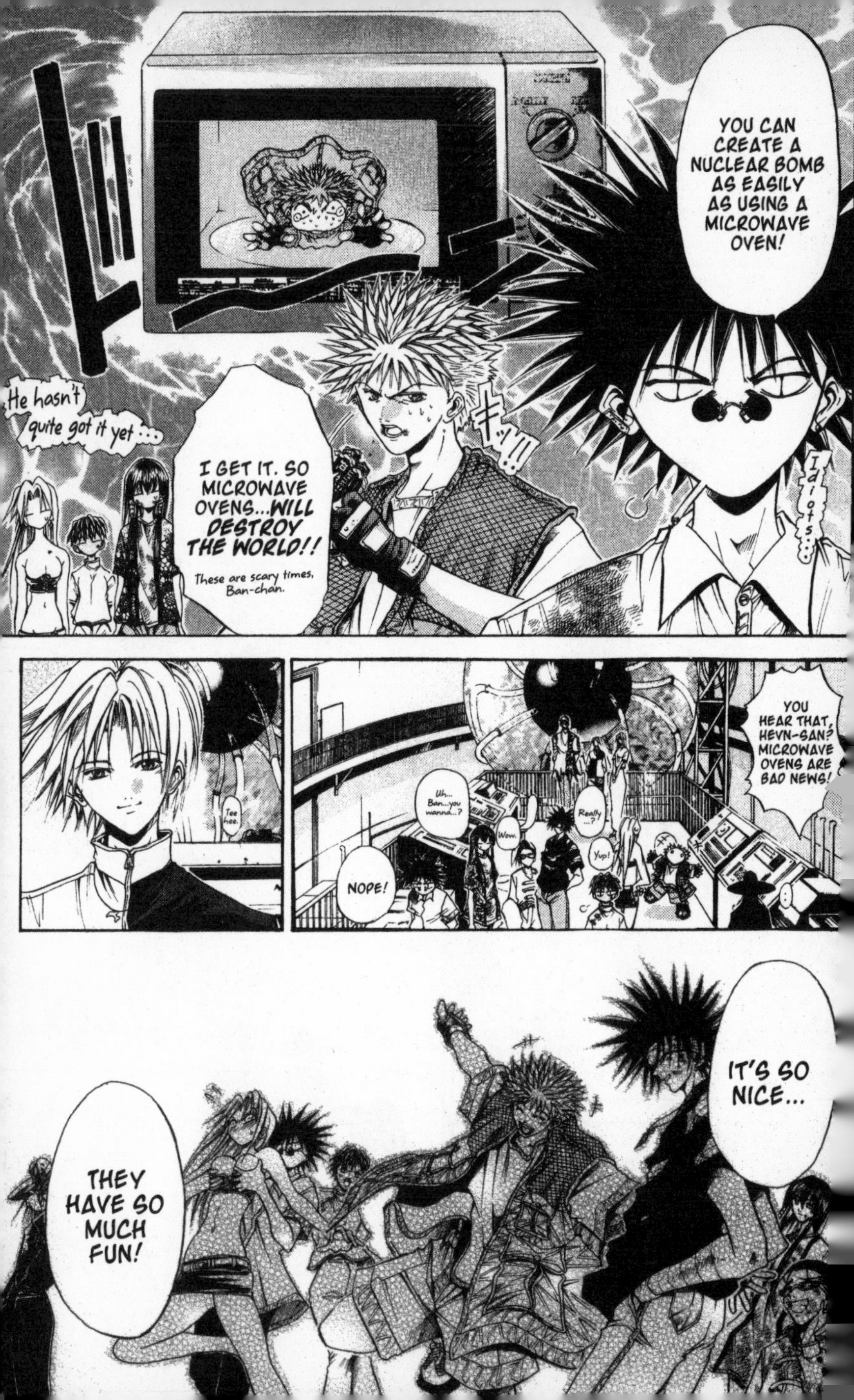
YOU CAN CREATE A NUCLEAR BOMB AS EASILY AS USING A MICROWAVE OVEN!
Idiots...
I GET IT. SO MICROWAVE OVENS...WILL DESTROY THE WORLD!!
These are scary times, Ban-chan.
He hasn't quite got it yet...
YOU HEAR THAT, HEVN-SAN? MICROWAVE OVENS ARE BAD NEWS!
Really ...?
Yup!
Wow.
Uh... Ban...you wanna...?
NOPE!
...
Tee hee.
IT'S SO NICE...
THEY HAVE SO MUCH FUN!

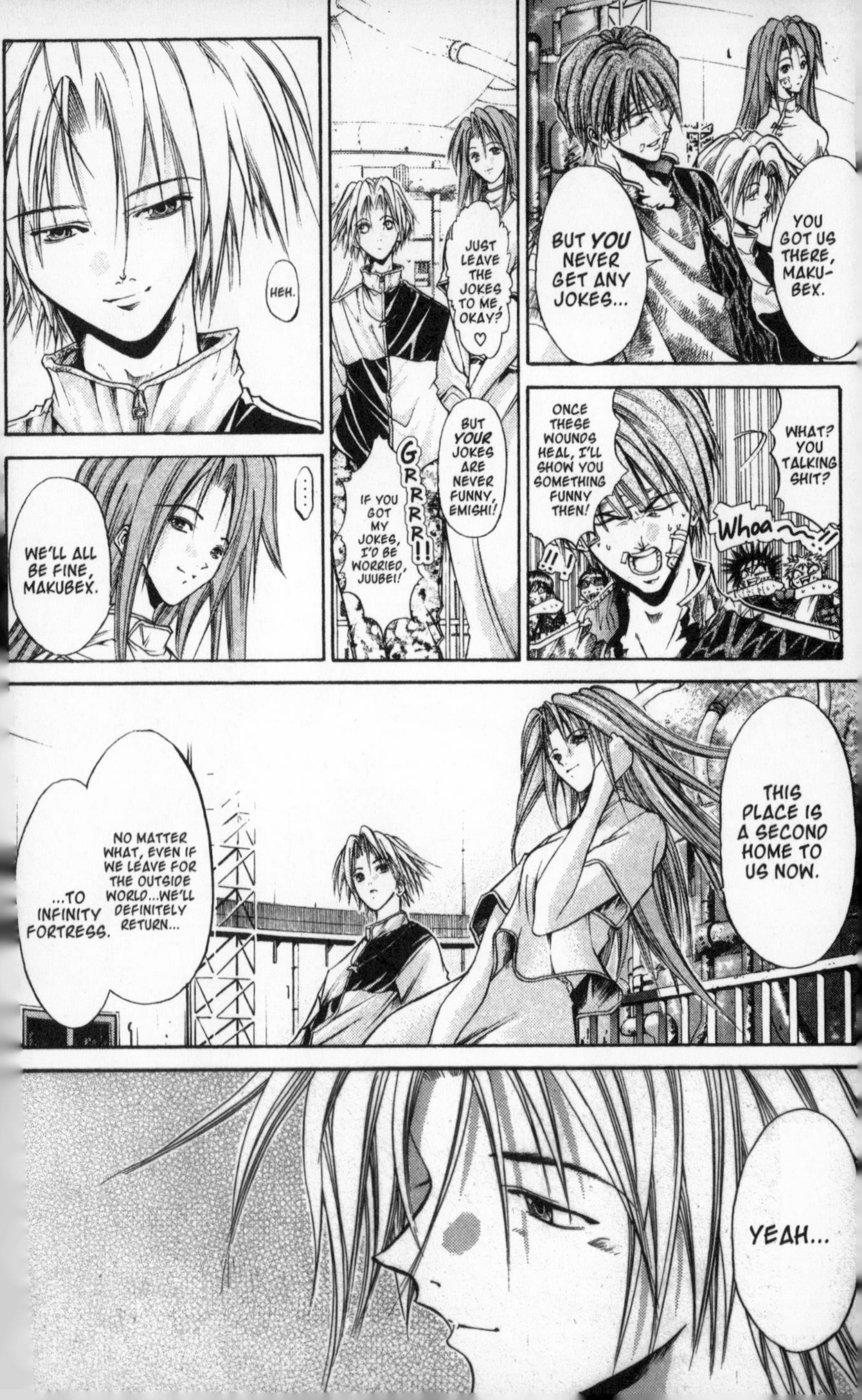
YOU GOT US THERE, MAKU-BEX.
BUT *YOU* NEVER GET ANY JOKES...
WHAT? YOU TALKING SHIT?
ONCE THESE WOUNDS HEAL, I'LL SHOW YOU SOMETHING FUNNY THEN!
Whoa~!!
JUST LEAVE THE JOKES TO ME, OKAY? ♡
BUT *YOUR* JOKES ARE NEVER FUNNY, EMISHI!
GRRRR!!
IF YOU GOT MY JOKES, I'D BE WORRIED, JUUBEI!
HEH.
...
WE'LL ALL BE FINE, MAKUBEX.
THIS PLACE IS A SECOND HOME TO US NOW.
NO MATTER WHAT, EVEN IF WE LEAVE FOR THE OUTSIDE WORLD...WE'LL DEFINITELY RETURN...
...TO INFINITY FORTRESS.
YEAH...

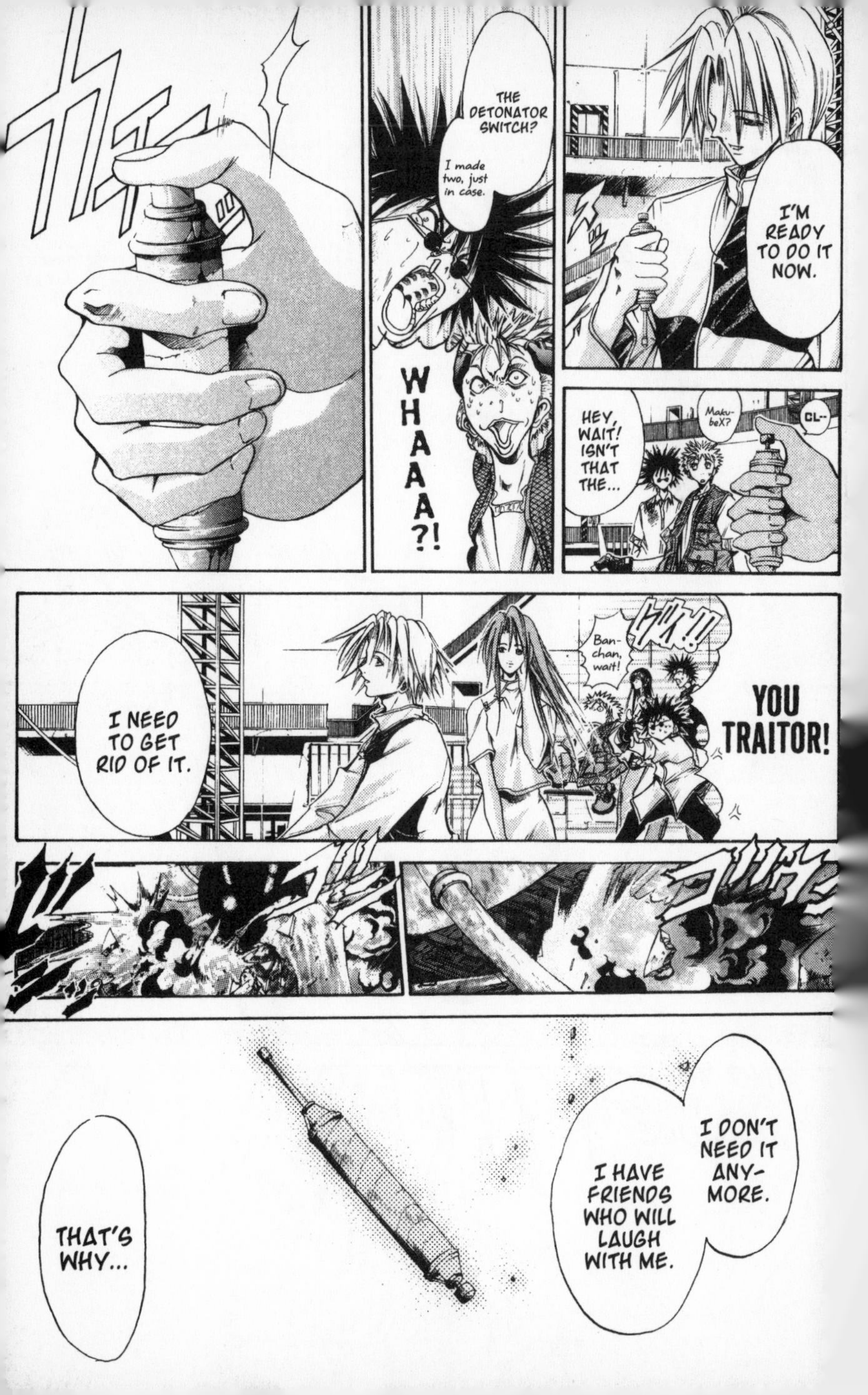
I'M READY TO DO IT NOW.
HEY, WAIT! ISN'T THAT THE...
Maku-beX?
CL--
THE DETONATOR SWITCH?
I made two, just in case.
WHAAAA?!
Ban-chan, wait!
YOU TRAITOR!
I NEED TO GET RID OF IT.
I DON'T NEED IT ANYMORE.
I HAVE FRIENDS WHO WILL LAUGH WITH ME.
THAT'S WHY...

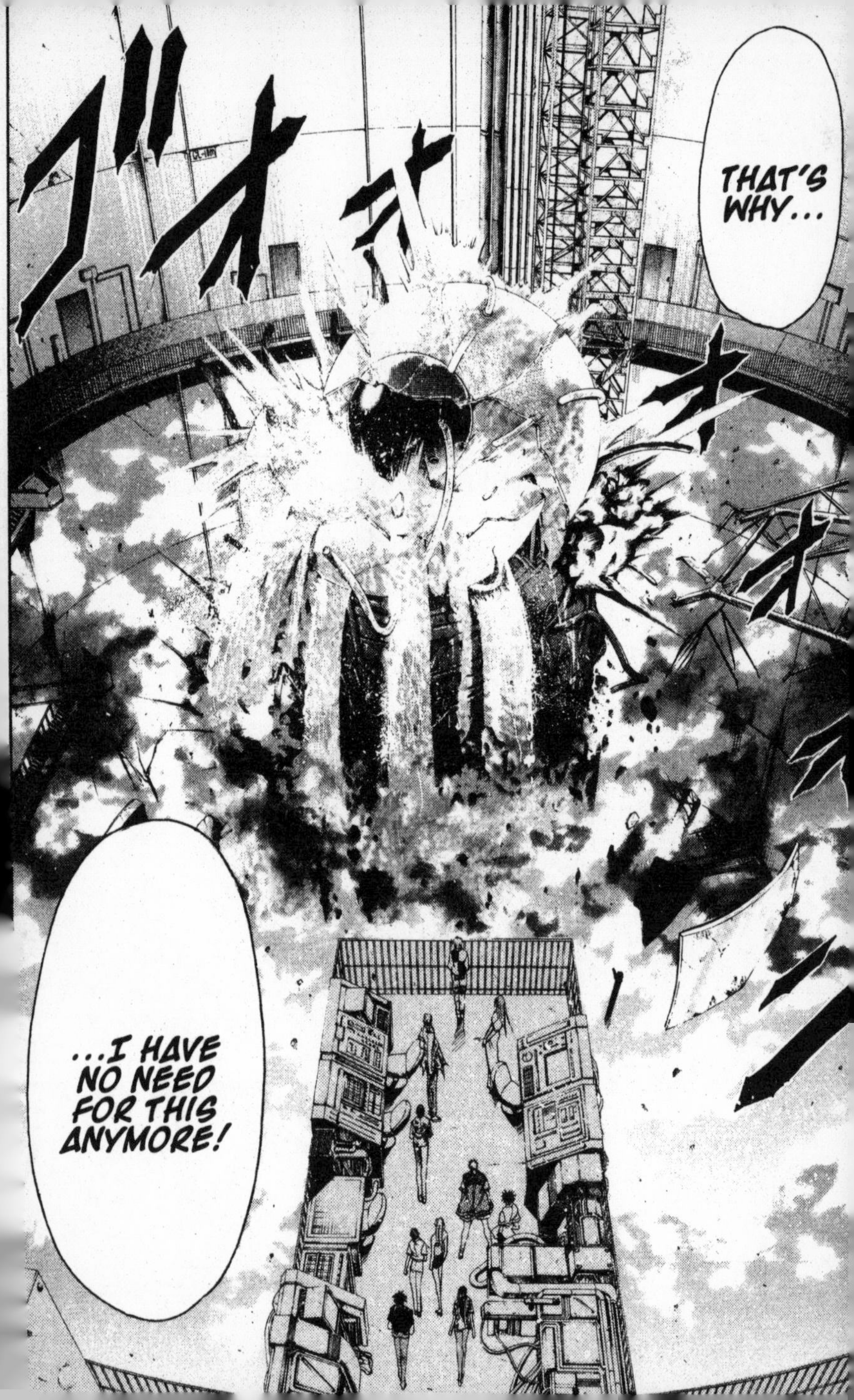
THAT'S WHY...
...I HAVE NO NEED FOR THIS ANYMORE!

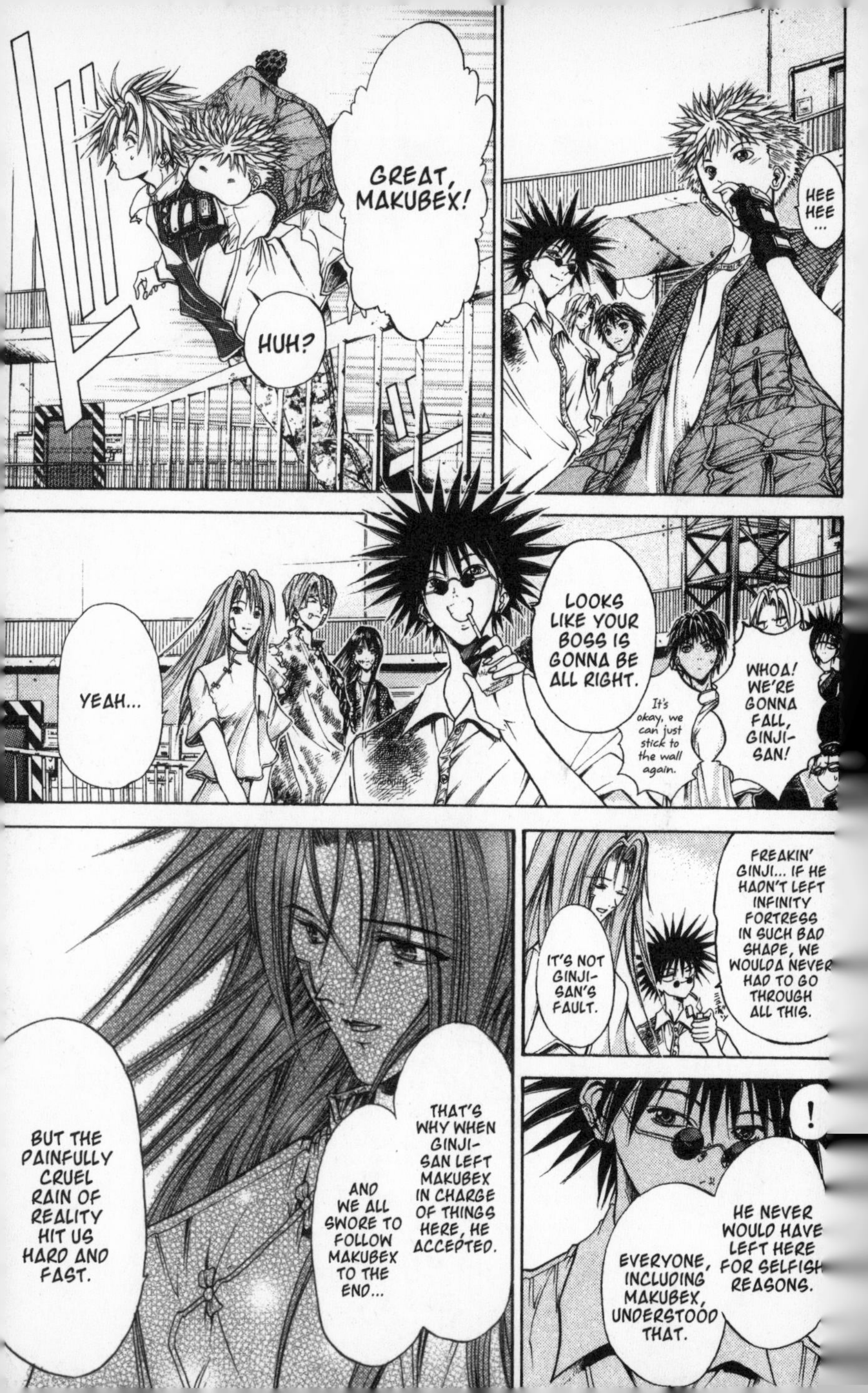
HEE HEE ...
GREAT, MAKUBEX!
HUH?
WHOA! WE'RE GONNA FALL, GINJI-SAN!
It's okay, we can just stick to the wall again.
LOOKS LIKE YOUR BOSS IS GONNA BE ALL RIGHT.
YEAH...
FREAKIN' GINJI... IF HE HADN'T LEFT INFINITY FORTRESS IN SUCH BAD SHAPE, WE WOULDA NEVER HAD TO GO THROUGH ALL THIS.
IT'S NOT GINJI-SAN'S FAULT.
!
HE NEVER WOULD HAVE LEFT HERE FOR SELFISH REASONS.
EVERYONE, INCLUDING MAKUBEX, UNDERSTOOD THAT.
THAT'S WHY WHEN GINJI-SAN LEFT MAKUBEX IN CHARGE OF THINGS HERE, HE ACCEPTED.
AND WE ALL SWORE TO FOLLOW MAKUBEX TO THE END...
BUT THE PAINFULLY CRUEL RAIN OF REALITY HIT US HARD AND FAST.

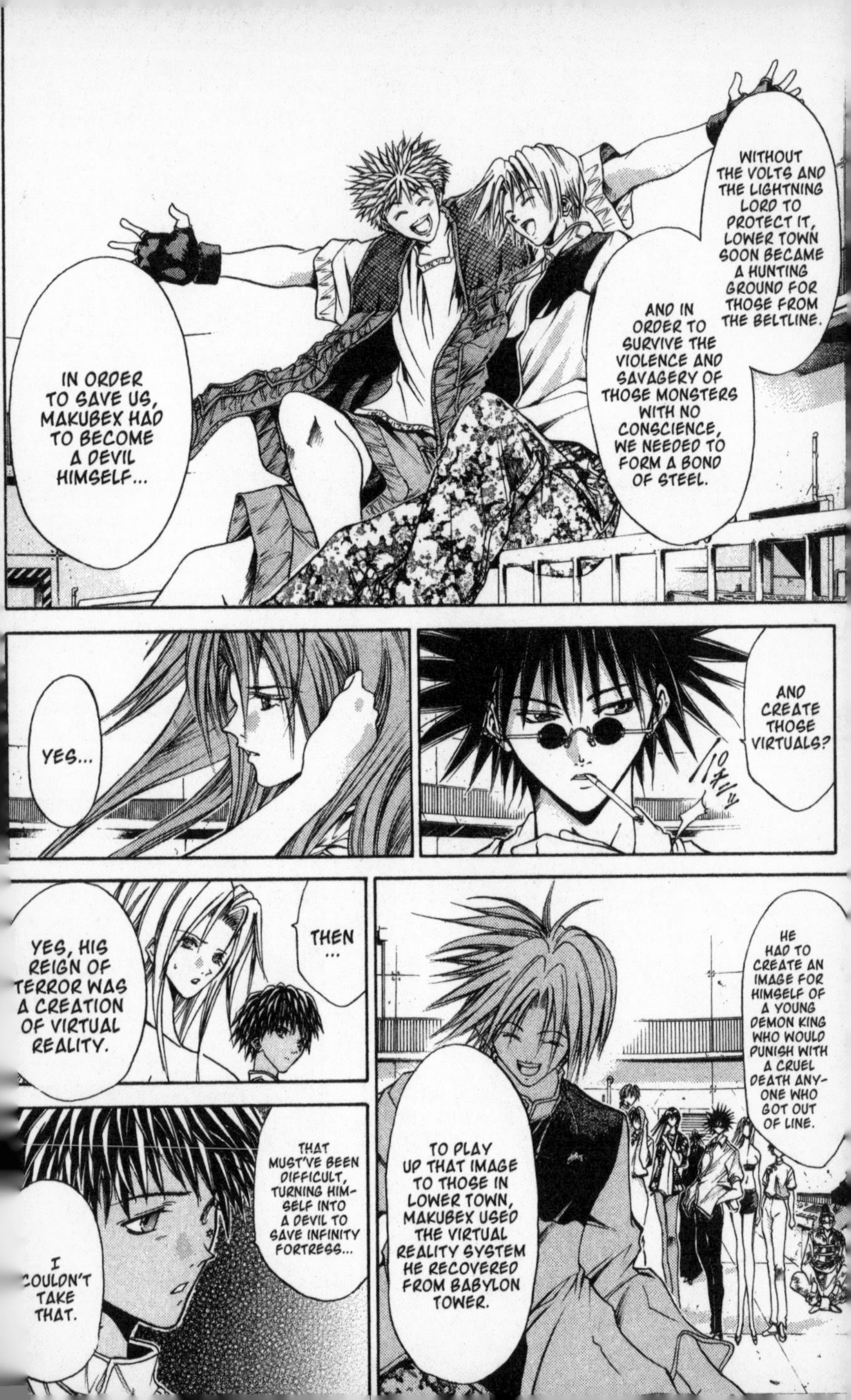
WITHOUT THE VOLTS AND THE LIGHTNING LORD TO PROTECT IT, LOWER TOWN SOON BECAME A HUNTING GROUND FOR THOSE FROM THE BELTLINE.
AND IN ORDER TO SURVIVE THE VIOLENCE AND SAVAGERY OF THOSE MONSTERS WITH NO CONSCIENCE, WE NEEDED TO FORM A BOND OF STEEL.
IN ORDER TO SAVE US, MAKUBEX HAD TO BECOME A DEVIL HIMSELF...
AND CREATE THOSE VIRTUALS?
YES...
HE HAD TO CREATE AN IMAGE FOR HIMSELF OF A YOUNG DEMON KING WHO WOULD PUNISH WITH A CRUEL DEATH ANYONE WHO GOT OUT OF LINE.
TO PLAY UP THAT IMAGE TO THOSE IN LOWER TOWN, MAKUBEX USED THE VIRTUAL REALITY SYSTEM HE RECOVERED FROM BABYLON TOWER.
THEN ...
YES, HIS REIGN OF TERROR WAS A CREATION OF VIRTUAL REALITY.
THAT MUST'VE BEEN DIFFICULT, TURNING HIMSELF INTO A DEVIL TO SAVE INFINITY FORTRESS...
I COULDN'T TAKE THAT.

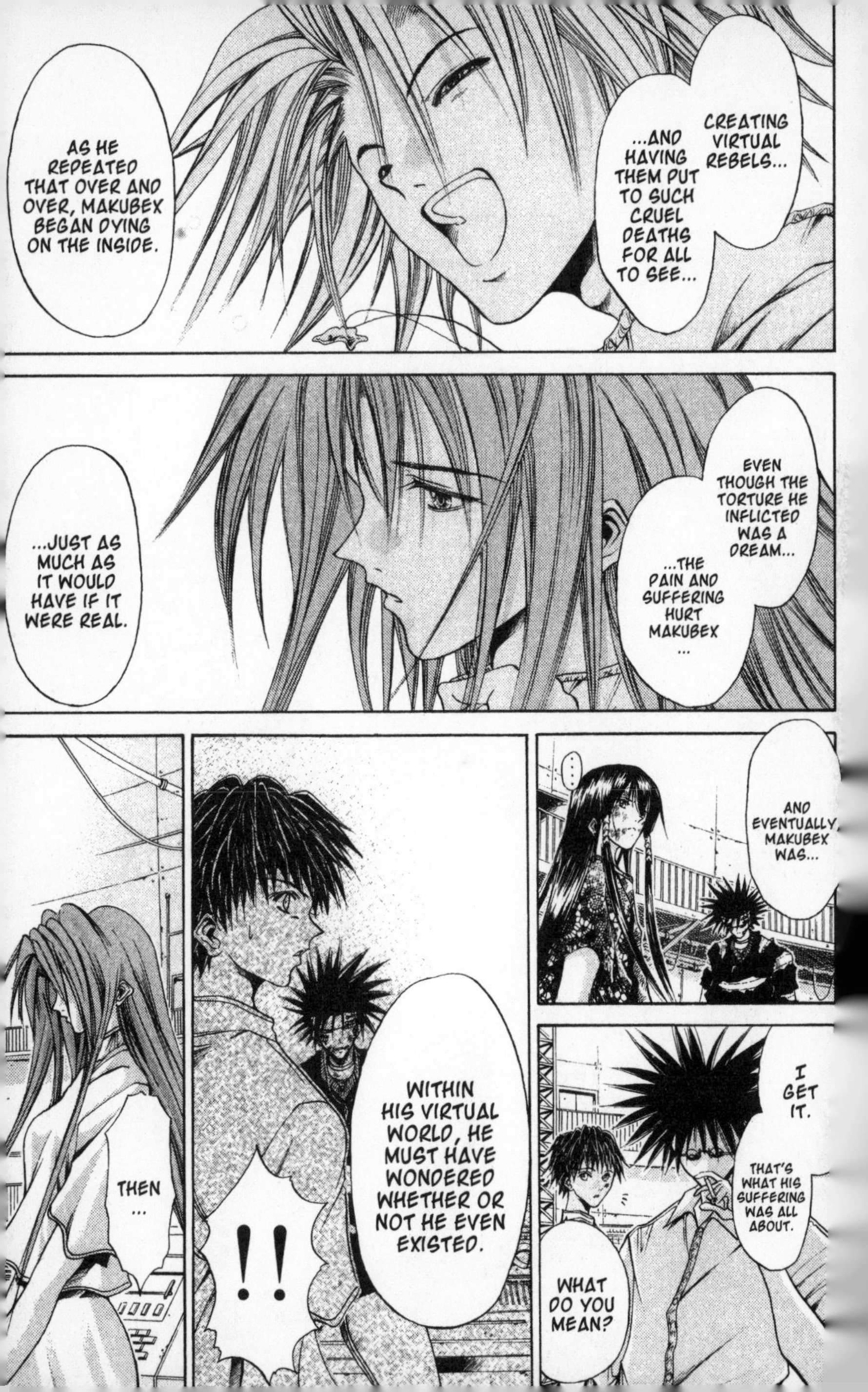
CREATING VIRTUAL REBELS...
...AND HAVING THEM PUT TO SUCH CRUEL DEATHS FOR ALL TO SEE...
AS HE REPEATED THAT OVER AND OVER, MAKUBEX BEGAN DYING ON THE INSIDE.
EVEN THOUGH THE TORTURE HE INFLICTED WAS A DREAM...
...THE PAIN AND SUFFERING HURT MAKUBEX ...
...JUST AS MUCH AS IT WOULD HAVE IF IT WERE REAL.
AND EVENTUALLY MAKUBEX WAS...
...
I GET IT.
THAT'S WHAT HIS SUFFERING WAS ALL ABOUT.
WHAT DO YOU MEAN?
WITHIN HIS VIRTUAL WORLD, HE MUST HAVE WONDERED WHETHER OR NOT HE EVEN EXISTED.
!!
THEN ...

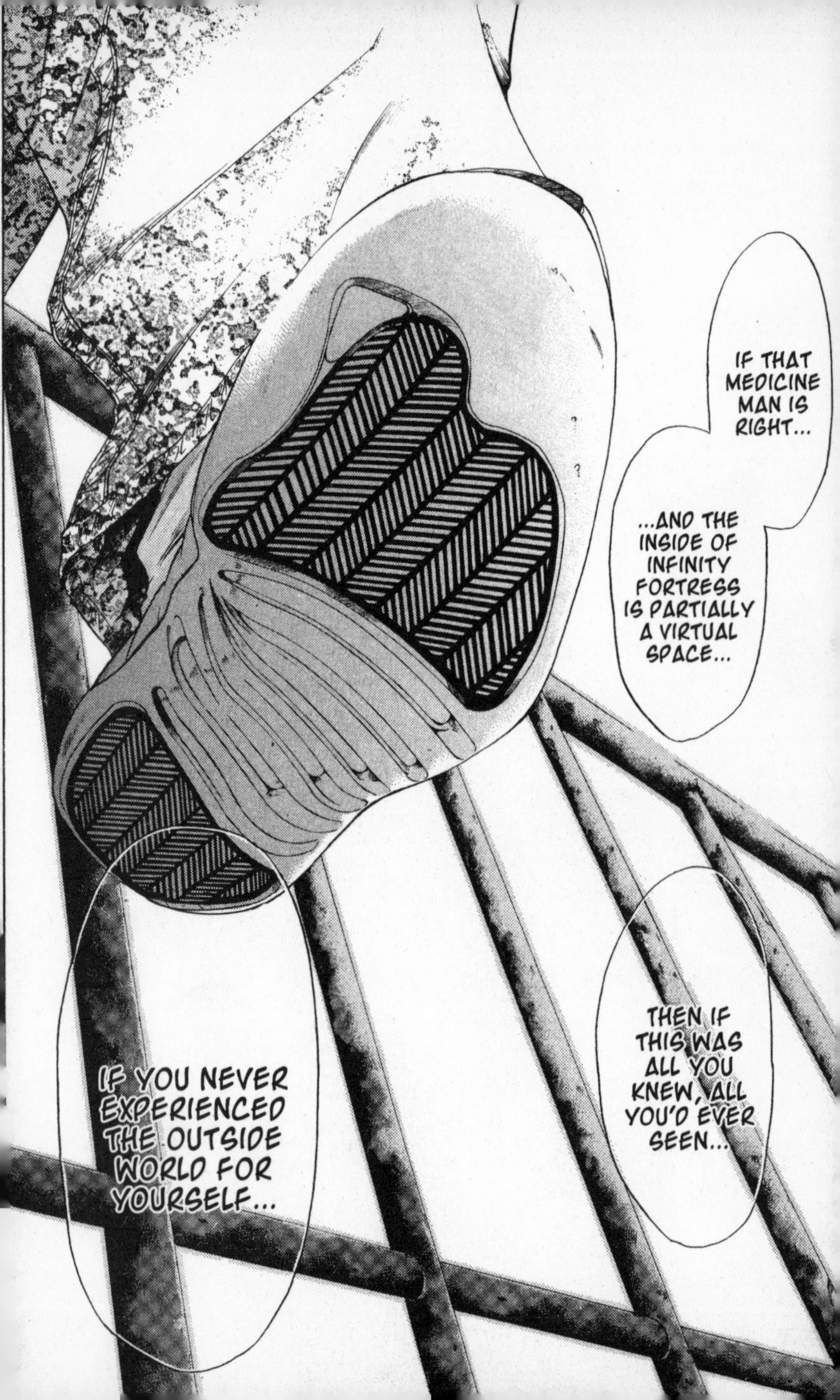
IF THAT MEDICINE MAN IS RIGHT...
...AND THE INSIDE OF INFINITY FORTRESS IS PARTIALLY A VIRTUAL SPACE...
THEN IF THIS WAS ALL YOU KNEW, ALL YOU'D EVER SEEN...
IF YOU NEVER EXPERIENCED THE OUTSIDE WORLD FOR YOURSELF...

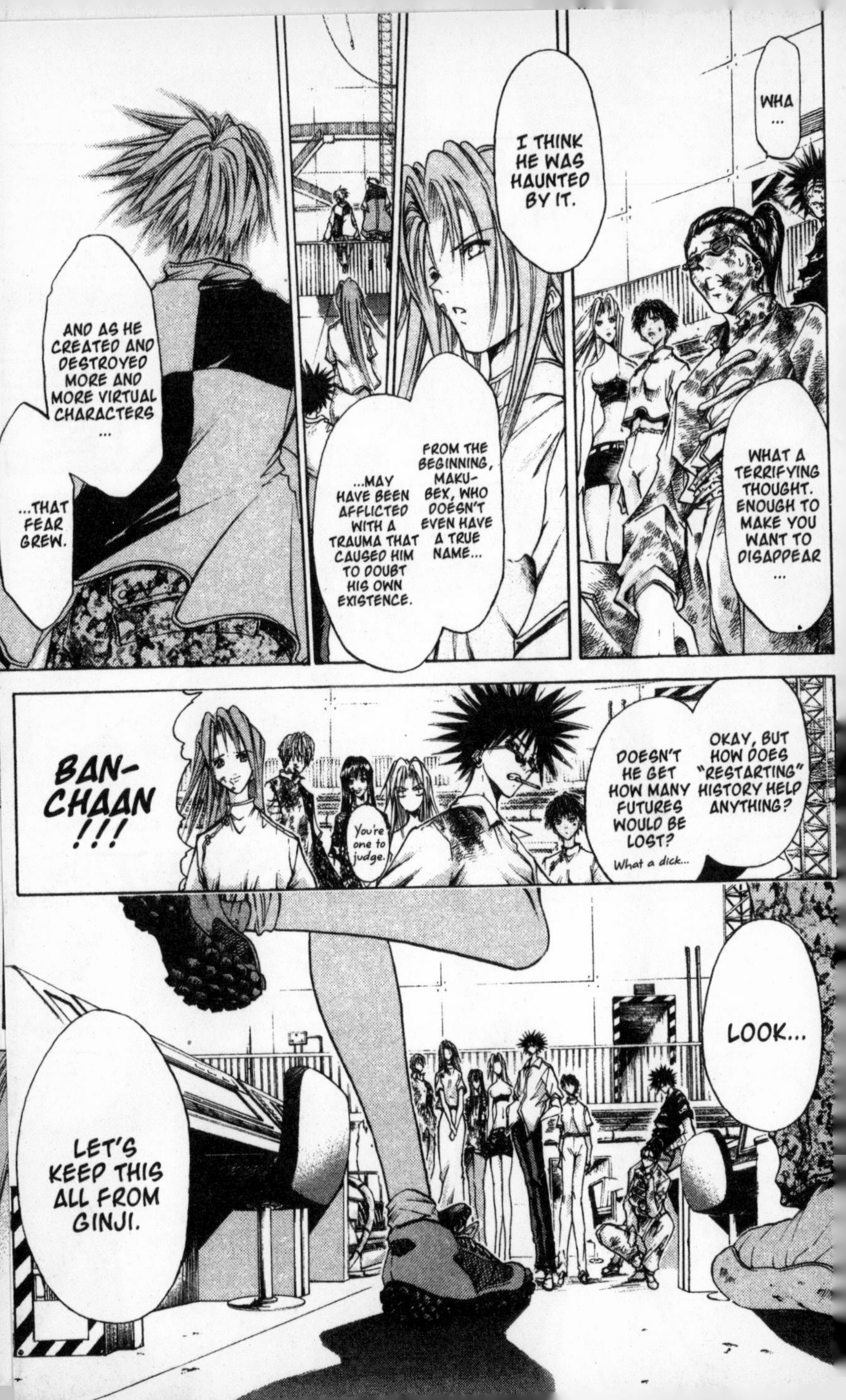
WHA ...
WHAT A TERRIFYING THOUGHT. ENOUGH TO MAKE YOU WANT TO DISAPPEAR ...
I THINK HE WAS HAUNTED BY IT.
FROM THE BEGINNING, MAKU-BEX, WHO DOESN'T EVEN HAVE A TRUE NAME...
...MAY HAVE BEEN AFFLICTED WITH A TRAUMA THAT CAUSED HIM TO DOUBT HIS OWN EXISTENCE.
AND AS HE CREATED AND DESTROYED MORE AND MORE VIRTUAL CHARACTERS ...
...THAT FEAR GREW.
OKAY, BUT HOW DOES "RESTARTING" HISTORY HELP ANYTHING?
DOESN'T HE GET HOW MANY FUTURES WOULD BE LOST?
What a dick...
You're one to judge.
BAN-CHAAN !!!
LOOK...
LET'S KEEP THIS ALL FROM GINJI.

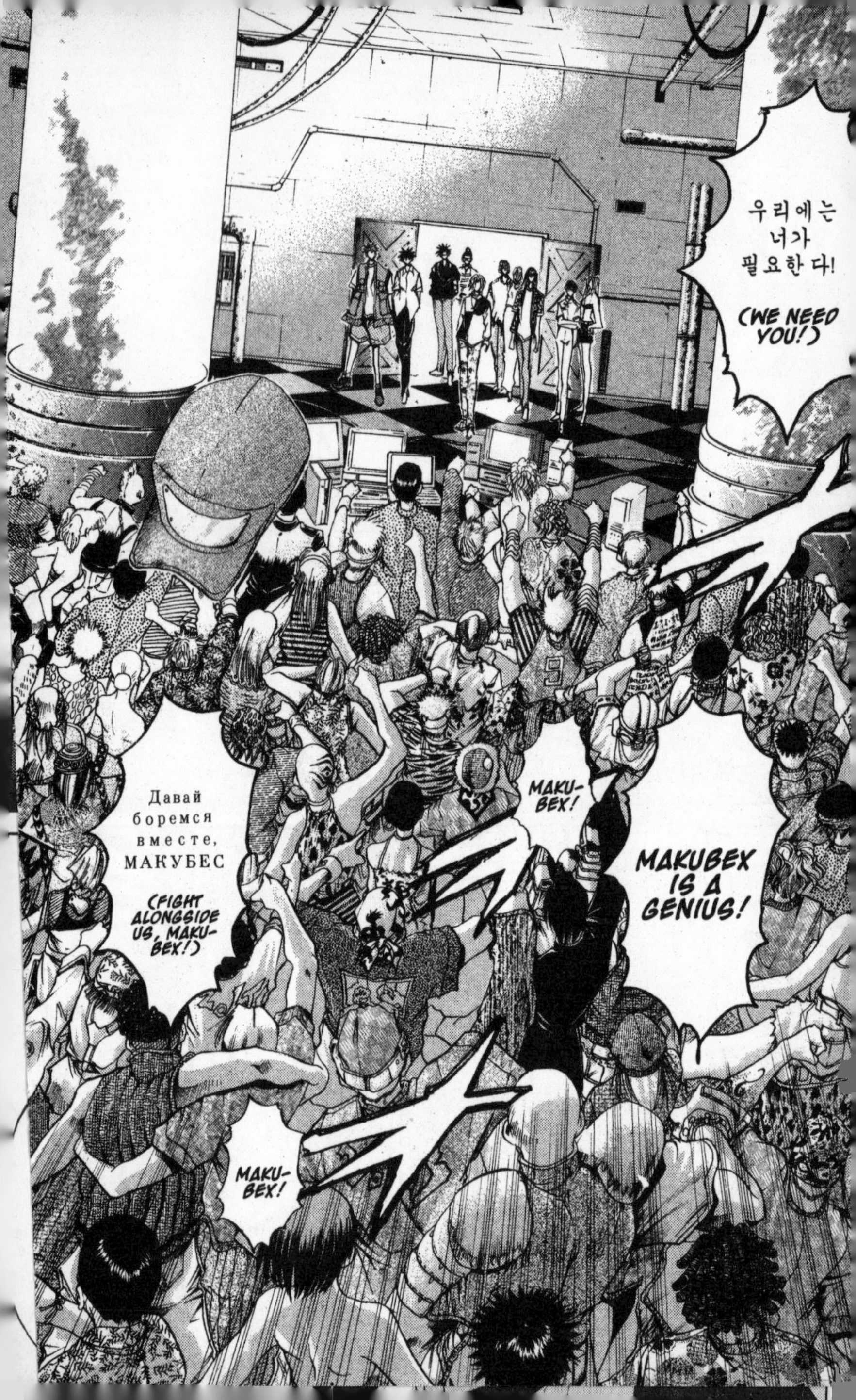
우리에는 너가 필요한 다!
(WE NEED YOU!)
MAKUBEX IS A GENIUS!
MAKU-BEX!
Давай боремся вместе, МАКУБЕС
(FIGHT ALONGSIDE US, MAKU-BEX!)
MAKU-BEX!

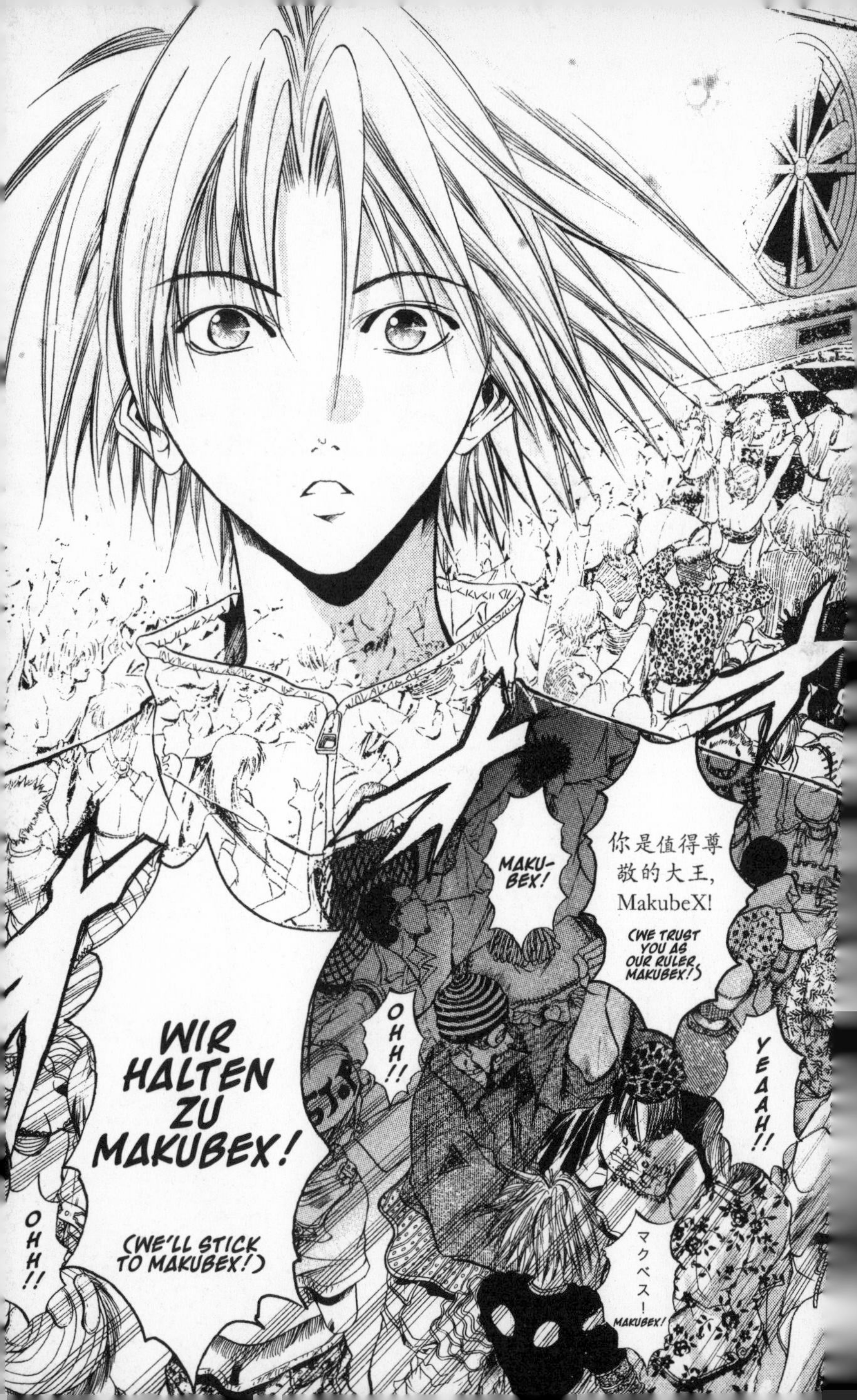
你是值得尊敬的大王, MakubeX!
(WE TRUST YOU AS OUR RULER, MAKUBEX!)
MAKU-BEX!
YEAAH!!
OHH!!
WIR HALTEN ZU MAKUBEX!
(WE'LL STICK TO MAKUBEX!)
マクベス！
MAKUBEX!
OHH!!

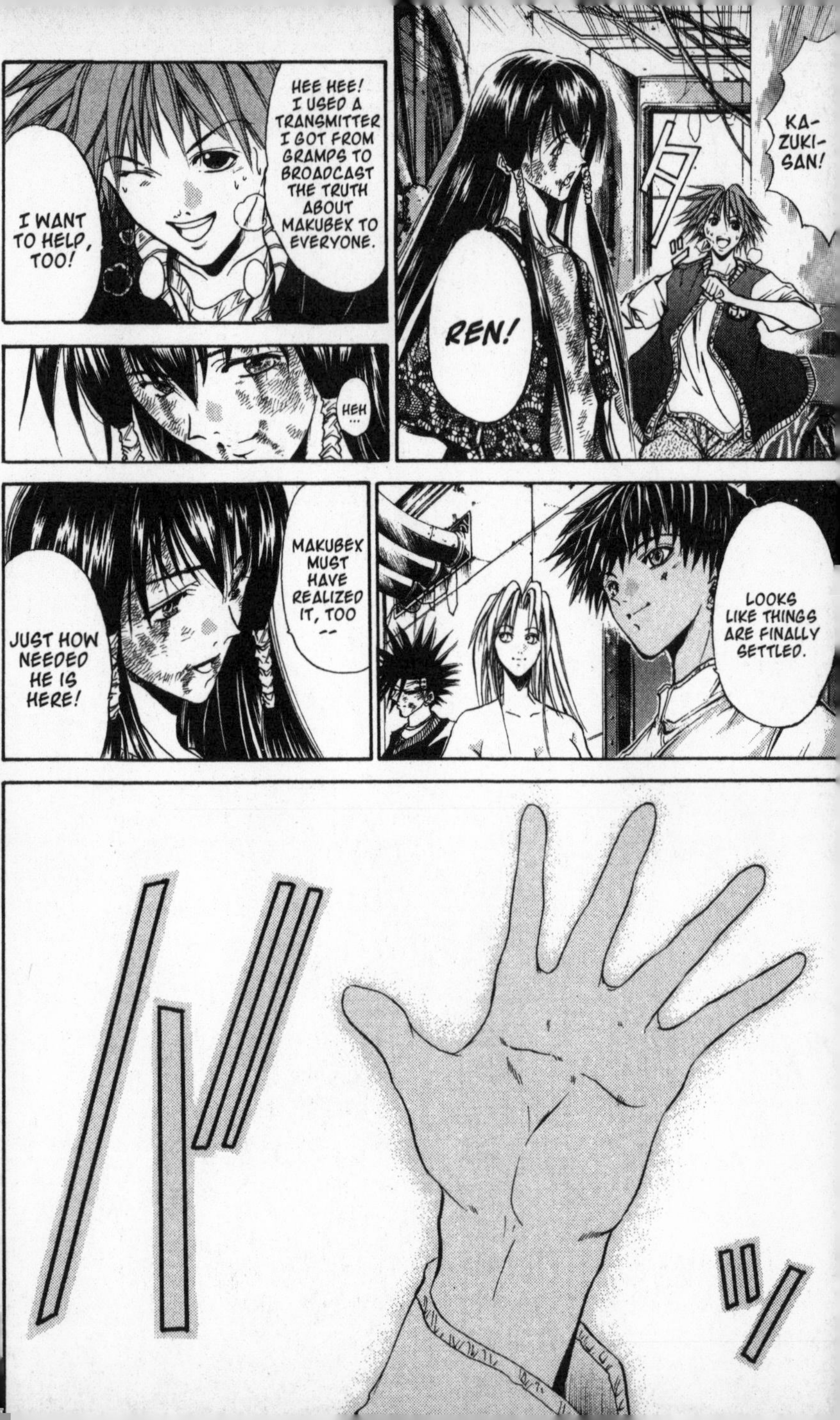
KA-ZUKI-SAN!
REN!
HEE HEE! I USED A TRANSMITTER I GOT FROM GRAMPS TO BROADCAST THE TRUTH ABOUT MAKUBEX TO EVERYONE.
I WANT TO HELP, TOO!
HEH...
LOOKS LIKE THINGS ARE FINALLY SETTLED.
MAKUBEX MUST HAVE REALIZED IT, TOO --
JUST HOW NEEDED HE IS HERE!

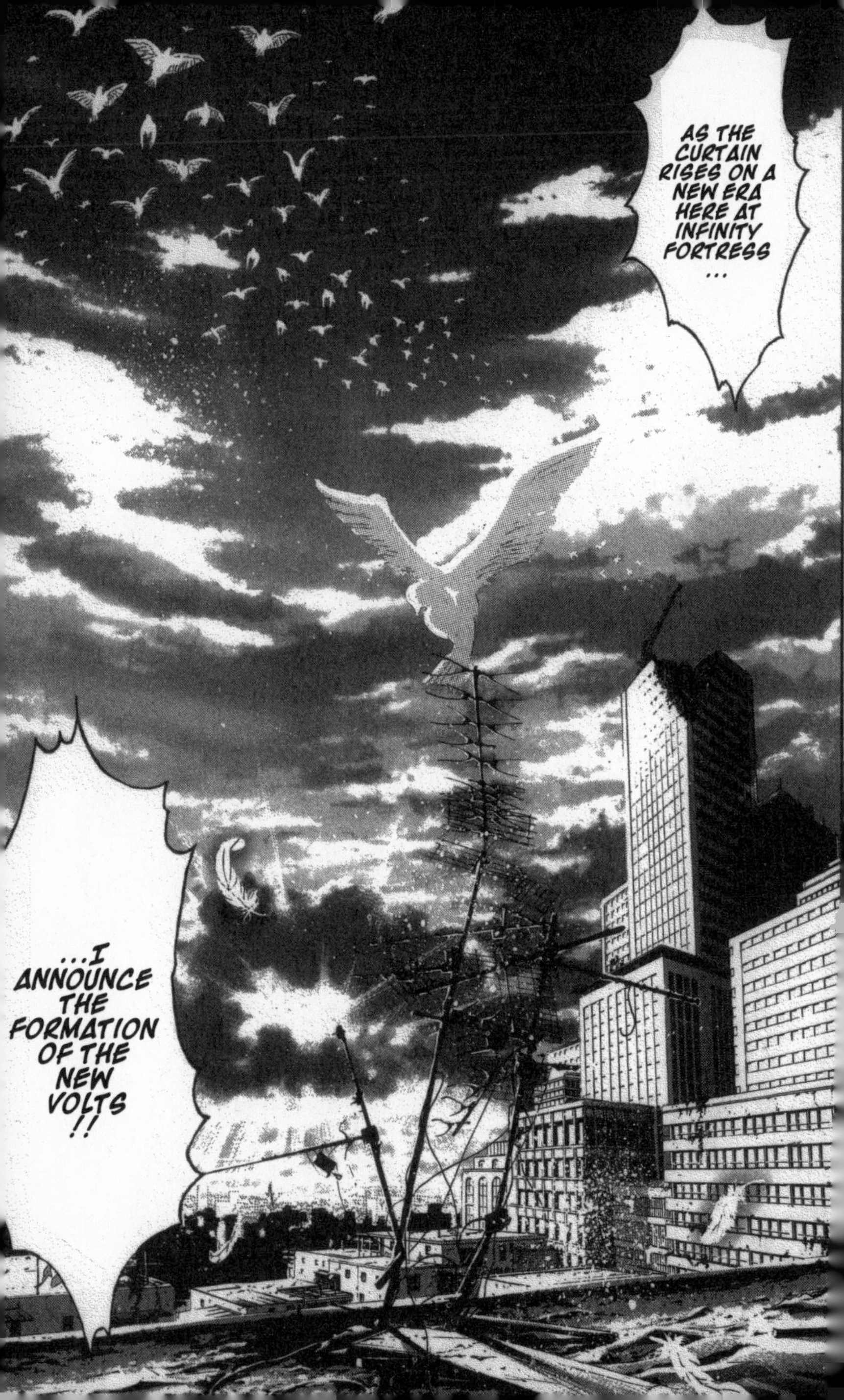
AS THE CURTAIN RISES ON A NEW ERA HERE AT INFINITY FORTRESS ...
...I ANNOUNCE THE FORMATION OF THE NEW VOLTS !!

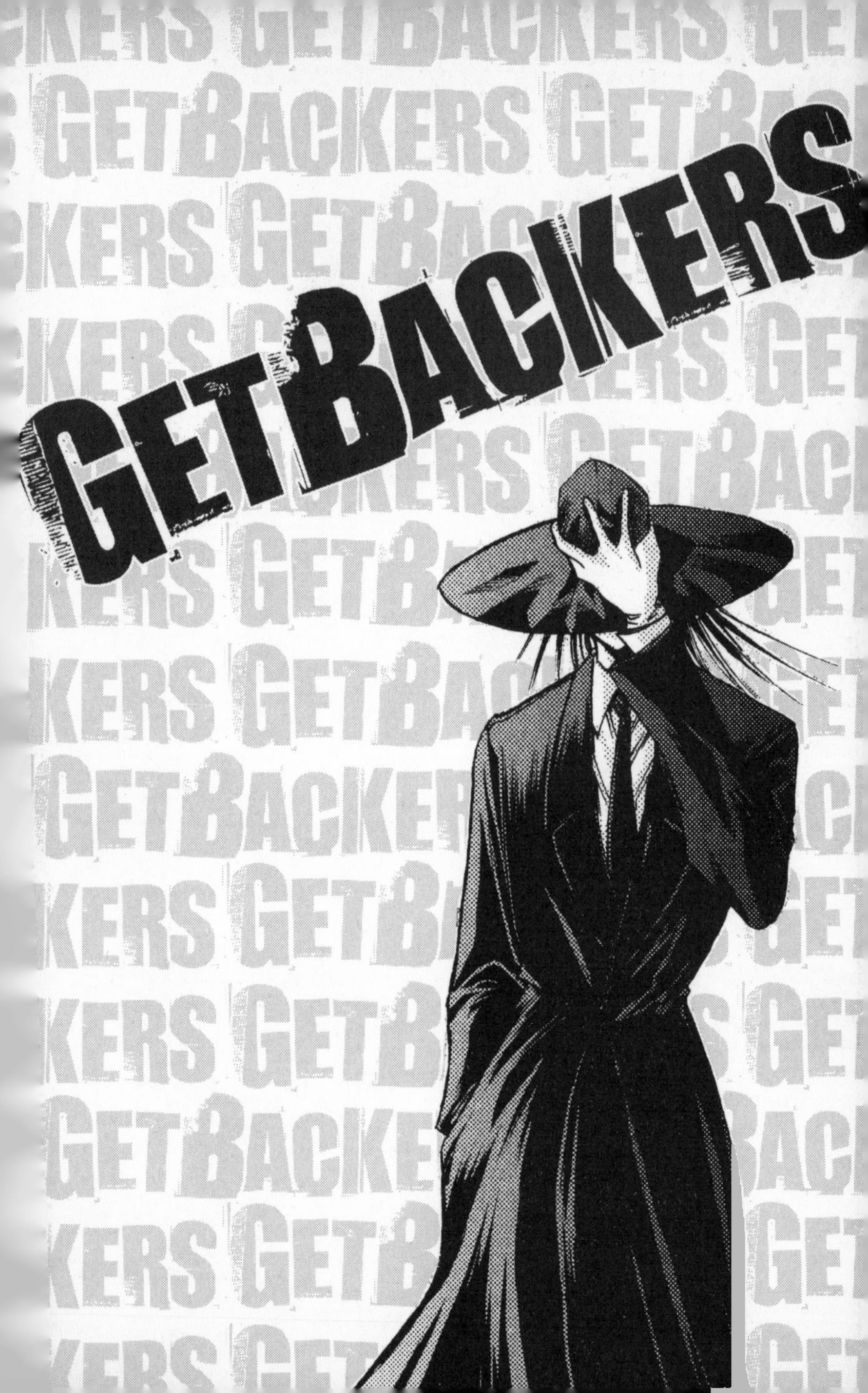
GETBACKERS

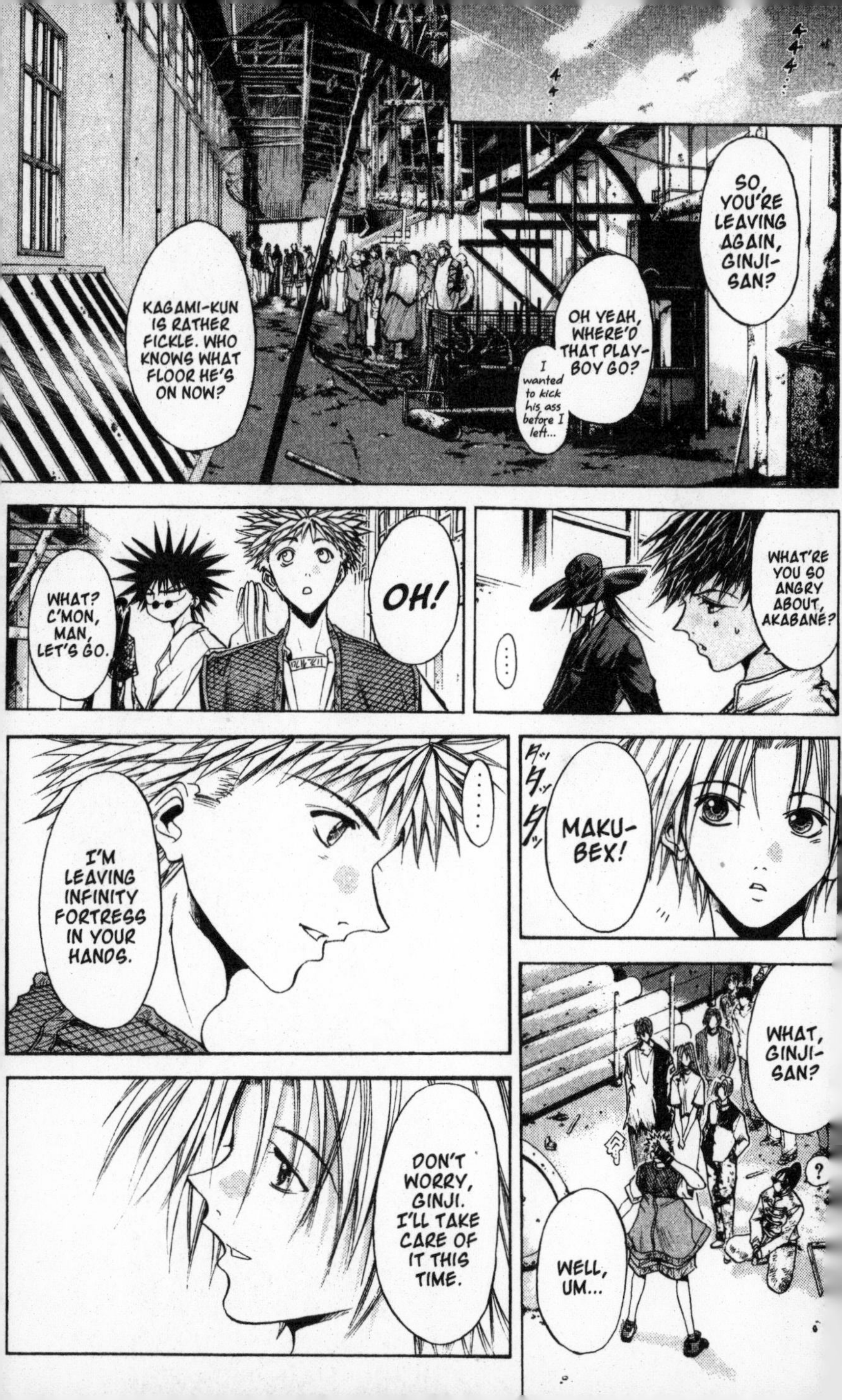
SO, YOU'RE LEAVING AGAIN, GINJI-SAN?
OH YEAH, WHERE'D THAT PLAYBOY GO?
I wanted to kick his ass before I left...
KAGAMI-KUN IS RATHER FICKLE. WHO KNOWS WHAT FLOOR HE'S ON NOW?
WHAT'RE YOU SO ANGRY ABOUT, AKABANE?
...
OH!
WHAT? C'MON, MAN, LET'S GO.
MAKU-BEX!
WHAT, GINJI-SAN?
?
WELL, UM...
...
I'M LEAVING INFINITY FORTRESS IN YOUR HANDS.
DON'T WORRY, GINJI. I'LL TAKE CARE OF IT THIS TIME.

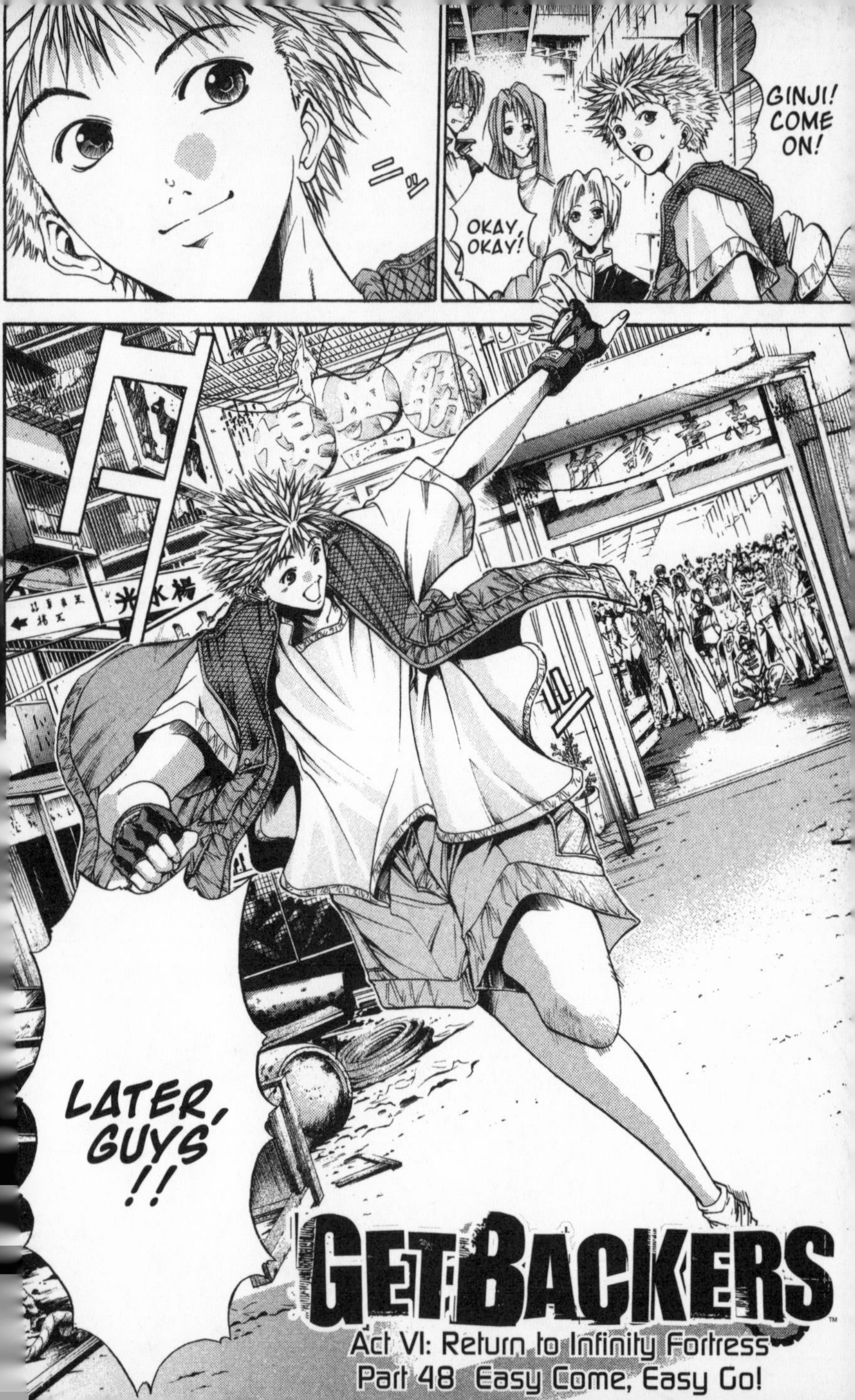
GINJI! COME ON!
OKAY, OKAY!
ニッ
LATER, GUYS!!
GETBACKERS™
Act VI: Return to Infinity Fortress
Part 48 Easy Come, Easy Go!

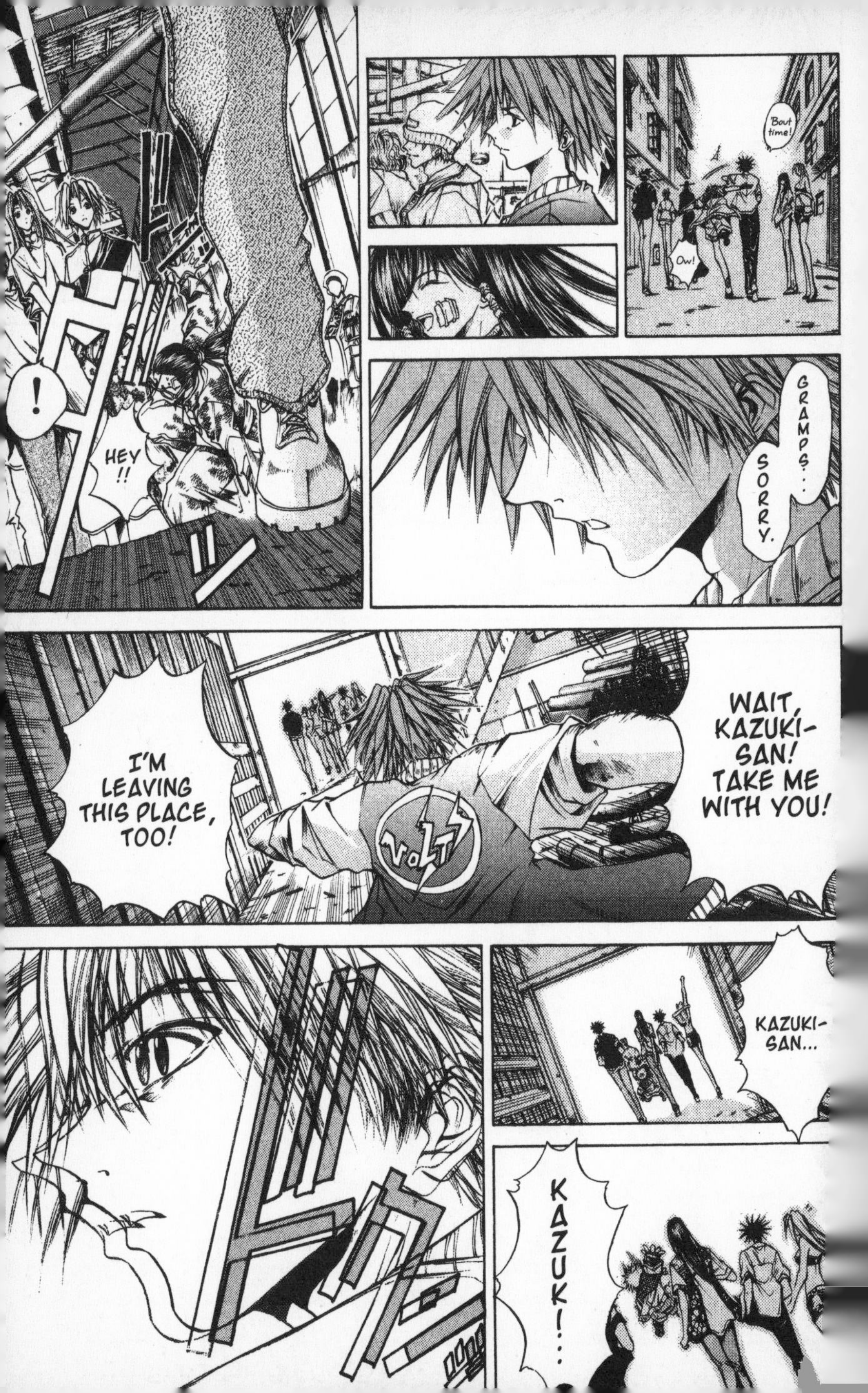
Bout time!
Ow!
GRAMPS...
SORRY.
!
HEY !!
WAIT, KAZUKI-SAN! TAKE ME WITH YOU!
I'M LEAVING THIS PLACE, TOO!
KAZUKI-SAN...
KAZUKI!...

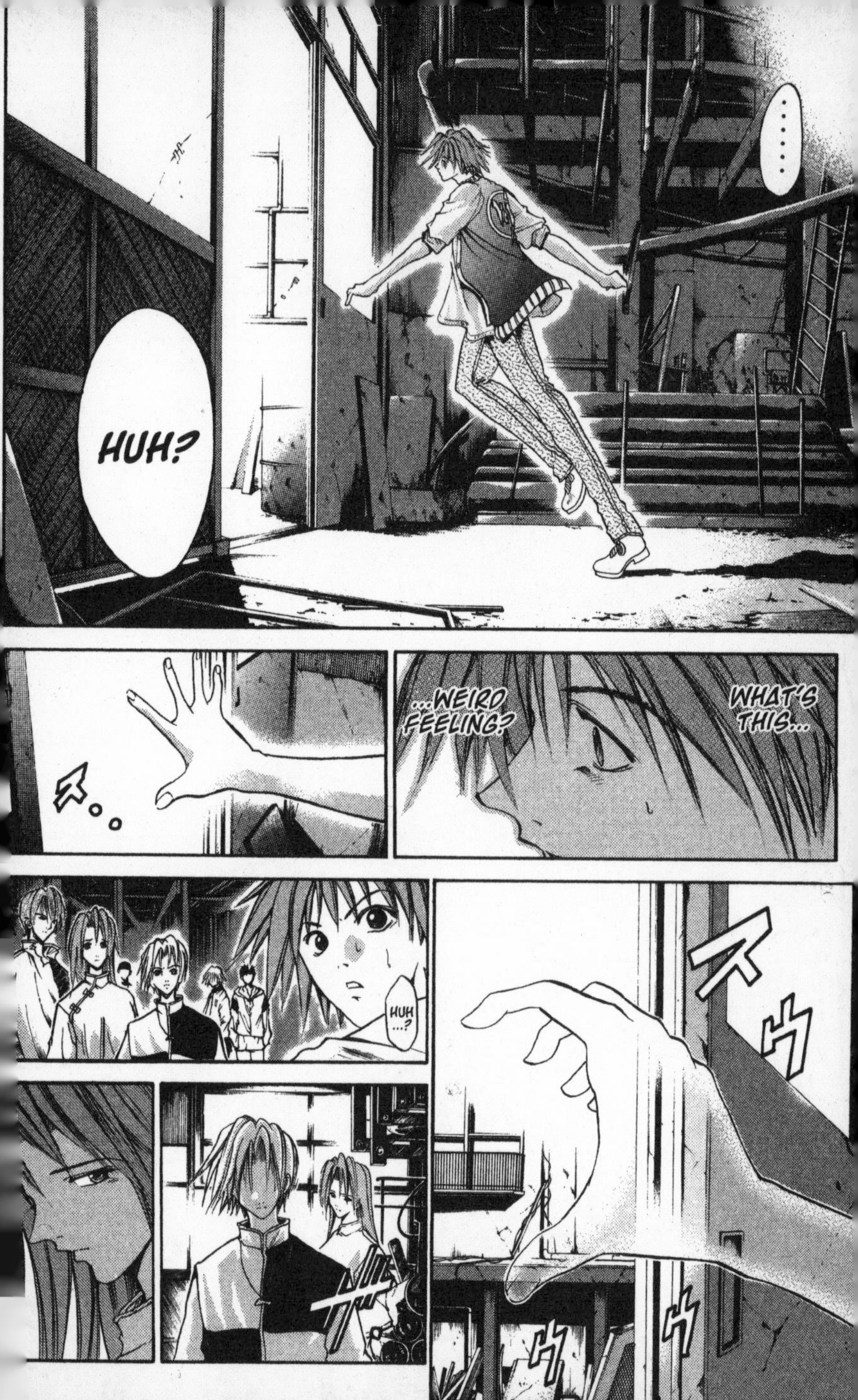
……
HUH?
WHAT'S THIS...
...WEIRD FEELING?
HUH ...?

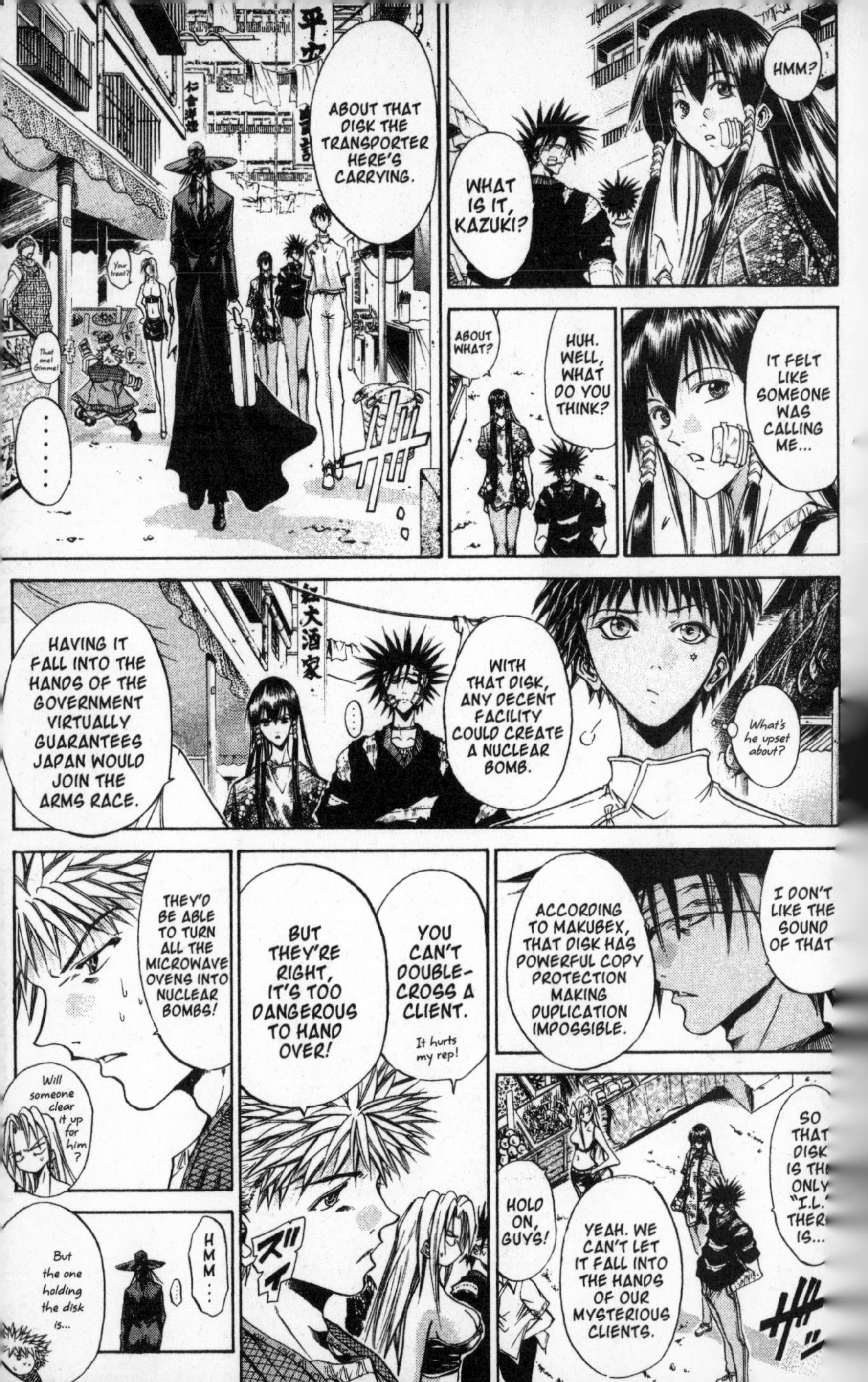
HMM?
WHAT IS IT, KAZUKI?
IT FELT LIKE SOMEONE WAS CALLING ME...
HUH. WELL, WHAT DO YOU THINK?
ABOUT WHAT?
ABOUT THAT DISK THE TRANSPORTER HERE'S CARRYING.
Your treat?
That one! Gimme!
......
WITH THAT DISK, ANY DECENT FACILITY COULD CREATE A NUCLEAR BOMB.
What's he upset about?
...
HAVING IT FALL INTO THE HANDS OF THE GOVERNMENT VIRTUALLY GUARANTEES JAPAN WOULD JOIN THE ARMS RACE.
I DON'T LIKE THE SOUND OF THAT
ACCORDING TO MAKUBEX, THAT DISK HAS POWERFUL COPY PROTECTION MAKING DUPLICATION IMPOSSIBLE.
SO THAT DISK IS THE ONLY "I.L." THERE IS...
YEAH. WE CAN'T LET IT FALL INTO THE HANDS OF OUR MYSTERIOUS CLIENTS.
HOLD ON, GUYS!
YOU CAN'T DOUBLE-CROSS A CLIENT.
It hurts my rep!
BUT THEY'RE RIGHT, IT'S TOO DANGEROUS TO HAND OVER!
ズイ
THEY'D BE ABLE TO TURN ALL THE MICROWAVE OVENS INTO NUCLEAR BOMBS!
Will someone clear it up for him?
HMM...
...
But the one holding the disk is...

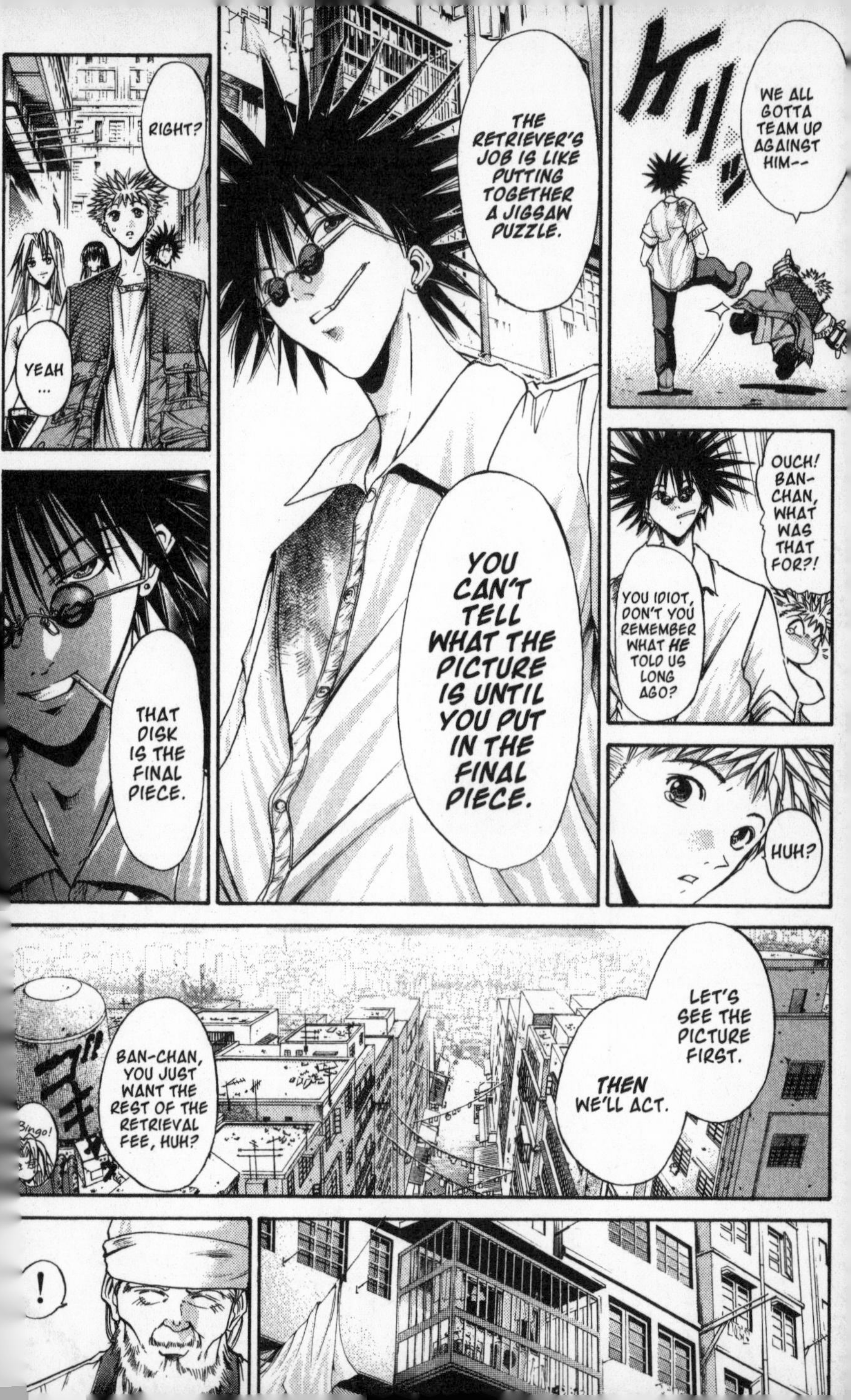
WE ALL GOTTA TEAM UP AGAINST HIM--
OUCH! BAN-CHAN, WHAT WAS THAT FOR?!
YOU IDIOT, DON'T YOU REMEMBER WHAT HE TOLD US LONG AGO?
HUH?
THE RETRIEVER'S JOB IS LIKE PUTTING TOGETHER A JIGSAW PUZZLE.
YOU CAN'T TELL WHAT THE PICTURE IS UNTIL YOU PUT IN THE FINAL PIECE.
RIGHT?
YEAH ...
THAT DISK IS THE FINAL PIECE.
LET'S SEE THE PICTURE FIRST.
THEN WE'LL ACT.
BAN-CHAN, YOU JUST WANT THE REST OF THE RETRIEVAL FEE, HUH?
Bingo!
!

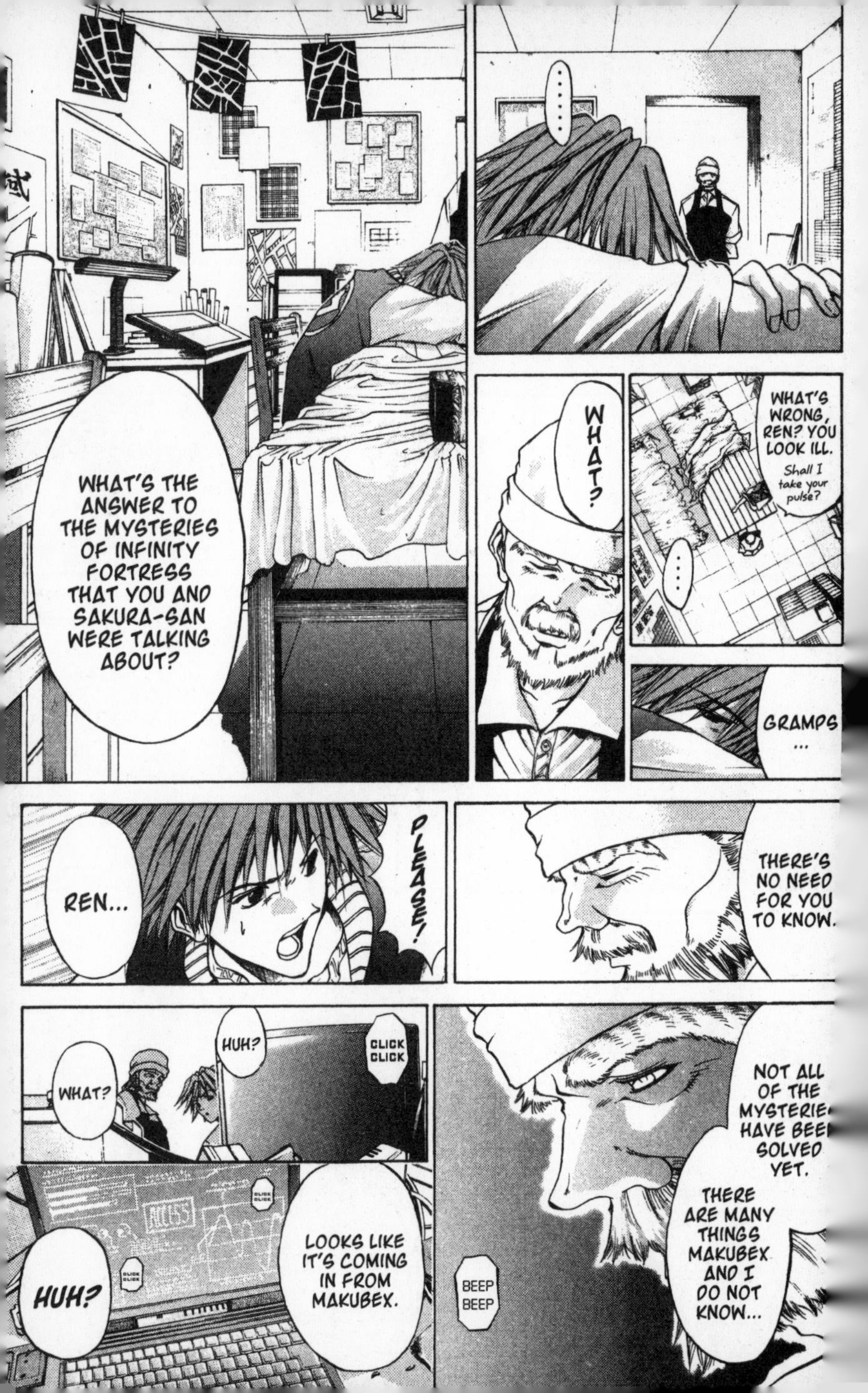
......
WHAT'S WRONG, REN? YOU LOOK ILL.
Shall I take your pulse?
......
GRAMPS ...
WHAT?
WHAT'S THE ANSWER TO THE MYSTERIES OF INFINITY FORTRESS THAT YOU AND SAKURA-SAN WERE TALKING ABOUT?
THERE'S NO NEED FOR YOU TO KNOW.
PLEASE!
REN...
NOT ALL OF THE MYSTERIE HAVE BEE SOLVED YET.
THERE ARE MANY THINGS MAKUBEX AND I DO NOT KNOW...
BEEP BEEP
CLICK CLICK
HUH?
WHAT?
CLICK CLICK
LOOKS LIKE IT'S COMING IN FROM MAKUBEX.
CLICK CLICK
HUH?

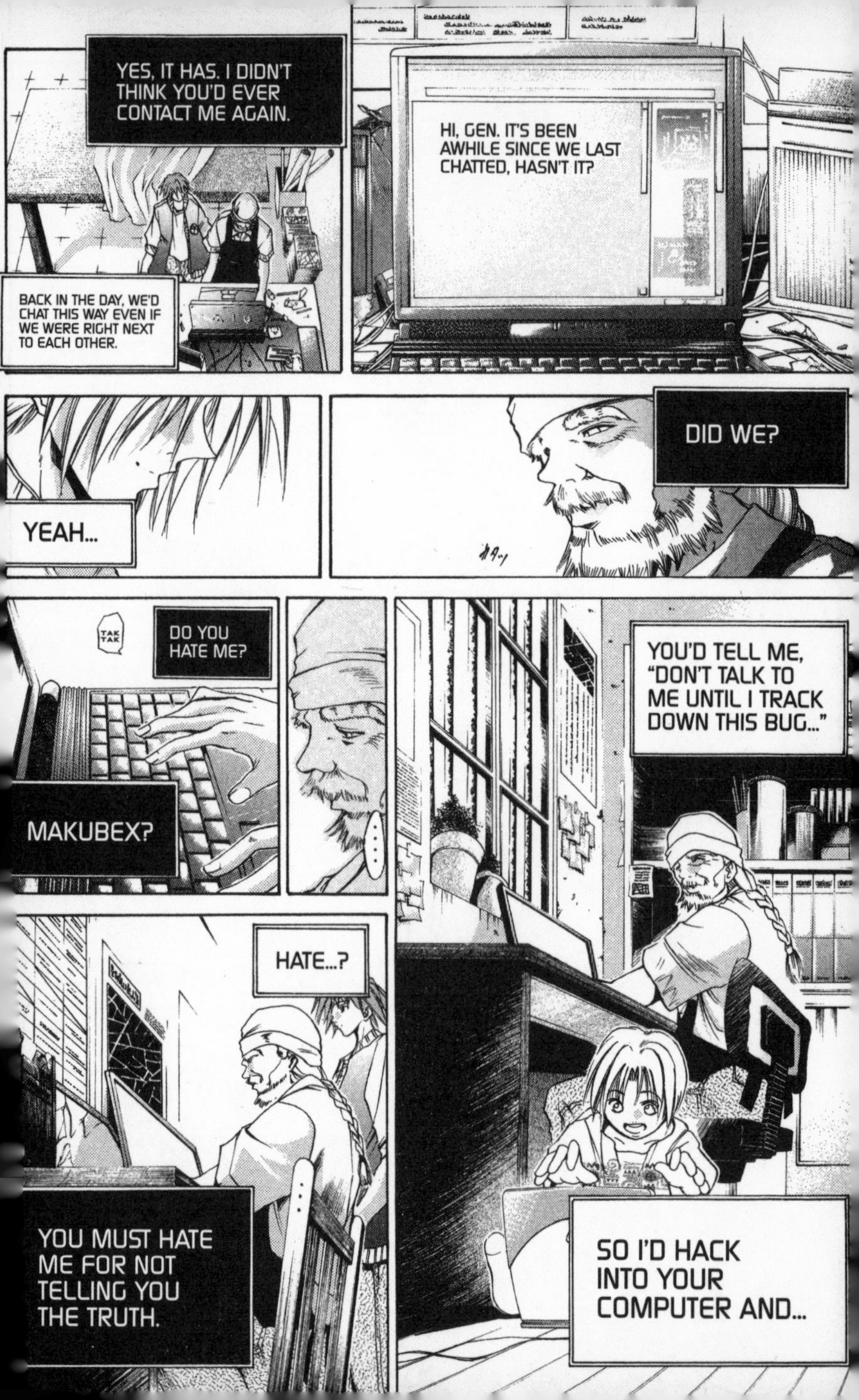
HI, GEN. IT'S BEEN AWHILE SINCE WE LAST CHATTED, HASN'T IT?
YES, IT HAS. I DIDN'T THINK YOU'D EVER CONTACT ME AGAIN.
BACK IN THE DAY, WE'D CHAT THIS WAY EVEN IF WE WERE RIGHT NEXT TO EACH OTHER.
DID WE?
YEAH...
YOU'D TELL ME, "DON'T TALK TO ME UNTIL I TRACK DOWN THIS BUG..."
SO I'D HACK INTO YOUR COMPUTER AND...
DO YOU HATE ME?
TAK TAK
MAKUBEX?
HATE...?
YOU MUST HATE ME FOR NOT TELLING YOU THE TRUTH.

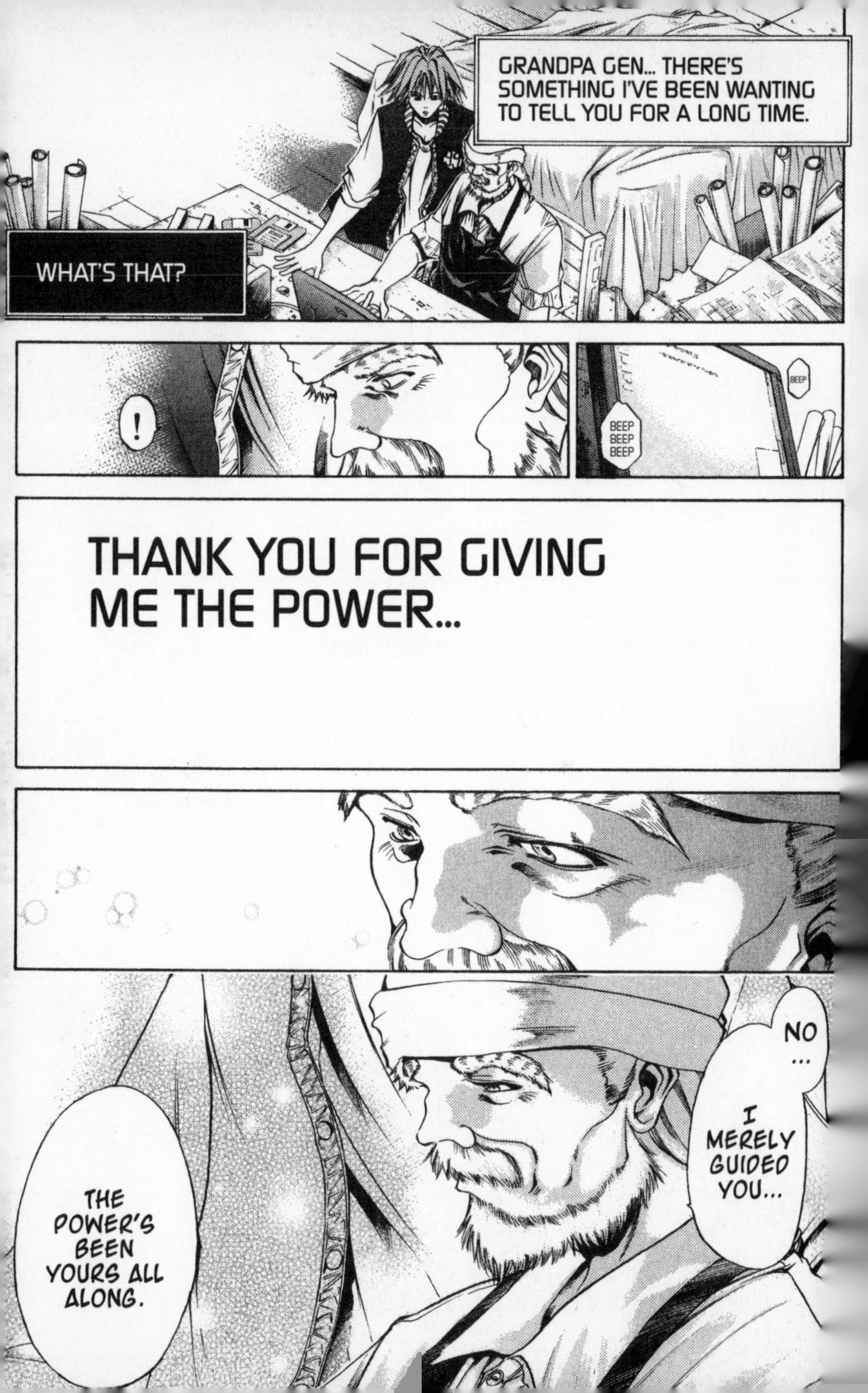
GRANDPA GEN... THERE'S SOMETHING I'VE BEEN WANTING TO TELL YOU FOR A LONG TIME.
WHAT'S THAT?
BEEP
BEEP BEEP BEEP
!
THANK YOU FOR GIVING ME THE POWER...
NO ...
I MERELY GUIDED YOU...
THE POWER'S BEEN YOURS ALL ALONG.

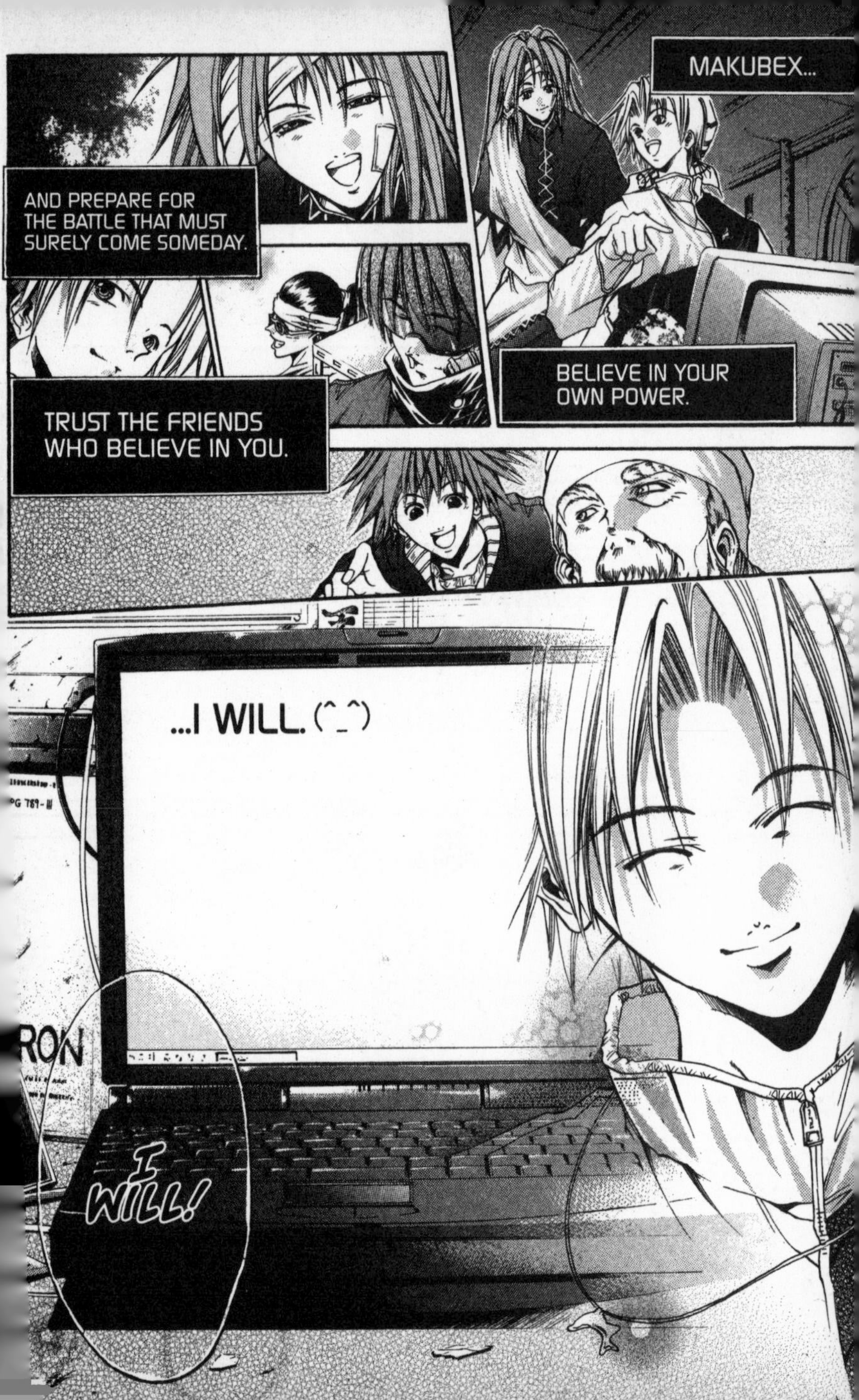
MAKUBEX...
BELIEVE IN YOUR OWN POWER.
TRUST THE FRIENDS WHO BELIEVE IN YOU.
AND PREPARE FOR THE BATTLE THAT MUST SURELY COME SOMEDAY.
...I WILL. (^_^)
I WILL!

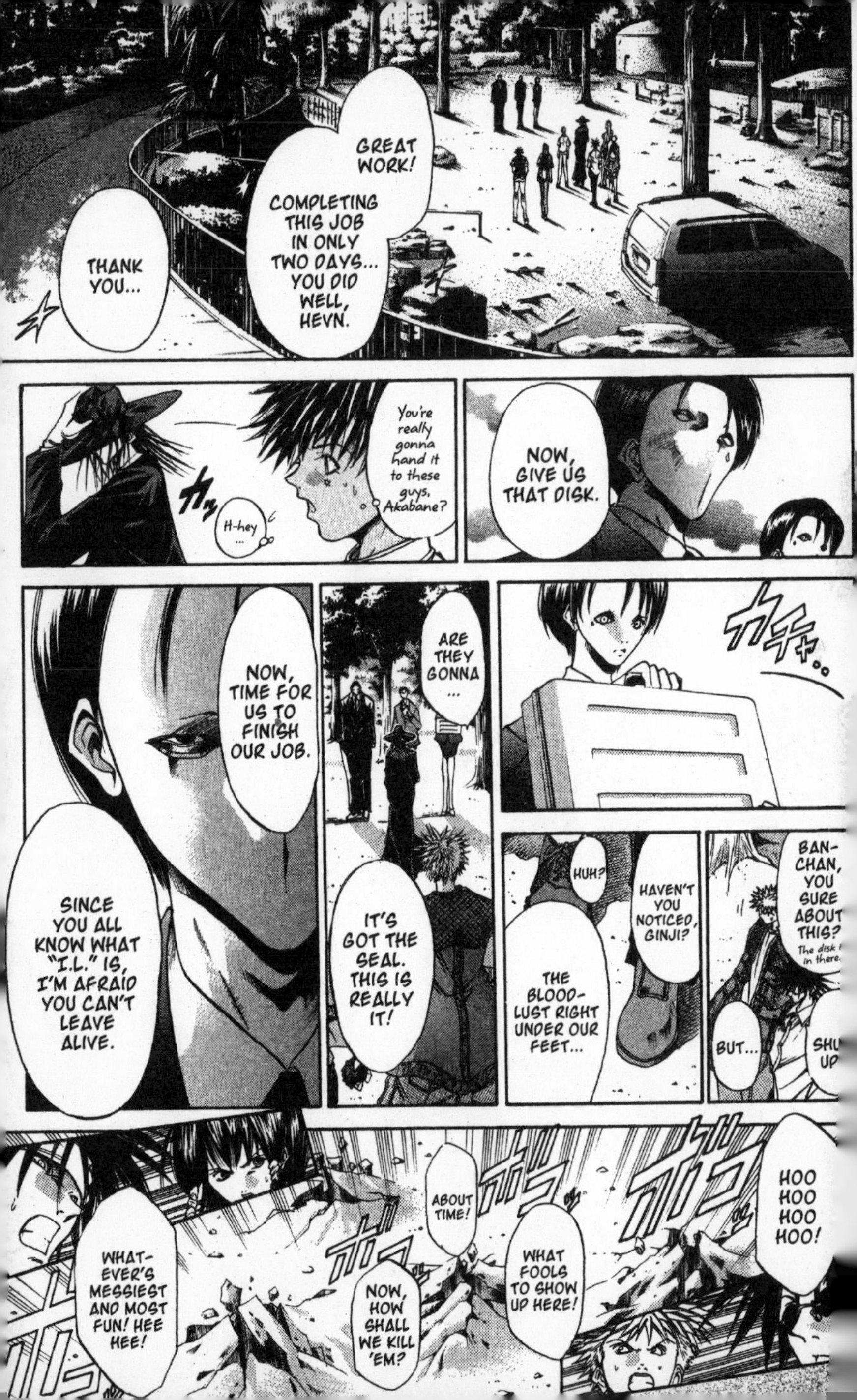
GREAT WORK!
COMPLETING THIS JOB IN ONLY TWO DAYS... YOU DID WELL, HEVN.
THANK YOU...
NOW, GIVE US THAT DISK.
You're really gonna hand it to these guys, Akabane?
H-hey...
カチャ..
BAN-CHAN, YOU SURE ABOUT THIS?
The disk i in there.
BUT...
SHU UP
HUH?
HAVEN'T YOU NOTICED, GINJI?
THE BLOOD-LUST RIGHT UNDER OUR FEET...
ARE THEY GONNA...
IT'S GOT THE SEAL. THIS IS REALLY IT!
NOW, TIME FOR US TO FINISH OUR JOB.
SINCE YOU ALL KNOW WHAT "I.L." IS, I'M AFRAID YOU CAN'T LEAVE ALIVE.
HOO HOO HOO HOO!
WHAT FOOLS TO SHOW UP HERE!
ABOUT TIME!
NOW, HOW SHALL WE KILL 'EM?
WHAT-EVER'S MESSIEST AND MOST FUN! HEE HEE!

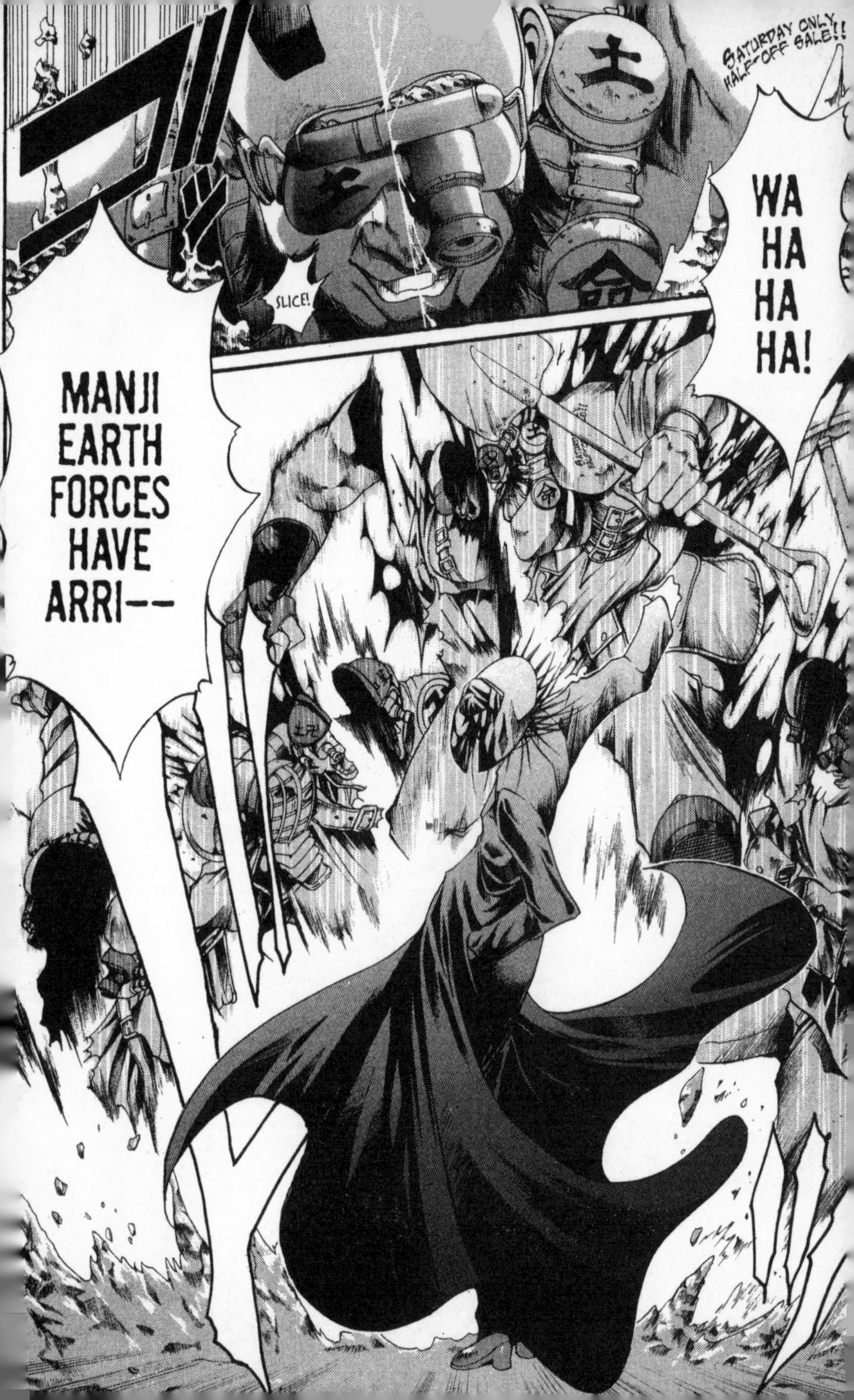
SATURDAY ONLY HALF-OFF SALE!!
WA HA HA HA!
MANJI EARTH FORCES HAVE ARRI--
SLICE!

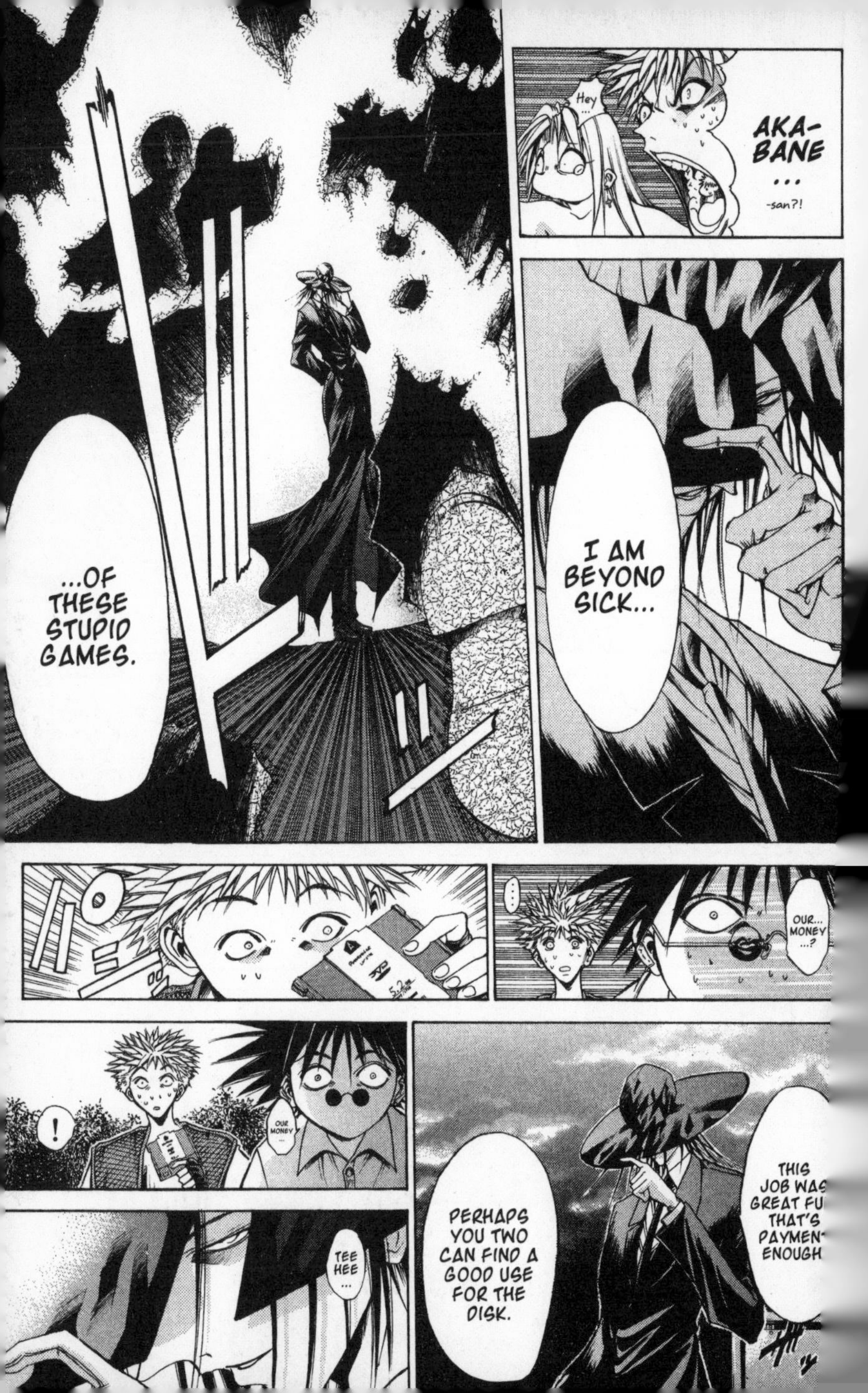
Hey ...
AKA-BANE ...
-san?!
I AM BEYOND SICK...
...OF THESE STUPID GAMES.
...
OUR... MONEY ...?
THIS JOB WAS GREAT FU THAT'S PAYMEN ENOUGH
PERHAPS YOU TWO CAN FIND A GOOD USE FOR THE DISK.
!
OUR MONEY ...
TEE HEE ...

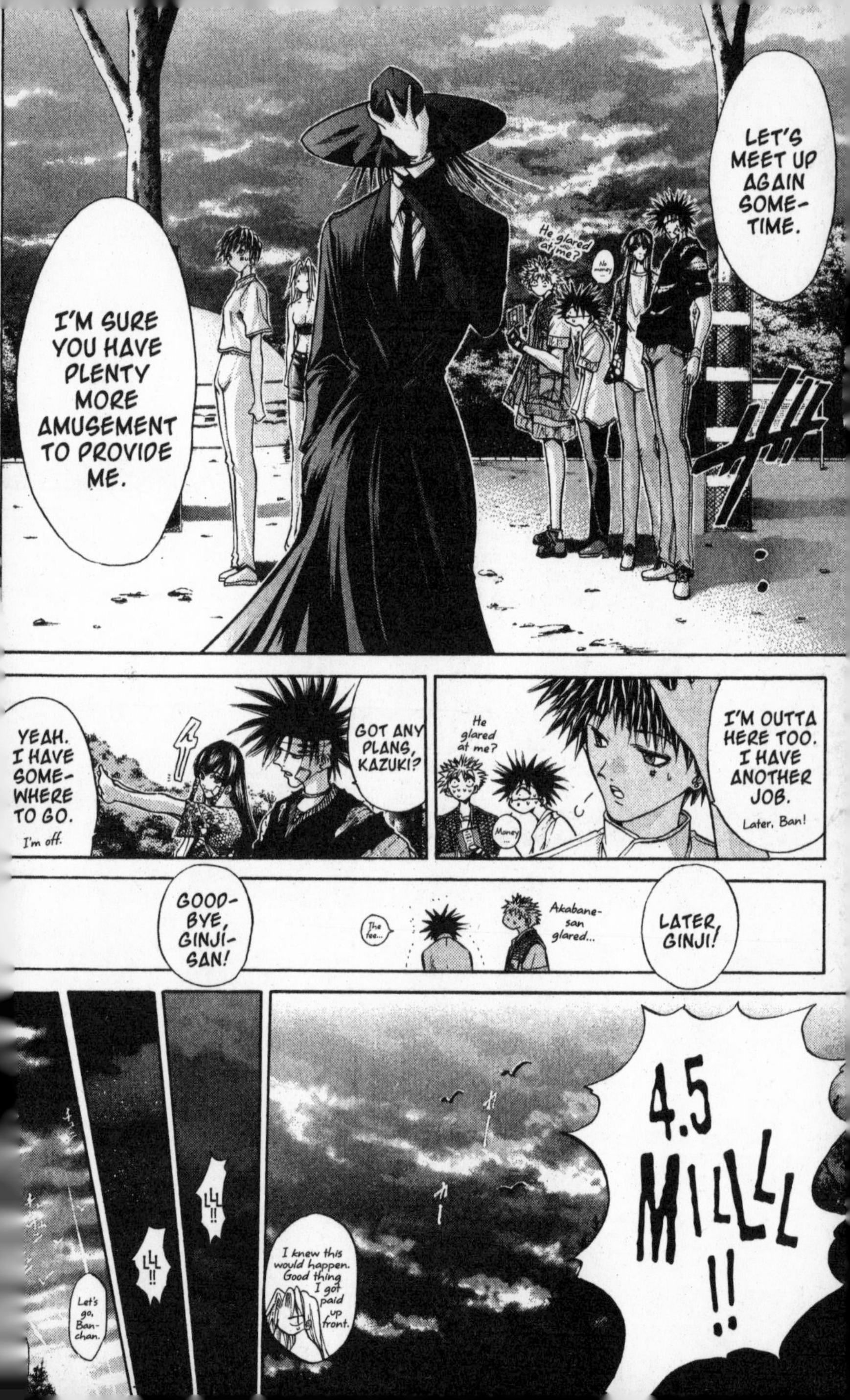
LET'S MEET UP AGAIN SOME-TIME.
He glared at me?
No money...
I'M SURE YOU HAVE PLENTY MORE AMUSEMENT TO PROVIDE ME.
I'M OUTTA HERE TOO. I HAVE ANOTHER JOB.
Later, Ban!
He glared at me?
Money...
GOT ANY PLANS, KAZUKI?
YEAH. I HAVE SOME-WHERE TO GO.
I'm off.
LATER, GINJI!
Akabane-san glared...
The fee...
GOOD-BYE, GINJI-SAN!
4.5 MILLL !!
I knew this would happen. Good thing I got paid up front.
LLL!!
LLL!!
Let's go, Ban-chan.

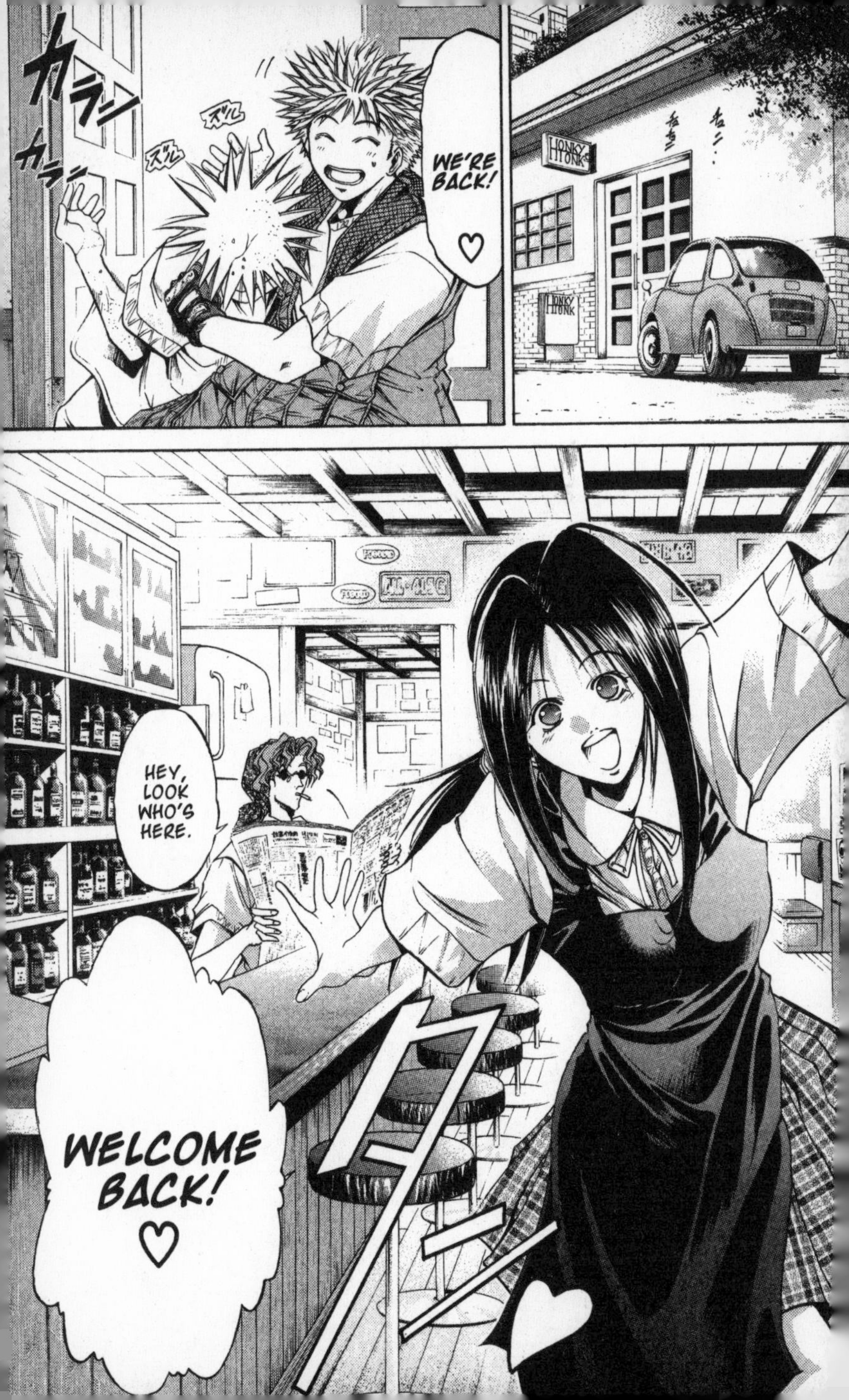
HONKY TONK
HONKY TONK
カラン
カラン
ズル
ズル
WE'RE BACK! ♡
HEY, LOOK WHO'S HERE.
WELCOME BACK! ♡

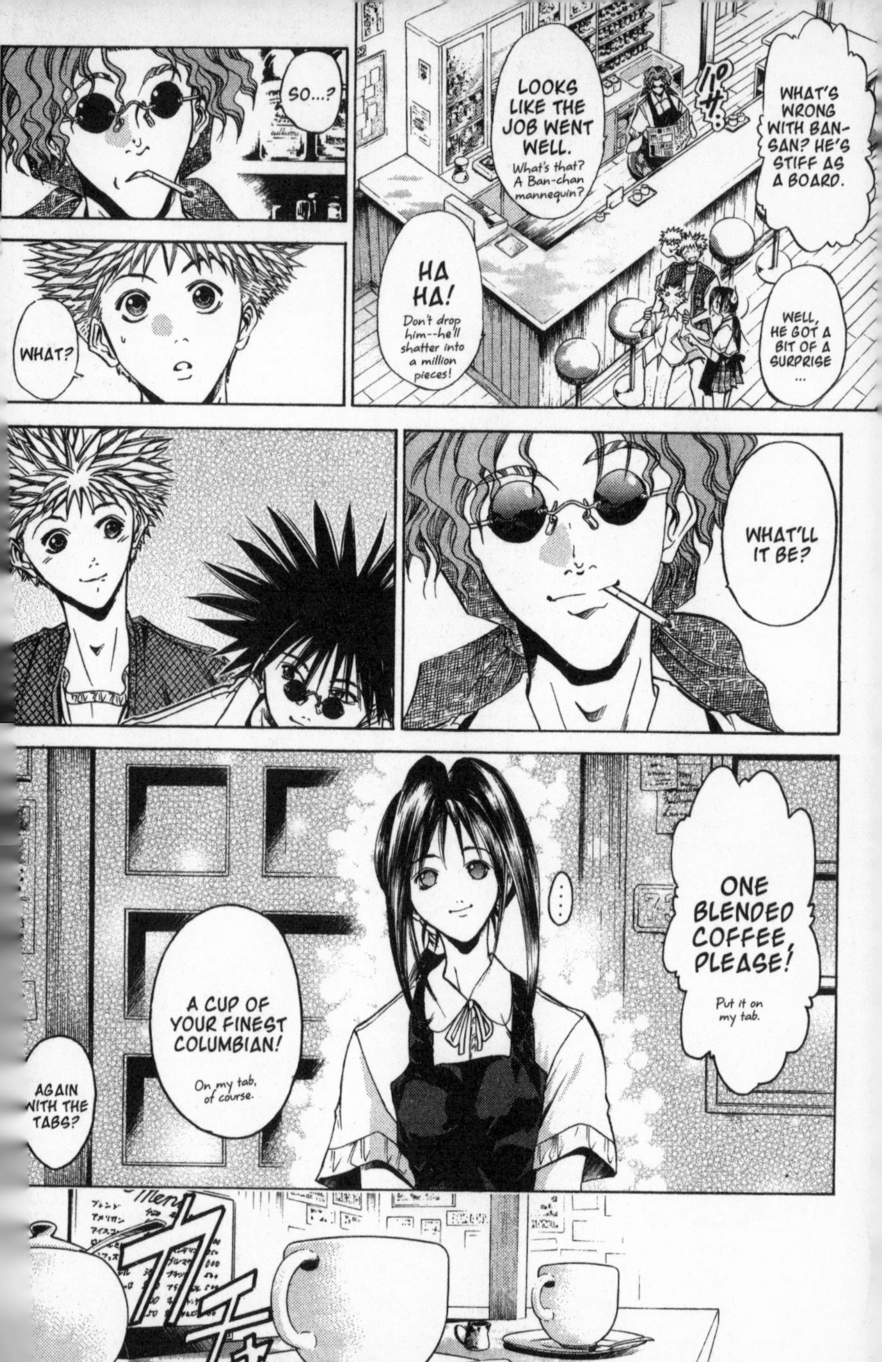
WHAT'S WRONG WITH BAN-SAN? HE'S STIFF AS A BOARD.
LOOKS LIKE THE JOB WENT WELL.
What's that? A Ban-chan mannequin?
WELL, HE GOT A BIT OF A SURPRISE...
HA HA!
Don't drop him--he'll shatter into a million pieces!
SO...?
WHAT?
WHAT'LL IT BE?
ONE BLENDED COFFEE, PLEASE!
Put it on my tab.
...
A CUP OF YOUR FINEST COLUMBIAN!
On my tab, of course.
AGAIN WITH THE TABS?

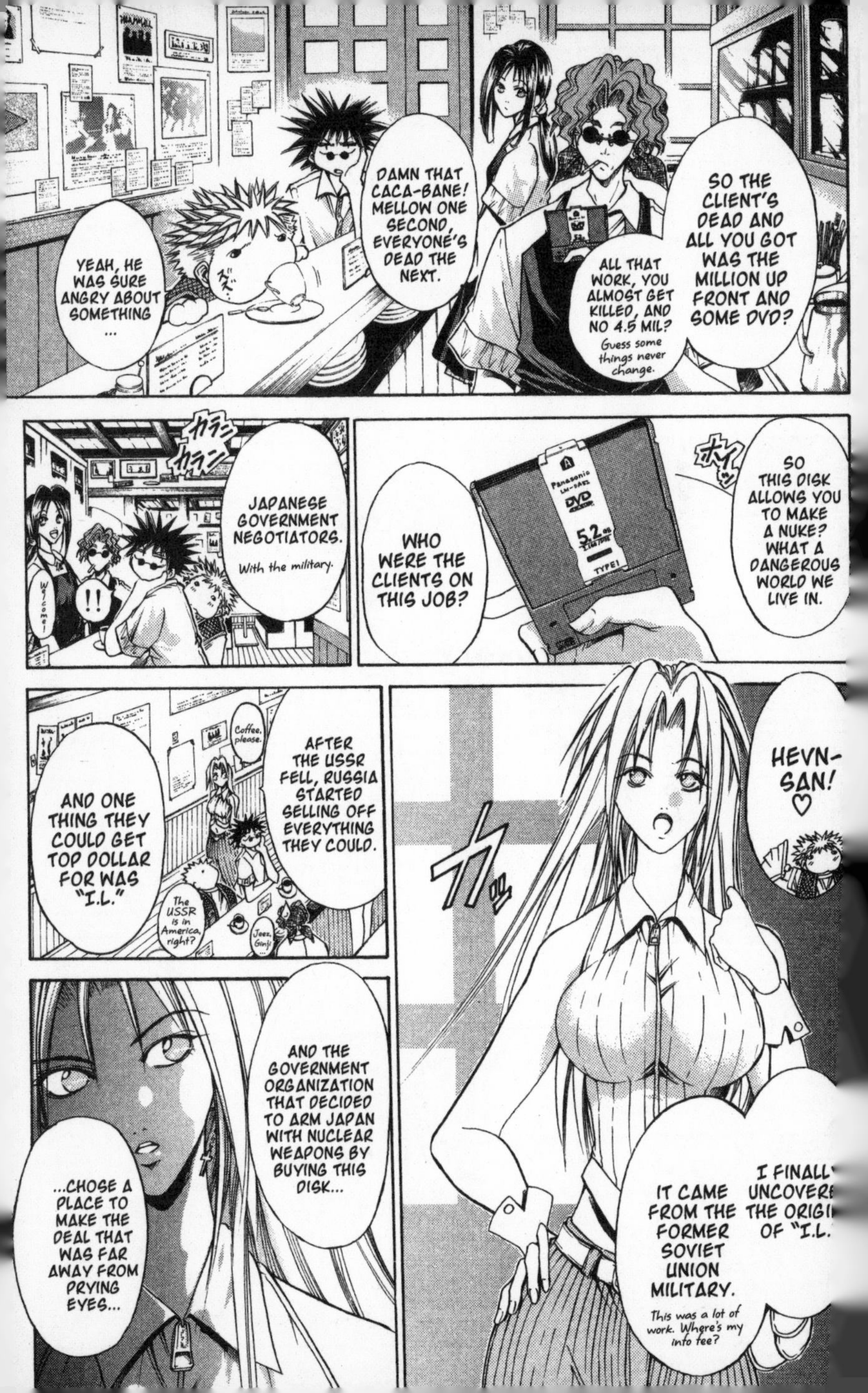
SO THE CLIENT'S DEAD AND ALL YOU GOT WAS THE MILLION UP FRONT AND SOME DVD?
ALL THAT WORK, YOU ALMOST GET KILLED, AND NO 4.5 MIL?
Guess some things never change.
DAMN THAT CACA-BANE! MELLOW ONE SECOND, EVERYONE'S DEAD THE NEXT.
YEAH, HE WAS SURE ANGRY ABOUT SOMETHING ...
SO THIS DISK ALLOWS YOU TO MAKE A NUKE? WHAT A DANGEROUS WORLD WE LIVE IN.
Panasonic
DVD
5.2 GB
TYPE1
WHO WERE THE CLIENTS ON THIS JOB?
JAPANESE GOVERNMENT NEGOTIATORS.
With the military.
!!
Welcome!
HEVN-SAN! ♡
I FINALLY UNCOVERE THE ORIGI OF "I.L.
IT CAME FROM THE FORMER SOVIET UNION MILITARY.
This was a lot of work. Where's my info fee?
Coffee, please.
AFTER THE USSR FELL, RUSSIA STARTED SELLING OFF EVERYTHING THEY COULD.
AND ONE THING THEY COULD GET TOP DOLLAR FOR WAS "I.L."
Jeez, Ginji ...
The USSR is in America, right?
AND THE GOVERNMENT ORGANIZATION THAT DECIDED TO ARM JAPAN WITH NUCLEAR WEAPONS BY BUYING THIS DISK...
...CHOSE A PLACE TO MAKE THE DEAL THAT WAS FAR AWAY FROM PRYING EYES...

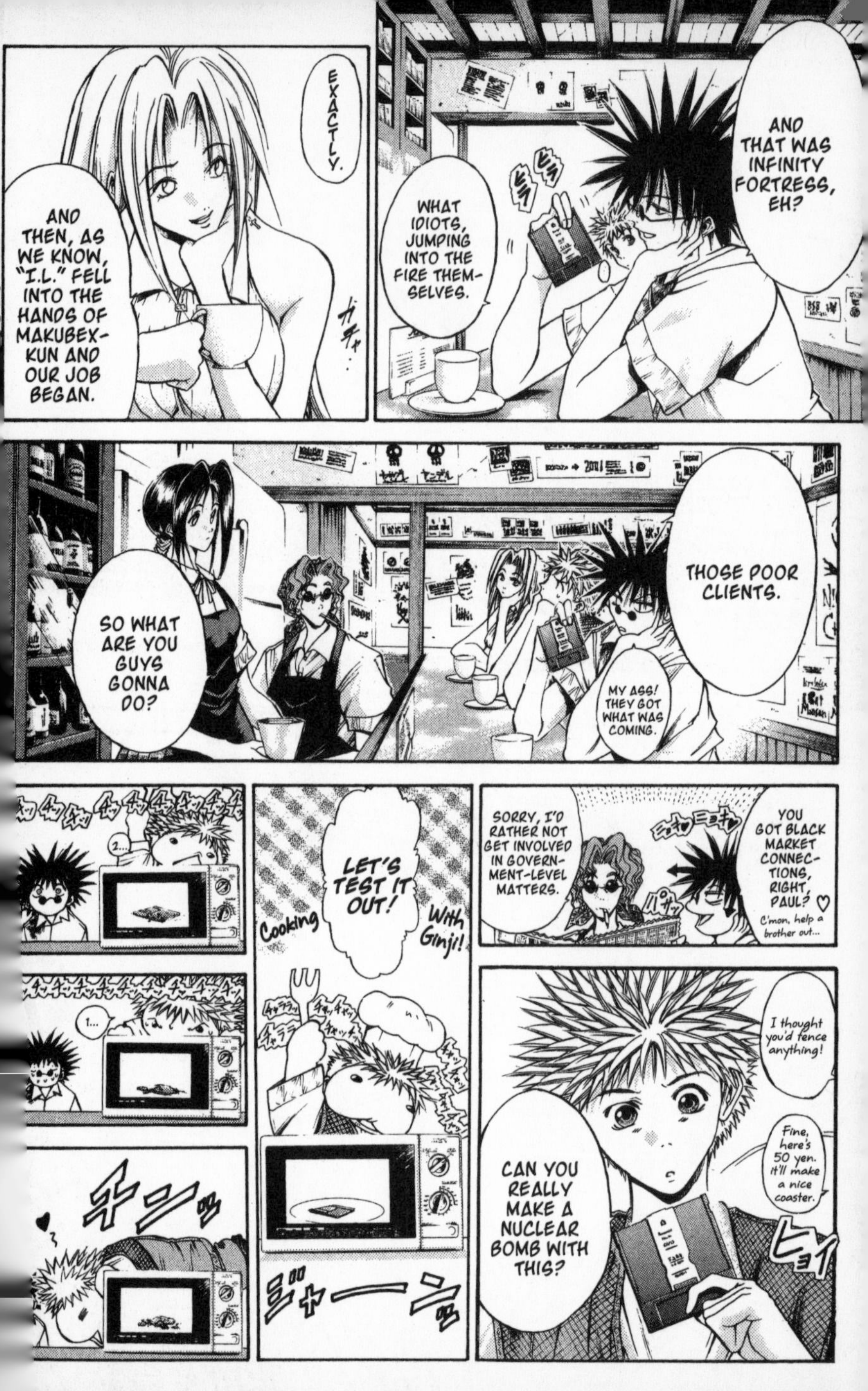
AND THAT WAS INFINITY FORTRESS, EH?
WHAT IDIOTS, JUMPING INTO THE FIRE THEM-SELVES.
EXACTLY.
AND THEN, AS WE KNOW, "I.L." FELL INTO THE HANDS OF MAKUBEX-KUN AND OUR JOB BEGAN.
THOSE POOR CLIENTS.
MY ASS! THEY GOT WHAT WAS COMING.
SO WHAT ARE YOU GUYS GONNA DO?
YOU GOT BLACK MARKET CONNEC-TIONS, RIGHT, PAUL? ♡
C'mon, help a brother out...
SORRY, I'D RATHER NOT GET INVOLVED IN GOVERN-MENT-LEVEL MATTERS.
I thought you'd fence anything!
Fine, here's 50 yen. It'll make a nice coaster.
CAN YOU REALLY MAKE A NUCLEAR BOMB WITH THIS?
LET'S TEST IT OUT!
Cooking With Ginji!
2...
1...

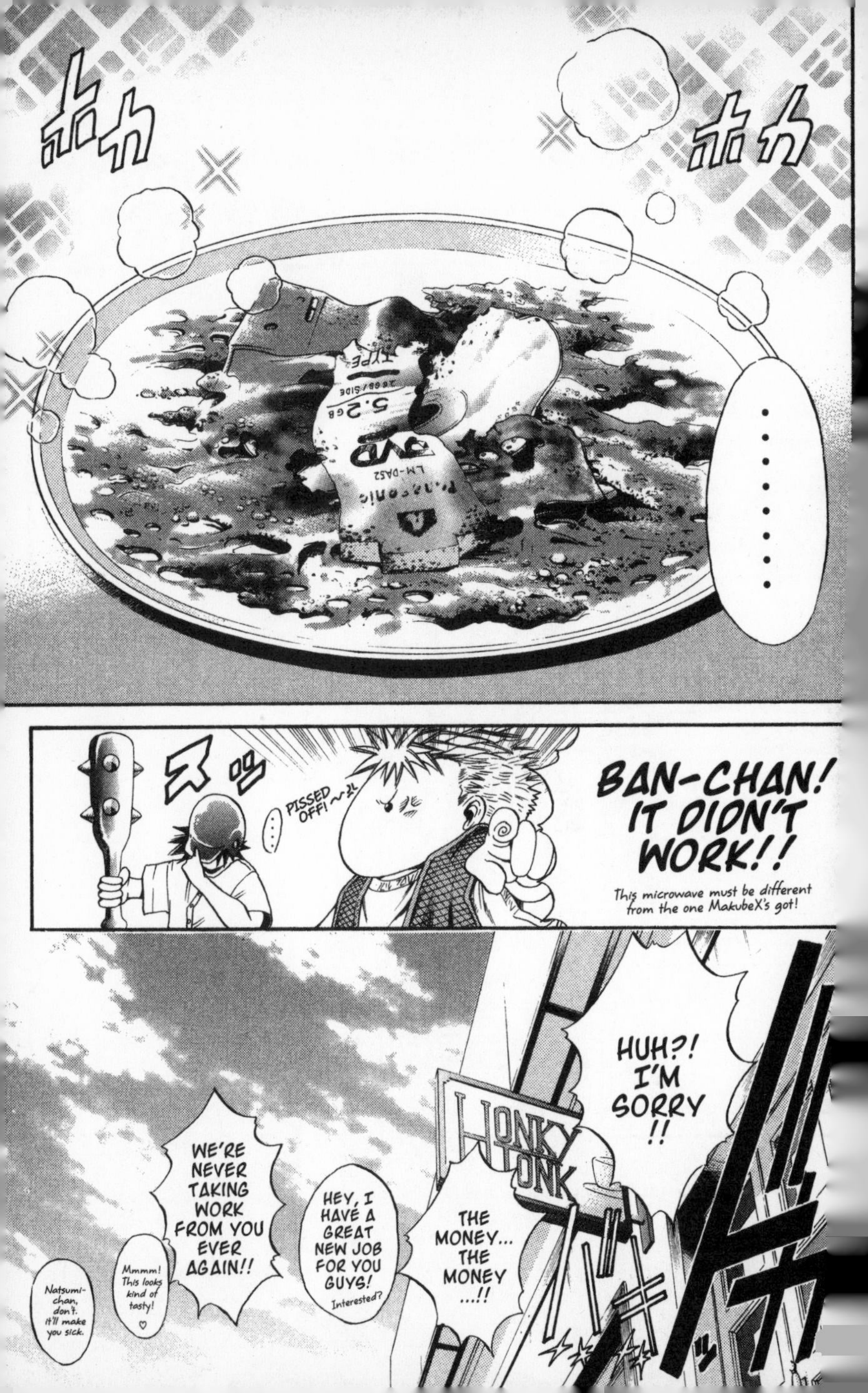
......
BAN-CHAN! IT DIDN'T WORK!!
This microwave must be different from the one MakubeX's got!
PISSED OFF!~
...
HUH?! I'M SORRY!!
HONKY TONK
THE MONEY... THE MONEY...!!
HEY, I HAVE A GREAT NEW JOB FOR YOU GUYS! Interested?
WE'RE NEVER TAKING WORK FROM YOU EVER AGAIN!!
Mmmm! This looks kind of tasty! ♡
Natsumi-chan, don't. It'll make you sick.

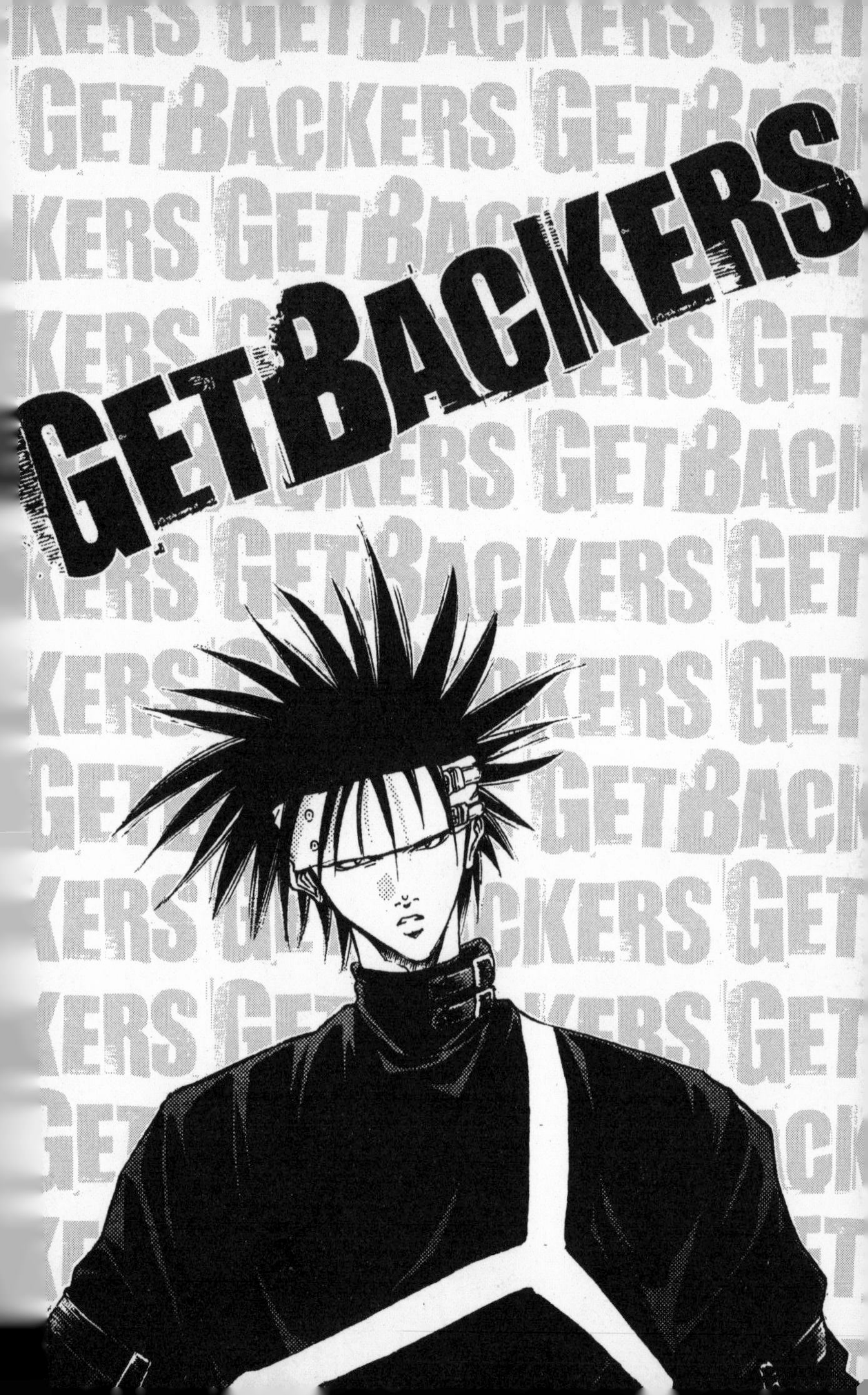
GETBACKERS

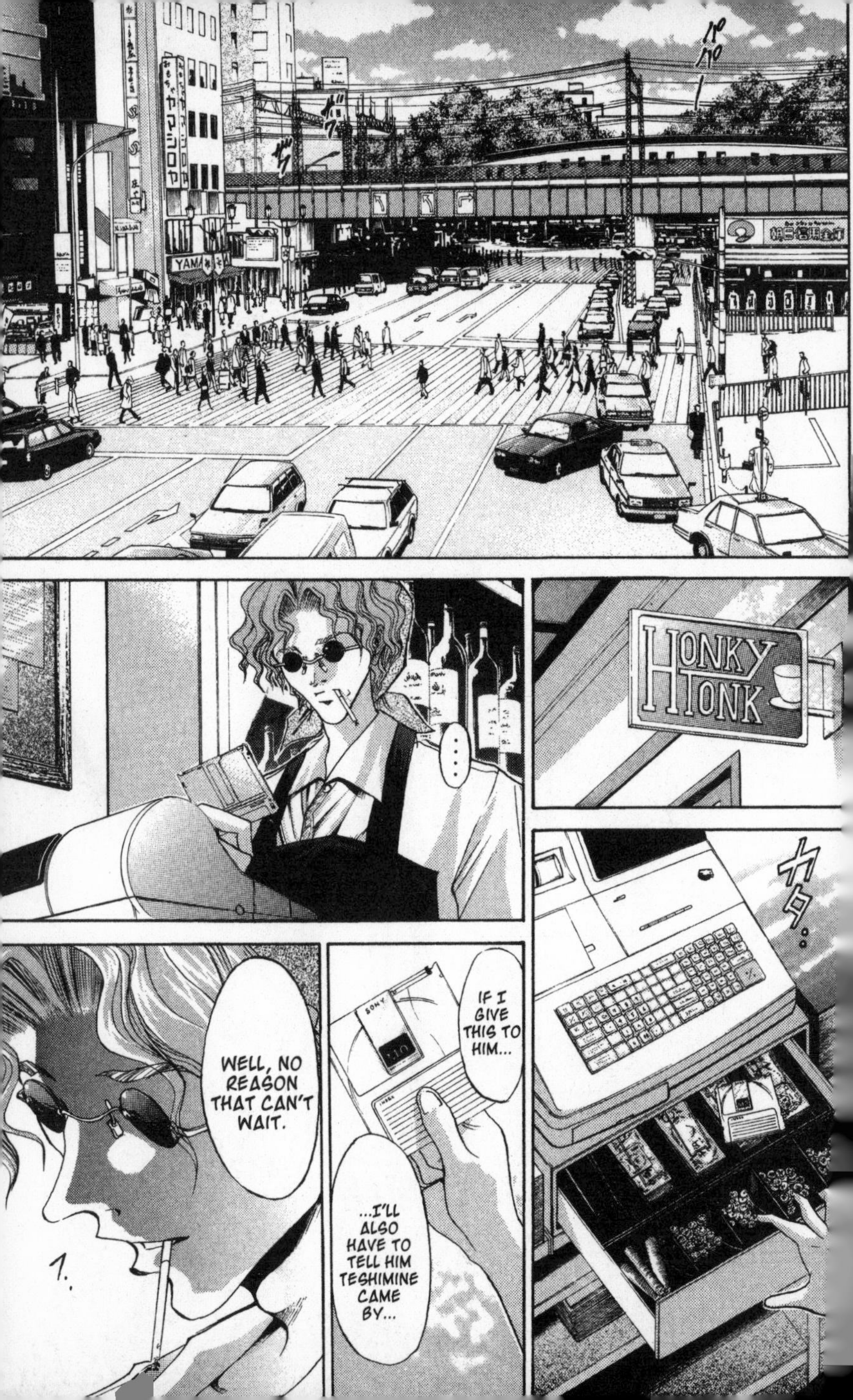
HONKY TONK
...
カタ
IF I GIVE THIS TO HIM...
...I'LL ALSO HAVE TO TELL HIM TESHIMINE CAME BY...
WELL, NO REASON THAT CAN'T WAIT.

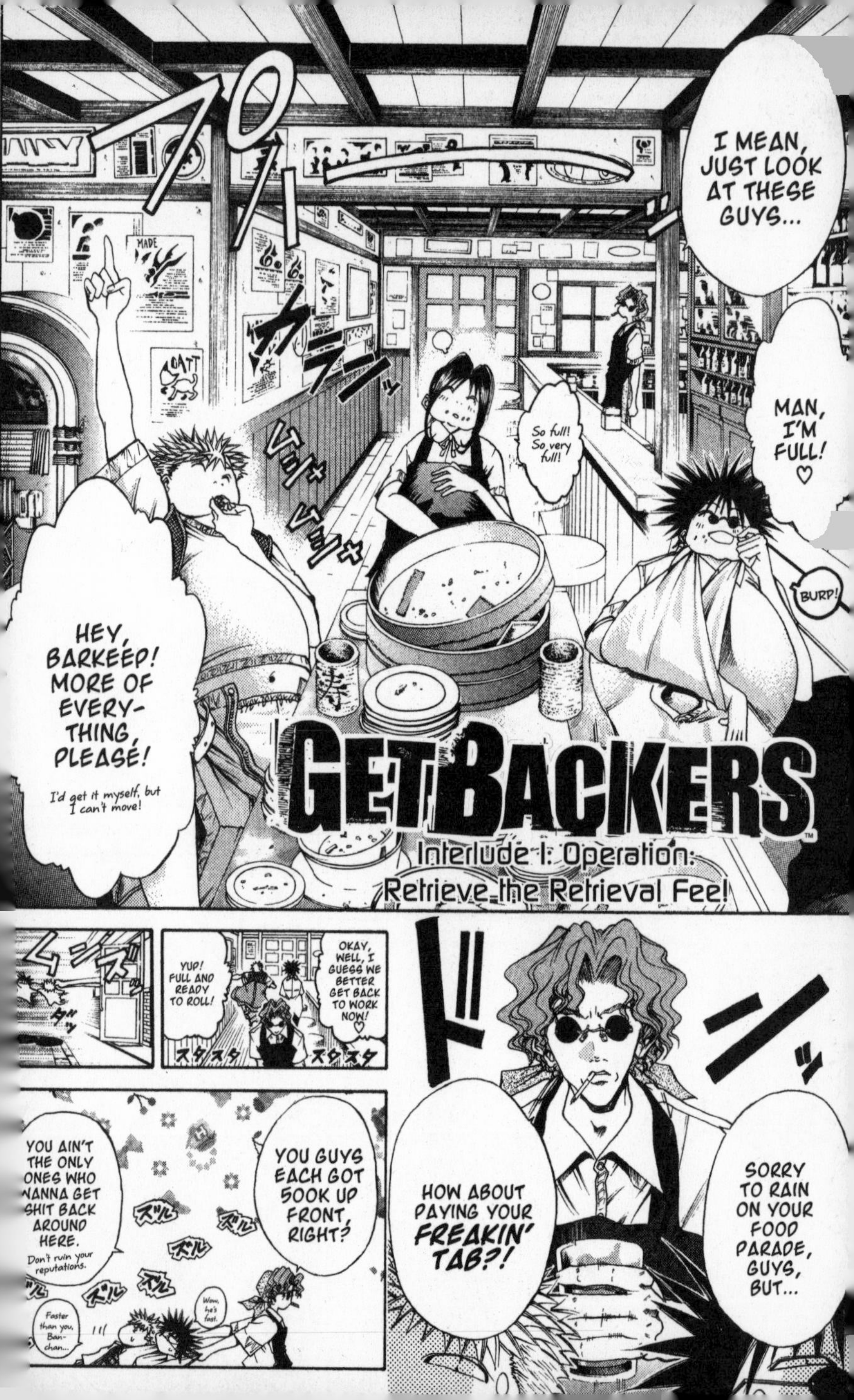
I MEAN, JUST LOOK AT THESE GUYS...
MAN, I'M FULL! ♡
BURP!
So full! So very full!
HEY, BARKEEP! MORE OF EVERY-THING, PLEASÉ!
I'd get it myself, but I can't move!
GETBACKERS™
Interlude I: Operation: Retrieve the Retrieval Fee!
SORRY TO RAIN ON YOUR FOOD PARADE, GUYS, BUT...
HOW ABOUT PAYING YOUR FREAKIN' TAB?!
OKAY, WELL, I GUESS WE BETTER GET BACK TO WORK NOW! ♡
YUP! FULL AND READY TO ROLL!
YOU GUYS EACH GOT 500K UP FRONT, RIGHT?
YOU AIN'T THE ONLY ONES WHO WANNA GET SHIT BACK AROUND HERE.
Don't ruin your reputations.
Wow, he's fast.
Faster than you, Ban-chan...

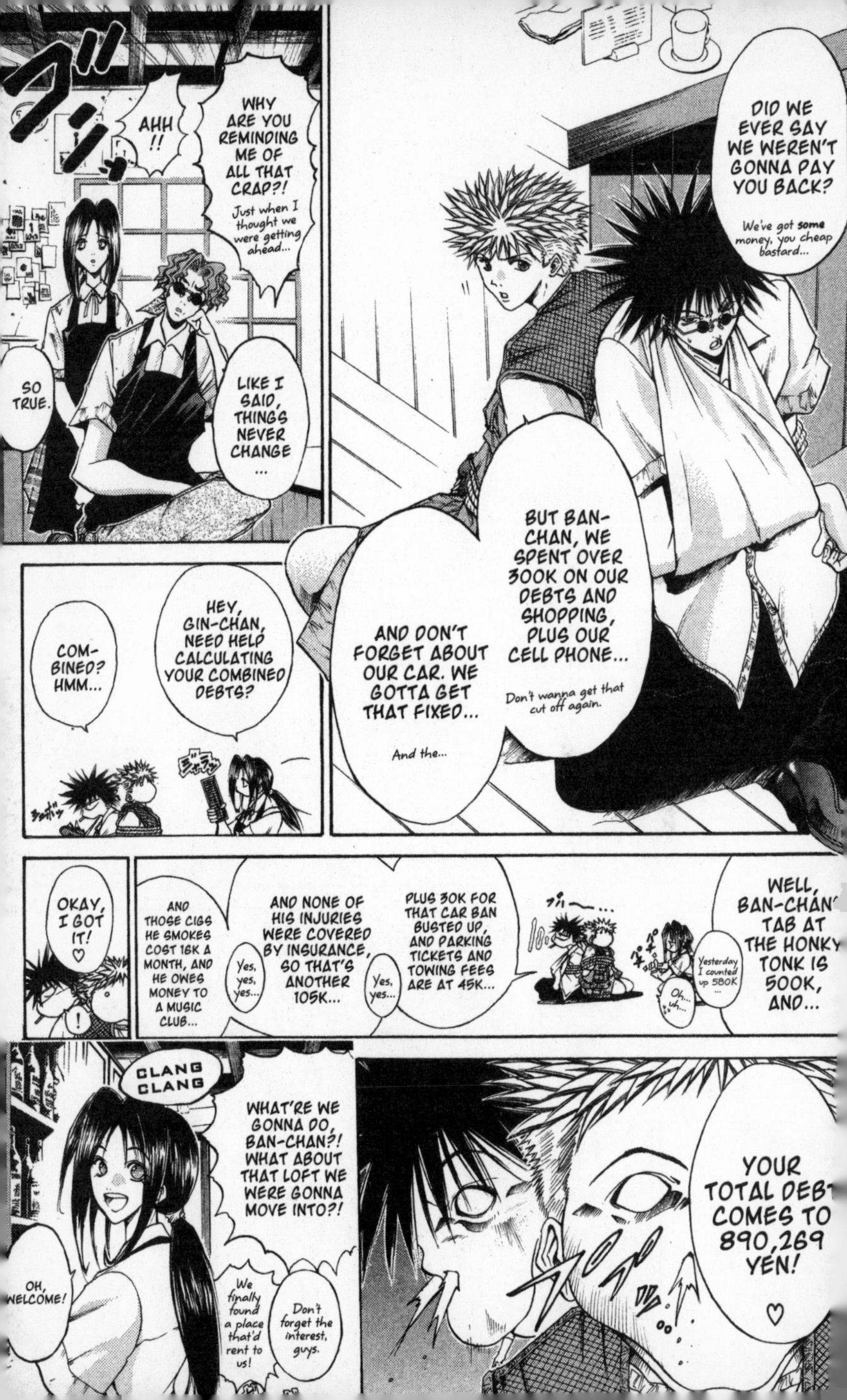
DID WE EVER SAY WE WEREN'T GONNA PAY YOU BACK?
We've got **some** money, you cheap bastard...
BUT BAN-CHAN, WE SPENT OVER 300K ON OUR DEBTS AND SHOPPING, PLUS OUR CELL PHONE...
Don't wanna get that cut off again.
AND DON'T FORGET ABOUT OUR CAR. WE GOTTA GET THAT FIXED...
And the...
WHY ARE YOU REMINDING ME OF ALL THAT CRAP?!
Just when I thought we were getting ahead...
AHH!!
LIKE I SAID, THING'S NEVER CHANGE...
SO TRUE.
HEY, GIN-CHAN, NEED HELP CALCULATING YOUR COMBINED DEBTS?
COMBINED? HMM...
WELL, BAN-CHAN'S TAB AT THE HONKY TONK IS 500K, AND...
Yesterday I counted up 580K...
Oh... uh...
PLUS 30K FOR THAT CAR BAN BUSTED UP, AND PARKING TICKETS AND TOWING FEES ARE AT 45K...
Yes, yes...
AND NONE OF HIS INJURIES WERE COVERED BY INSURANCE, SO THAT'S ANOTHER 105K...
Yes, yes, yes...
AND THOSE CIGS HE SMOKES COST 16K A MONTH, AND HE OWES MONEY TO A MUSIC CLUB...
OKAY, I GOT IT! ♡
!
YOUR TOTAL DEBT COMES TO 890,269 YEN! ♡
CLANG CLANG
WHAT'RE WE GONNA DO, BAN-CHAN?! WHAT ABOUT THAT LOFT WE WERE GONNA MOVE INTO?!
Don't forget the interest, guys.
We finally found a place that'd rent to us!
OH, WELCOME!

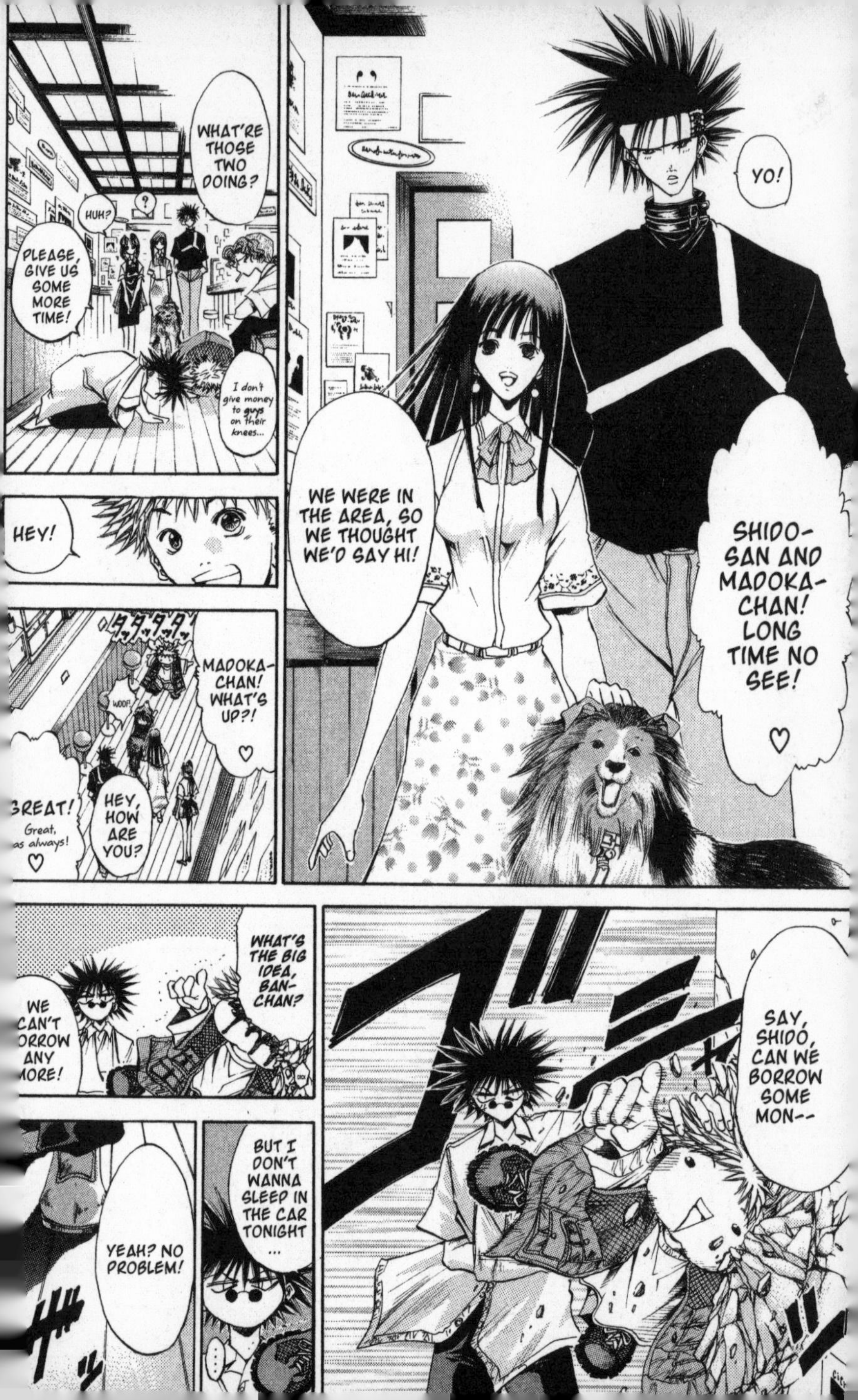
YO!
SHIDO-SAN AND MADOKA-CHAN! LONG TIME NO SEE! ♡
WE WERE IN THE AREA, SO WE THOUGHT WE'D SAY HI!
WHAT'RE THOSE TWO DOING?
HUH?
?
PLEASE, GIVE US SOME MORE TIME!
I don't give money to guys on their knees...
HEY!
MADOKA-CHAN! WHAT'S UP?! ♡
WOOF!
HEY, HOW ARE YOU?
GREAT! Great, as always! ♡
SAY, SHIDO, CAN WE BORROW SOME MON--
WHAT'S THE BIG IDEA, BAN-CHAN?
WE CAN'T ORROW ANY MORE!
BUT I DON'T WANNA SLEEP IN THE CAR TONIGHT...
YEAH? NO PROBLEM!
...

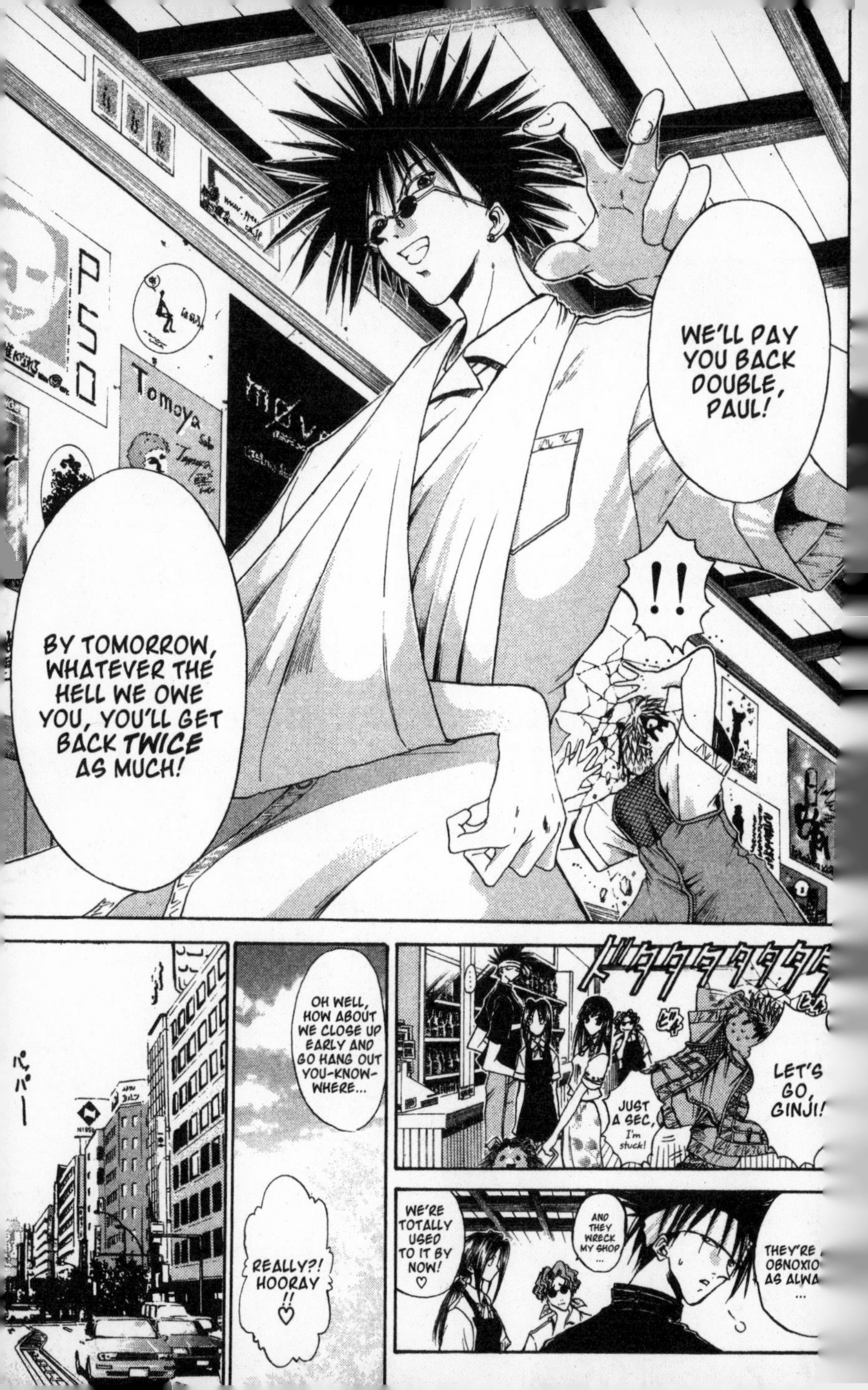
WE'LL PAY YOU BACK DOUBLE, PAUL!
!!
BY TOMORROW, WHATEVER THE HELL WE OWE YOU, YOU'LL GET BACK TWICE AS MUCH!
LET'S GO, GINJI!
JUST A SEC, I'm stuck!
THEY'RE OBNOXIO AS ALWA ...
AND THEY WRECK MY SHOP ...
WE'RE TOTALLY USED TO IT BY NOW! ♡
OH WELL, HOW ABOUT WE CLOSE UP EARLY AND GO HANG OUT YOU-KNOW-WHERE...
REALLY?! HOORAY!! ♡
パパー

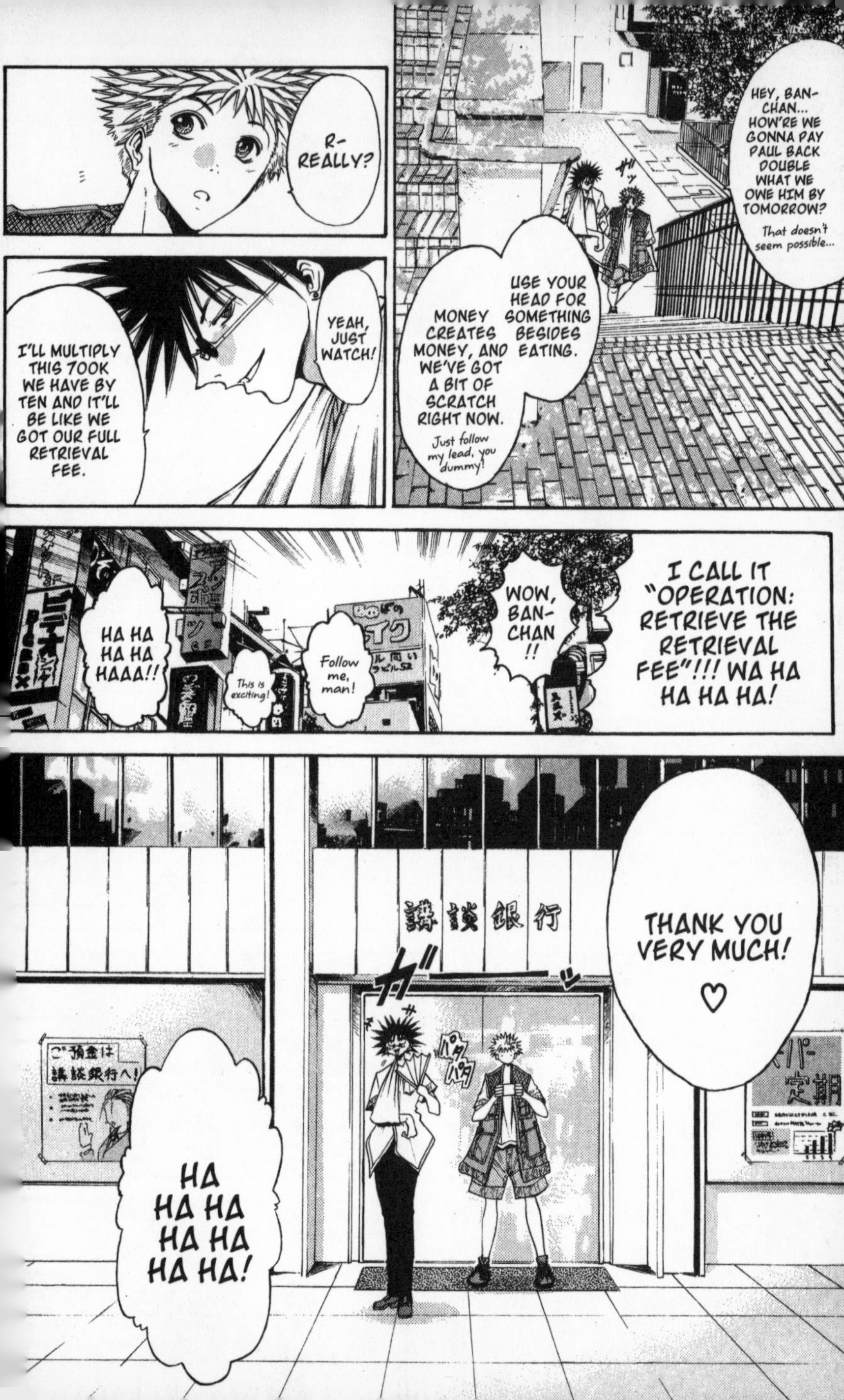
HEY, BAN-CHAN... HOW'RE WE GONNA PAY PAUL BACK DOUBLE WHAT WE OWE HIM BY TOMORROW?
That doesn't seem possible...
USE YOUR HEAD FOR SOMETHING BESIDES EATING.
MONEY CREATES MONEY, AND WE'VE GOT A BIT OF SCRATCH RIGHT NOW.
Just follow my lead, you dummy!
R-REALLY?
YEAH, JUST WATCH!
I'LL MULTIPLY THIS 700K WE HAVE BY TEN AND IT'LL BE LIKE WE GOT OUR FULL RETRIEVAL FEE.
I CALL IT "OPERATION: RETRIEVE THE RETRIEVAL FEE"!!! WA HA HA HA HA!
WOW, BAN-CHAN!!
Follow me, man!
This is exciting!
HA HA HA HA HAAA!!
講談銀行
THANK YOU VERY MUCH! ♡
HA HA HA HA HA HA HA HA HA!

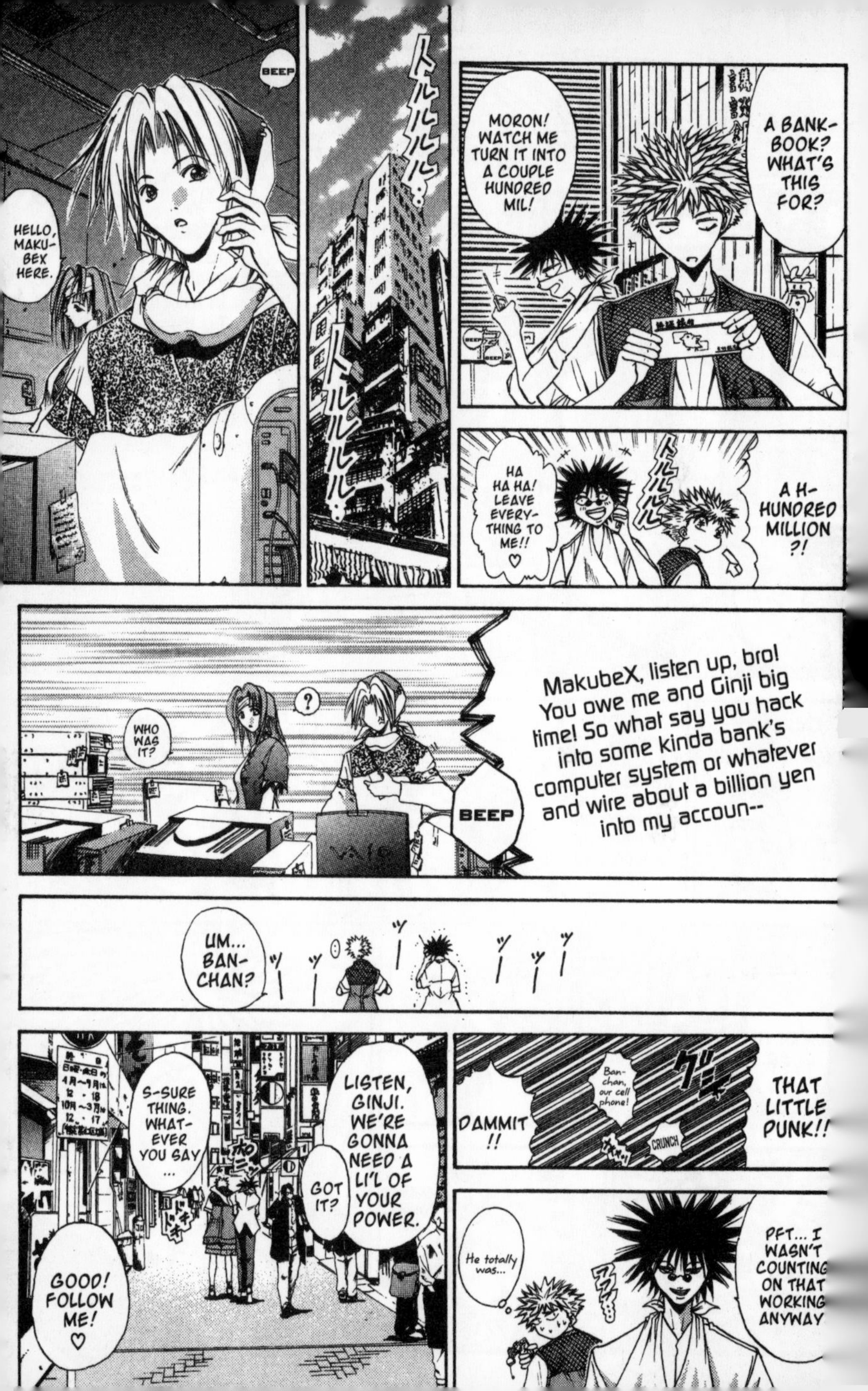
A BANK-BOOK? WHAT'S THIS FOR?
MORON! WATCH ME TURN IT INTO A COUPLE HUNDRED MIL!
BEEP
A H-HUNDRED MILLION?!
HA HA HA! LEAVE EVERYTHING TO ME!! ♡
BEEP
HELLO, MAKU-BEX HERE.
MakubeX, listen up, bro! You owe me and Ginji big time! So what say you hack into some kinda bank's computer system or whatever and wire about a billion yen into my accoun--
BEEP
?
WHO WAS IT?
UM... BAN-CHAN?
THAT LITTLE PUNK!!
Ban-chan, our cell phone!
CRUNCH
DAMMIT!!
PFT... I WASN'T COUNTING ON THAT WORKING ANYWAY
He totally was...
LISTEN, GINJI. WE'RE GONNA NEED A LI'L OF YOUR POWER.
GOT IT?
S-SURE THING. WHATEVER YOU SAY...
GOOD! FOLLOW ME! ♡

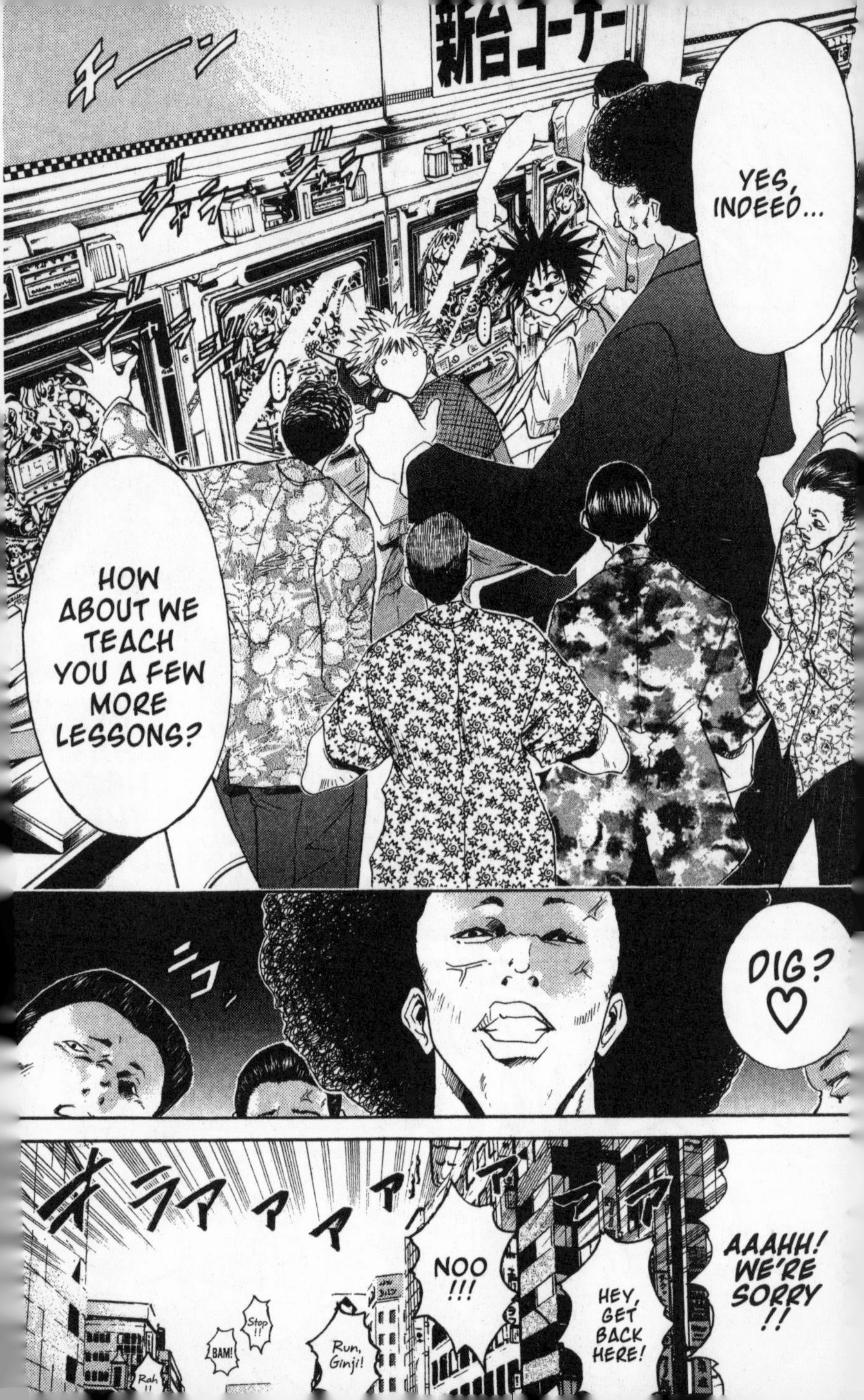
新台コーナー
チーーン
YES, INDEED...
HOW ABOUT WE TEACH YOU A FEW MORE LESSONS?
DIG? ♥
AAAHH! WE'RE SORRY!!
HEY, GET BACK HERE!
NOO!!!
Run, Ginji!
Stop!!
BAM!
Rah!!

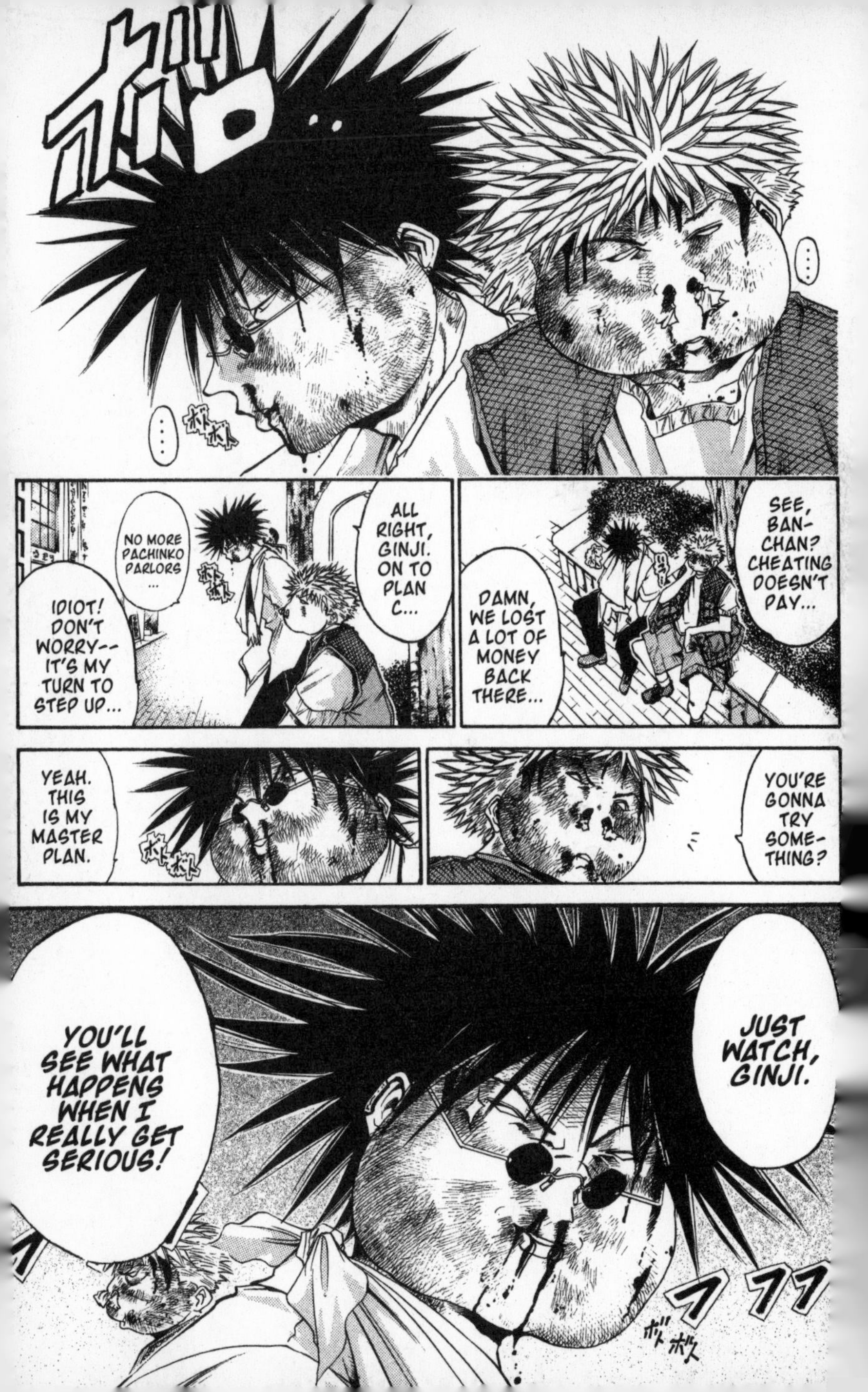
...
...
SEE, BAN-CHAN? CHEATING DOESN'T PAY...
DAMN, WE LOST A LOT OF MONEY BACK THERE...
ALL RIGHT, GINJI. ON TO PLAN C...
NO MORE PACHINKO PARLORS ...
IDIOT! DON'T WORRY--IT'S MY TURN TO STEP UP...
YOU'RE GONNA TRY SOME-THING?
YEAH. THIS IS MY MASTER PLAN.
JUST WATCH, GINJI.
YOU'LL SEE WHAT HAPPENS WHEN I REALLY GET SERIOUS!

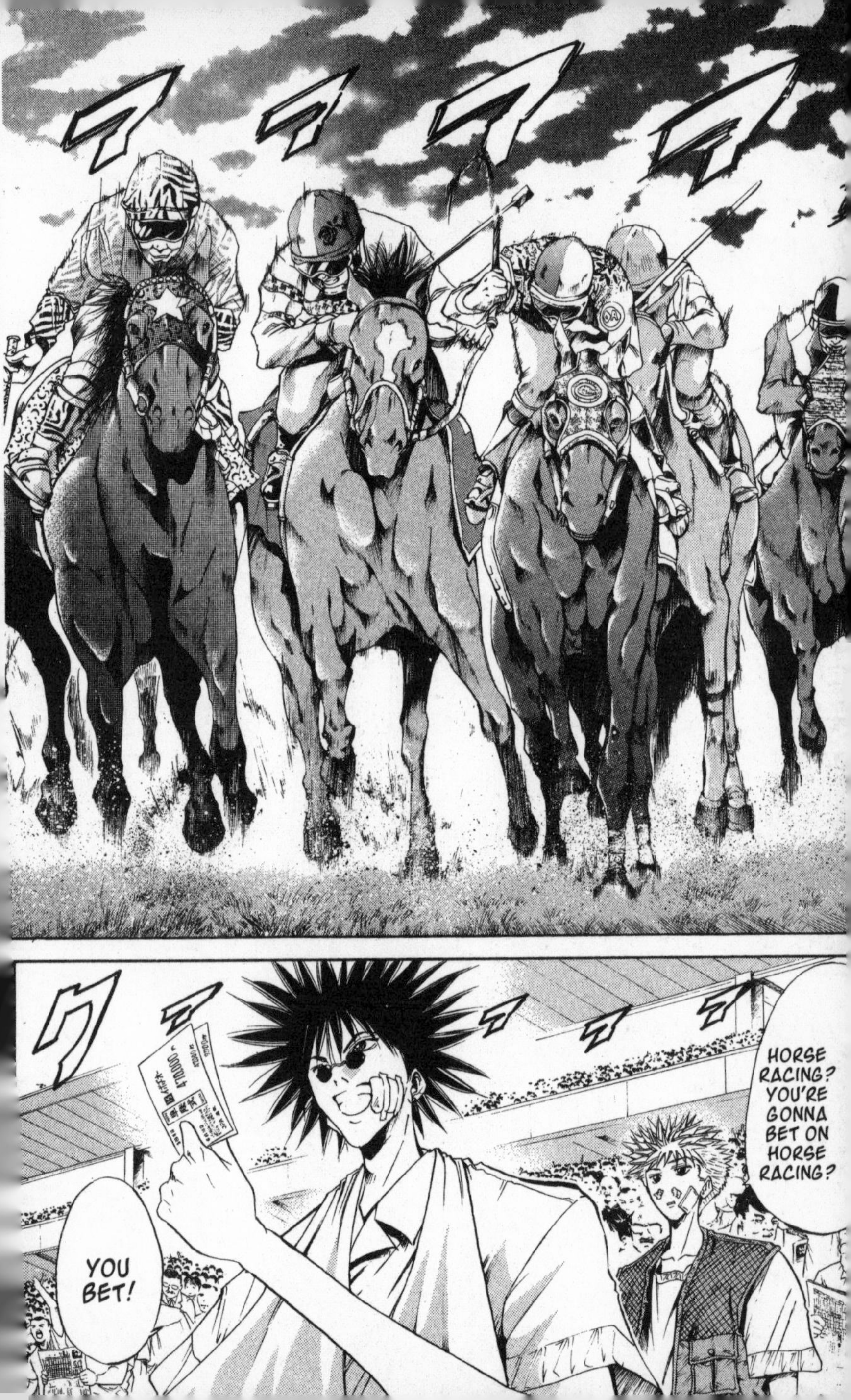
HORSE RACING? YOU'RE GONNA BET ON HORSE RACING?
YOU BET!

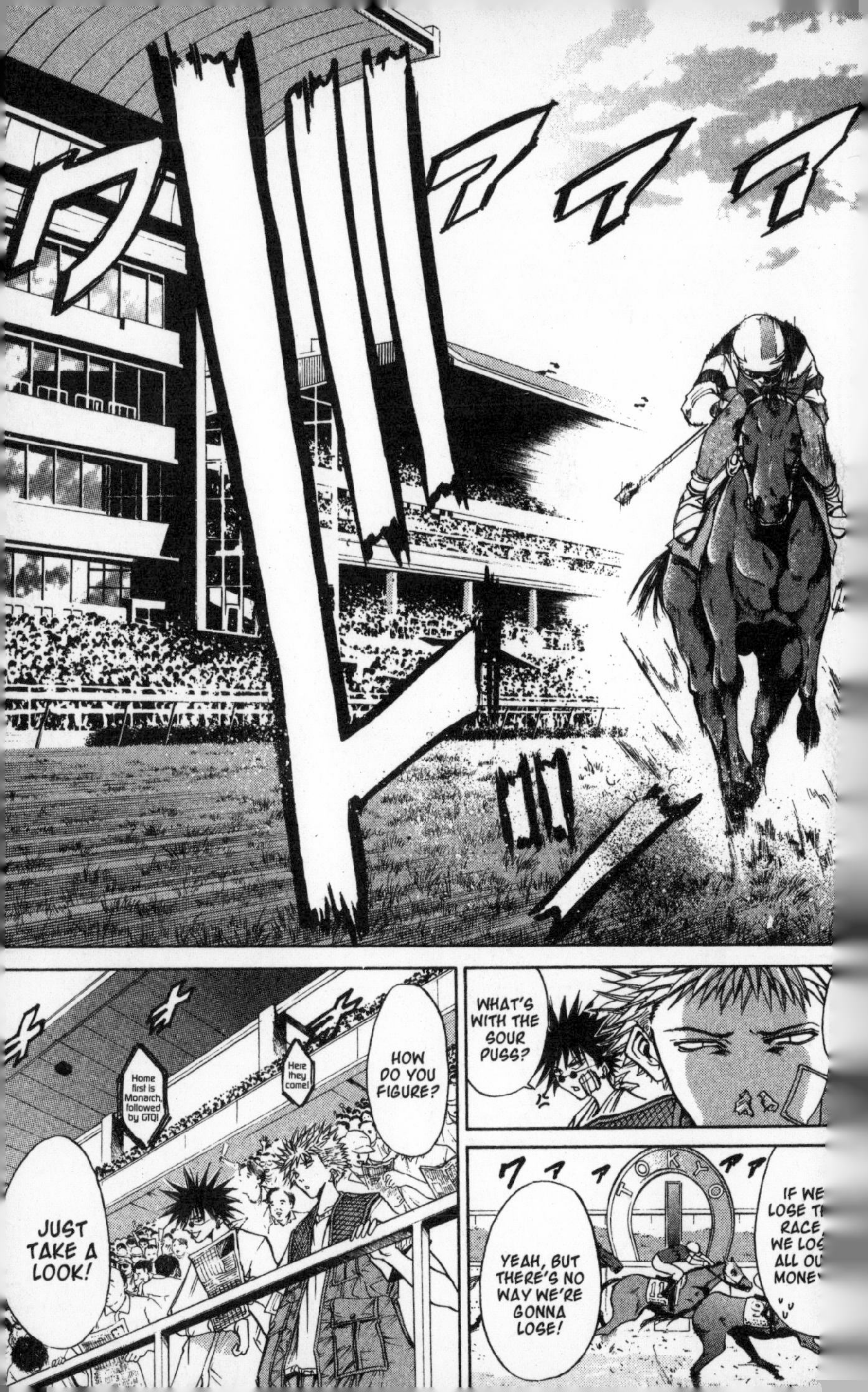
WHAT'S WITH THE SOUR PUSS?
IF WE LOSE T RACE WE LOS ALL OU MONE
YEAH, BUT THERE'S NO WAY WE'RE GONNA LOSE!
HOW DO YOU FIGURE?
Here they come!
Home first is Monarch, followed by GTO!
JUST TAKE A LOOK!

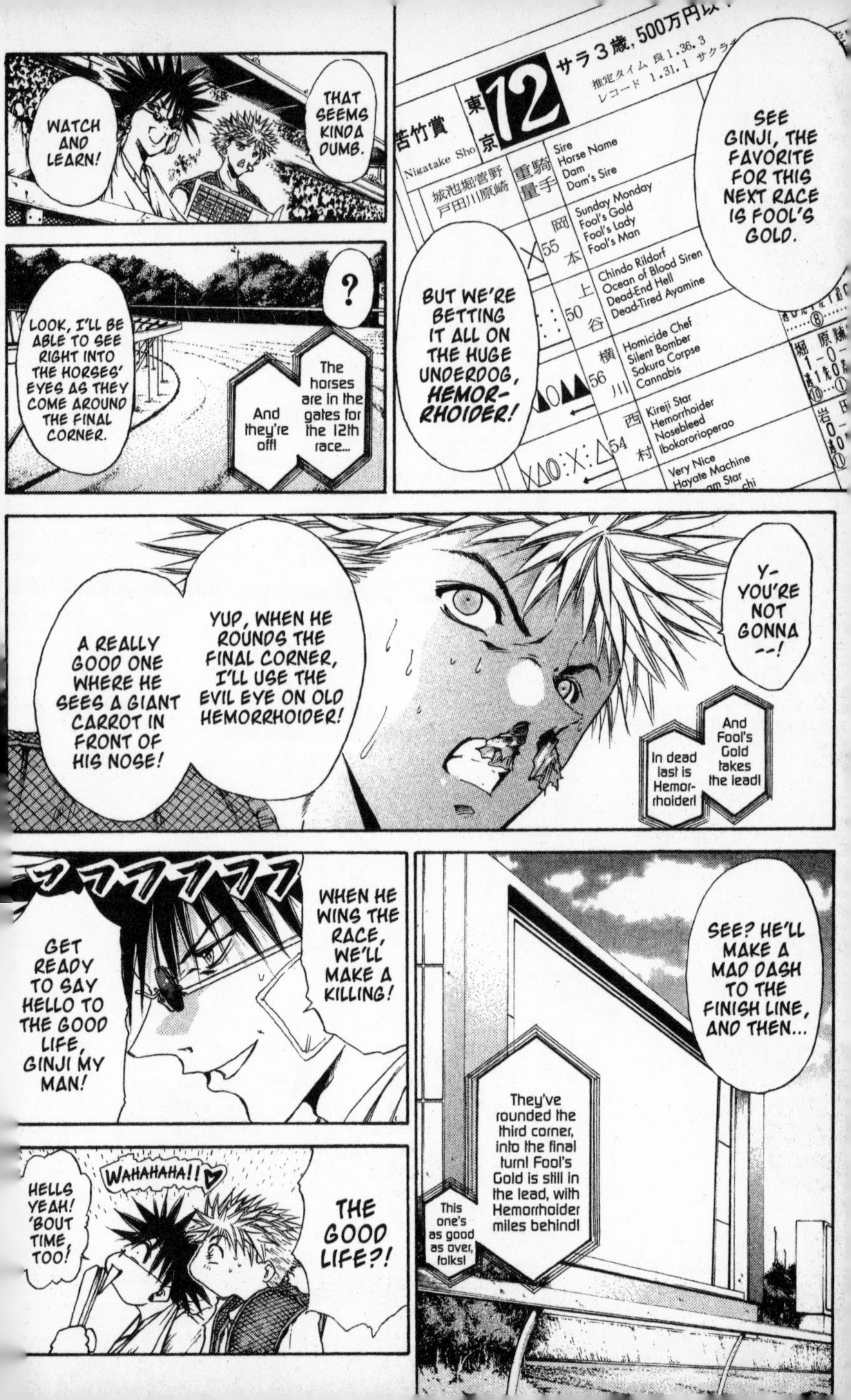
SEE GINJI, THE FAVORITE FOR THIS NEXT RACE IS FOOL'S GOLD.
サラ3歳, 500万円以
推定タイム 良 1.36.3
レコード 1.31.1 サクラ
東京 12
苦竹賞
Nigatake Sho
重騎 量手
城池堀菅野 戸田川原崎
Sire
Horse Name
Dam
Dam's Sire
岡本 55
Sunday Monday
Fool's Gold
Fool's Lady
Fool's Man
上谷 50
Chindo Rildorf
Ocean of Blood Siren
Dead-End Hell
Dead-Tired Ayamine
横川 56
Homicide Chef
Silent Bomber
Sakura Corpse
Cannabis
西村 54
Kireji Star
Hemorrhoider
Nosebleed
Ibokororioperao
Very Nice
Hayate Machine
BUT WE'RE BETTING IT ALL ON THE HUGE UNDERDOG, HEMORRHOIDER!
THAT SEEMS KINDA DUMB.
WATCH AND LEARN!
?
The horses are in the gates for the 12th race...
And they're off!
LOOK, I'LL BE ABLE TO SEE RIGHT INTO THE HORSES' EYES AS THEY COME AROUND THE FINAL CORNER.
Y-YOU'RE NOT GONNA--!
And Fool's Gold takes the lead!
In dead last is Hemorrhoider!
YUP, WHEN HE ROUNDS THE FINAL CORNER, I'LL USE THE EVIL EYE ON OLD HEMORRHOIDER!
A REALLY GOOD ONE WHERE HE SEES A GIANT CARROT IN FRONT OF HIS NOSE!
SEE? HE'LL MAKE A MAD DASH TO THE FINISH LINE, AND THEN...
They've rounded the third corner, into the final turn! Fool's Gold is still in the lead, with Hemorrhoider miles behind!
This one's as good as over, folks!
WHEN HE WINS THE RACE, WE'LL MAKE A KILLING!
GET READY TO SAY HELLO TO THE GOOD LIFE, GINJI MY MAN!
THE GOOD LIFE?!
WAHAHAHA!!♥
HELLS YEAH! 'BOUT TIME, TOO!

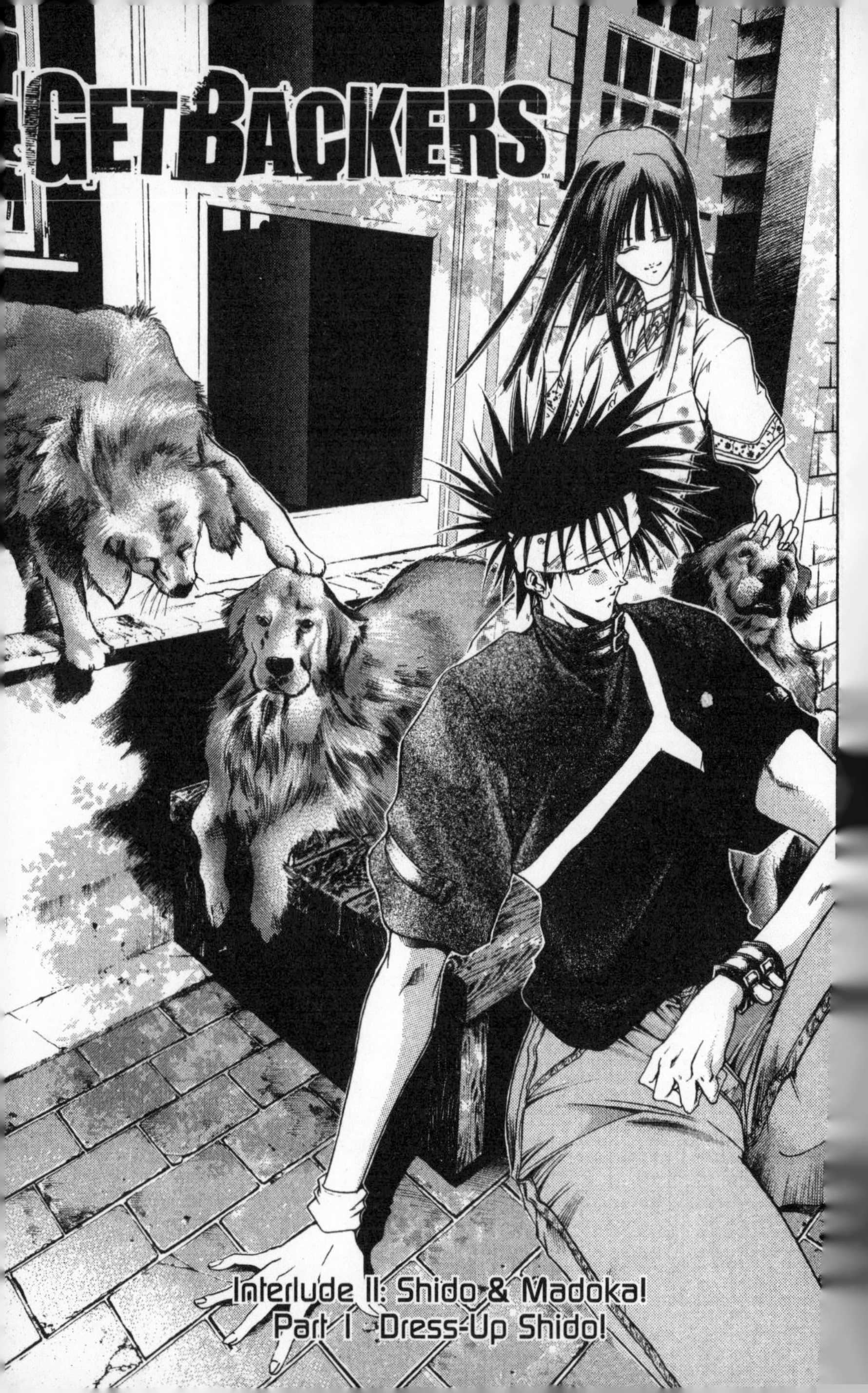
GetBackers
Interlude II: Shido & Madoka!
Part I Dress-Up Shido!

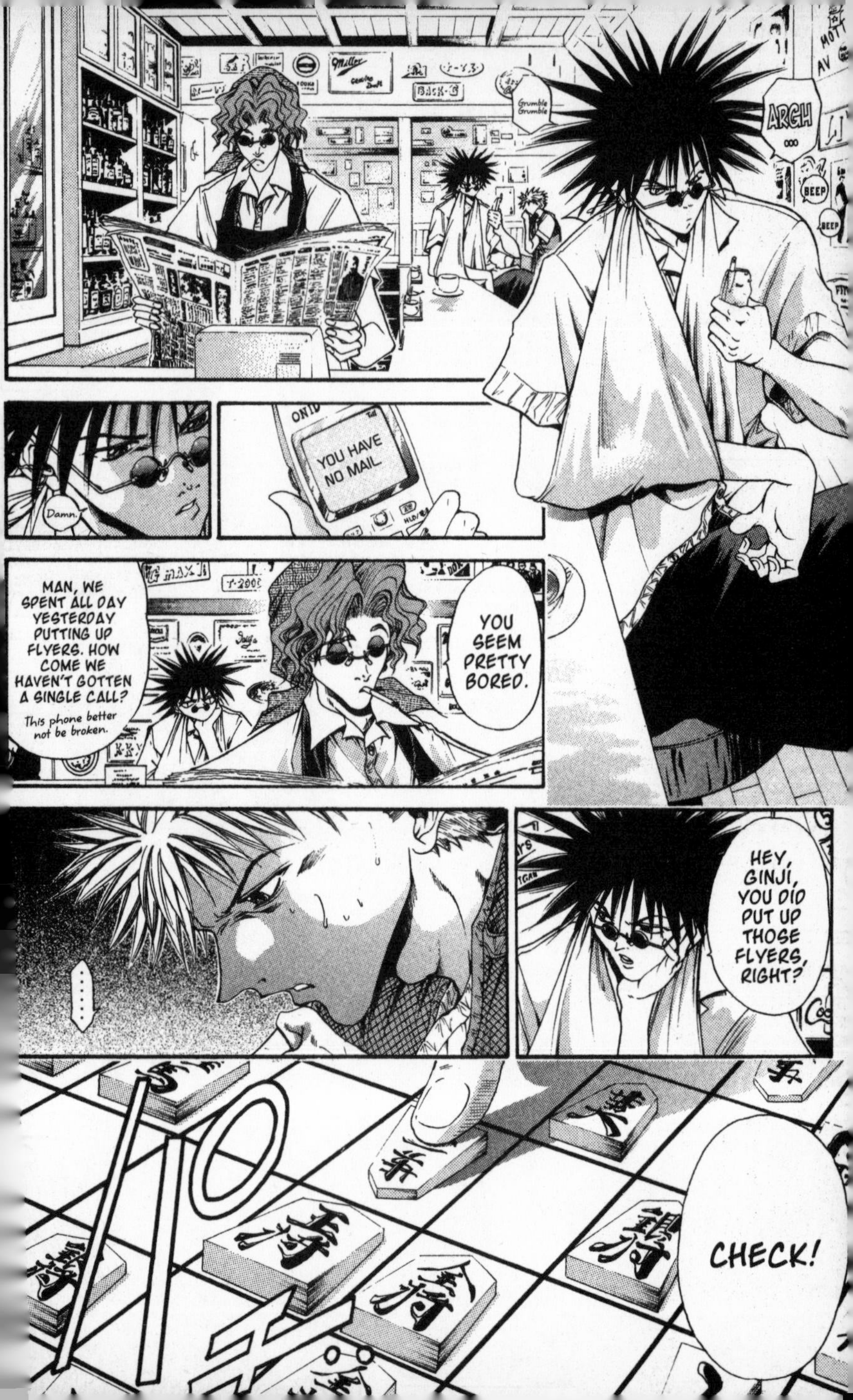
ARGH
BEEP
BEEP
Grumble Grumble
YOU HAVE NO MAIL
Damn.
YOU SEEM PRETTY BORED.
MAN, WE SPENT ALL DAY YESTERDAY PUTTING UP FLYERS. HOW COME WE HAVEN'T GOTTEN A SINGLE CALL?
This phone better not be broken.
HEY, GINJI, YOU DID PUT UP THOSE FLYERS, RIGHT?
......
CHECK!

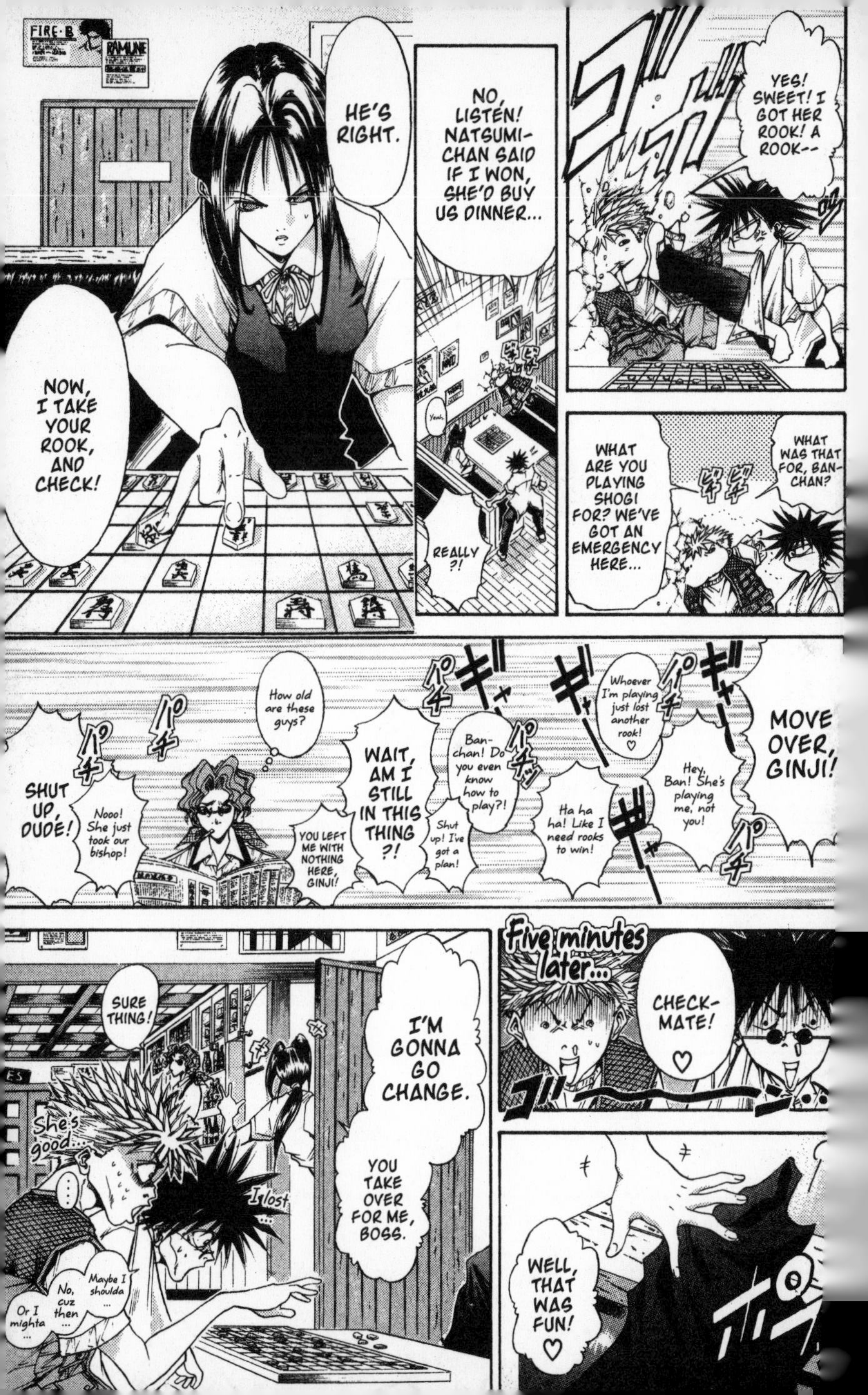
YES! SWEET! I GOT HER ROOK! A ROOK--
WHAT WAS THAT FOR, BAN-CHAN?
WHAT ARE YOU PLAYING SHOGI FOR? WE'VE GOT AN EMERGENCY HERE...
NO, LISTEN! NATSUMI-CHAN SAID IF I WON, SHE'D BUY US DINNER...
Yeah.
REALLY?!
FIRE-B
RAMUNE
HE'S RIGHT.
NOW, I TAKE YOUR ROOK, AND CHECK!
MOVE OVER, GINJI!
Hey, Ban! She's playing me, not you!
Whoever I'm playing just lost another rook! ♡
Ha ha ha! Like I need rooks to win!
Ban-chan! Do you even know how to play?!
Shut up! I've got a plan!
WAIT, AM I STILL IN THIS THING?!
YOU LEFT ME WITH NOTHING HERE, GINJI!
How old are these guys?
Nooo! She just took our bishop!
SHUT UP, DUDE!
Five minutes later...
CHECKMATE! ♡
WELL, THAT WAS FUN! ♡
I'M GONNA GO CHANGE.
YOU TAKE OVER FOR ME, BOSS.
SURE THING!
She's good...
I lost...
...
Maybe I shoulda...
No, cuz then...
Or I mighta...

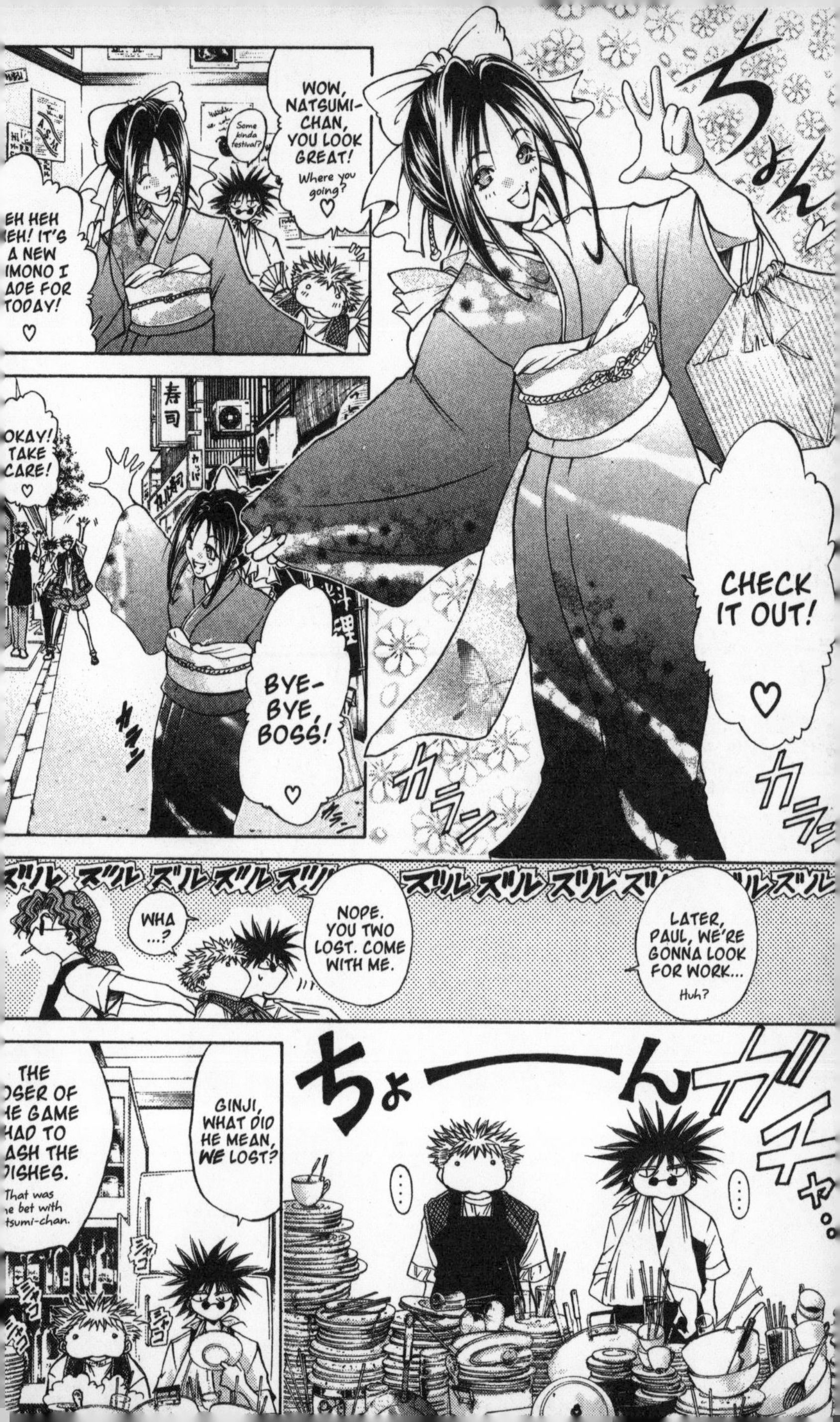
CHECK IT OUT! ♥
WOW, NATSUMI-CHAN, YOU LOOK GREAT! Where you going? ♥
Some kinda festival?
EH HEH HEH! IT'S A NEW IMONO I ADE FOR TODAY! ♥
BYE-BYE, BOSS! ♥
OKAY! TAKE CARE! ♥
LATER, PAUL, WE'RE GONNA LOOK FOR WORK... Huh?
NOPE. YOU TWO LOST. COME WITH ME.
WHA ...?
ちょーーん
...
...
GINJI, WHAT DID HE MEAN, WE LOST?
THE OSER OF HE GAME HAD TO ASH THE ISHES. That was e bet with tsumi-chan.

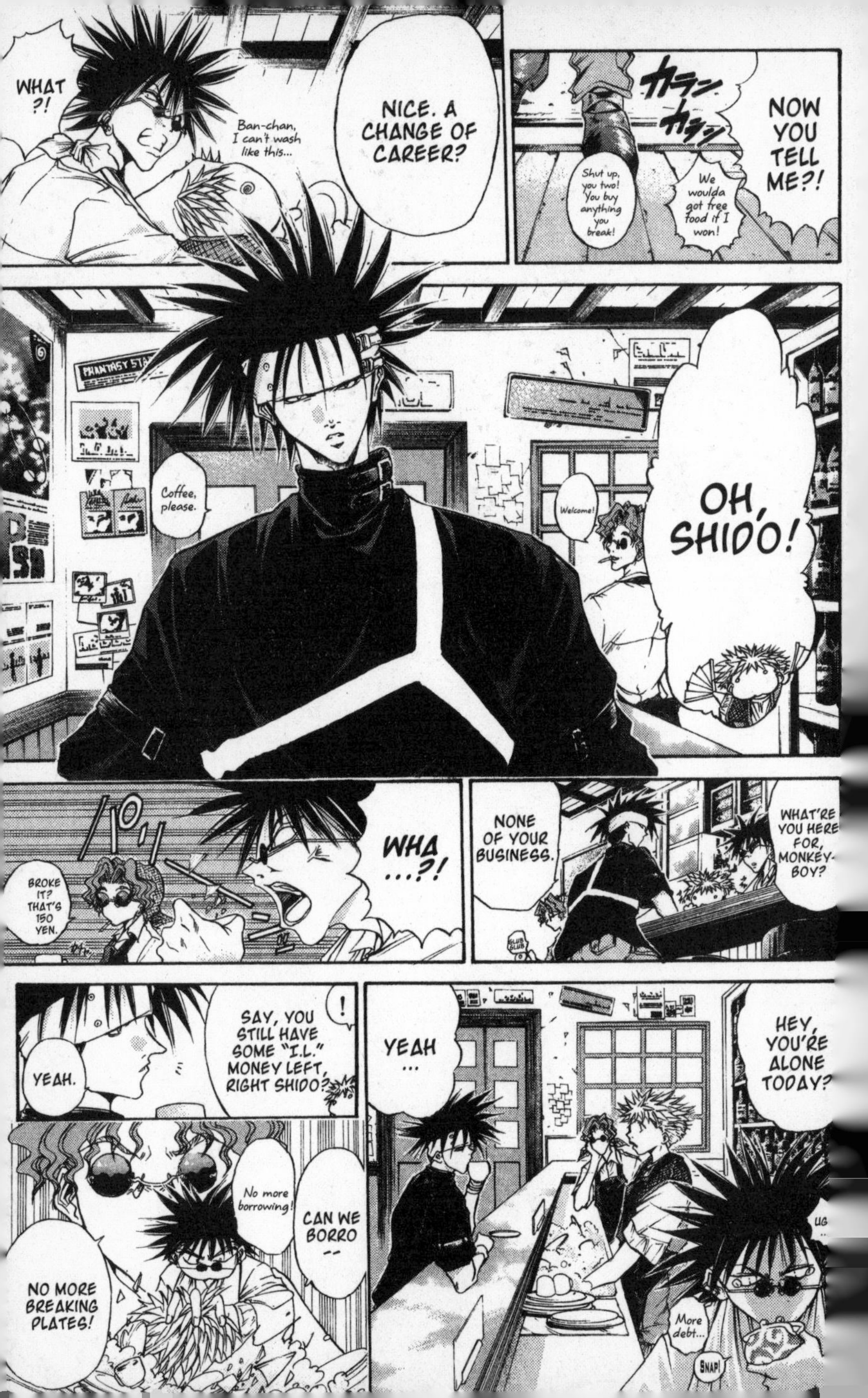
NOW YOU TELL ME?!
We woulda got free food if I won!
Shut up, you two! You buy anything you break!
NICE. A CHANGE OF CAREER?
Ban-chan, I can't wash like this...
WHAT ?!
OH, SHIDO!
Welcome!
Coffee, please.
WHAT'RE YOU HERE FOR, MONKEY-BOY?
NONE OF YOUR BUSINESS.
GLUB GLUB
WHA ...?!
BROKE IT? THAT'S 150 YEN.
HEY, YOU'RE ALONE TODAY?
YEAH ...
UG ...
More debt...
SNAP!
!
SAY, YOU STILL HAVE SOME "I.L." MONEY LEFT, RIGHT SHIDO?
YEAH.
CAN WE BORRO --
No more borrowing!
NO MORE BREAKING PLATES!

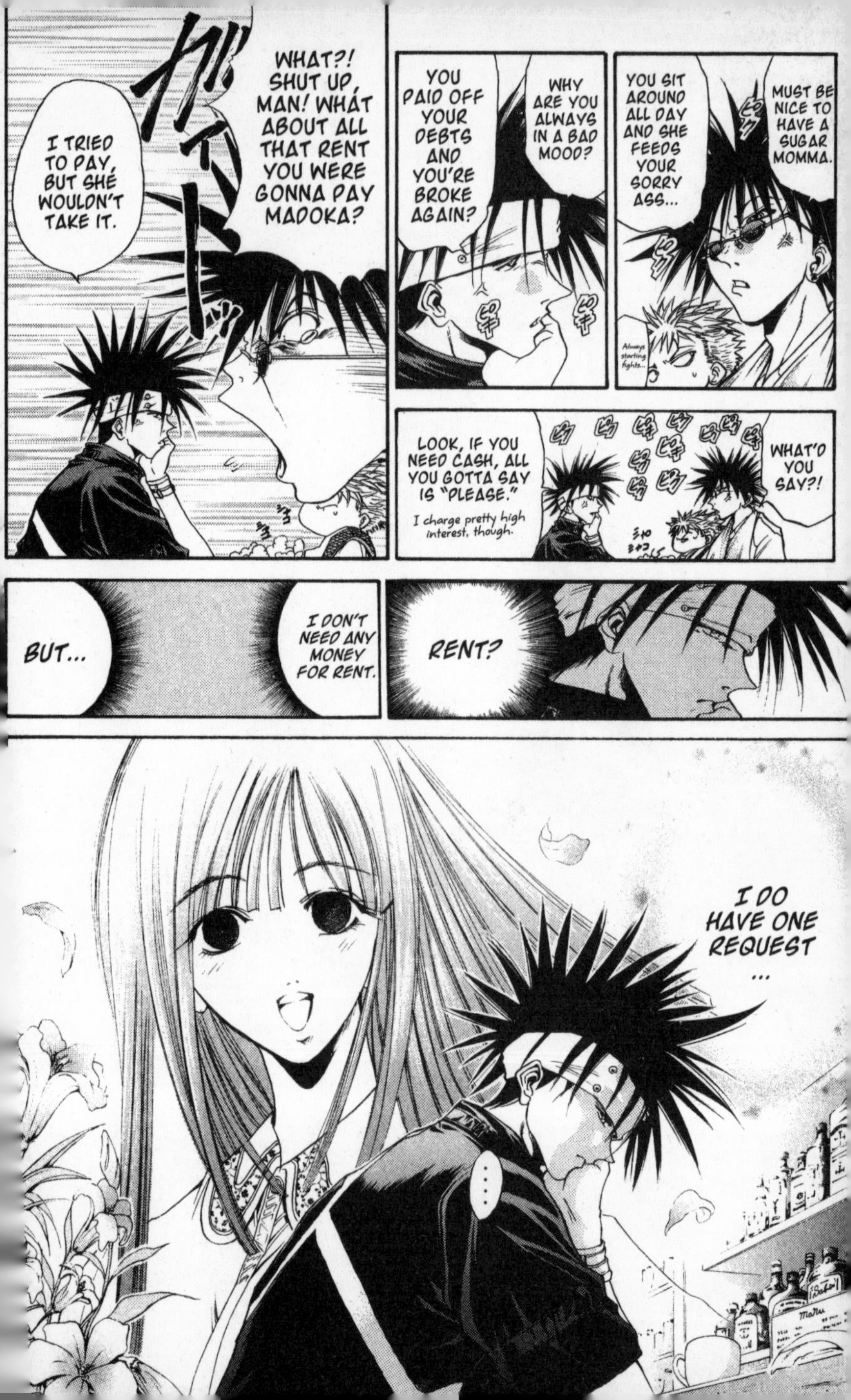
MUST BE NICE TO HAVE A SUGAR MOMMA.
YOU SIT AROUND ALL DAY AND SHE FEEDS YOUR SORRY ASS...
Always starting fights...
WHY ARE YOU ALWAYS IN A BAD MOOD?
YOU PAID OFF YOUR DEBTS AND YOU'RE BROKE AGAIN?
WHAT'D YOU SAY?!
LOOK, IF YOU NEED CASH, ALL YOU GOTTA SAY IS "PLEASE."
I charge pretty high interest, though.
WHAT?! SHUT UP, MAN! WHAT ABOUT ALL THAT RENT YOU WERE GONNA PAY MADOKA?
I TRIED TO PAY, BUT SHE WOULDN'T TAKE IT.
RENT?
I DON'T NEED ANY MONEY FOR RENT.
BUT...
I DO HAVE ONE REQUEST ...
...

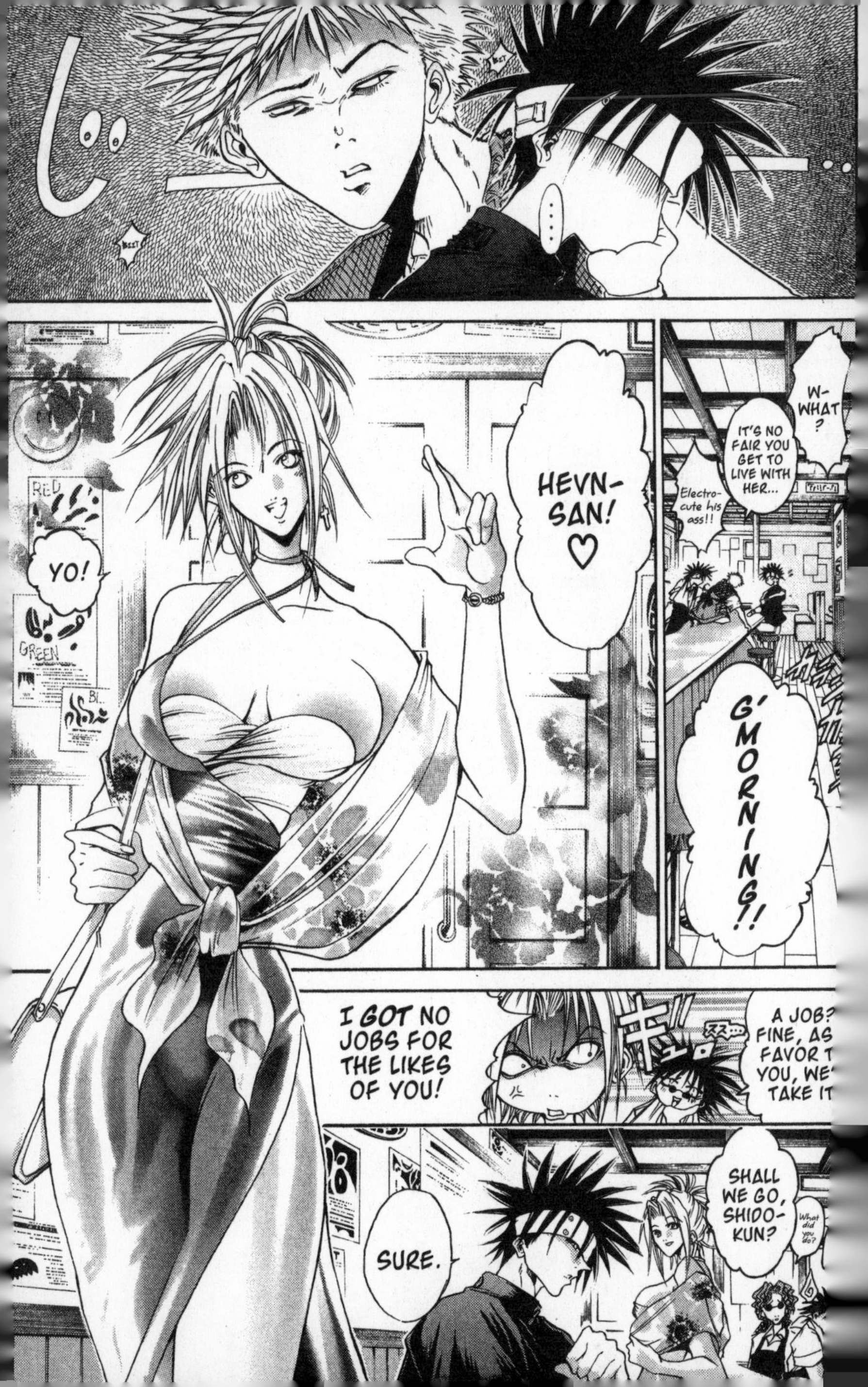
...
...
W-WHAT?
IT'S NO FAIR YOU GET TO LIVE WITH HER...
Electro-cute his ass!!
G'MORNING!!
HEVN-SAN! ♡
YO!
A JOB? FINE, AS FAVOR T YOU, WE' TAKE IT
I GOT NO JOBS FOR THE LIKES OF YOU!
What did you do?
SHALL WE GO, SHIDO-KUN?
SURE.

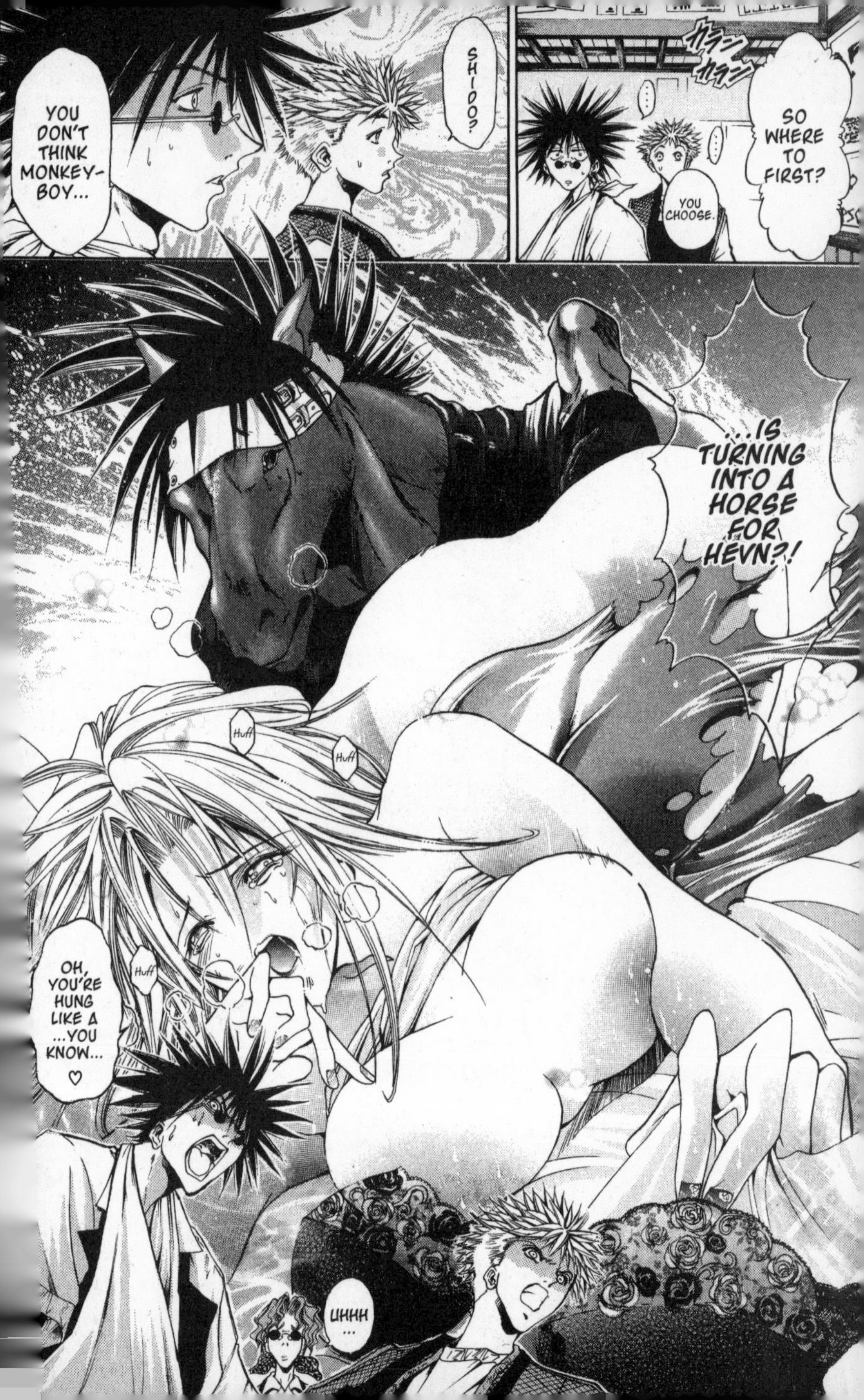
SO WHERE TO FIRST?
YOU CHOOSE.
...
...
SHIDO?
YOU DON'T THINK MONKEY-BOY...
...IS TURNING INTO A HORSE FOR HEVN?!
Huff
Huff
Huff
OH, YOU'RE HUNG LIKE A ...YOU KNOW... ♡
UHHH ...

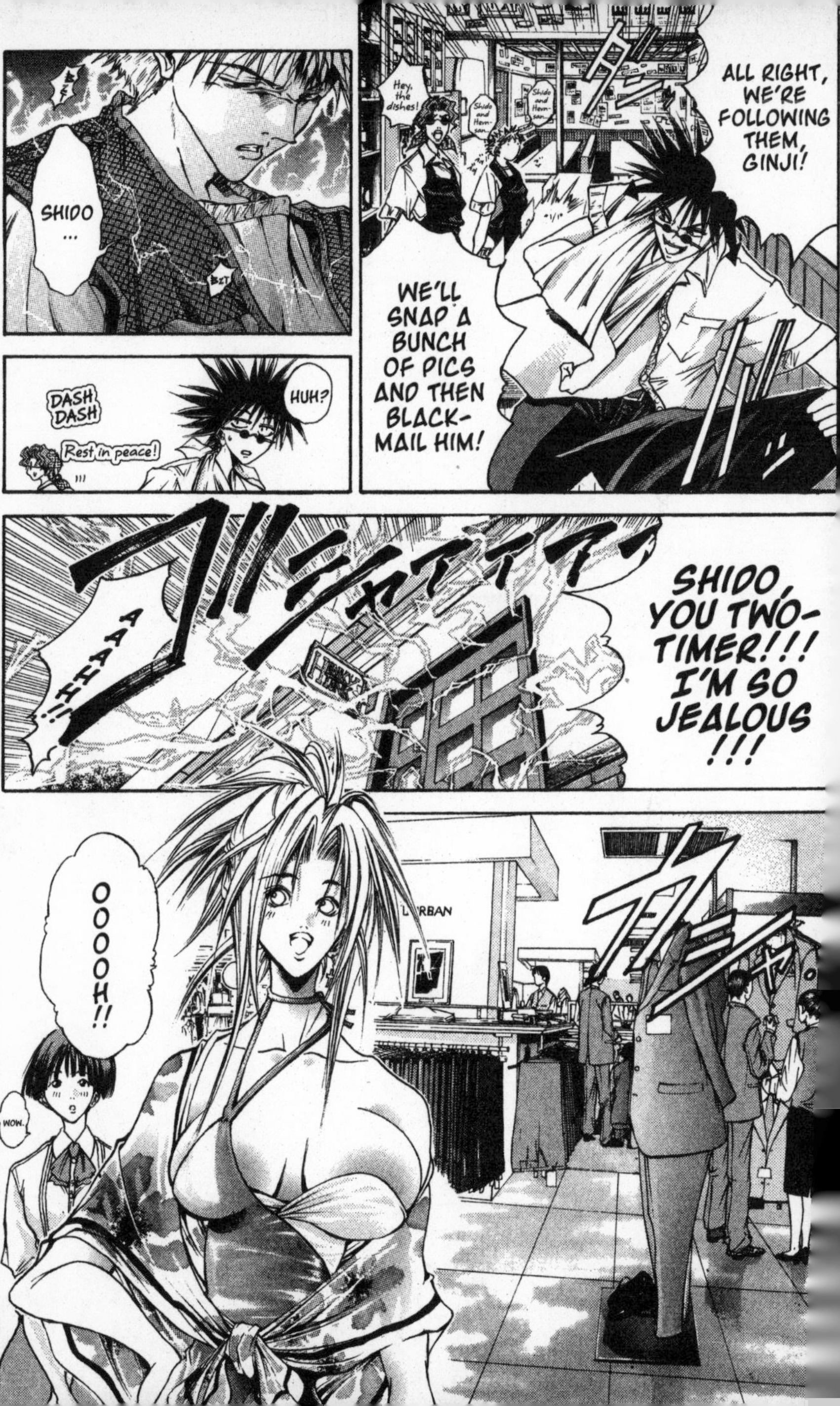

ALL RIGHT, WE'RE FOLLOWING THEM, GINJI!
Hey, the dishes!
Shido and Hevn-san...
WE'LL SNAP A BUNCH OF PICS AND THEN BLACK-MAIL HIM!
SHIDO ...
HUH?
DASH DASH
Rest in peace!
SHIDO, YOU TWO-TIMER!!! I'M SO JEALOUS!!!
AAAHH!!!
OOOOOH!!
WOW.

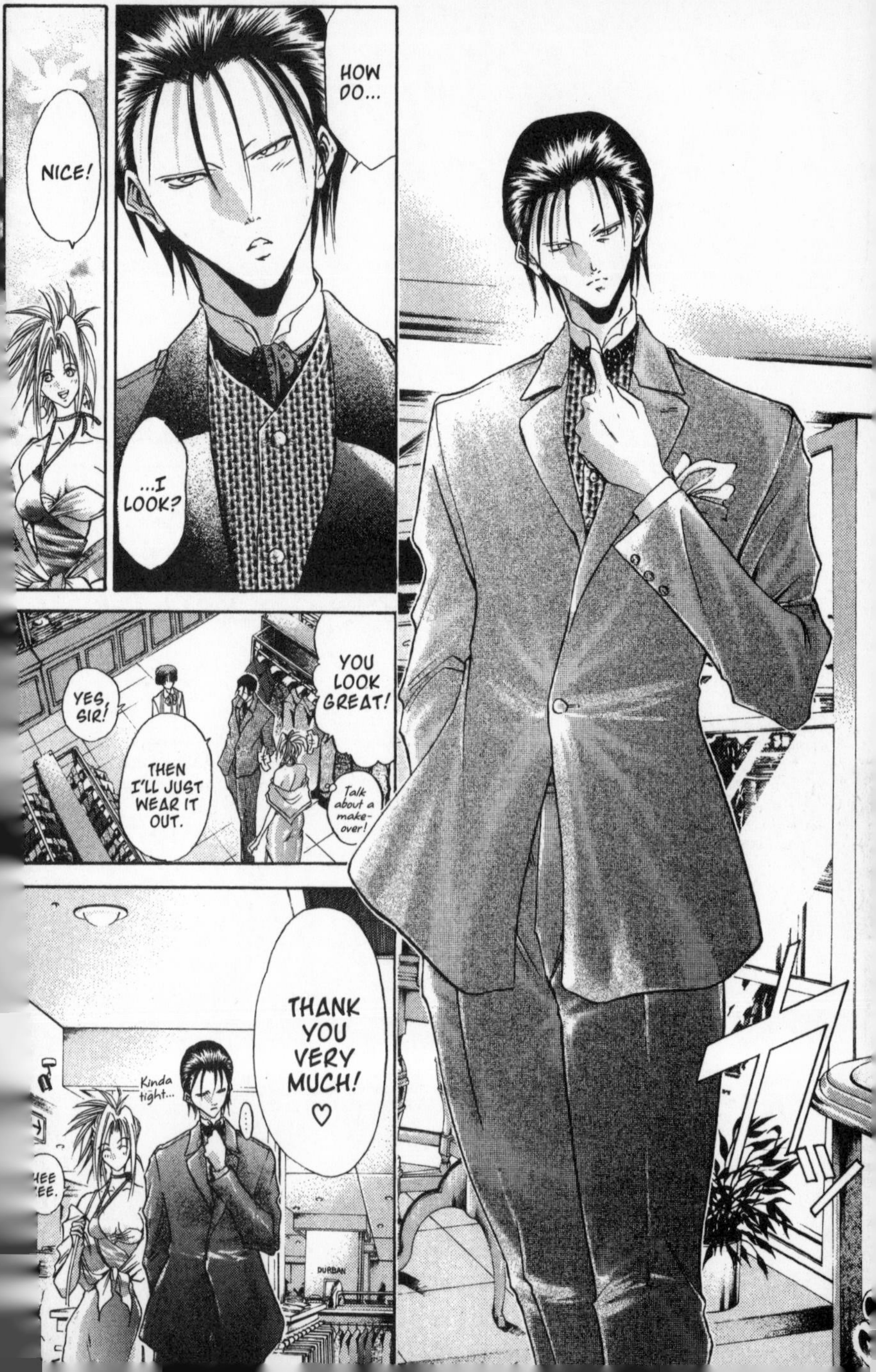
HOW DO...
...I LOOK?
NICE!
YOU LOOK GREAT!
YES, SIR!
Talk about a make-over!
THEN I'LL JUST WEAR IT OUT.
THANK YOU VERY MUCH! ♡
Kinda tight...
...
HEE HEE.
DURBAN

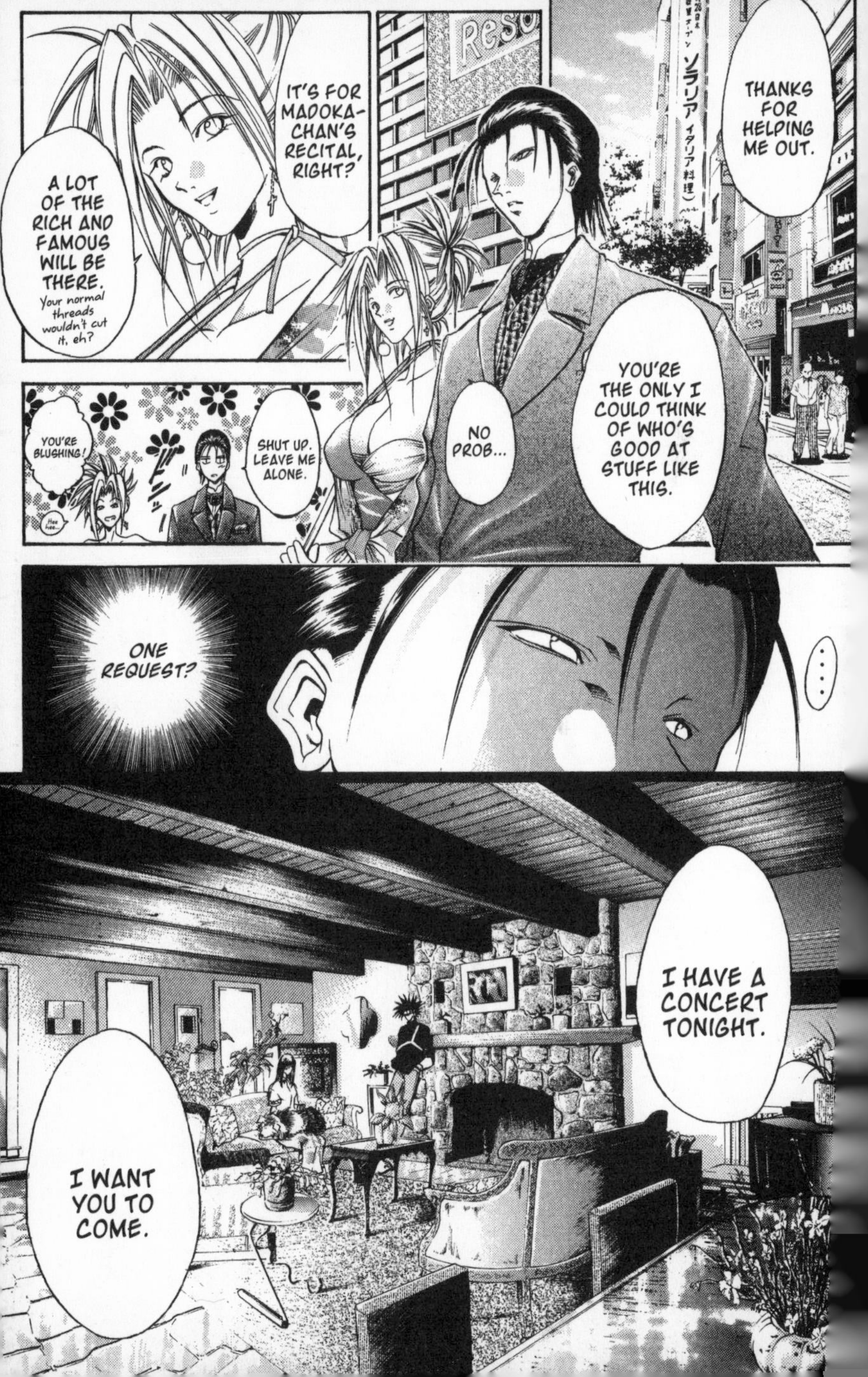
THANKS FOR HELPING ME OUT.
YOU'RE THE ONLY I COULD THINK OF WHO'S GOOD AT STUFF LIKE THIS.
NO PROB...
IT'S FOR MADOKA-CHAN'S RECITAL, RIGHT?
A LOT OF THE RICH AND FAMOUS WILL BE THERE.
Your normal threads wouldn't cut it, eh?
SHUT UP. LEAVE ME ALONE.
YOU'RE BLUSHING!
Hee hee...
...
ONE REQUEST?
I HAVE A CONCERT TONIGHT.
I WANT YOU TO COME.

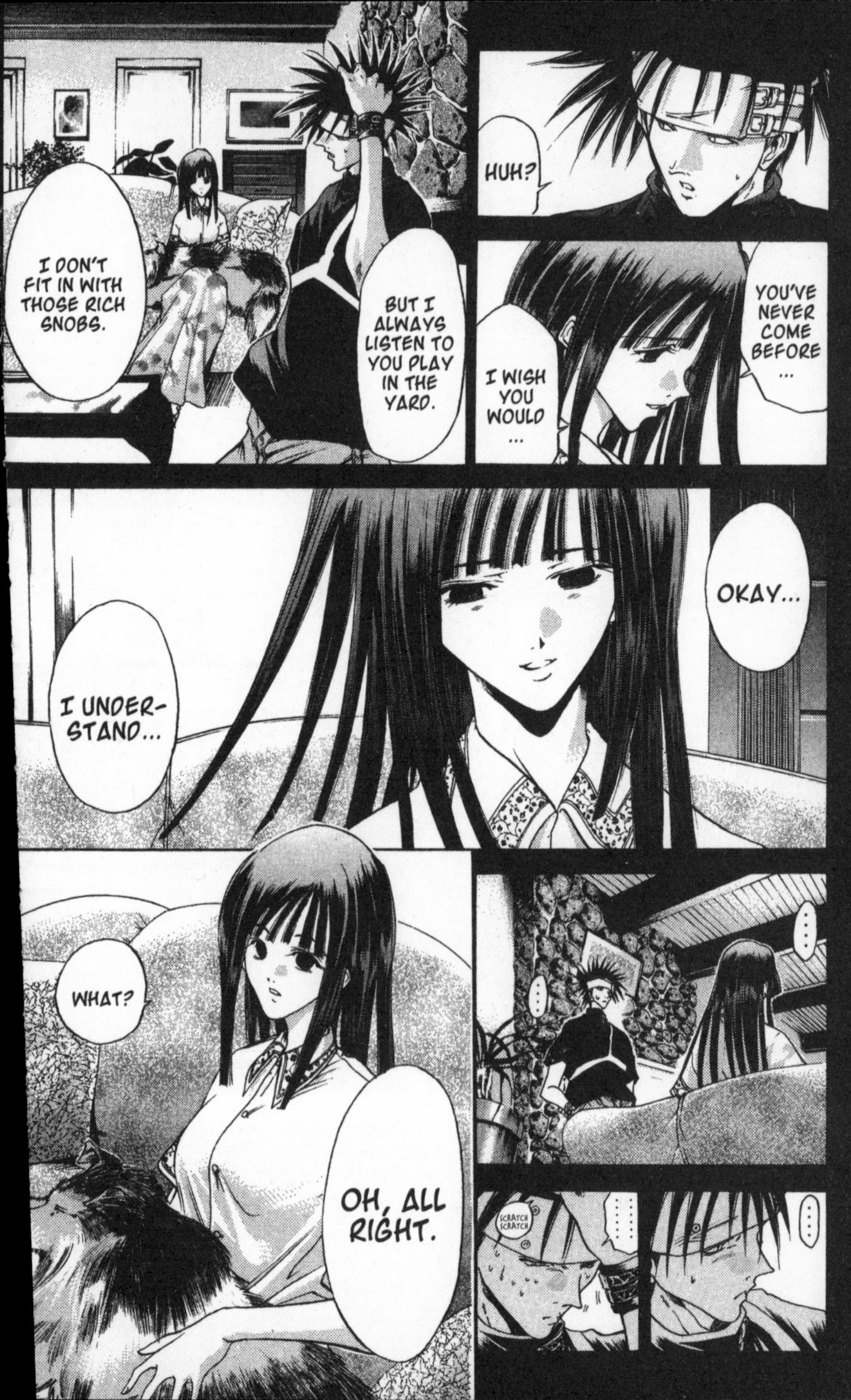
HUH?
YOU'VE NEVER COME BEFORE ...
I WISH YOU WOULD ...
I DON'T FIT IN WITH THOSE RICH SNOBS.
BUT I ALWAYS LISTEN TO YOU PLAY IN THE YARD.
OKAY...
I UNDER-STAND...
...
...
...
SCRATCH SCRATCH
...
WHAT?
OH, ALL RIGHT.

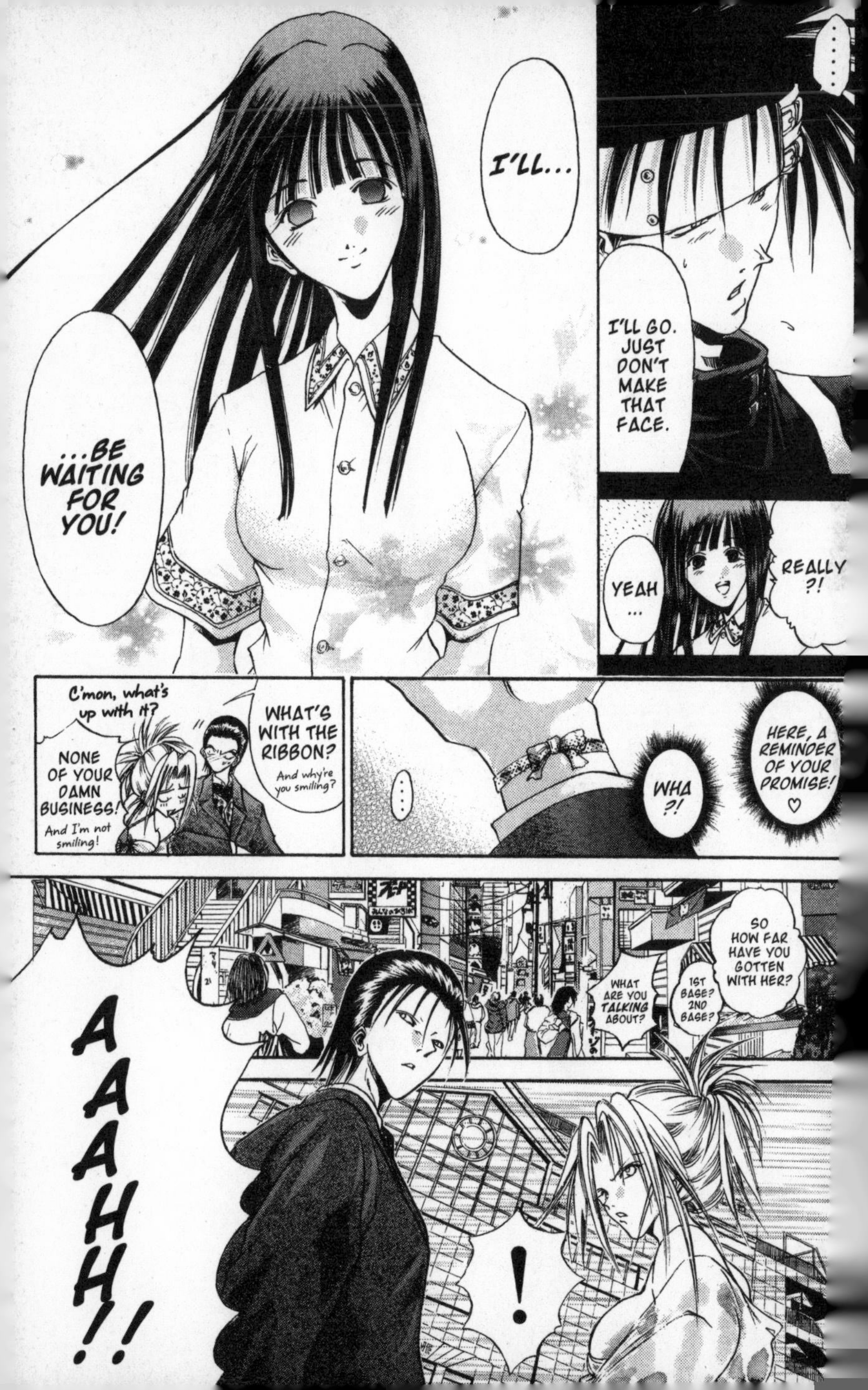
......
I'LL GO. JUST DON'T MAKE THAT FACE.
REALLY?!
YEAH...
I'LL...
...BE WAITING FOR YOU!
HERE, A REMINDER OF YOUR PROMISE! ♡
WHA?!
....
WHAT'S WITH THE RIBBON?
And why're you smiling?
C'mon, what's up with it?
NONE OF YOUR DAMN BUSINESS!
And I'm not smiling!
SO HOW FAR HAVE YOU GOTTEN WITH HER?
1ST BASE? 2ND BASE?
WHAT ARE YOU TALKING ABOUT?
!
AAAHH!!

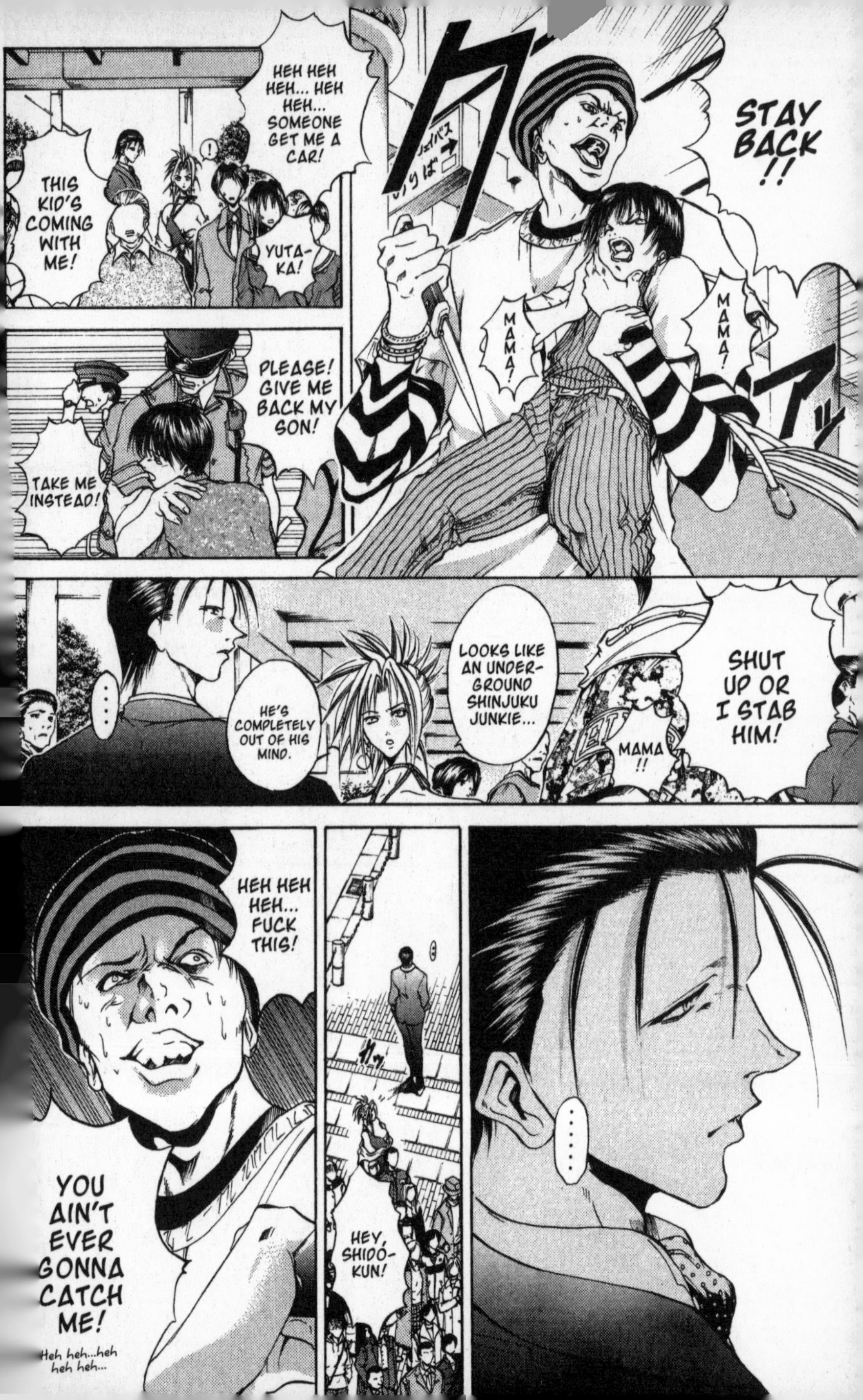
STAY BACK!!
MAMA!
MAMA!
HEH HEH HEH... HEH HEH... SOMEONE GET ME A CAR!
THIS KID'S COMING WITH ME!
!
YUTA-KA!
PLEASE! GIVE ME BACK MY SON!
TAKE ME INSTEAD!
SHUT UP OR I STAB HIM!
MAMA!!
LOOKS LIKE AN UNDER-GROUND SHINJUKU JUNKIE...
HE'S COMPLETELY OUT OF HIS MIND.
....
....
HEY, SHIDO-KUN!
HEH HEH HEH... FUCK THIS!
YOU AIN'T EVER GONNA CATCH ME!
Heh heh...heh heh heh...

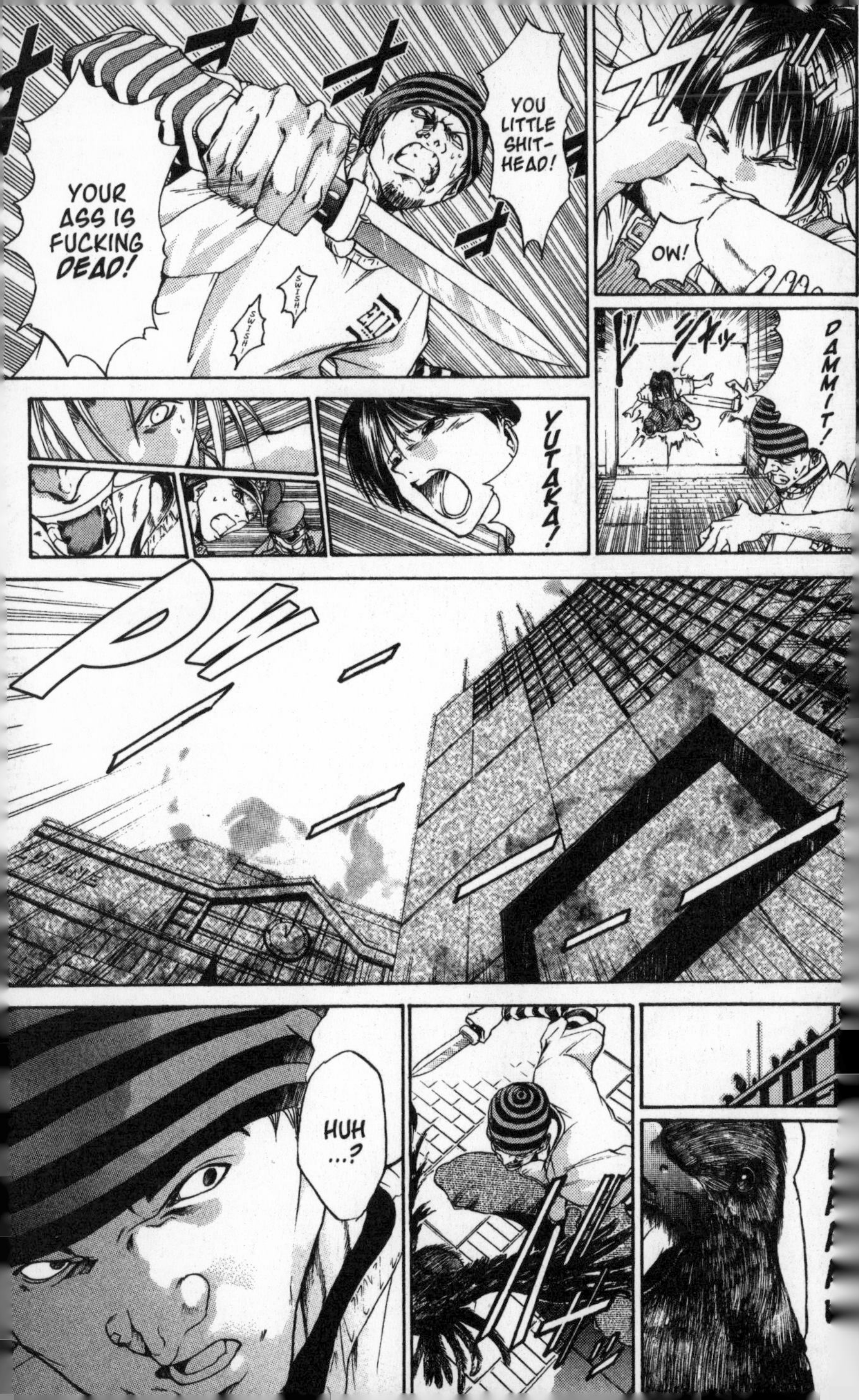
OW!
YOU LITTLE SHIT-HEAD!
YOUR ASS IS FUCKING DEAD!
SWISH!
SWISH!
DAMMIT!
YUTAKA!
HUH ...?

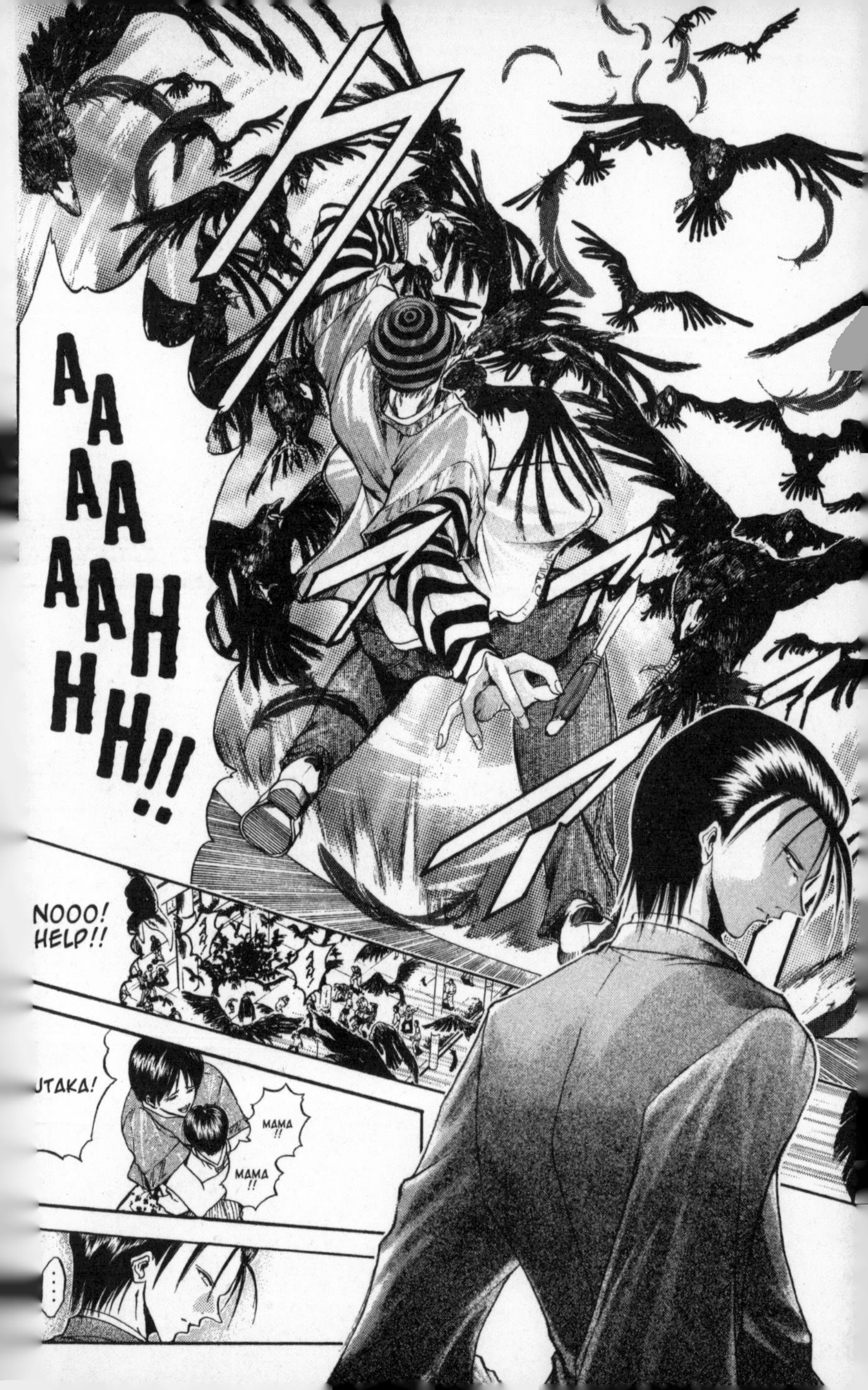
AAAAAAHHH!!
NOOO! HELP!!
UTAKA!
MAMA !!
MAMA !!
...

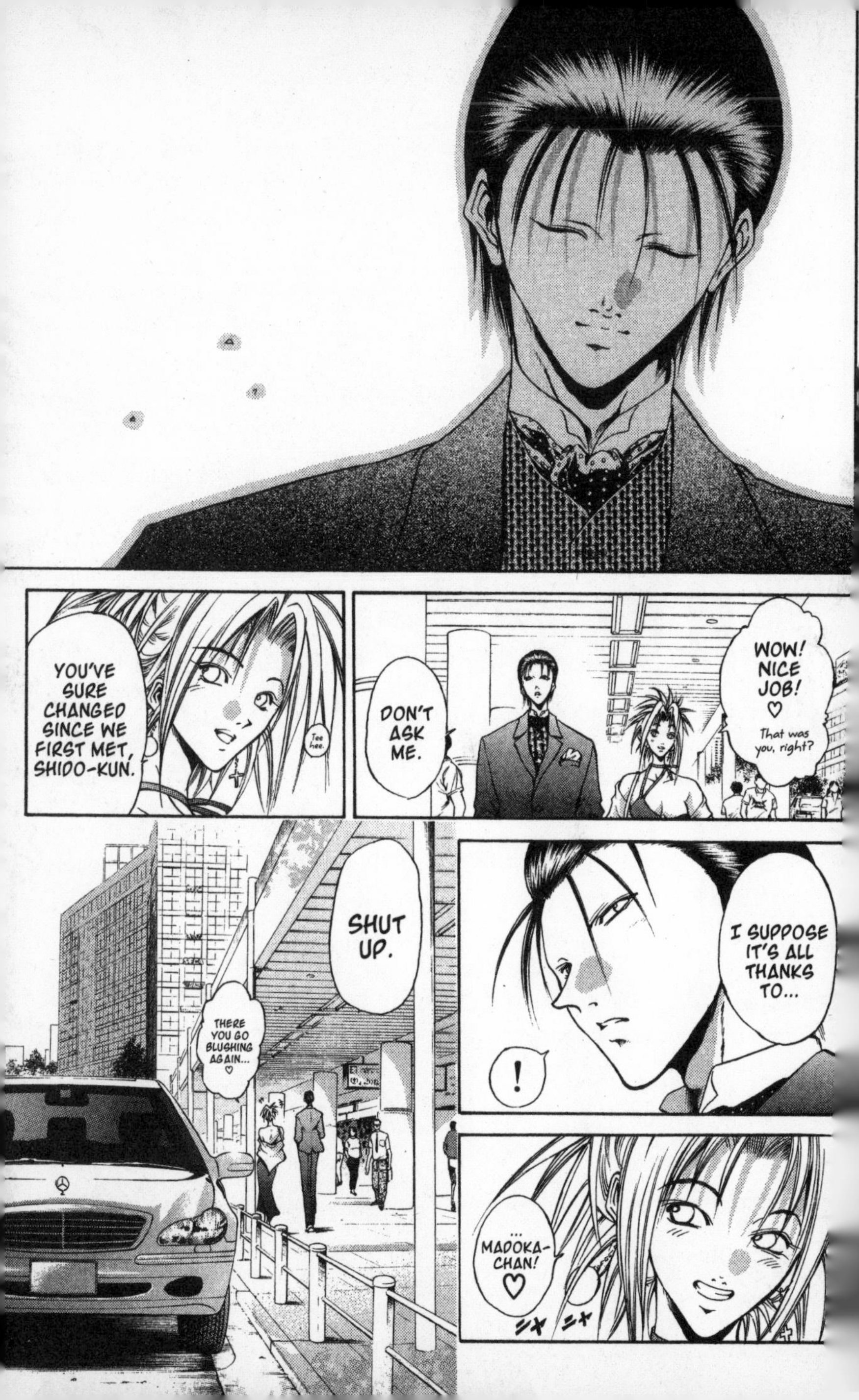
WOW! NICE JOB! ♡
That was you, right?
DON'T ASK ME.
YOU'VE SURE CHANGED SINCE WE FIRST MET, SHIDO-KUN.
Tee hee.
I SUPPOSE IT'S ALL THANKS TO...
!
...MADOKA-CHAN! ♡
ニヤ ニヤ
SHUT UP.
THERE YOU GO BLUSHING AGAIN... ♡

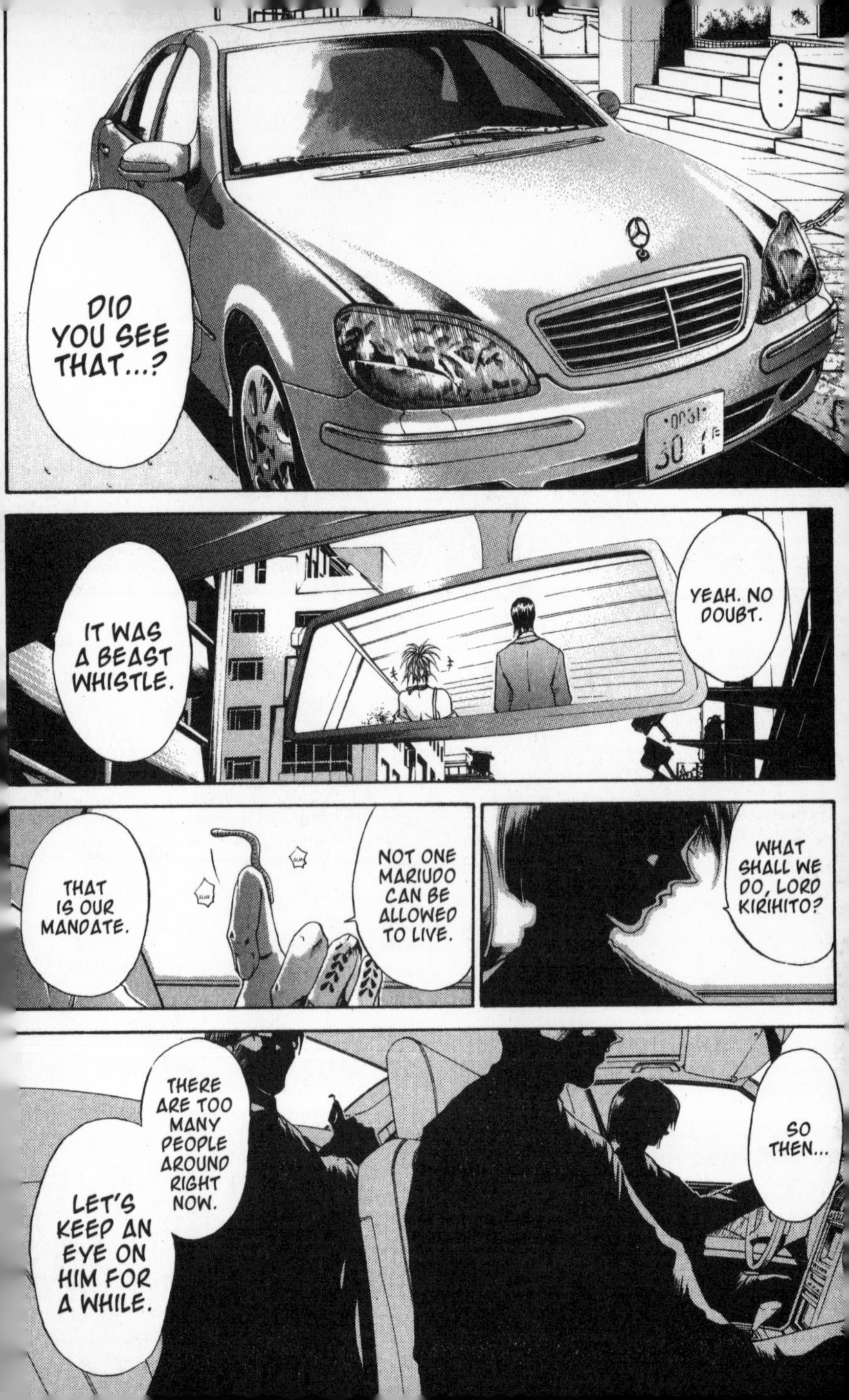
...
DID YOU SEE THAT...?
YEAH. NO DOUBT.
IT WAS A BEAST WHISTLE.
WHAT SHALL WE DO, LORD KIRIHITO?
NOT ONE MARIUDO CAN BE ALLOWED TO LIVE.
THAT IS OUR MANDATE.
SO THEN...
THERE ARE TOO MANY PEOPLE AROUND RIGHT NOW.
LET'S KEEP AN EYE ON HIM FOR A WHILE.

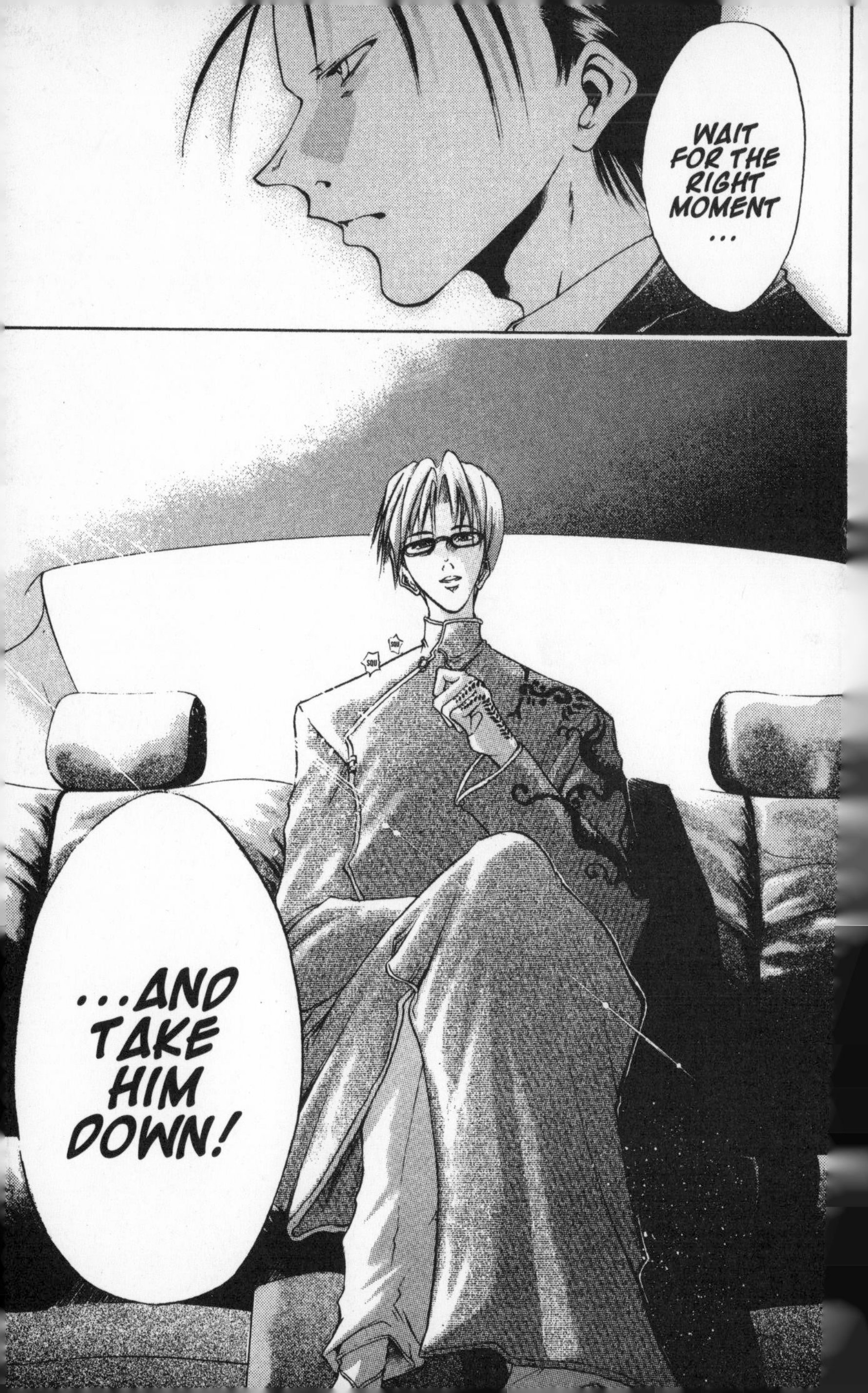
WAIT FOR THE RIGHT MOMENT ...
SQU
SQU
...AND TAKE HIM DOWN!

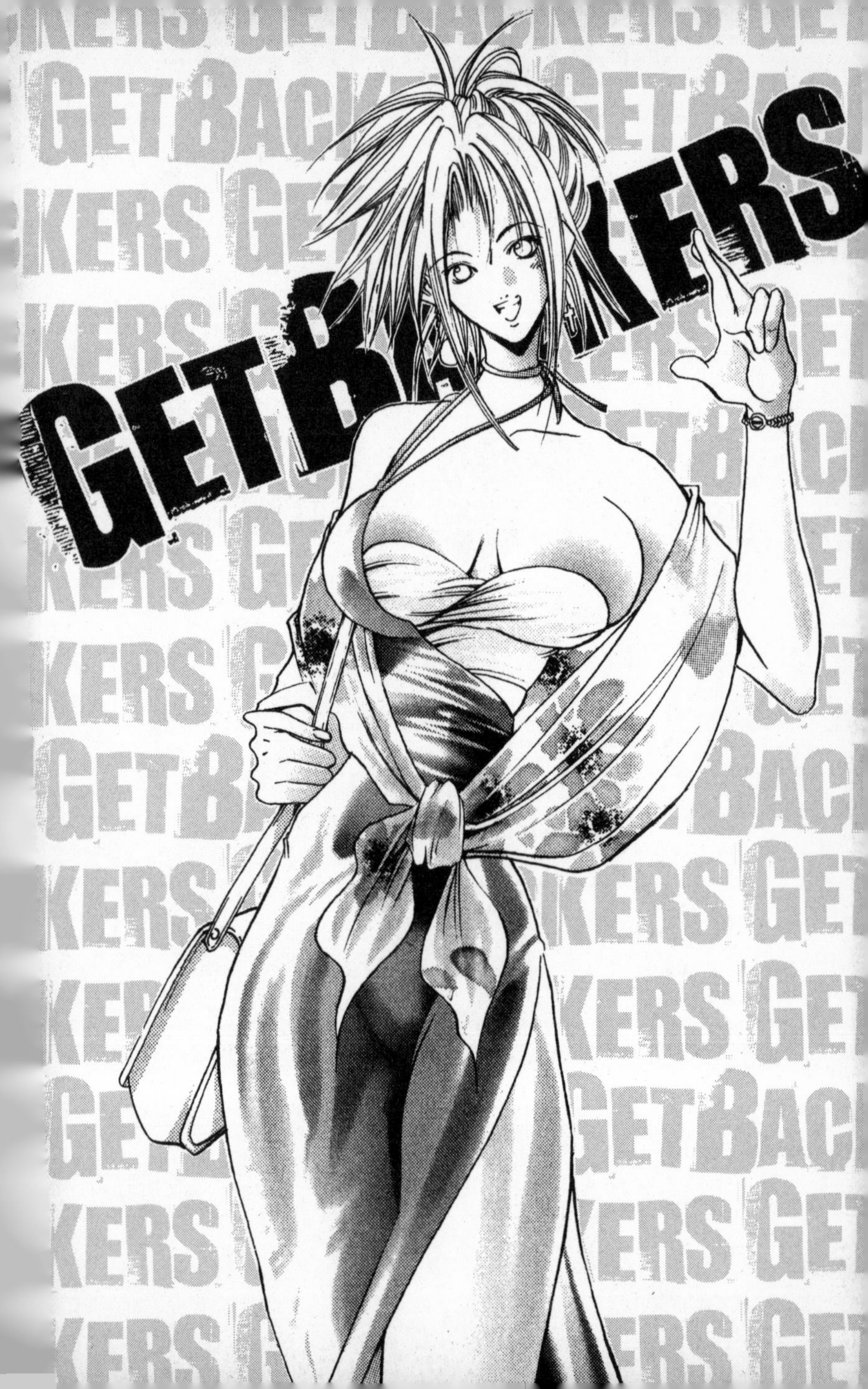
GETBACKERS

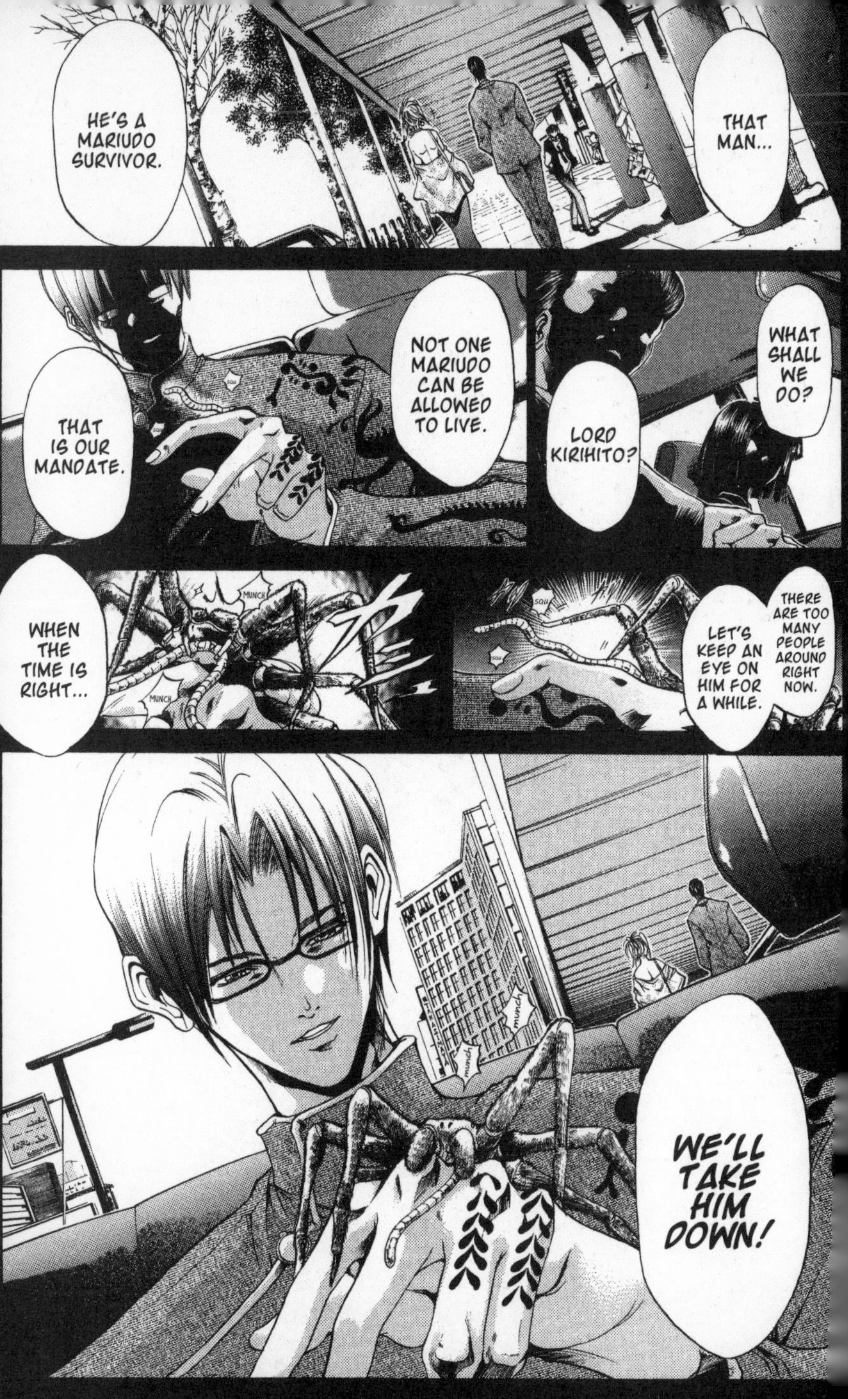
THAT MAN...
HE'S A MARIUDO SURVIVOR.
WHAT SHALL WE DO?
LORD KIRIHITO?
NOT ONE MARIUDO CAN BE ALLOWED TO LIVE.
THAT IS OUR MANDATE.
THERE ARE TOO MANY PEOPLE AROUND RIGHT NOW.
LET'S KEEP AN EYE ON HIM FOR A WHILE.
SQU
SQU
MUNCH
MUNCH
WHEN THE TIME IS RIGHT...
munch
munch
WE'LL TAKE HIM DOWN!

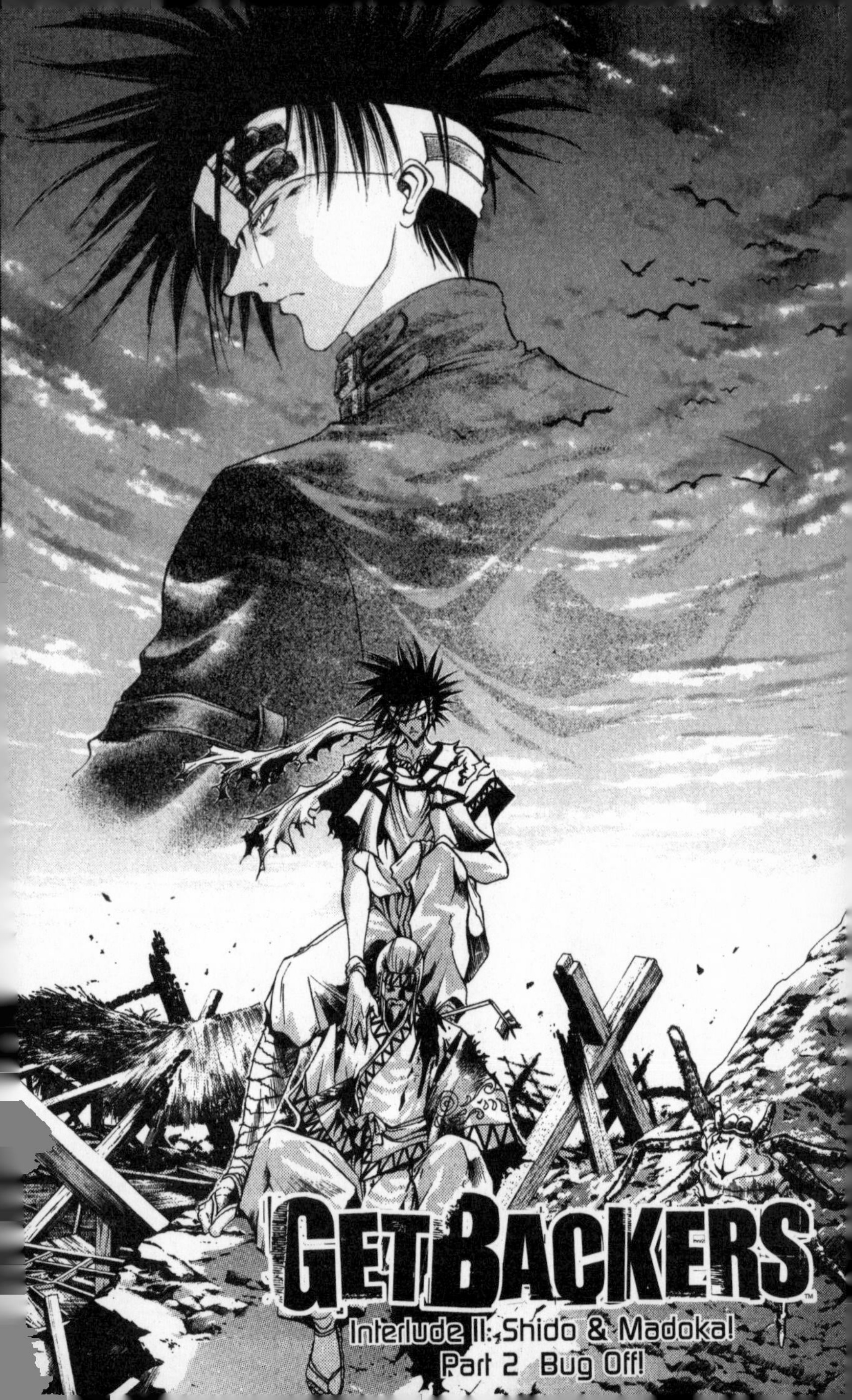
GETBACKERS
Interlude II: Shido & Madoka!
Part 2 Bug Off!

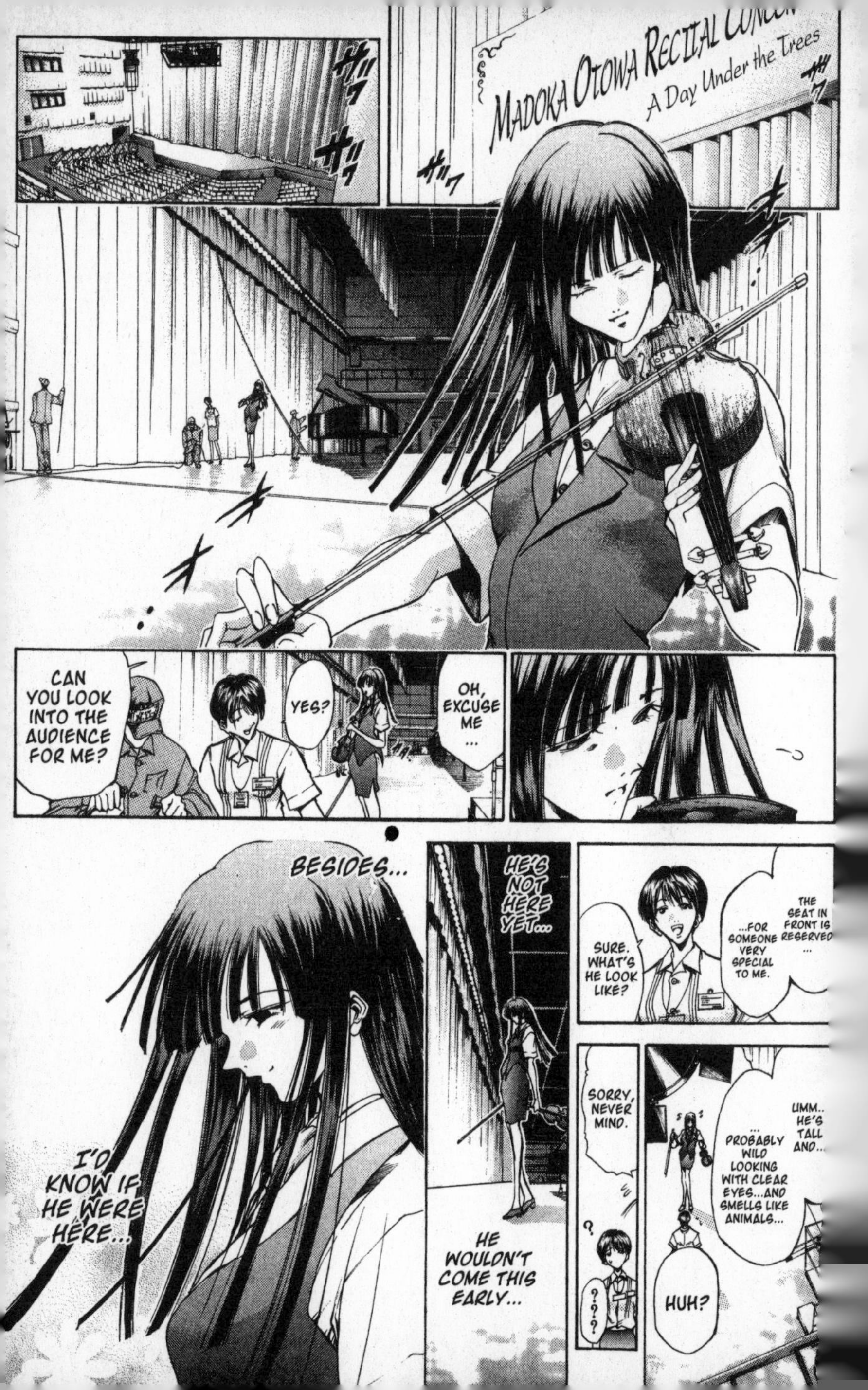

MADOKA OTOWA RECITAL CONC
A Day Under the Trees
OH, EXCUSE ME ...
YES?
CAN YOU LOOK INTO THE AUDIENCE FOR ME?
THE SEAT IN FRONT IS RESERVED ...
...FOR SOMEONE VERY SPECIAL TO ME.
SURE. WHAT'S HE LOOK LIKE?
UMM.. HE'S TALL AND...
... PROBABLY WILD LOOKING WITH CLEAR EYES...AND SMELLS LIKE ANIMALS...
HUH?
SORRY, NEVER MIND.
?
???
HE'S NOT HERE YET...
HE WOULDN'T COME THIS EARLY...
BESIDES...
I'D KNOW IF HE WERE HERE...

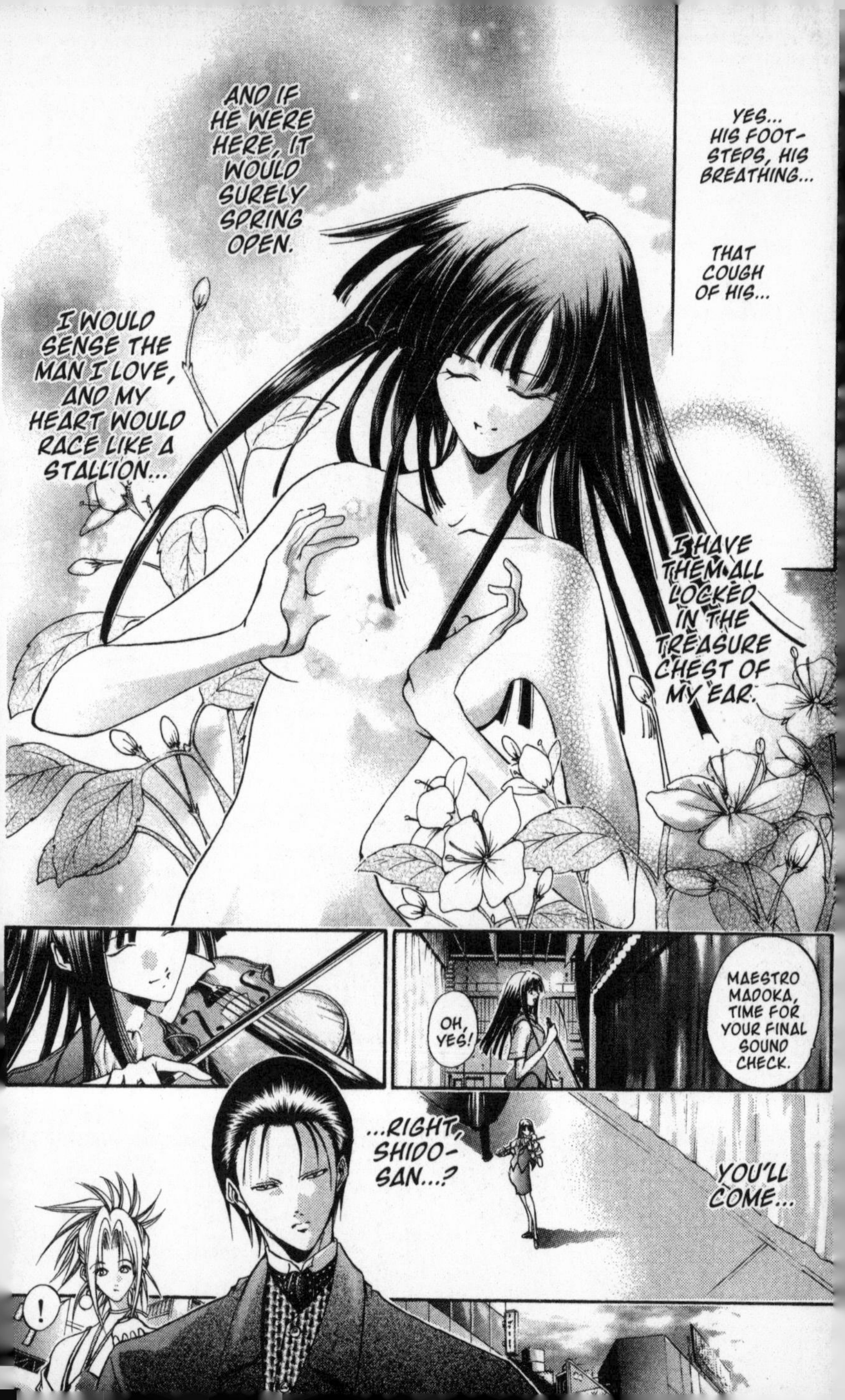
YES... HIS FOOT-STEPS, HIS BREATHING...
THAT COUGH OF HIS...
I HAVE THEM ALL LOCKED IN THE TREASURE CHEST OF MY EAR.
AND IF HE WERE HERE, IT WOULD SURELY SPRING OPEN.
I WOULD SENSE THE MAN I LOVE, AND MY HEART WOULD RACE LIKE A STALLION...
MAESTRO MADOKA, TIME FOR YOUR FINAL SOUND CHECK.
OH, YES!
YOU'LL COME...
...RIGHT, SHIDO-SAN...?
!

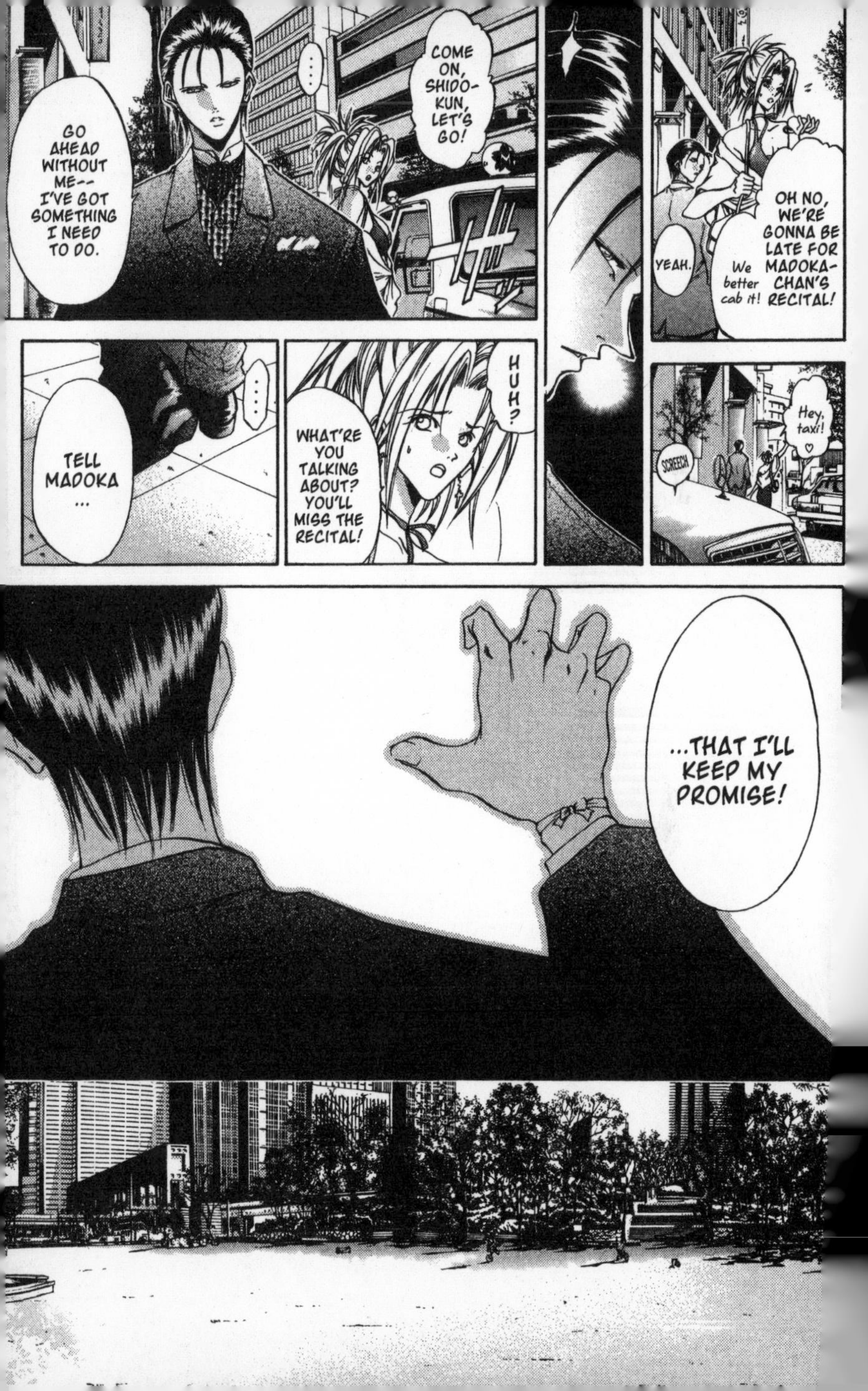
OH NO, WE'RE GONNA BE LATE FOR MADOKA-CHAN'S RECITAL!
We better cab it!
YEAH.
Hey, taxi! ♡
SCREECH
COME ON, SHIDO-KUN, LET'S GO!
...
GO AHEAD WITHOUT ME-- I'VE GOT SOMETHING I NEED TO DO.
HUH?
WHAT'RE YOU TALKING ABOUT? YOU'LL MISS THE RECITAL!
...
TELL MADOKA ...
...THAT I'LL KEEP MY PROMISE!

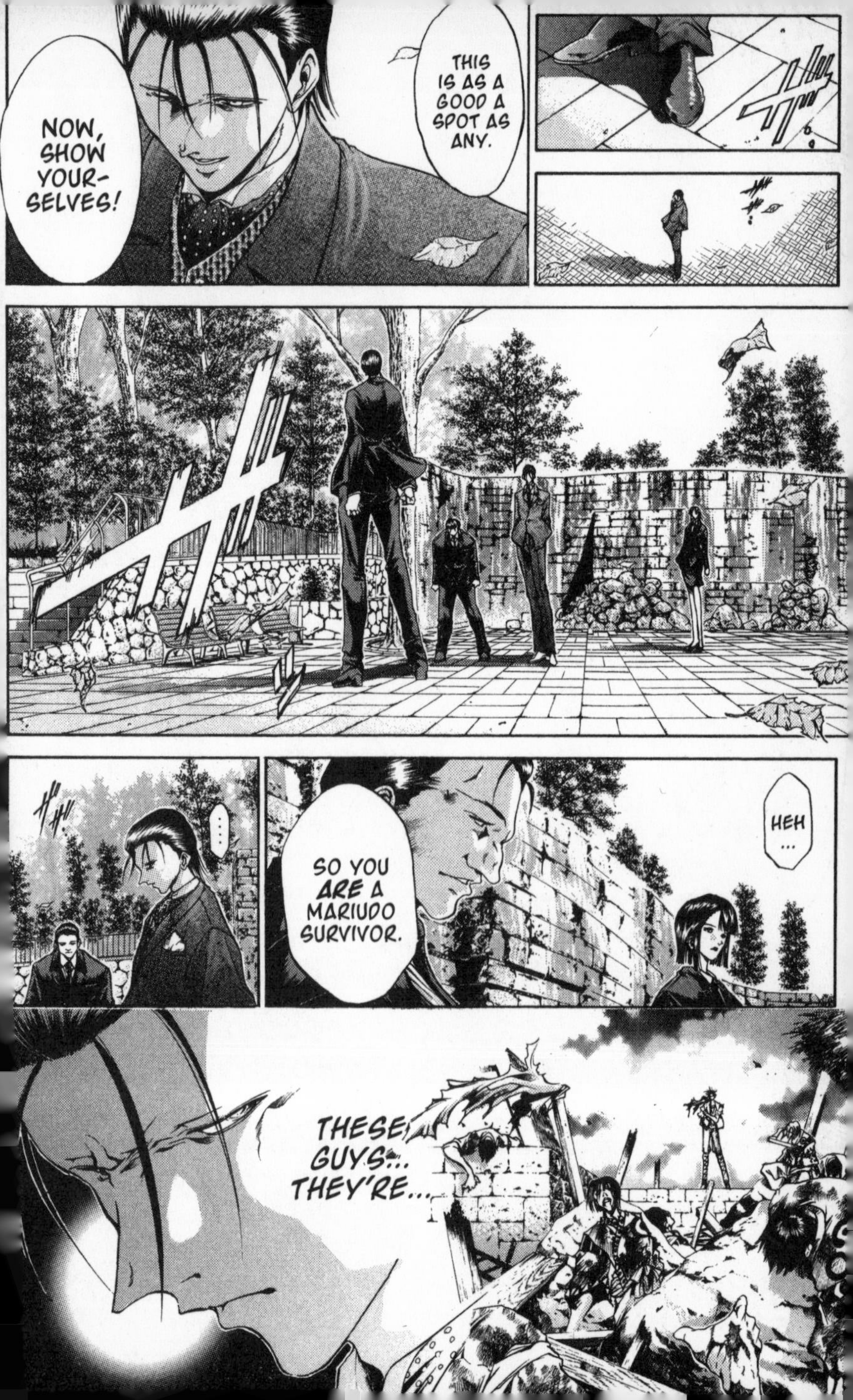
THIS IS AS A GOOD A SPOT AS ANY.
NOW, SHOW YOUR-SELVES!
HEH ...
SO YOU ARE A MARIUDO SURVIVOR.
...
THESE GUYS... THEY'RE...

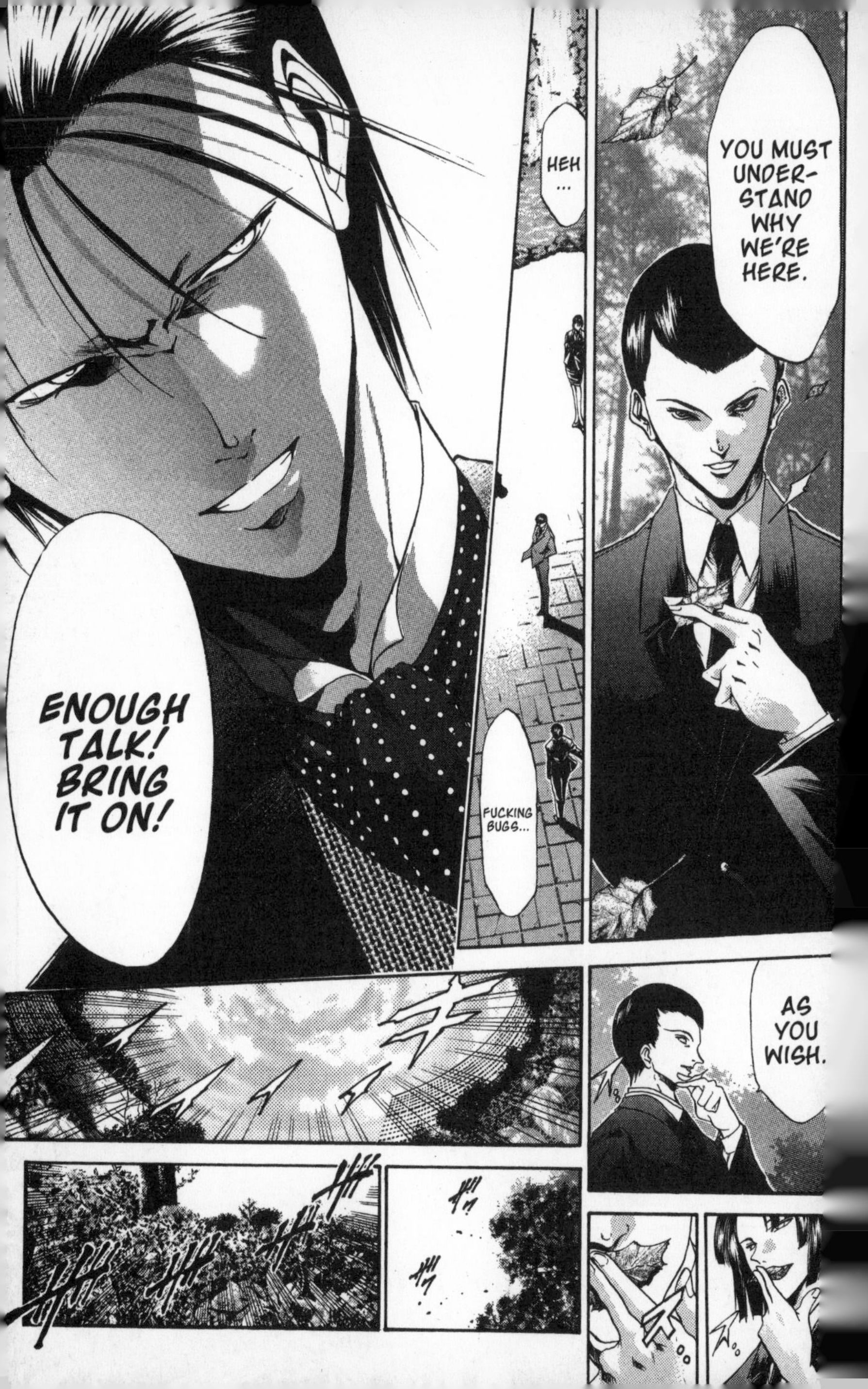
YOU MUST UNDER-STAND WHY WE'RE HERE.
HEH ...
FUCKING BUGS...
ENOUGH TALK! BRING IT ON!
AS YOU WISH.

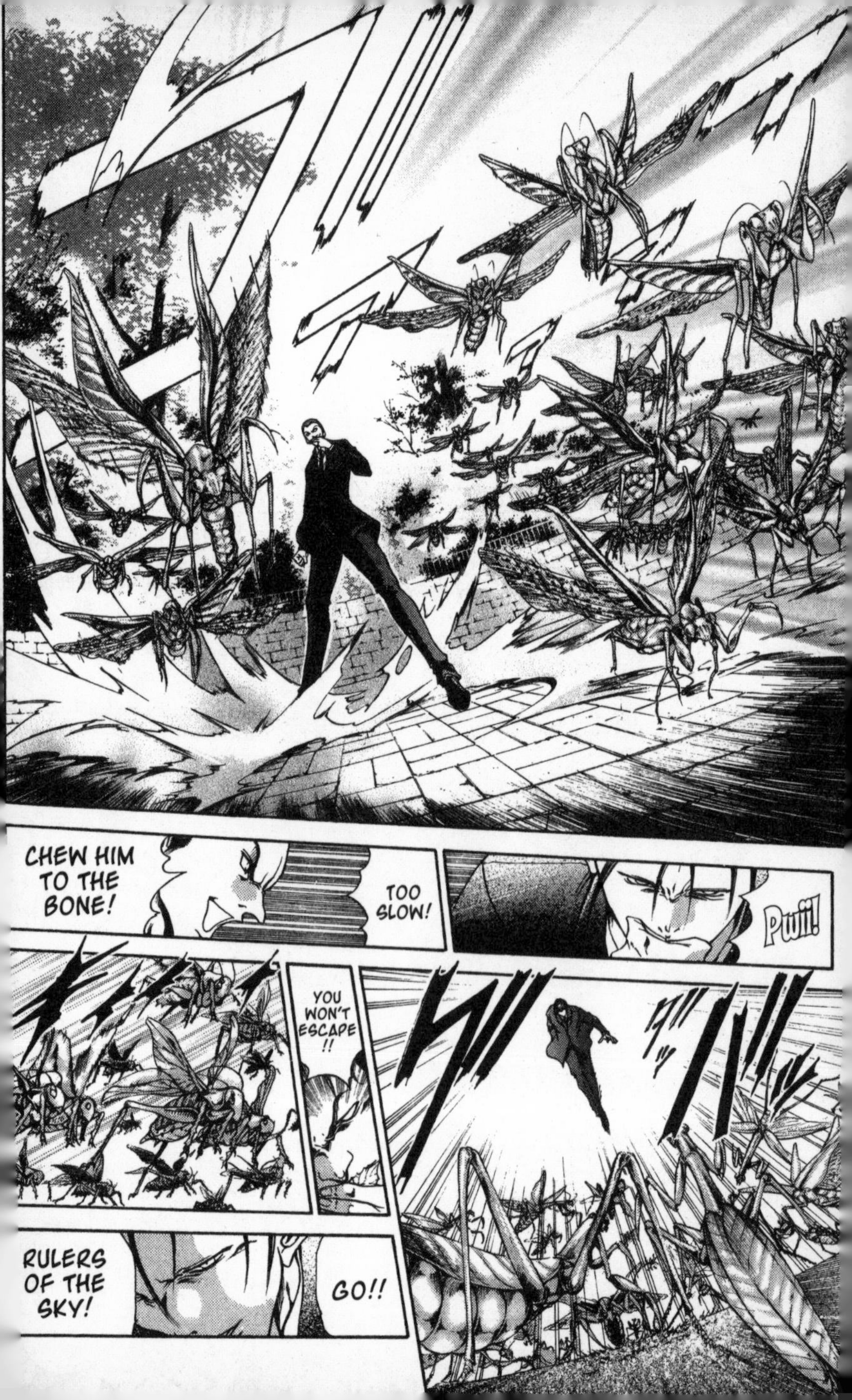
Pwii!
CHEW HIM TO THE BONE!
TOO SLOW!
YOU WON'T ESCAPE!!
RULERS OF THE SKY!
GO!!

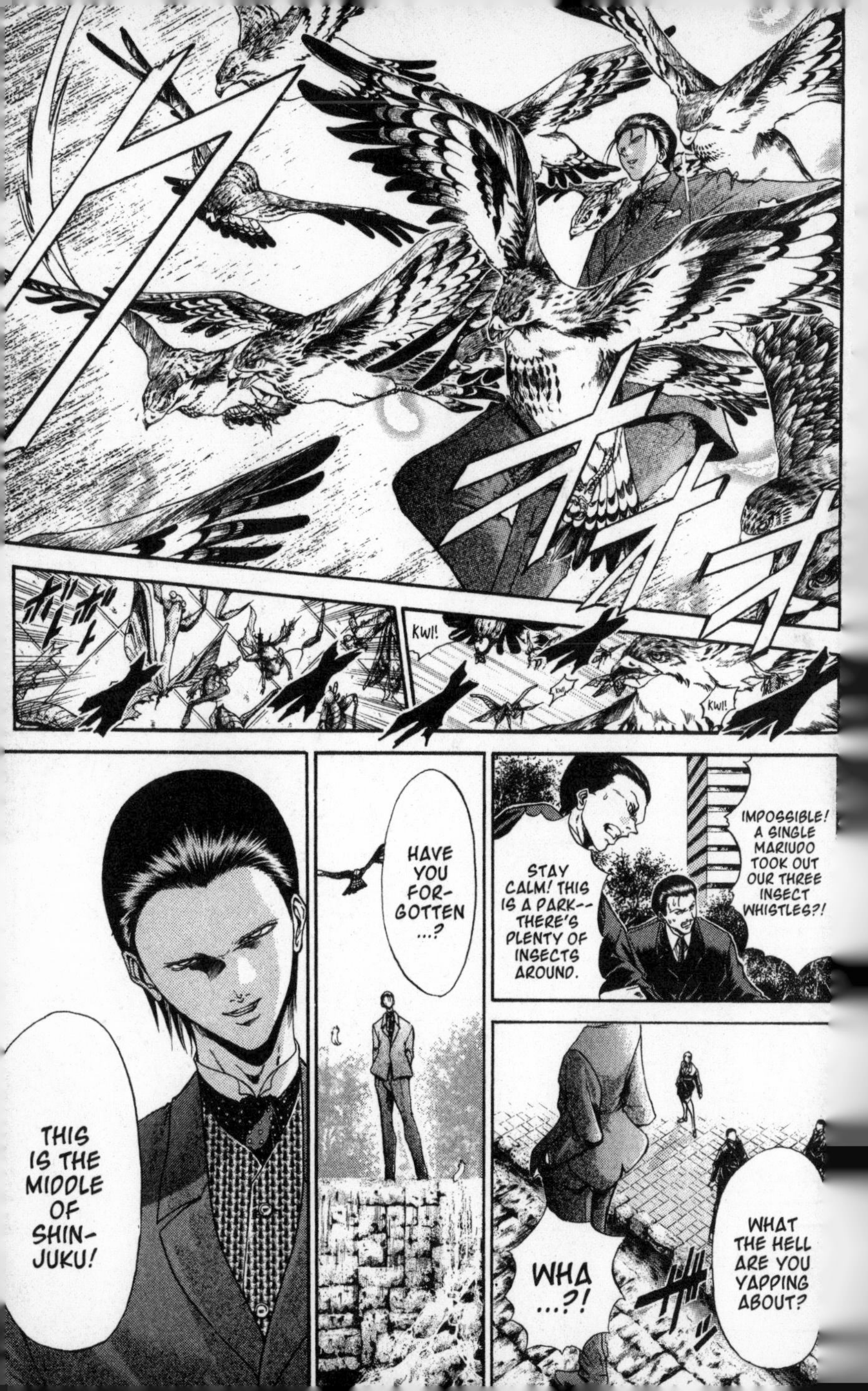
KWI!
KWI!
KWI!
IMPOSSIBLE! A SINGLE MARIUDO TOOK OUT OUR THREE INSECT WHISTLES?!
STAY CALM! THIS IS A PARK-- THERE'S PLENTY OF INSECTS AROUND.
WHAT THE HELL ARE YOU YAPPING ABOUT?
WHA ...?!
HAVE YOU FOR-GOTTEN ...?
THIS IS THE MIDDLE OF SHIN-JUKU!

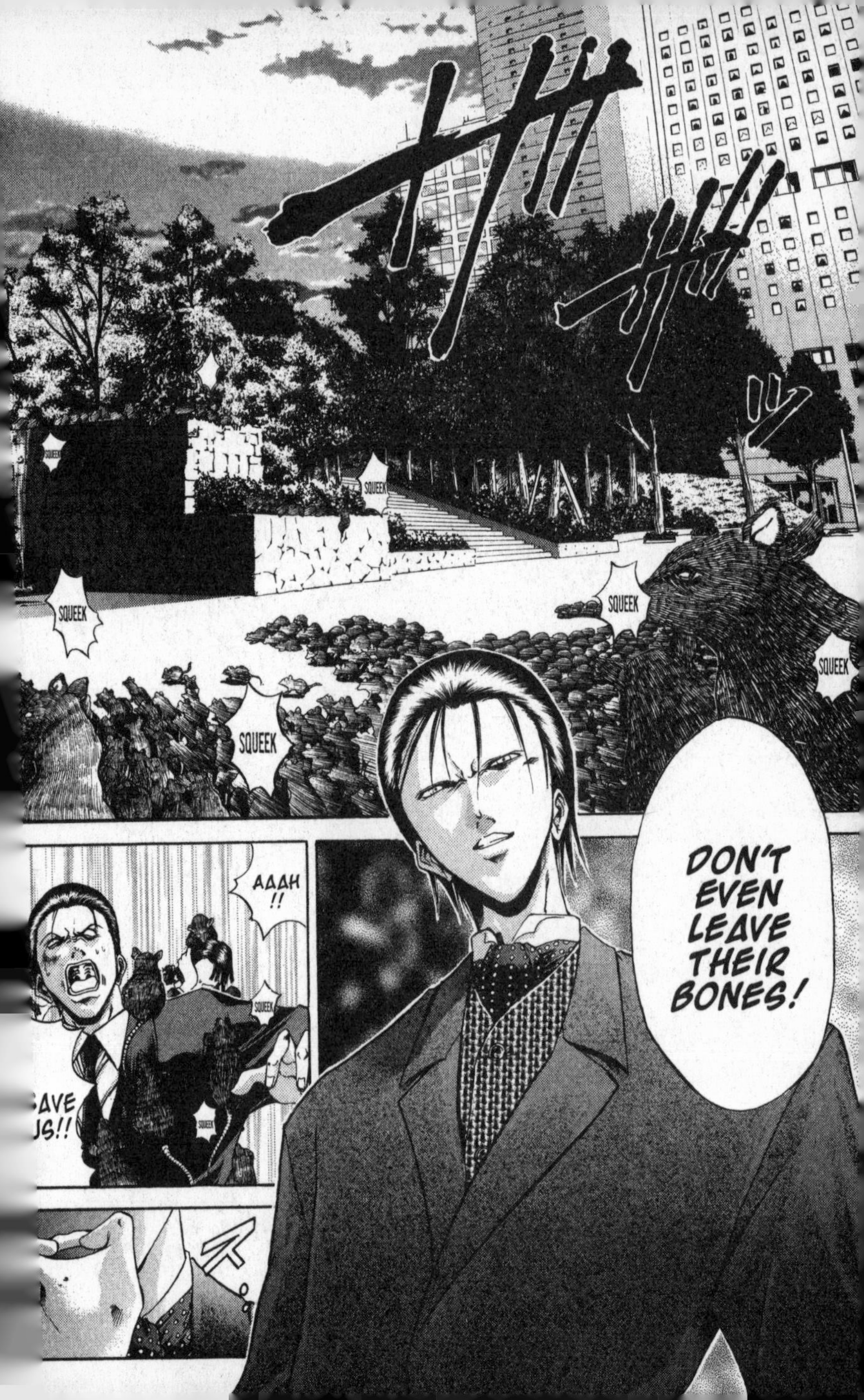
SQUEEK
SQUEEK
SQUEEK
SQUEEK
SQUEEK
SQUEEK
DON'T EVEN LEAVE THEIR BONES!
AAAH!!
SQUEEK
SAVE US!!
SQUEEK

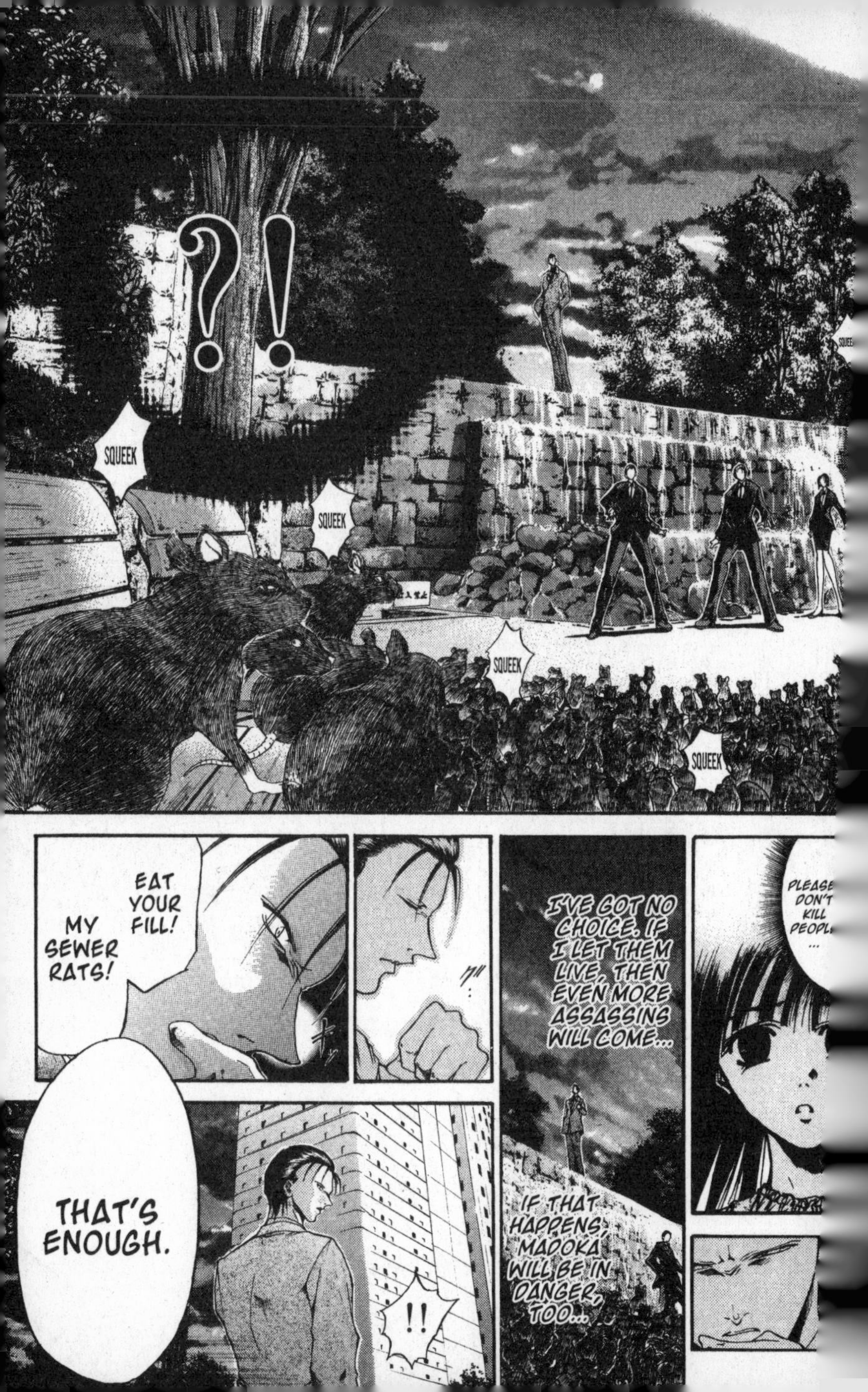

?!
SQUEEK
SQUEEK
SQUEEK
SQUEEK
PLEASE DON'T KILL PEOPL ...
I'VE GOT NO CHOICE. IF I LET THEM LIVE, THEN EVEN MORE ASSASSINS WILL COME...
IF THAT HAPPENS, MADOKA WILL BE IN DANGER, TOO...
EAT YOUR FILL!
MY SEWER RATS!
THAT'S ENOUGH.
!!

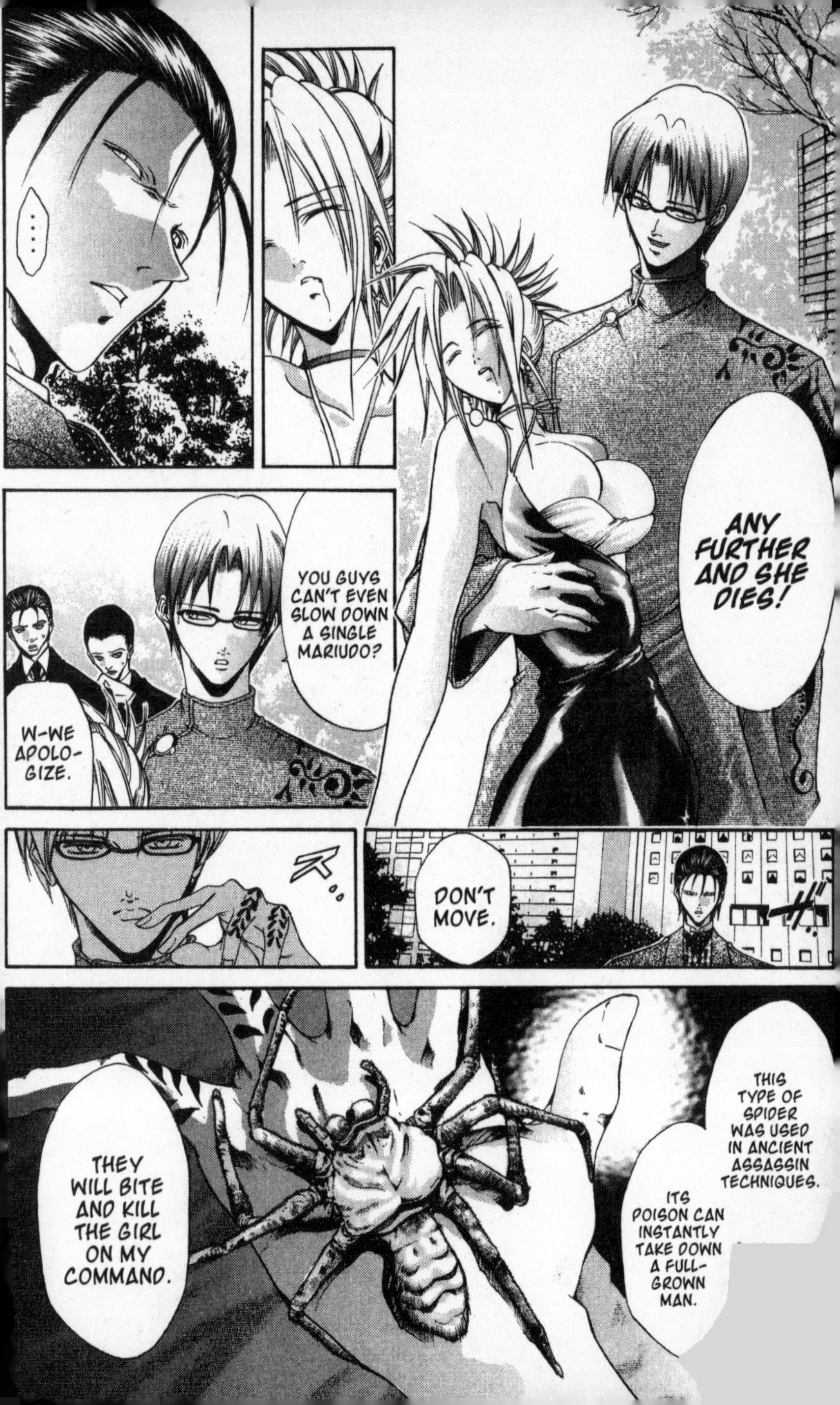
ANY FURTHER AND SHE DIES!
....
YOU GUYS CAN'T EVEN SLOW DOWN A SINGLE MARIUDO?
W-WE APOLOGIZE.
DON'T MOVE.
THIS TYPE OF SPIDER WAS USED IN ANCIENT ASSASSIN TECHNIQUES.
ITS POISON CAN INSTANTLY TAKE DOWN A FULL-GROWN MAN.
THEY WILL BITE AND KILL THE GIRL ON MY COMMAND.

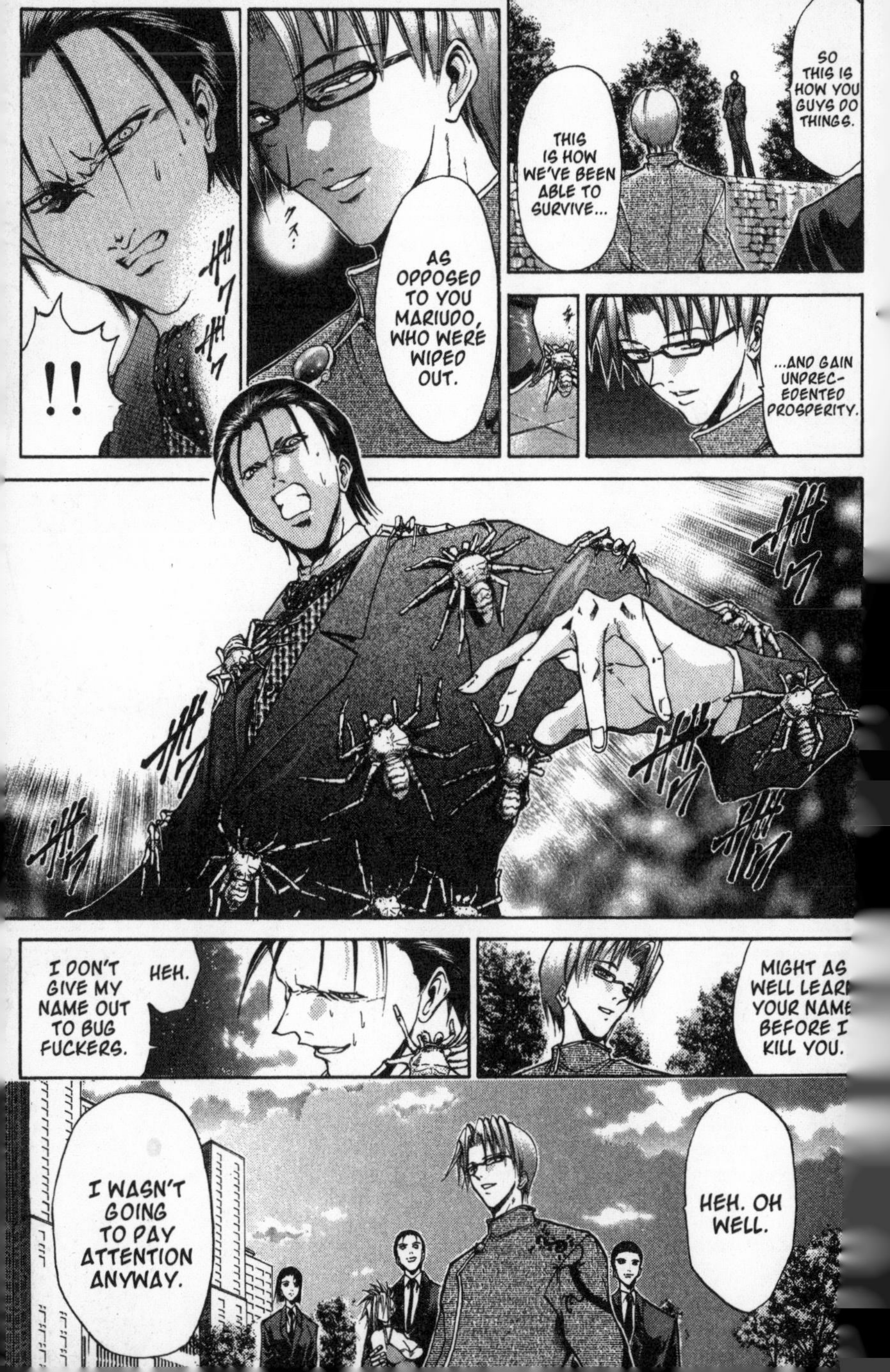

SO THIS IS HOW YOU GUYS DO THINGS.
THIS IS HOW WE'VE BEEN ABLE TO SURVIVE...
...AND GAIN UNPRECEDENTED PROSPERITY.
AS OPPOSED TO YOU MARIUDO, WHO WERE WIPED OUT.
!!
MIGHT AS WELL LEARN YOUR NAME BEFORE I KILL YOU.
HEH.
I DON'T GIVE MY NAME OUT TO BUG FUCKERS.
HEH. OH WELL.
I WASN'T GOING TO PAY ATTENTION ANYWAY.

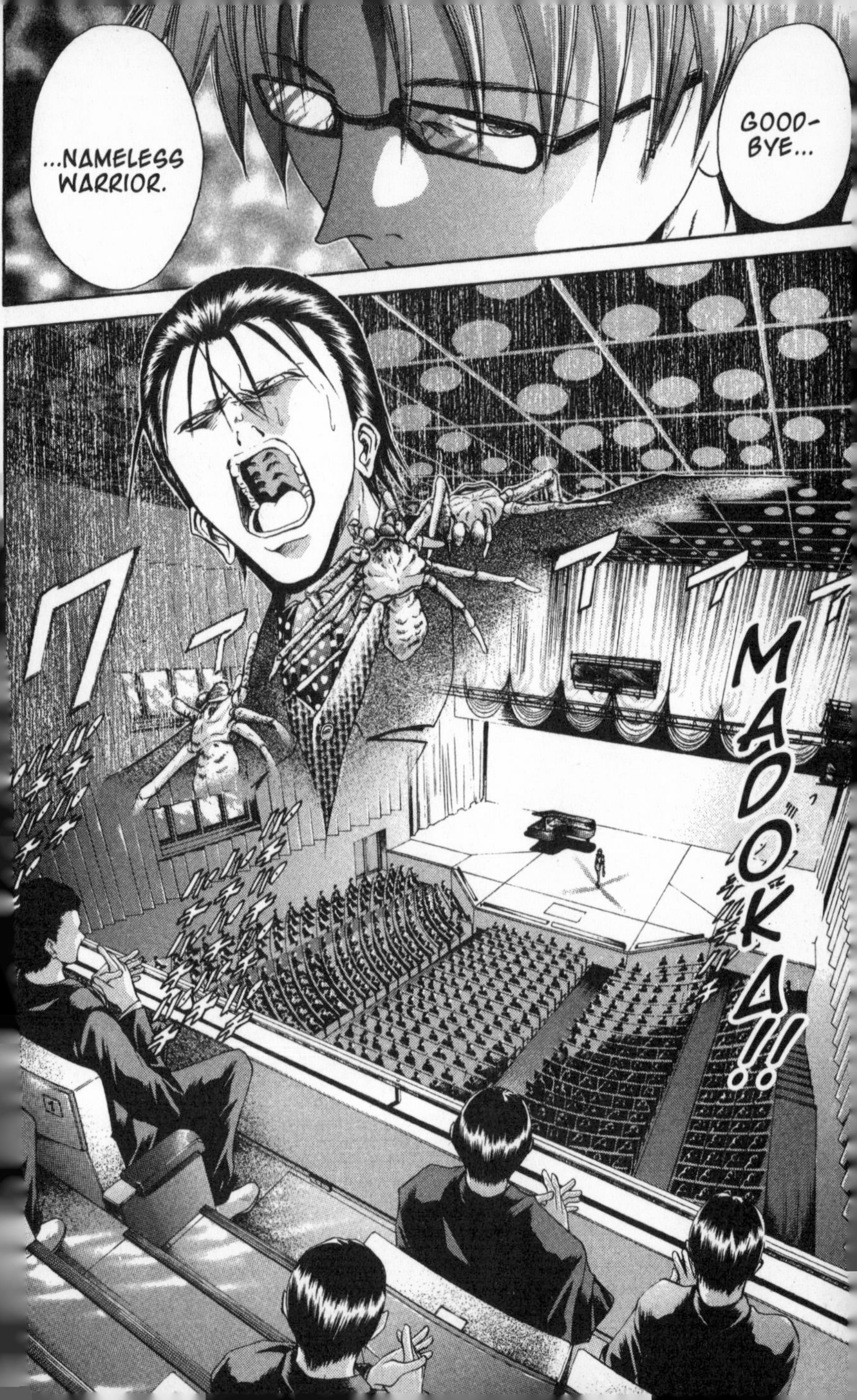
GOOD-BYE...
...NAMELESS WARRIOR.
MAOOKA!!

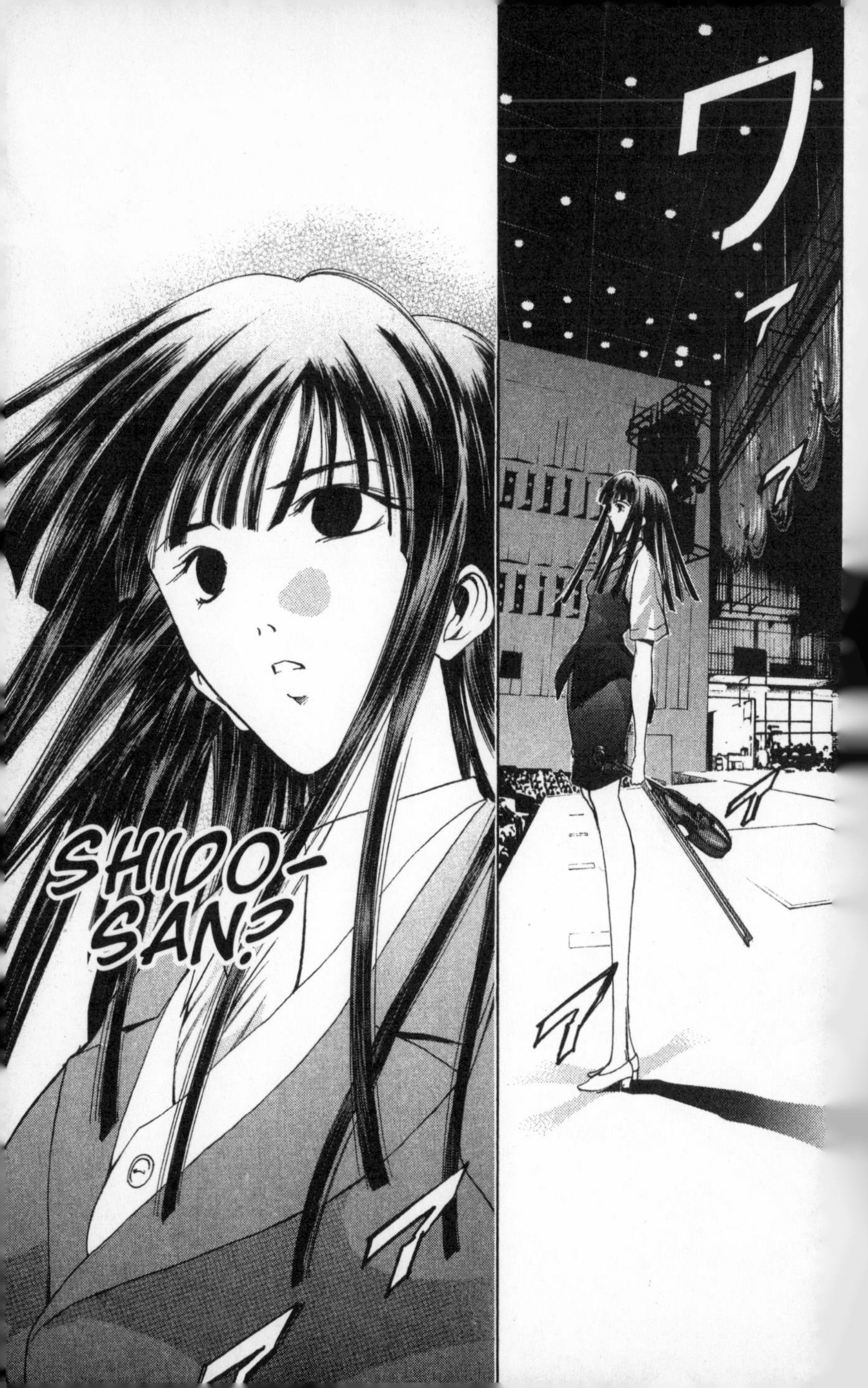
ワァァァァ
SHIDO-SAN?
ァァ

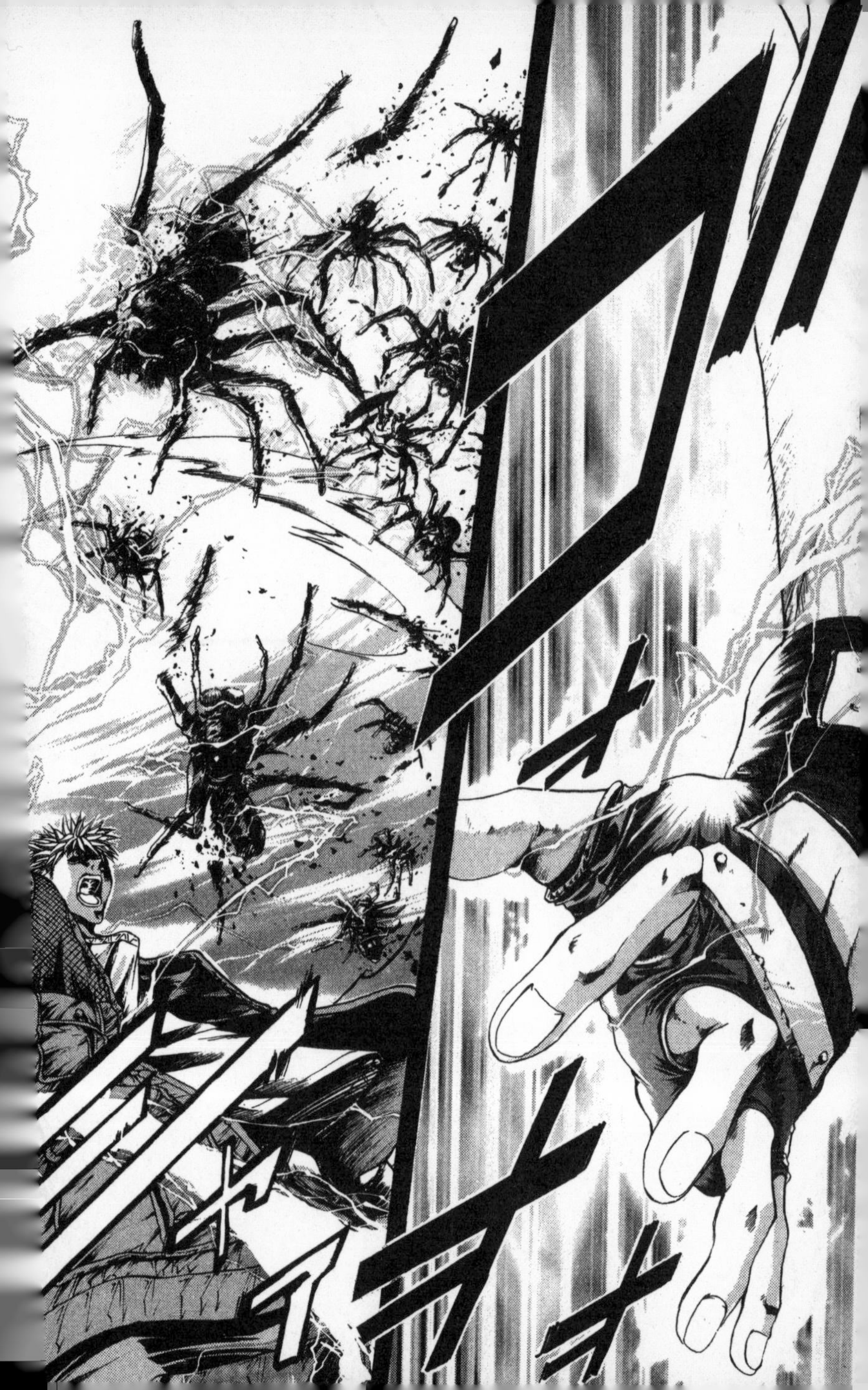

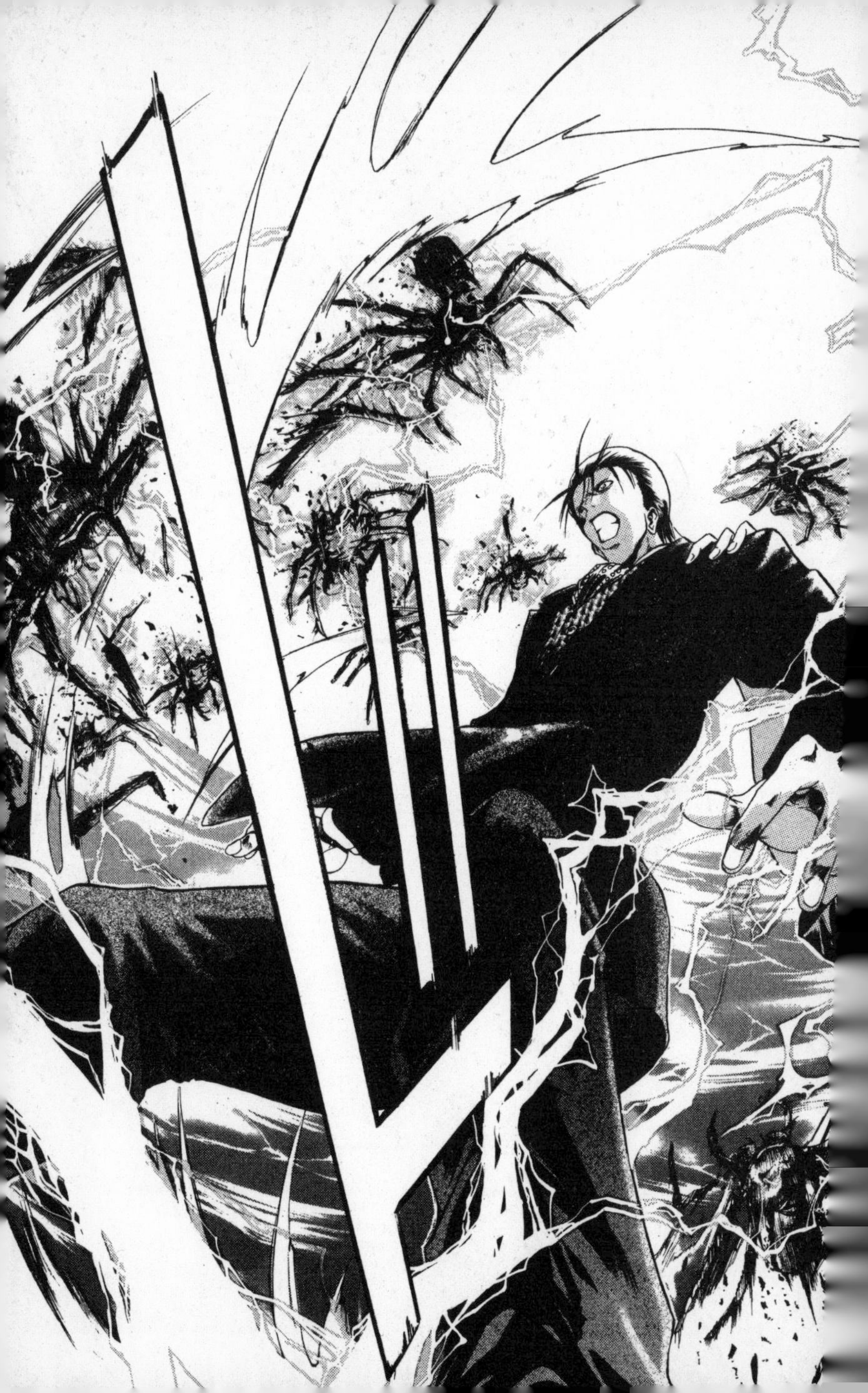

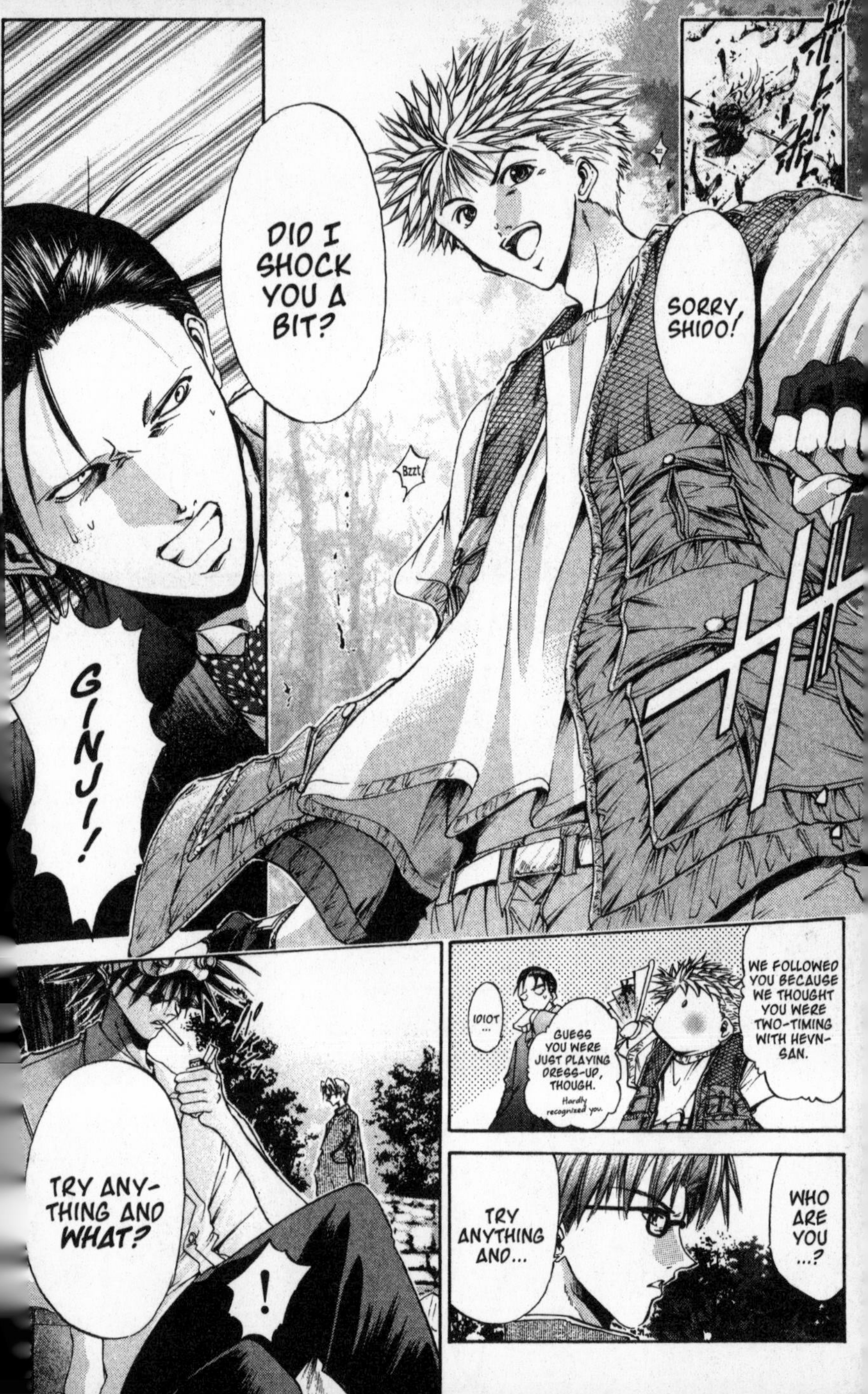
SORRY, SHIDO!
DID I SHOCK YOU A BIT?
Bzzt
GINJI!
WE FOLLOWED YOU BECAUSE WE THOUGHT YOU WERE TWO-TIMING WITH HEVN-SAN.
GUESS YOU WERE JUST PLAYING DRESS-UP, THOUGH.
Hardly recognized you.
IDIOT...
WHO ARE YOU ...?
TRY ANYTHING AND...
TRY ANY-THING AND WHAT?
!

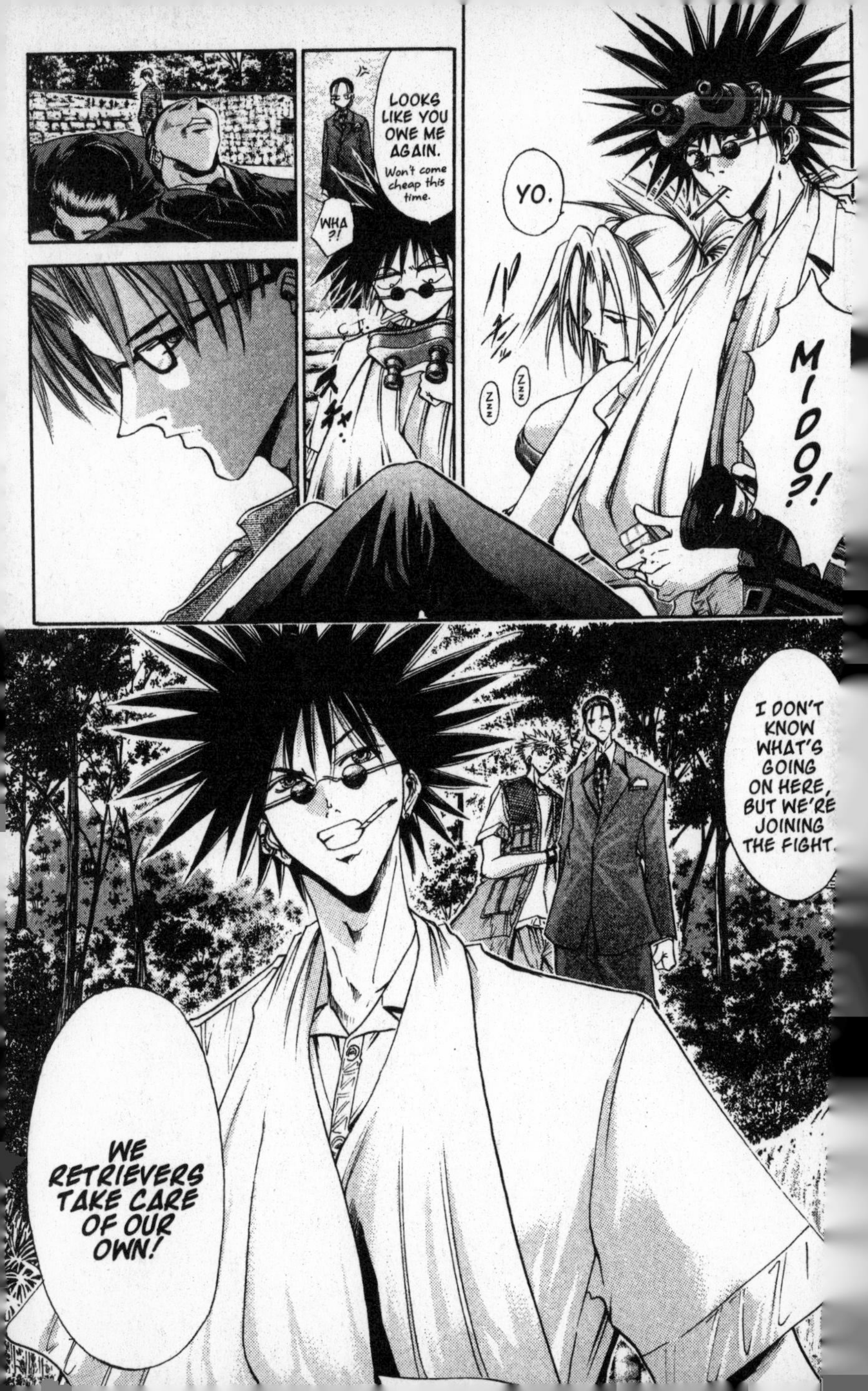
YO.
MIDOO?!
LOOKS LIKE YOU OWE ME AGAIN.
Won't come cheap this time.
WHA ?!
I DON'T KNOW WHAT'S GOING ON HERE, BUT WE'RE JOINING THE FIGHT.
WE RETRIEVERS TAKE CARE OF OUR OWN!

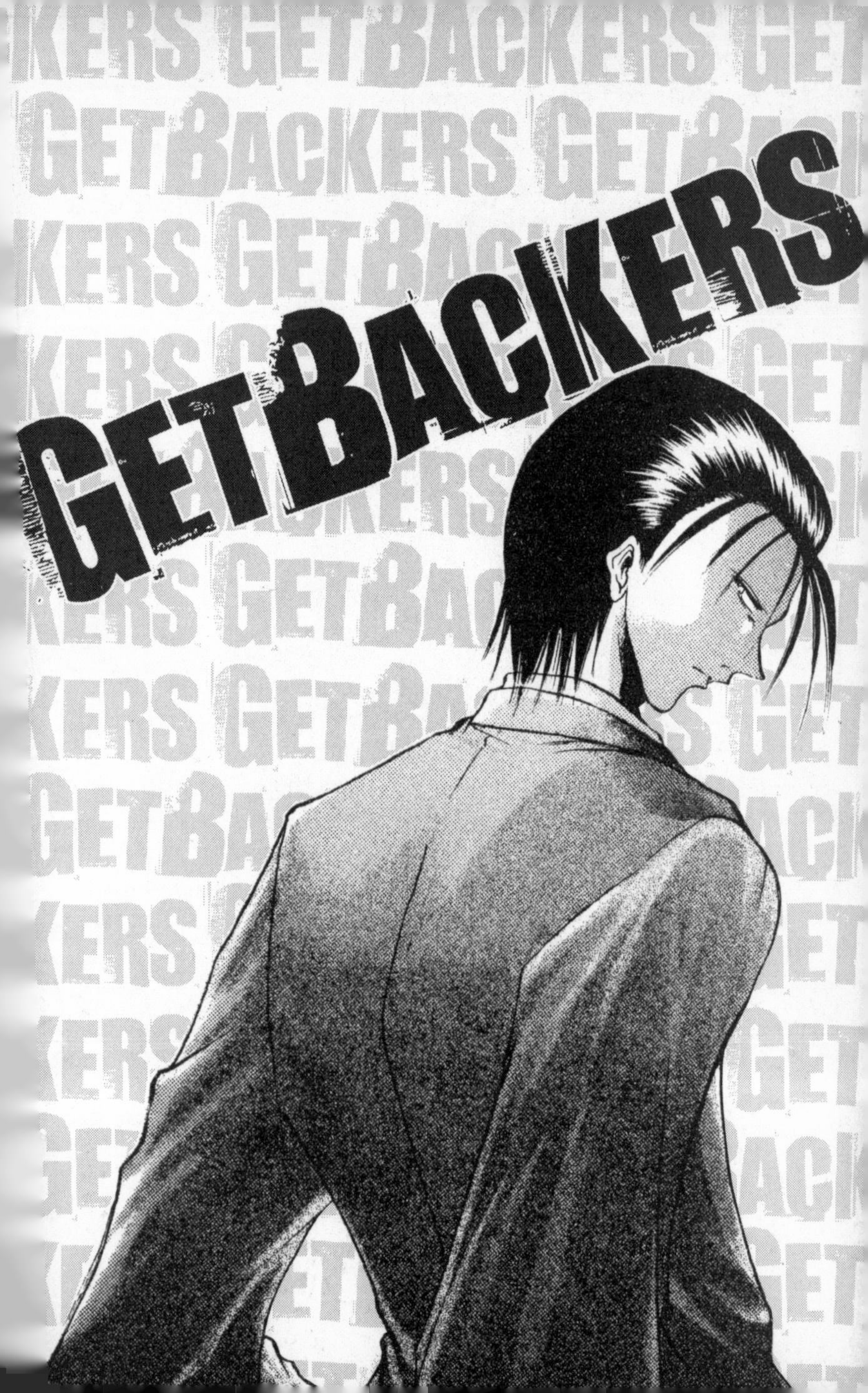
GETBACKERS

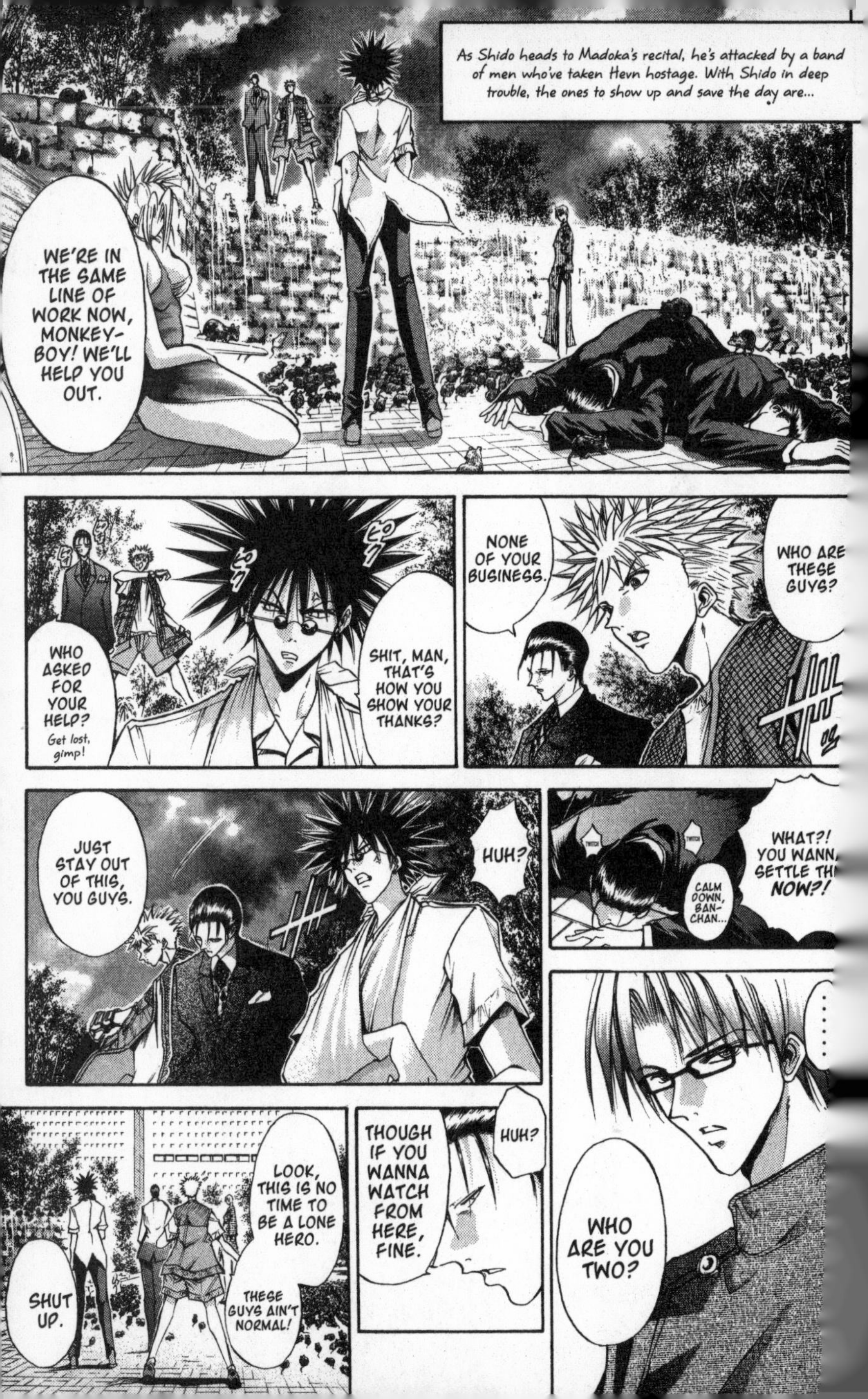
As Shido heads to Madoka's recital, he's attacked by a band of men who've taken Hevn hostage. With Shido in deep trouble, the ones to show up and save the day are...
WE'RE IN THE SAME LINE OF WORK NOW, MONKEY-BOY! WE'LL HELP YOU OUT.
WHO ARE THESE GUYS?
NONE OF YOUR BUSINESS.
SHIT, MAN, THAT'S HOW YOU SHOW YOUR THANKS?
WHO ASKED FOR YOUR HELP? Get lost, gimp!
WHAT?! YOU WANNA SETTLE THI NOW?!
TWITCH
TWITCH
CALM DOWN, BAN-CHAN...
.....
WHO ARE YOU TWO?
HUH?
JUST STAY OUT OF THIS, YOU GUYS.
HUH?
THOUGH IF YOU WANNA WATCH FROM HERE, FINE.
LOOK, THIS IS NO TIME TO BE A LONE HERO.
THESE GUYS AIN'T NORMAL!
SHUT UP.

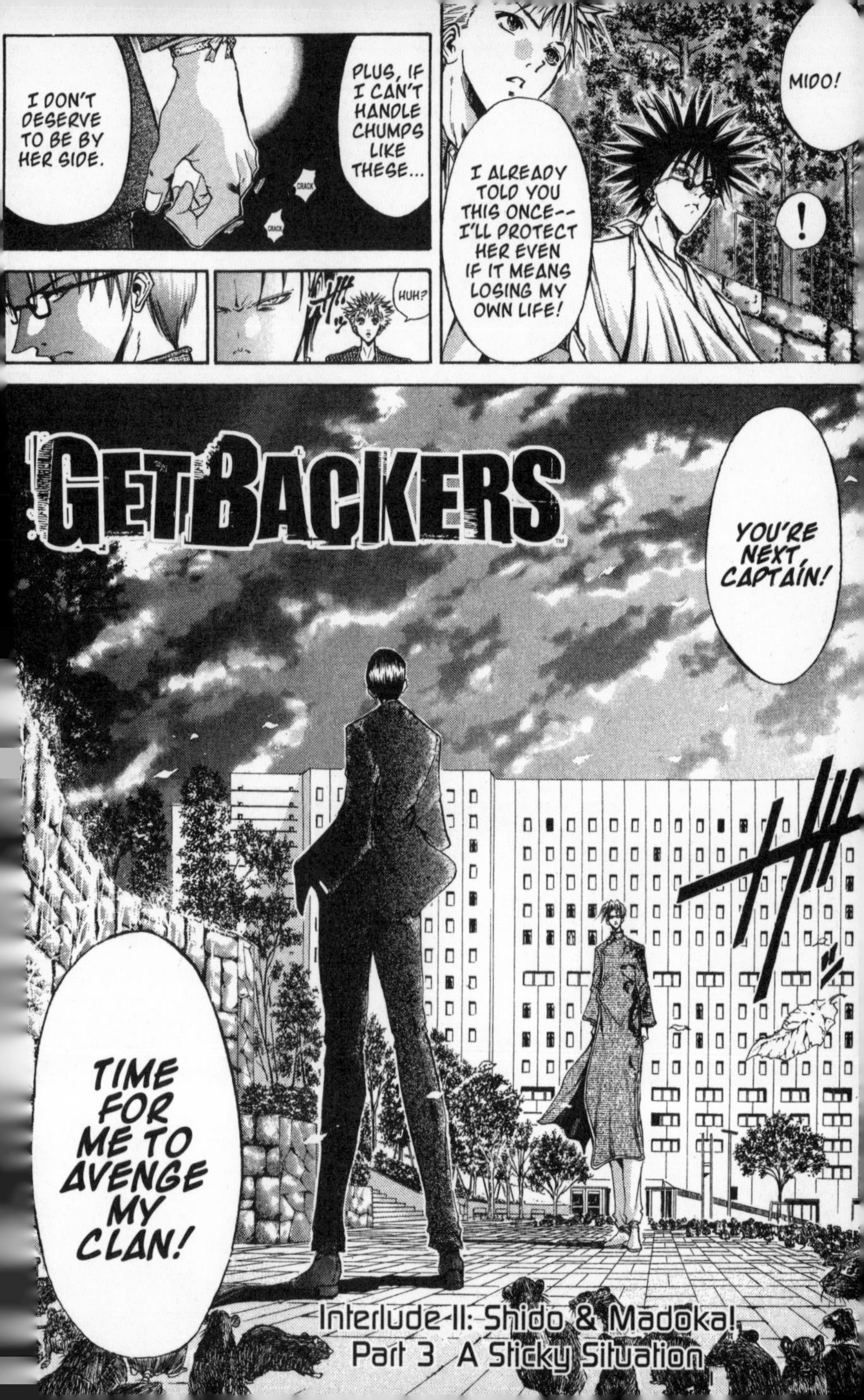
MIDO!
!
I ALREADY TOLD YOU THIS ONCE-- I'LL PROTECT HER EVEN IF IT MEANS LOSING MY OWN LIFE!
PLUS, IF I CAN'T HANDLE CHUMPS LIKE THESE...
CRACK
CRACK
I DON'T DESERVE TO BE BY HER SIDE.
HUH?
GETBACKERS
YOU'RE NEXT, CAPTAIN!
TIME FOR ME TO AVENGE MY CLAN!
Interlude II: Shido & Madoka!
Part 3 A Sticky Situation

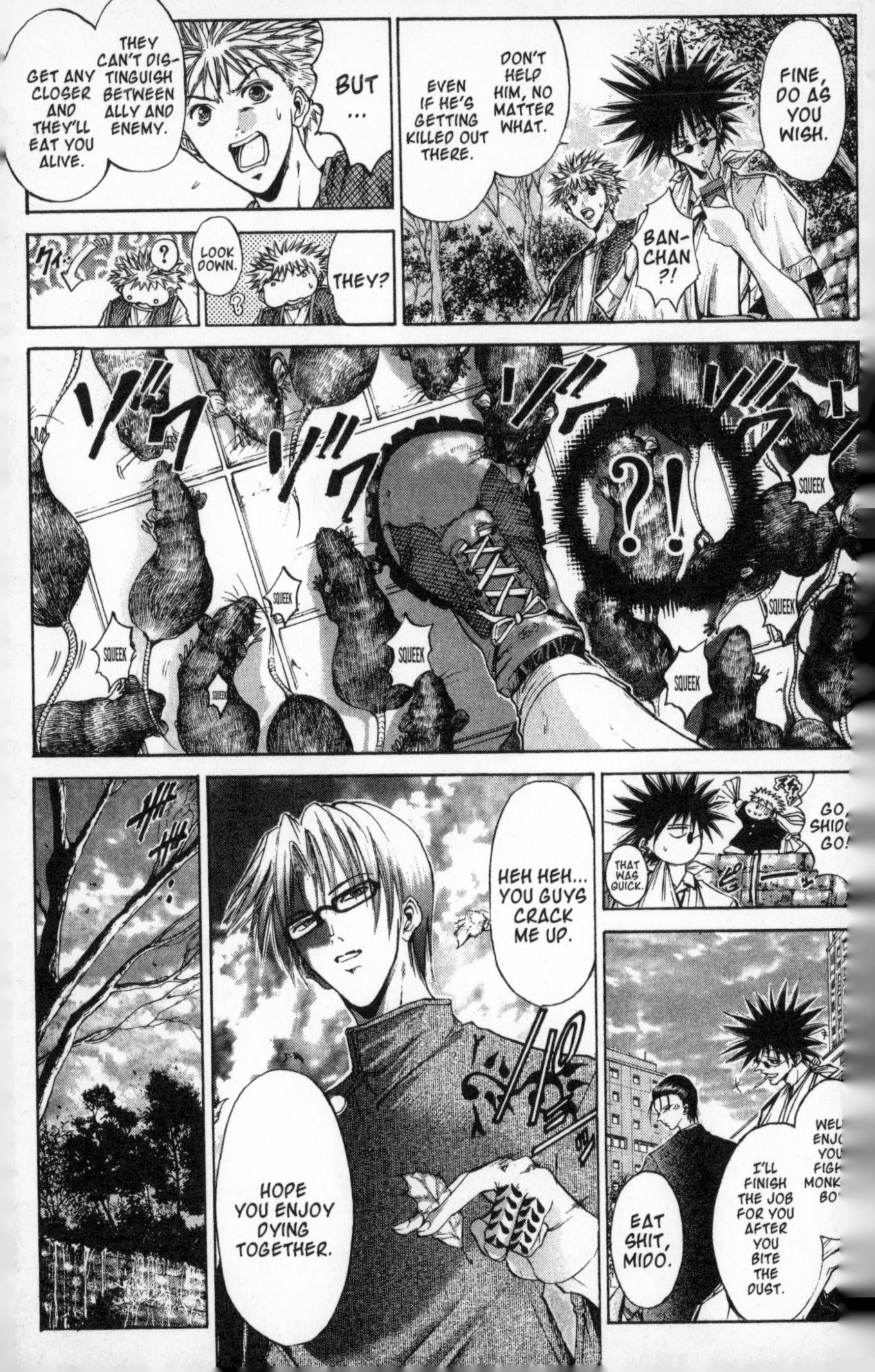
FINE, DO AS YOU WISH.
DON'T HELP HIM, NO MATTER WHAT.
EVEN IF HE'S GETTING KILLED OUT THERE.
BAN-CHAN?!
BUT ...
THEY CAN'T DIS-TINGUISH BETWEEN ALLY AND ENEMY.
GET ANY CLOSER AND THEY'LL EAT YOU ALIVE.
THEY?
LOOK DOWN.
?
?!
SQUEEK
SQUEEK
SQUEEK
SQUEEK
SQUEEK
SQUEEK
GO, SHIDO GO!
THAT WAS QUICK.
WEL ENJO YOU FIGH MONK BO
I'LL FINISH THE JOB FOR YOU AFTER YOU BITE THE DUST.
EAT SHIT, MIDO.
HEH HEH... YOU GUYS CRACK ME UP.
HOPE YOU ENJOY DYING TOGETHER.

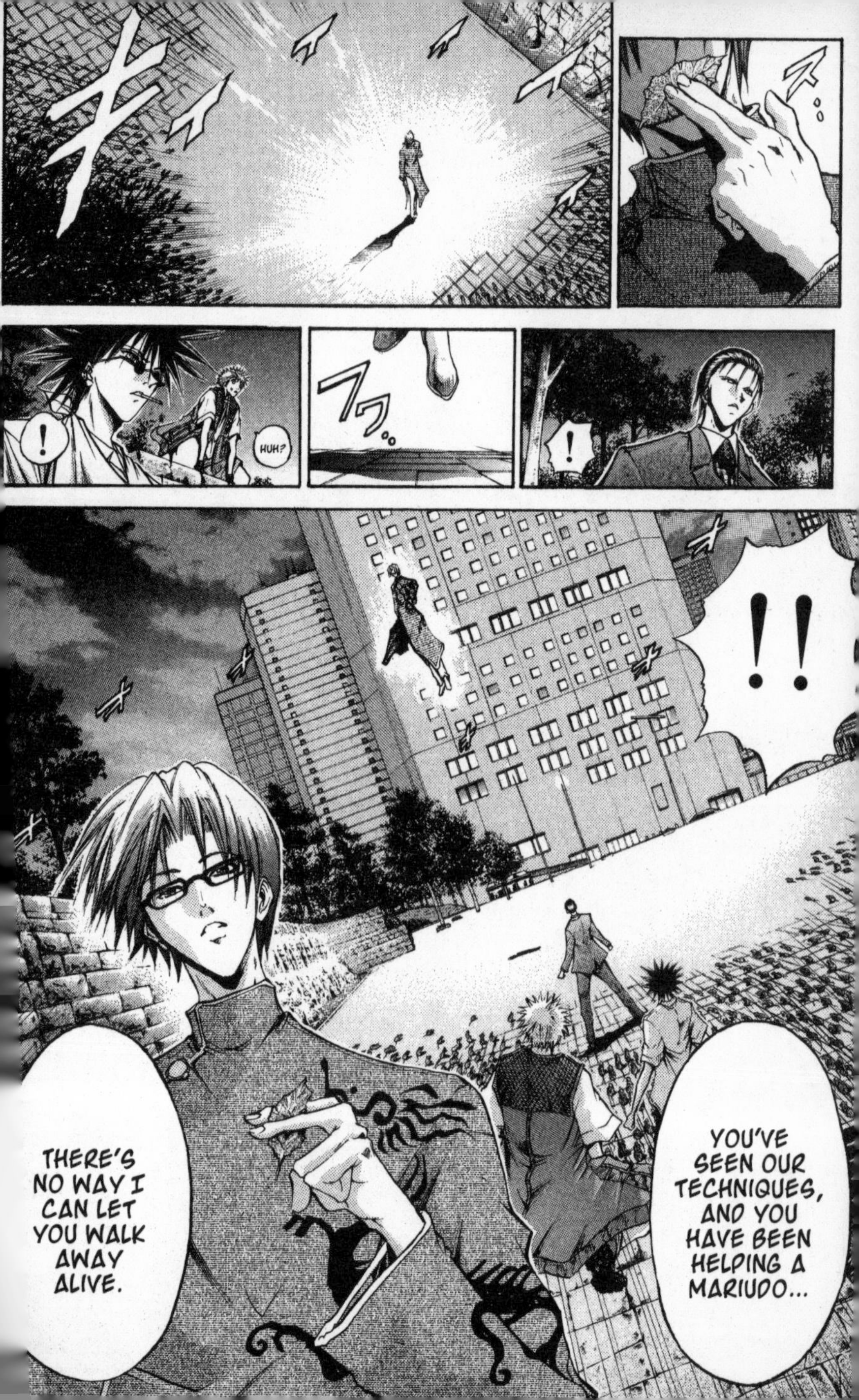
!
HUH?
!
!!
YOU'VE SEEN OUR TECHNIQUES, AND YOU HAVE BEEN HELPING A MARIUDO...
THERE'S NO WAY I CAN LET YOU WALK AWAY ALIVE.

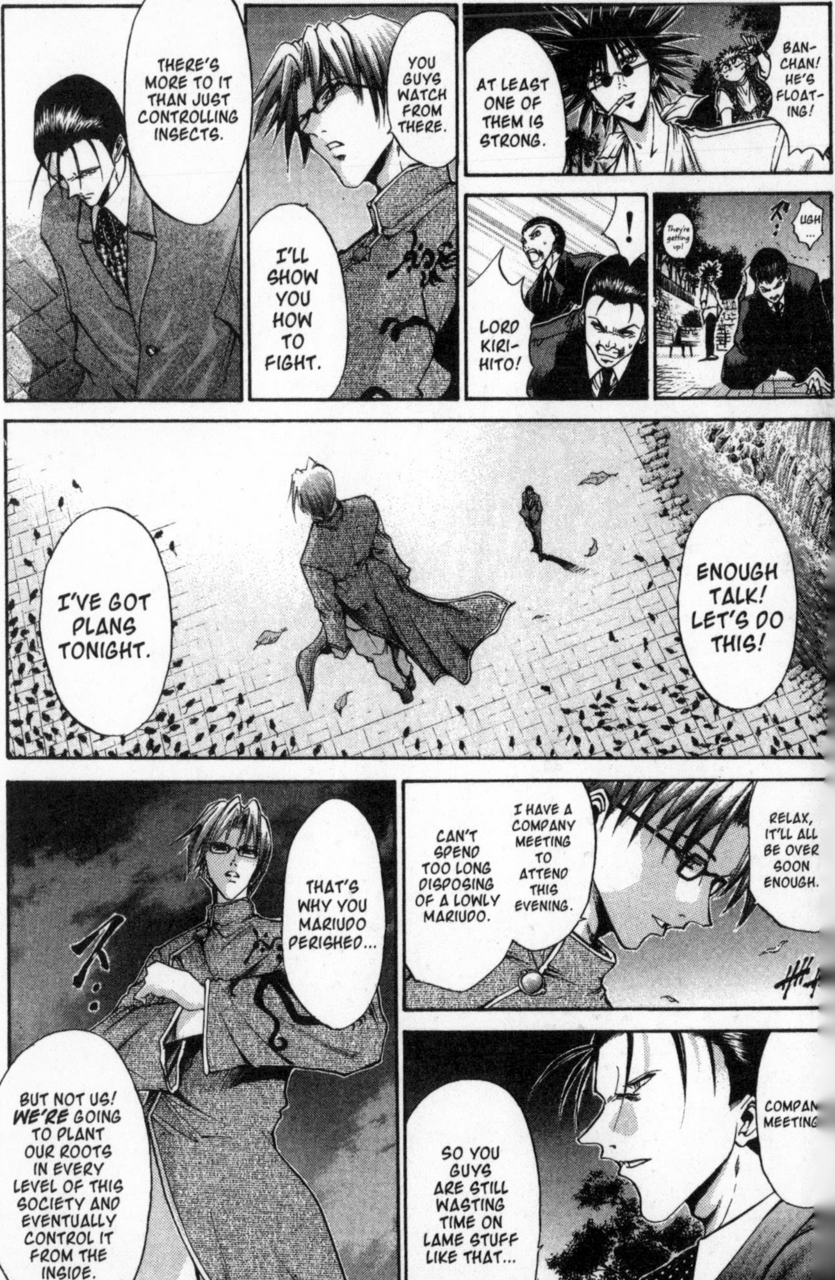
BAN-CHAN! HE'S FLOAT-ING!
AT LEAST ONE OF THEM IS STRONG.
UGH ...
They're getting up!
!
LORD KIRI-HITO!
YOU GUYS WATCH FROM THERE.
I'LL SHOW YOU HOW TO FIGHT.
THERE'S MORE TO IT THAN JUST CONTROLLING INSECTS.
ENOUGH TALK! LET'S DO THIS!
I'VE GOT PLANS TONIGHT.
RELAX, IT'LL ALL BE OVER SOON ENOUGH.
I HAVE A COMPANY MEETING TO ATTEND THIS EVENING.
CAN'T SPEND TOO LONG DISPOSING OF A LOWLY MARIUDO.
COMPAN MEETING
SO YOU GUYS ARE STILL WASTING TIME ON LAME STUFF LIKE THAT...
THAT'S WHY YOU MARIUDO PERISHED...
BUT NOT US! *WE'RE* GOING TO PLANT OUR ROOTS IN EVERY LEVEL OF THIS SOCIETY AND EVENTUALLY CONTROL IT FROM THE INSIDE.

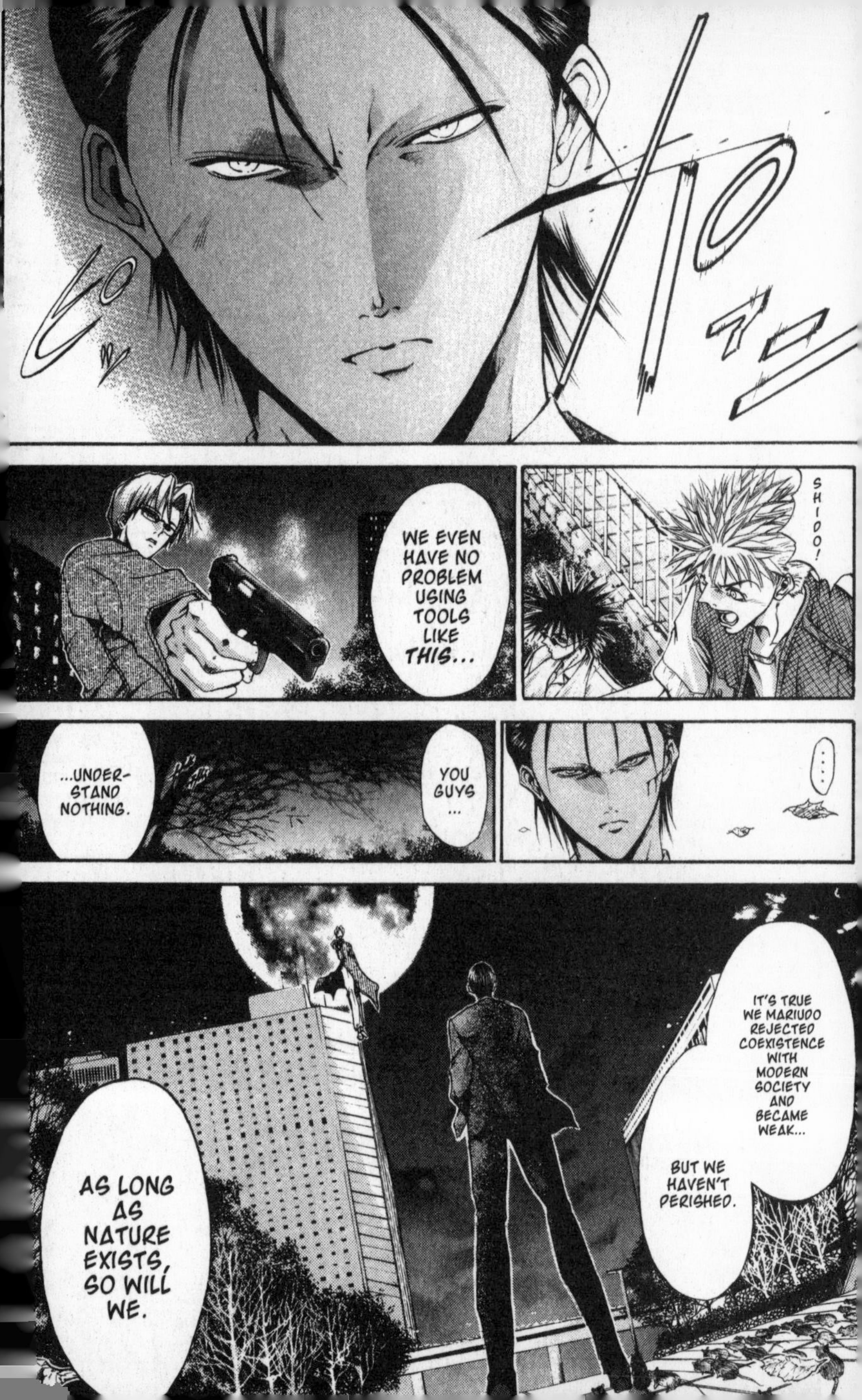
SHIDO!
WE EVEN HAVE NO PROBLEM USING TOOLS LIKE THIS...
...
YOU GUYS ...
...UNDER-STAND NOTHING.
IT'S TRUE WE MARIUDO REJECTED COEXISTENCE WITH MODERN SOCIETY AND BECAME WEAK...
BUT WE HAVEN'T PERISHED.
AS LONG AS NATURE EXISTS, SO WILL WE.

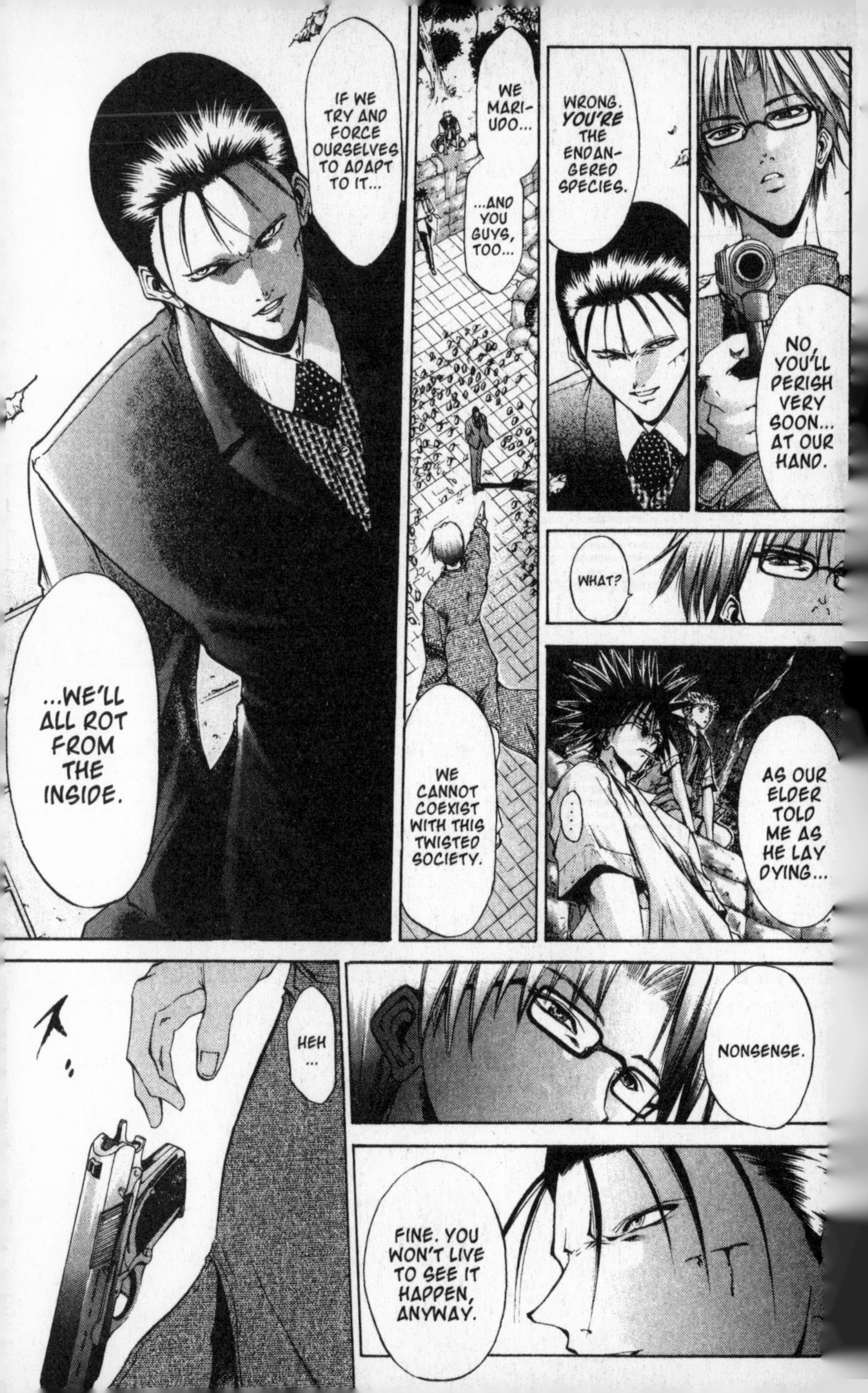
NO, YOU'LL PERISH VERY SOON... AT OUR HAND.
WRONG. YOU'RE THE ENDANGERED SPECIES.
WHAT?
...
AS OUR ELDER TOLD ME AS HE LAY DYING...
WE CANNOT COEXIST WITH THIS TWISTED SOCIETY.
WE MARIUDO...
...AND YOU GUYS, TOO...
IF WE TRY AND FORCE OURSELVES TO ADAPT TO IT...
...WE'LL ALL ROT FROM THE INSIDE.
NONSENSE.
HEH...
FINE. YOU WON'T LIVE TO SEE IT HAPPEN, ANYWAY.

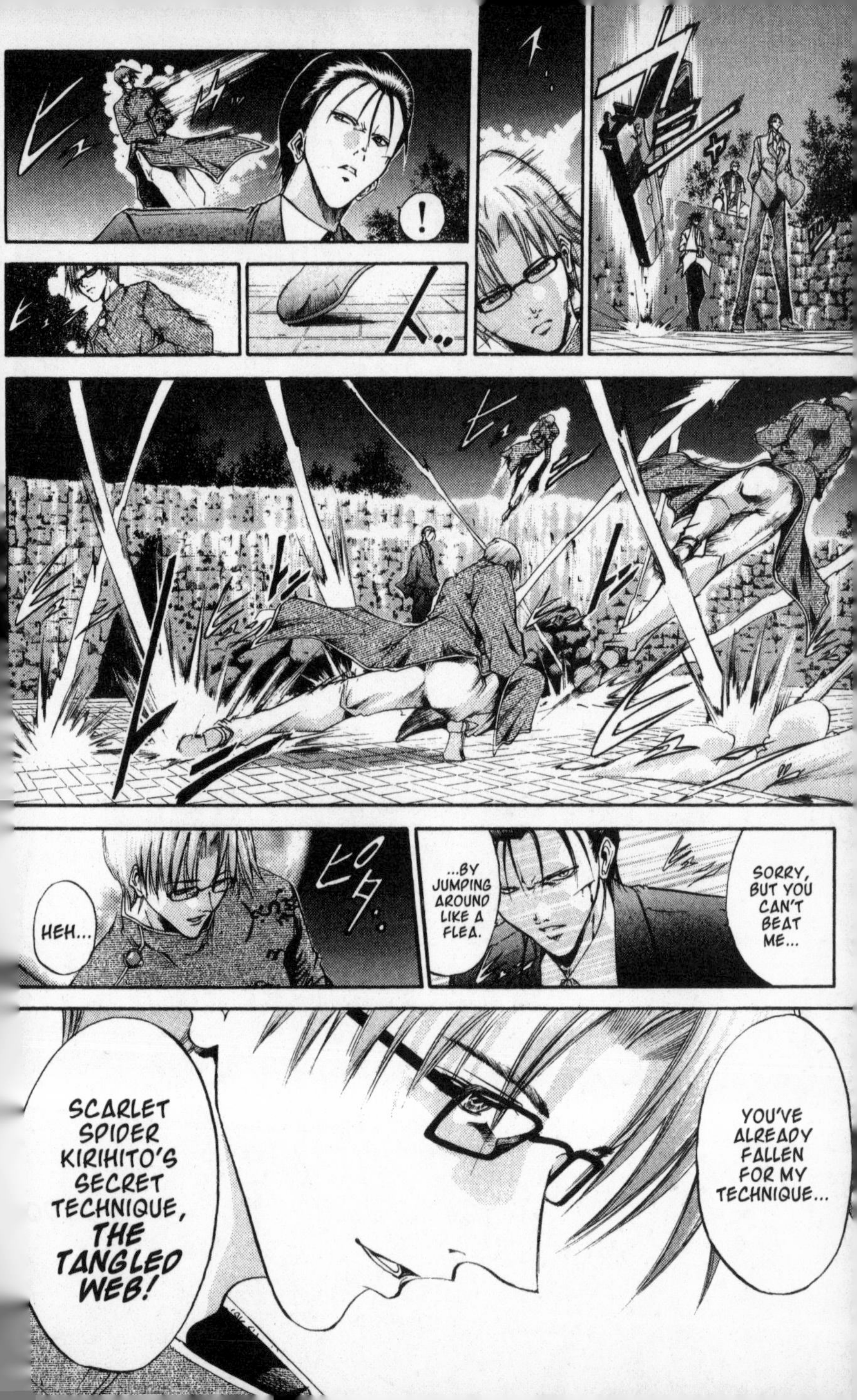
!
SORRY, BUT YOU CAN'T BEAT ME...
...BY JUMPING AROUND LIKE A FLEA.
HEH...
YOU'VE ALREADY FALLEN FOR MY TECHNIQUE...
SCARLET SPIDER KIRIHITO'S SECRET TECHNIQUE, **THE TANGLED WEB!**

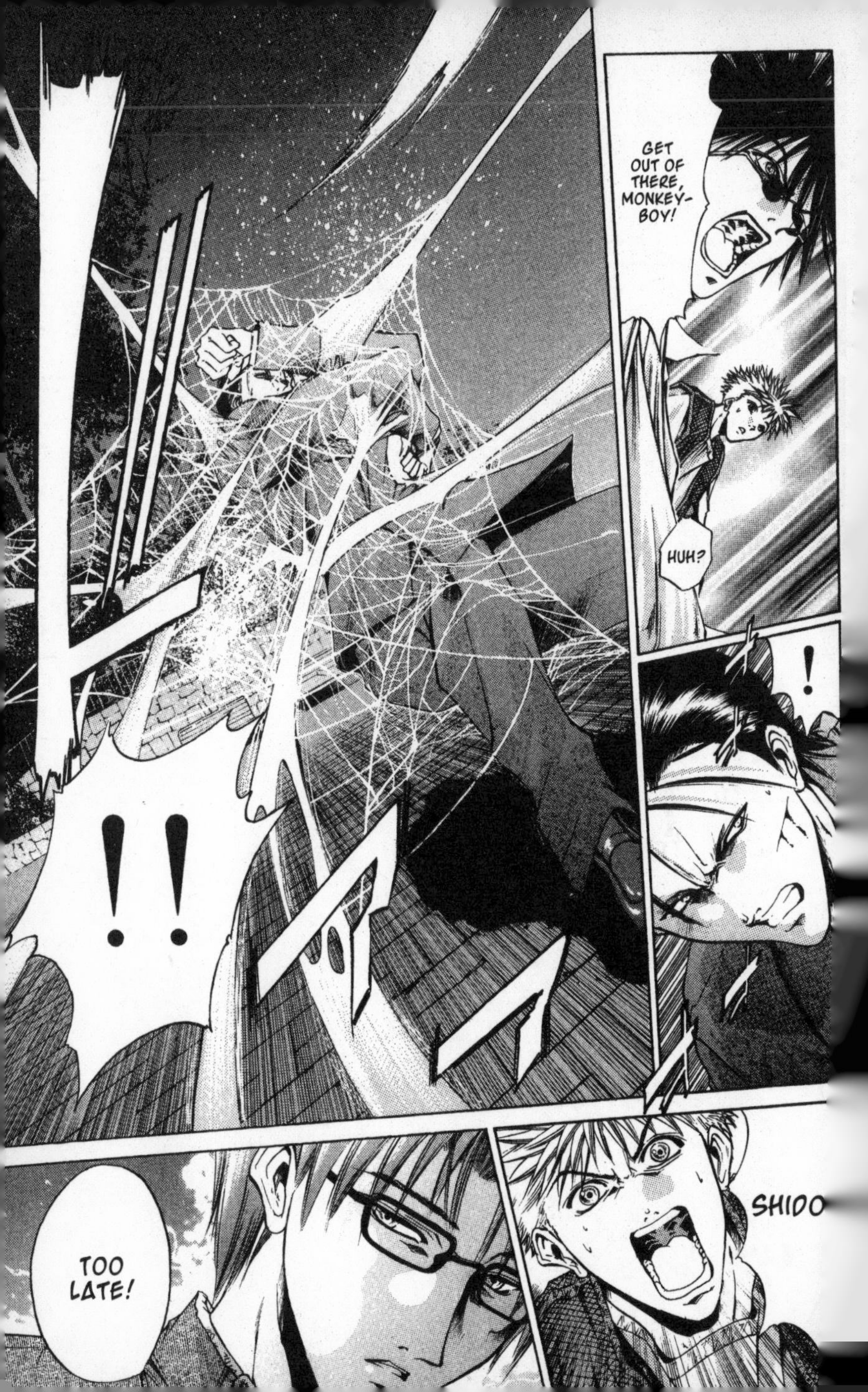

GET OUT OF THERE, MONKEY-BOY!
HUH?
!
!!
SHIDO
TOO LATE!

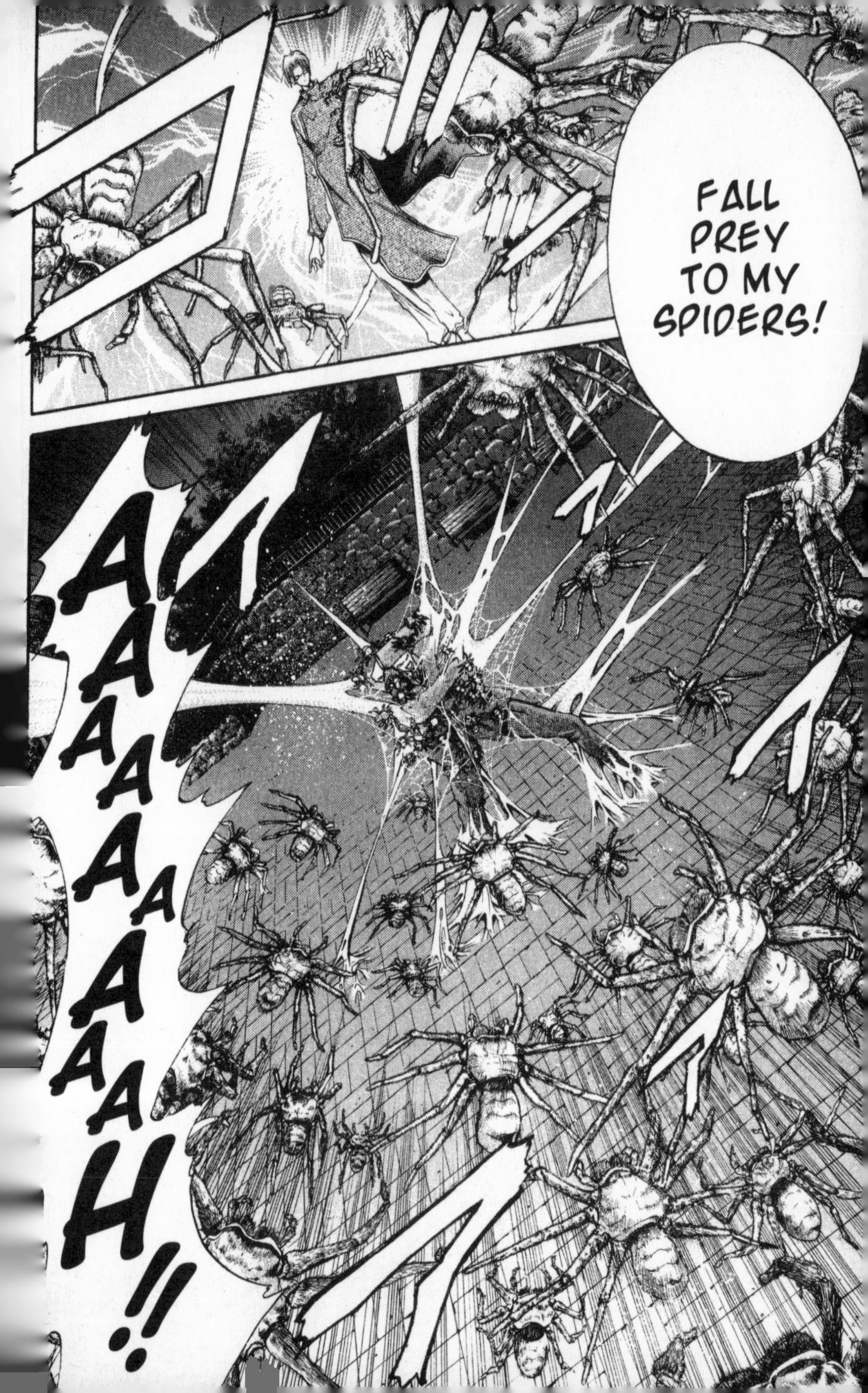
FALL PREY TO MY SPIDERS!
AAAAAAAAAAAH!!

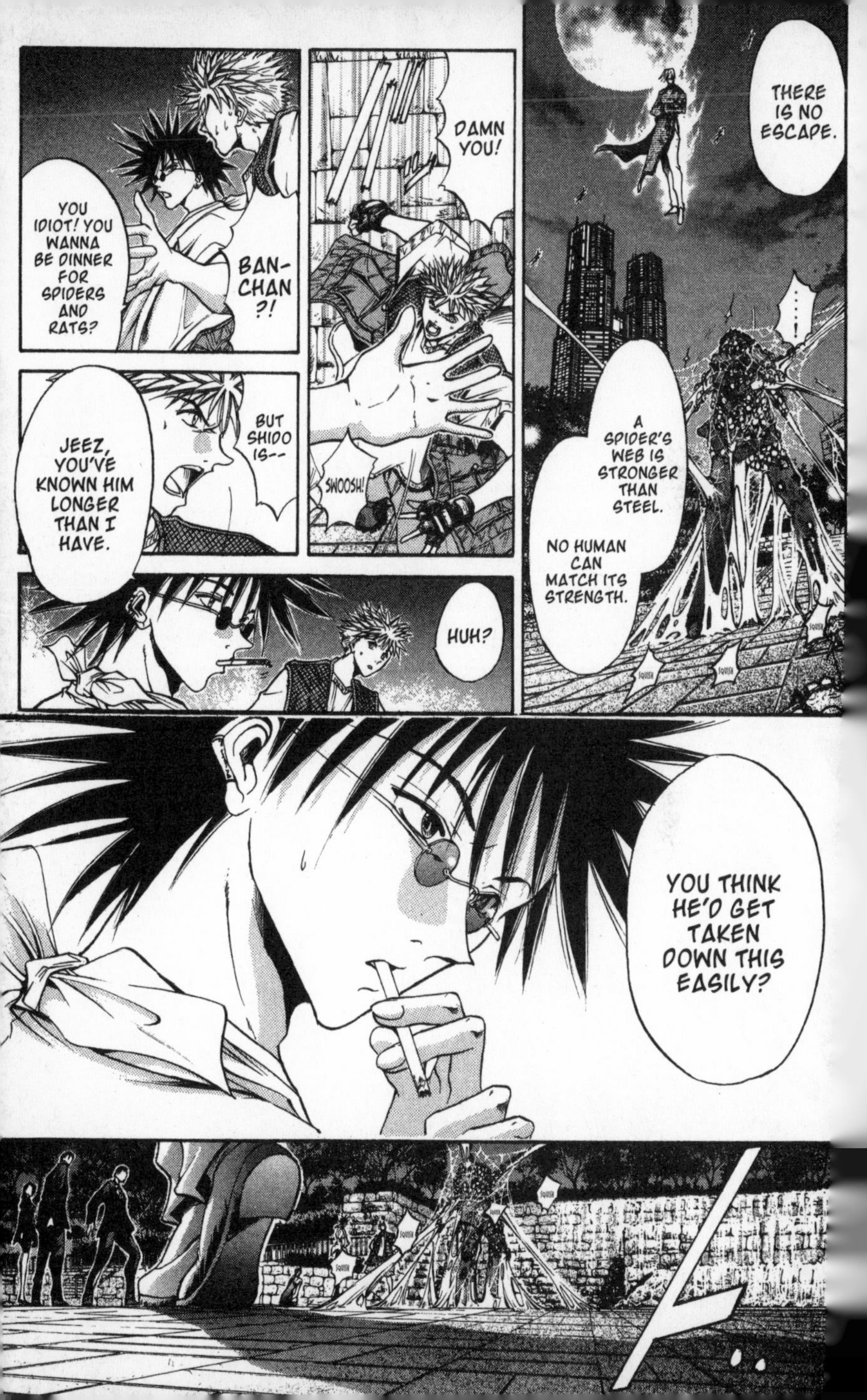
THERE IS NO ESCAPE.
...!
A SPIDER'S WEB IS STRONGER THAN STEEL.
NO HUMAN CAN MATCH ITS STRENGTH.
SQUISH
SQUISH
SQUISH
DAMN YOU!
SWOOSH!
BAN-CHAN?!
YOU IDIOT! YOU WANNA BE DINNER FOR SPIDERS AND RATS?
BUT SHIDO IS--
JEEZ, YOU'VE KNOWN HIM LONGER THAN I HAVE.
HUH?
YOU THINK HE'D GET TAKEN DOWN THIS EASILY?
SQUISH
SQUISH
SQUISH
SQUISH

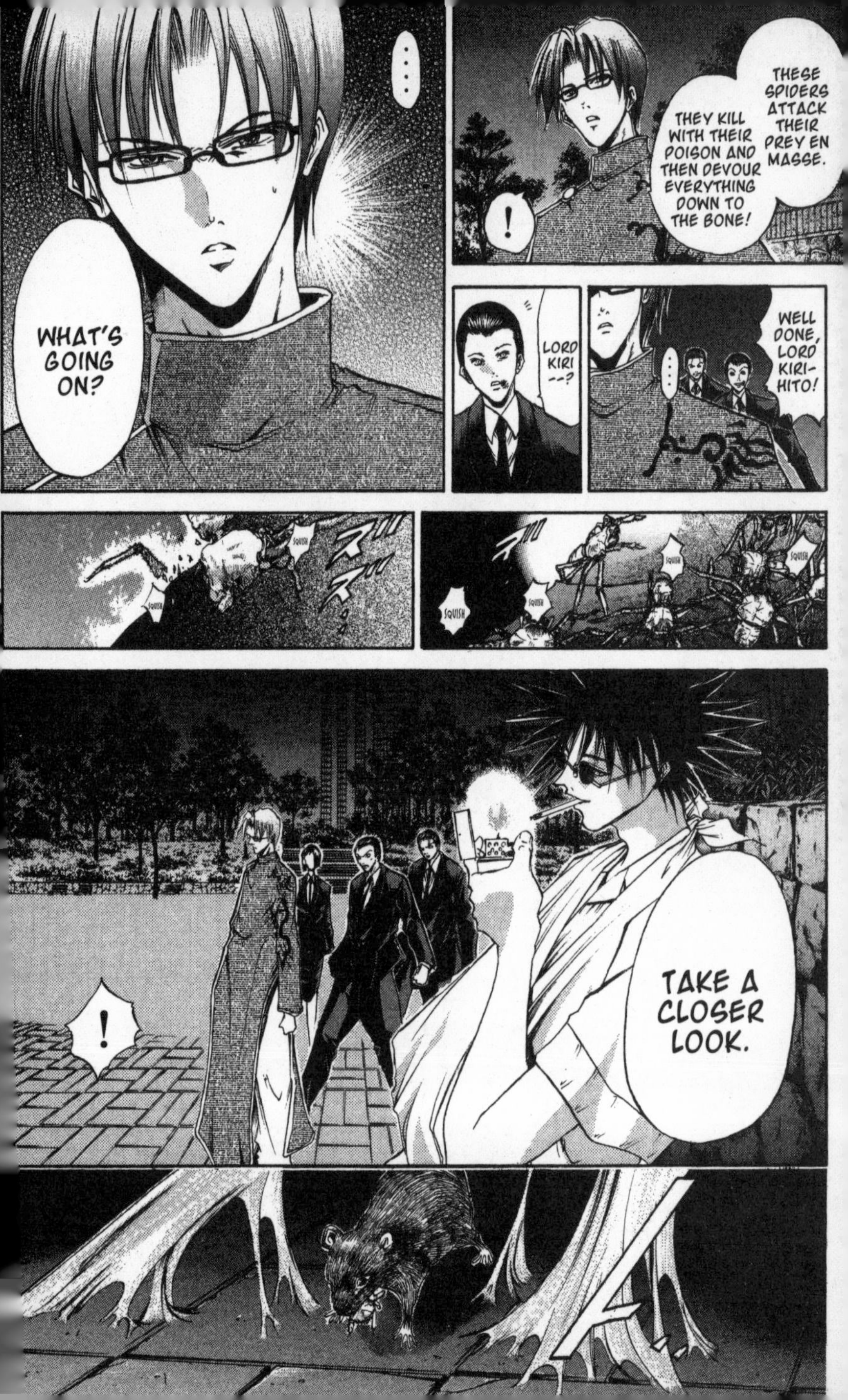
THESE SPIDERS ATTACK THEIR PREY EN MASSE.
THEY KILL WITH THEIR POISON AND THEN DEVOUR EVERYTHING DOWN TO THE BONE!
!
WELL DONE, LORD KIRIHITO!
...
LORD KIRI--?
...
WHAT'S GOING ON?
SQUISH
SQUISH
SQUISH
SQUISH
SQUISH
SQUISH
TAKE A CLOSER LOOK.
!

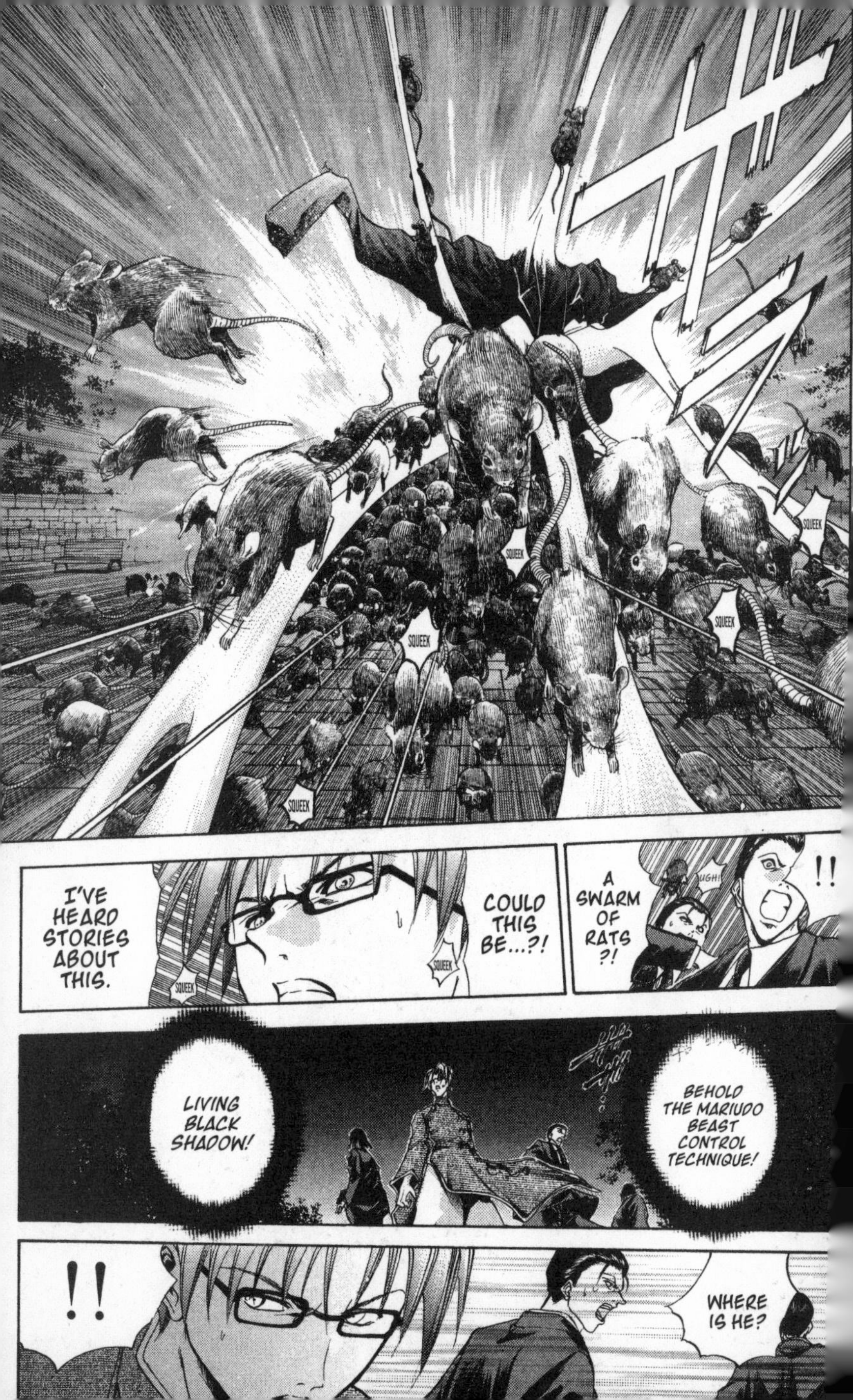
SQUEEK
SQUEEK
SQUEEK
SQUEEK
SQUEEK
!!
UGH!
A SWARM OF RATS ?!
COULD THIS BE...?!
SQUEEK
I'VE HEARD STORIES ABOUT THIS.
SQUEEK
BEHOLD THE MARIUDO BEAST CONTROL TECHNIQUE!
LIVING BLACK SHADOW!
WHERE IS HE?
!!

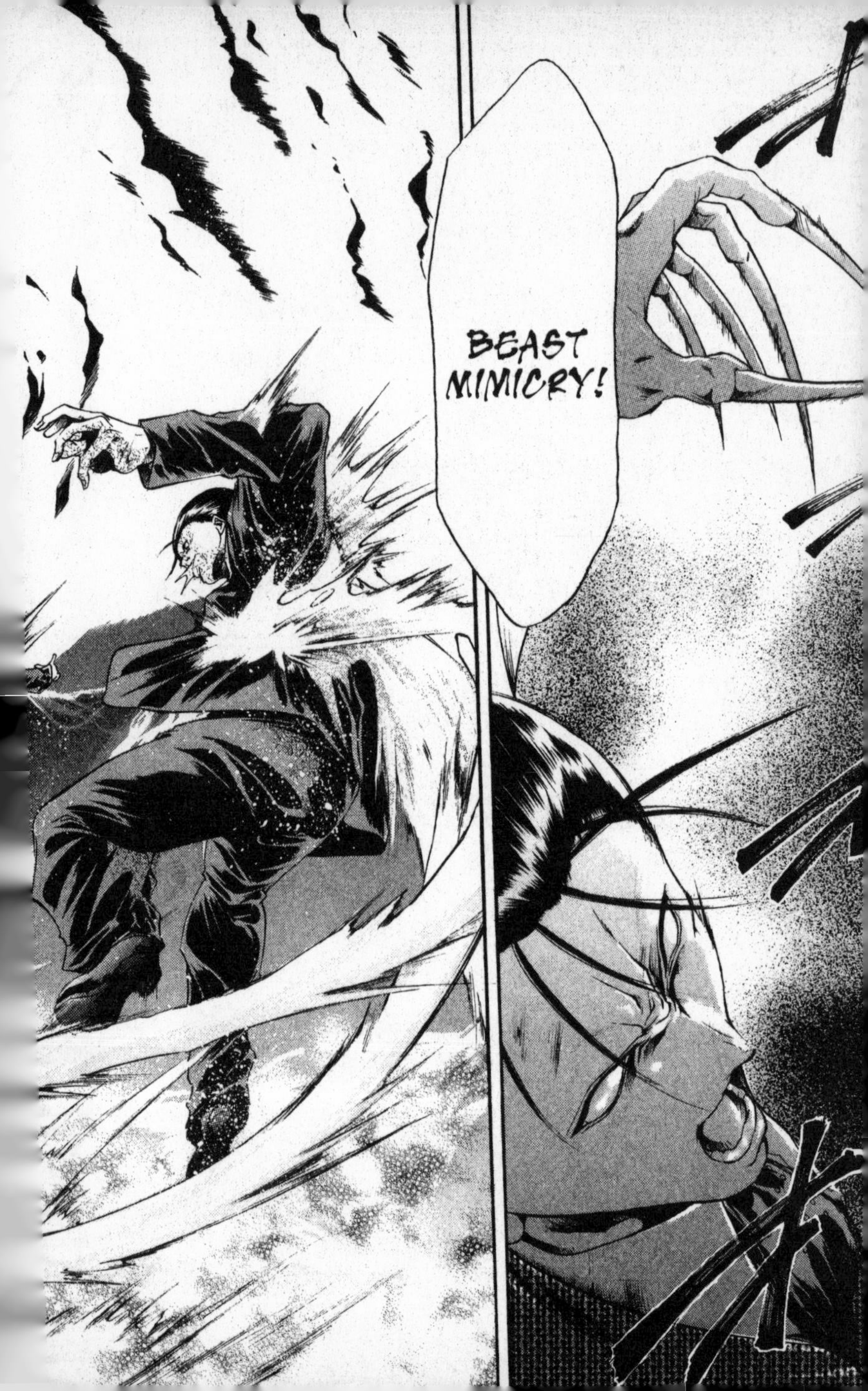
BEAST MIMICRY!

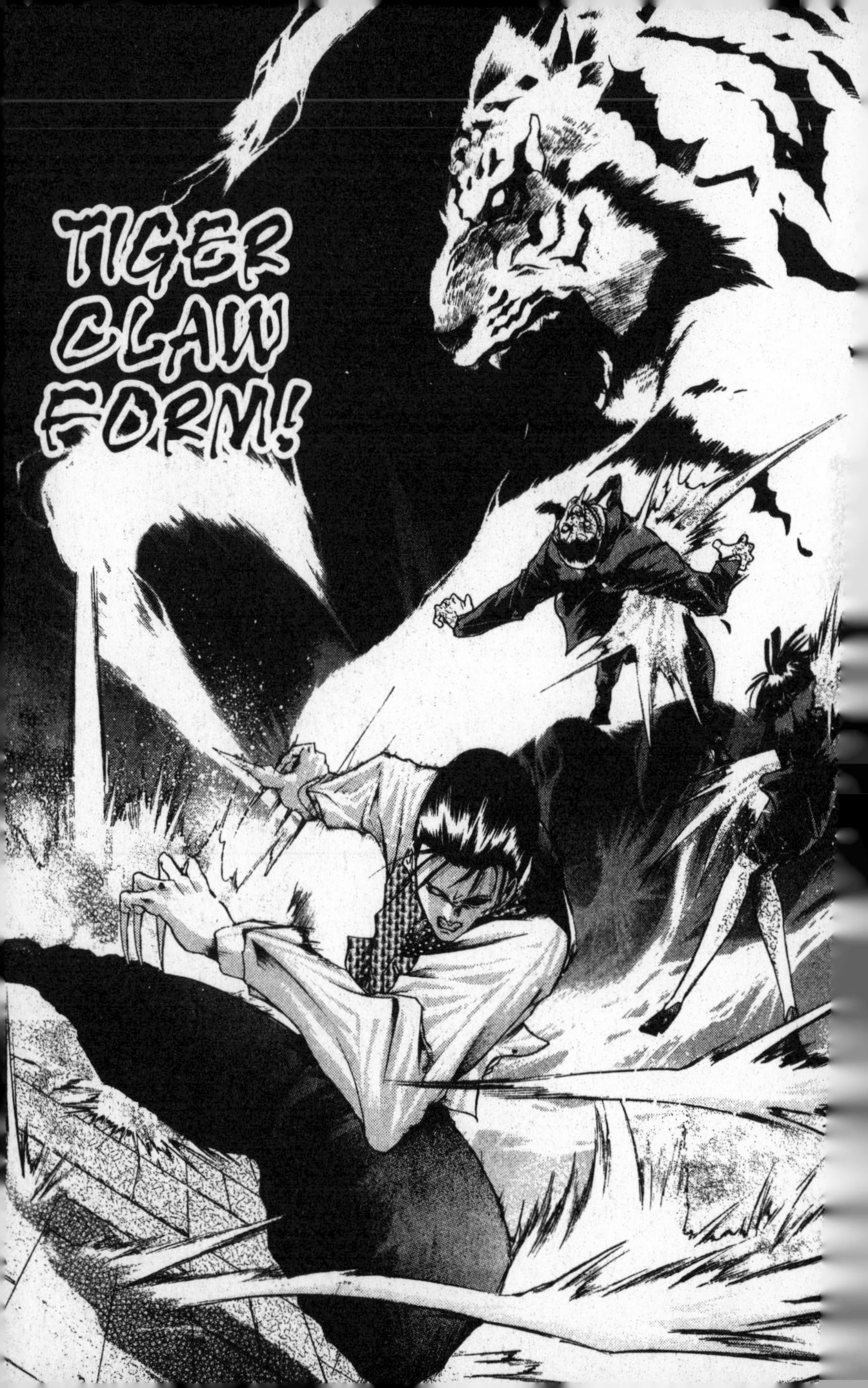
TIGER CLAW FORM!

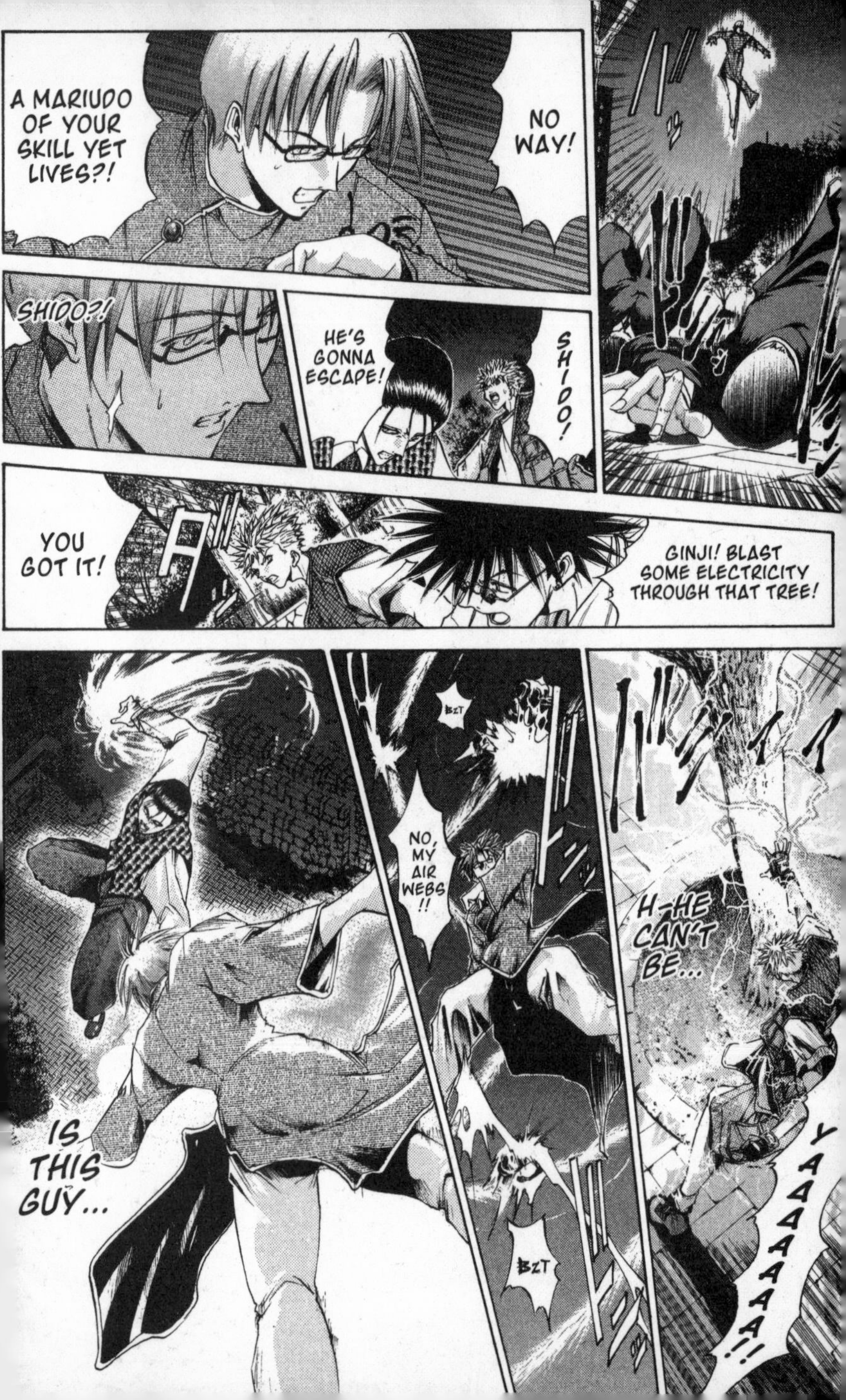
NO WAY!
A MARIUDO OF YOUR SKILL YET LIVES?!
SHIDO!
HE'S GONNA ESCAPE!
SHIDO?!
GINJI! BLAST SOME ELECTRICITY THROUGH THAT TREE!
YOU GOT IT!
H-HE CAN'T BE...
YAAAAAAAA!!
BZT
NO, MY AIR WEBS!!
BZT
IS THIS GUY...

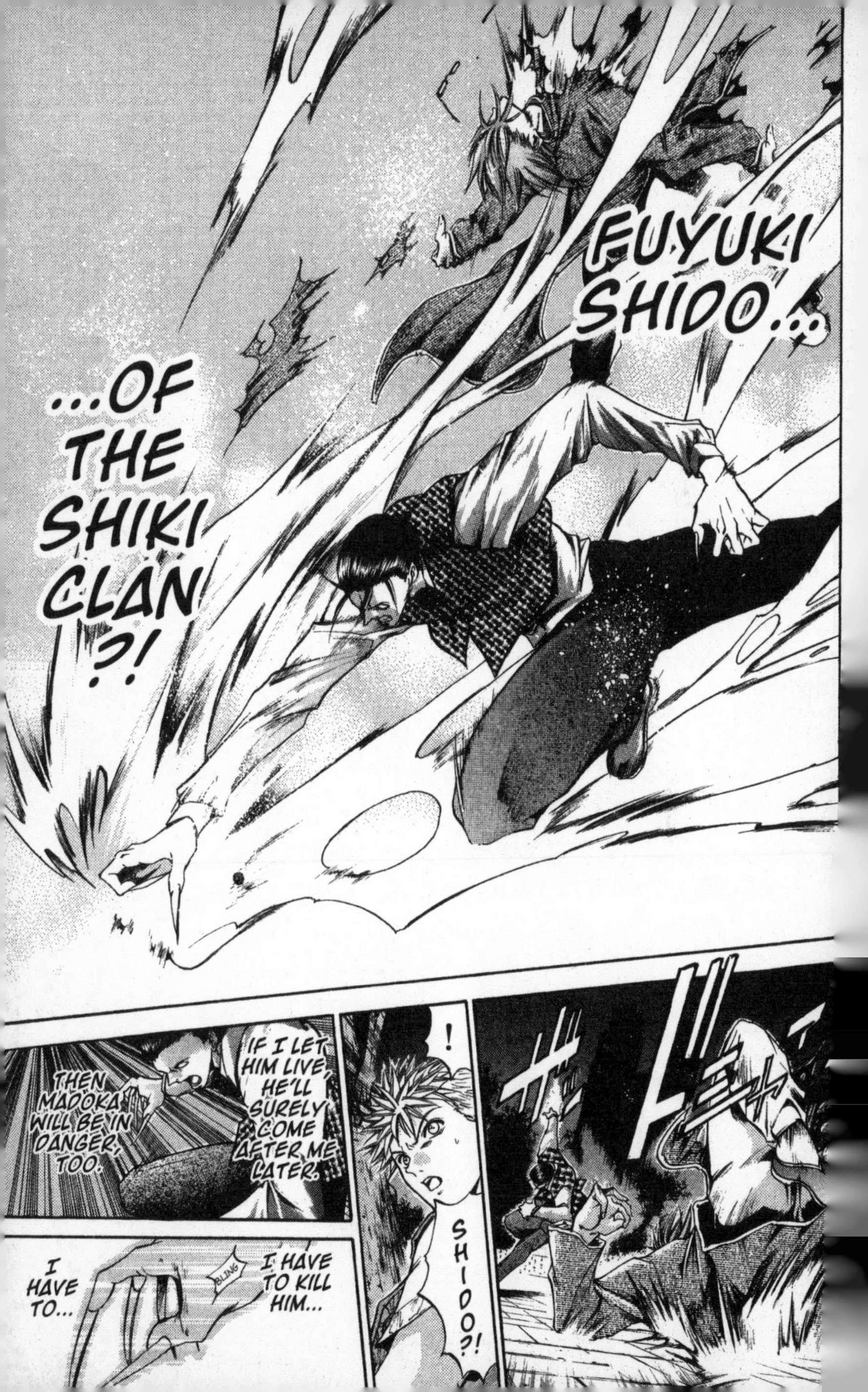
FUYUKI SHIDO...
...OF THE SHIKI CLAN?!
!
SHIDOO?!
IF I LET HIM LIVE, HE'LL SURELY COME AFTER ME LATER.
THEN MADOKA WILL BE IN DANGER, TOO.
I HAVE TO KILL HIM...
BLING
I HAVE TO...

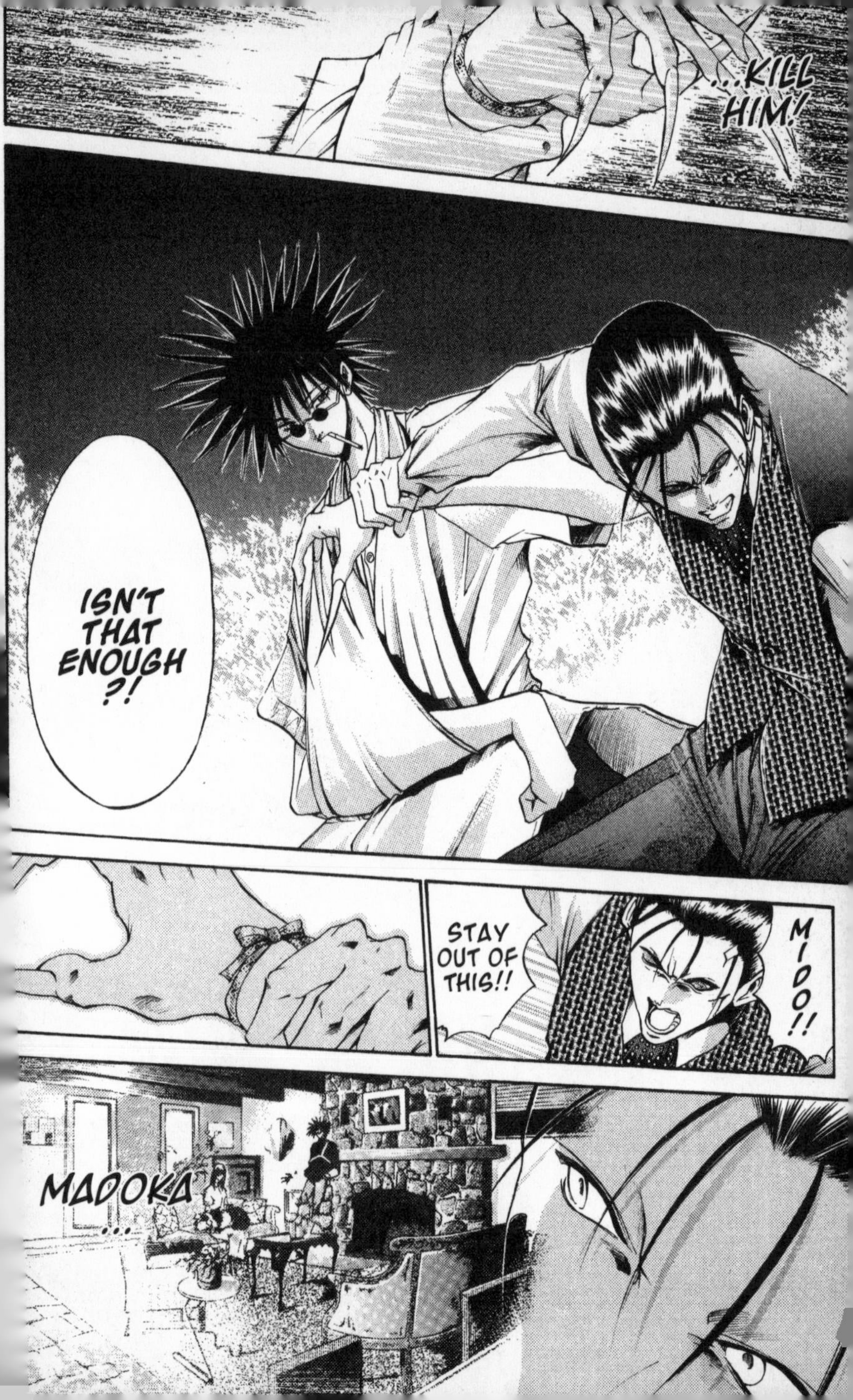
...KILL HIM!
ISN'T THAT ENOUGH?!
MIDO!!
STAY OUT OF THIS!!
MADOKA...

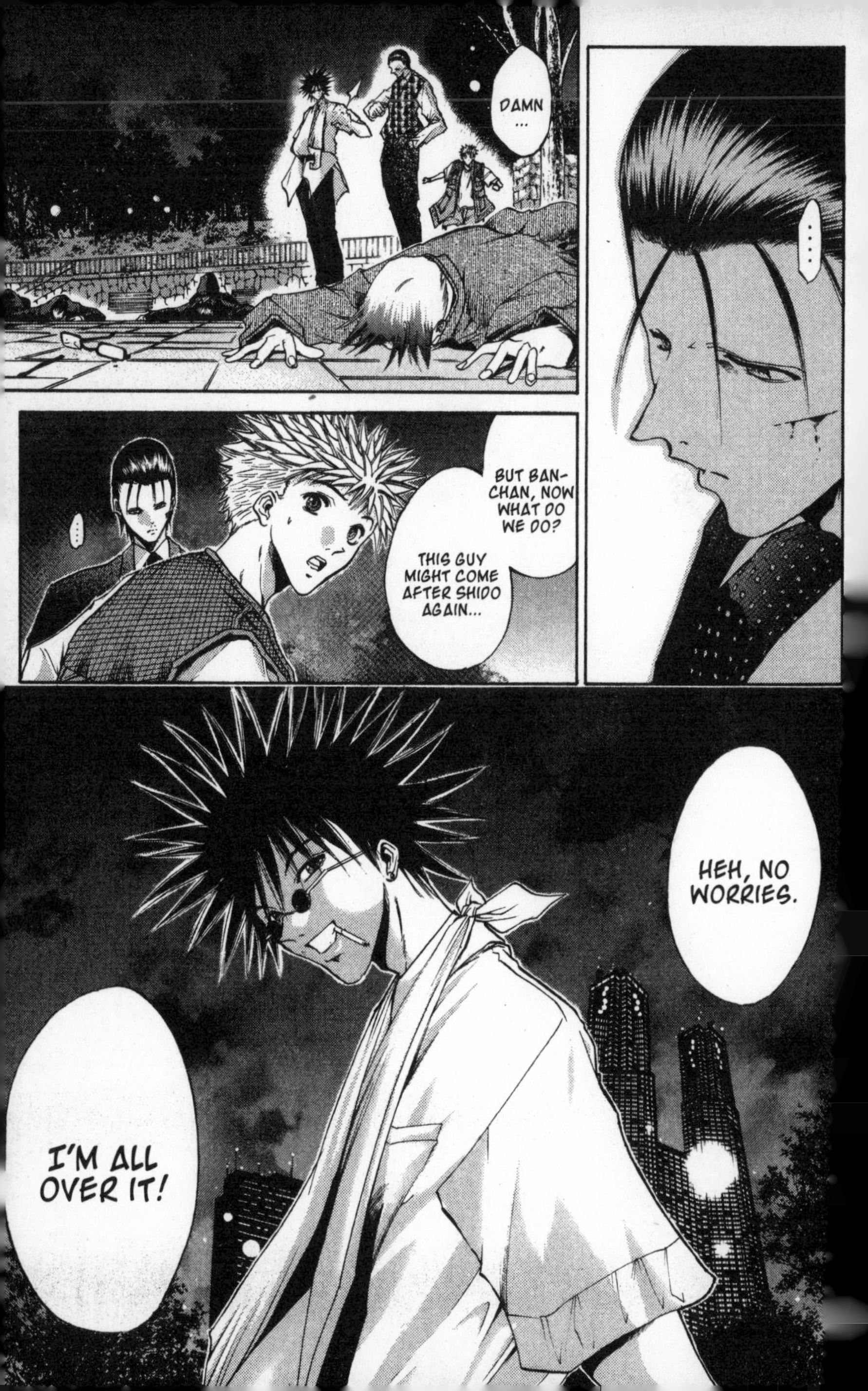
...
DAMN ...
BUT BAN-CHAN, NOW WHAT DO WE DO?
THIS GUY MIGHT COME AFTER SHIDO AGAIN...
...
HEH, NO WORRIES.
I'M ALL OVER IT!

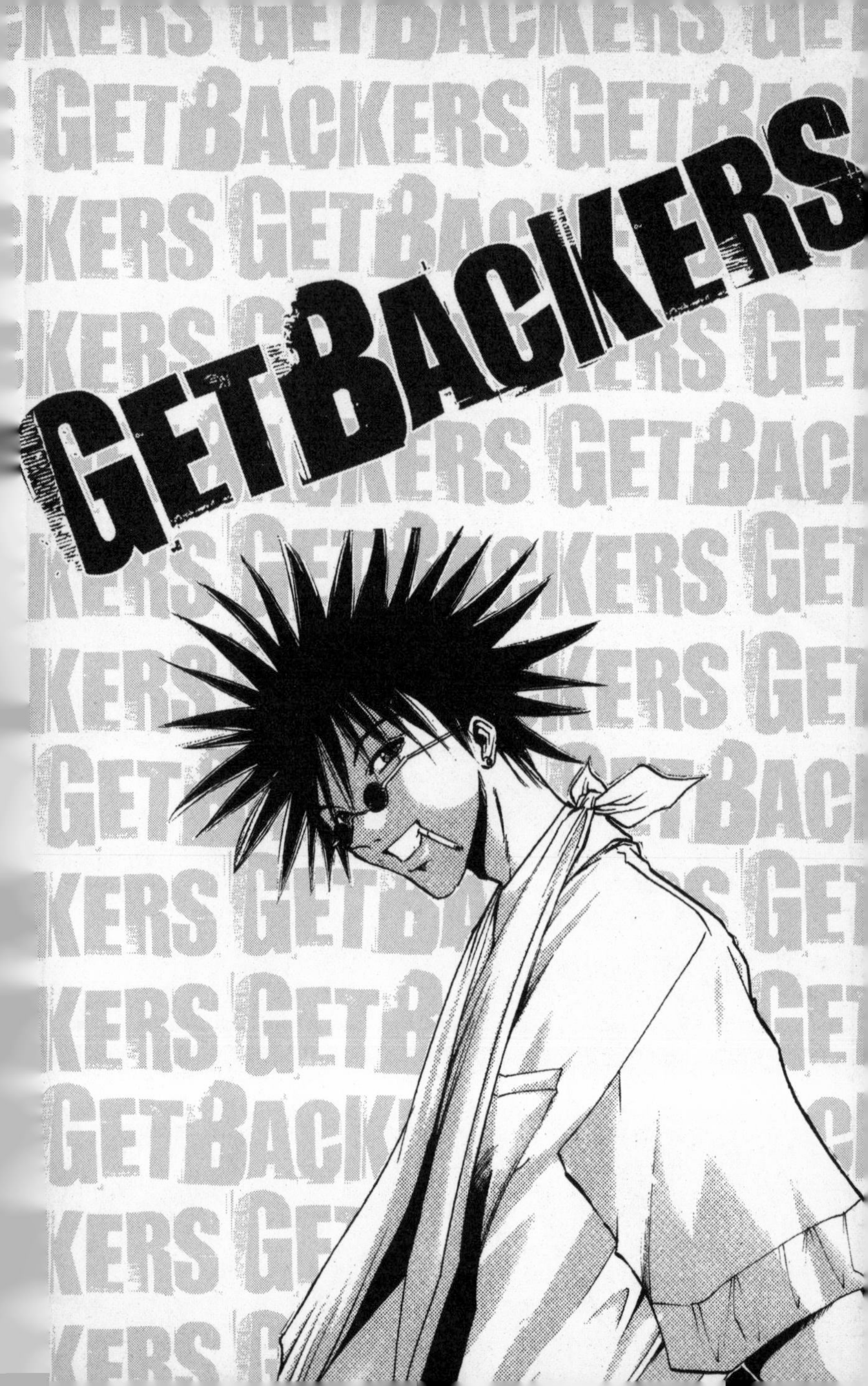
GETBACKERS

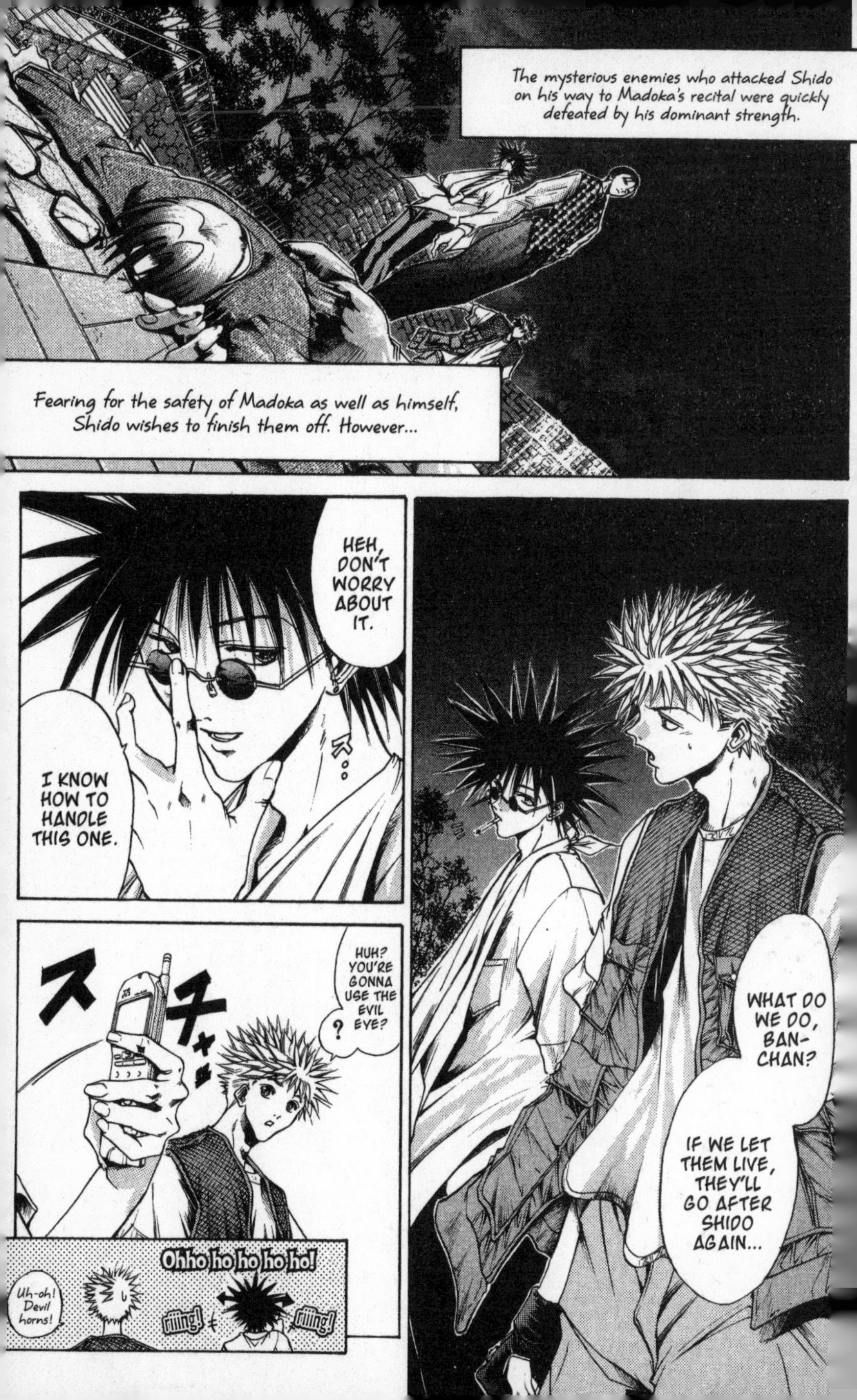
The mysterious enemies who attacked Shido on his way to Madoka's recital were quickly defeated by his dominant strength.
Fearing for the safety of Madoka as well as himself, Shido wishes to finish them off. However...
WHAT DO WE DO, BAN-CHAN?
IF WE LET THEM LIVE, THEY'LL GO AFTER SHIDO AGAIN...
HEH, DON'T WORRY ABOUT IT.
I KNOW HOW TO HANDLE THIS ONE.
HUH? YOU'RE GONNA USE THE EVIL EYE?
?
スチャ
Ohho ho ho ho ho!
riiing!
riiing!
Uh-oh! Devil horns!

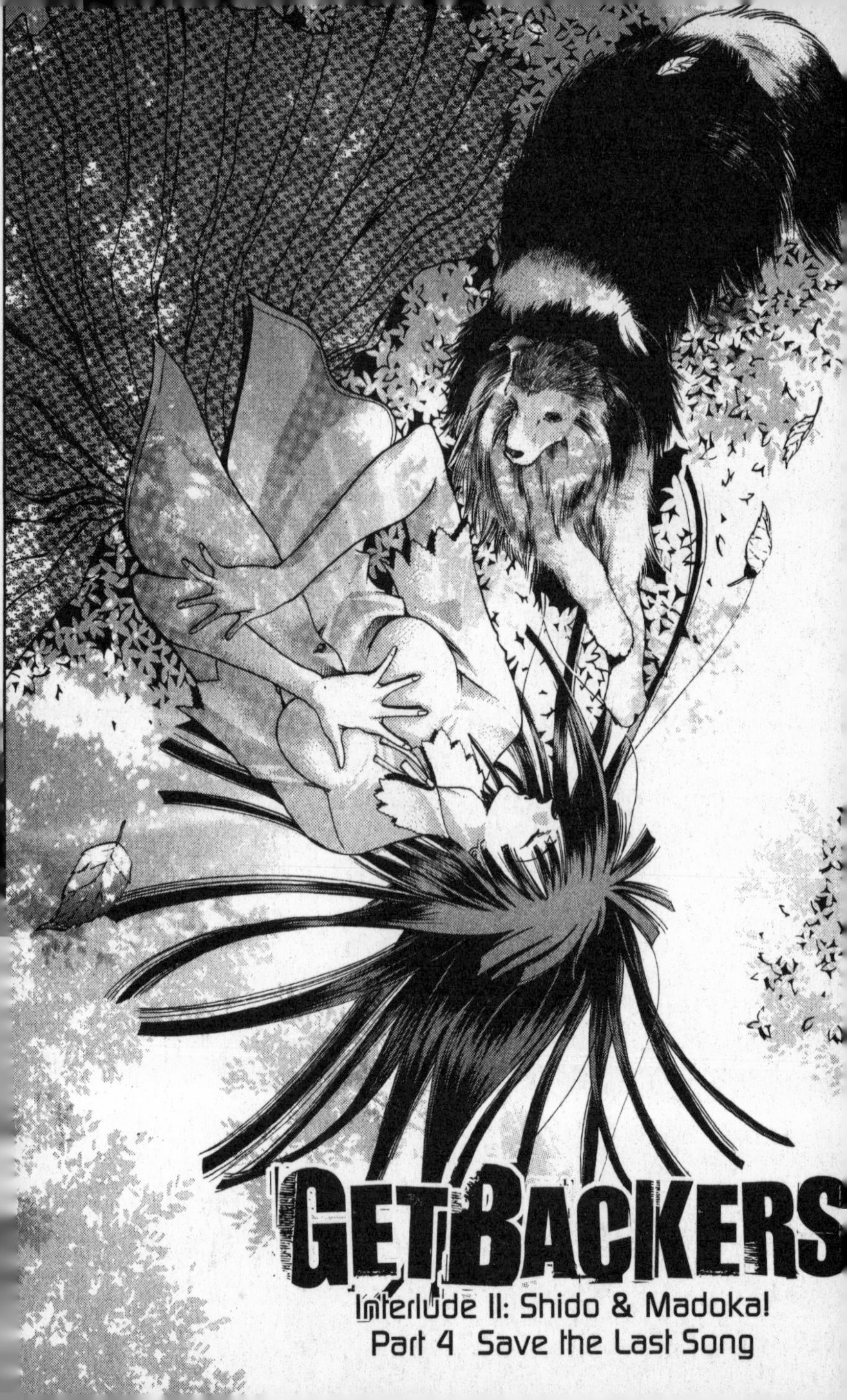
GETBACKERS
Interlude II: Shido & Madoka!
Part 4 Save the Last Song

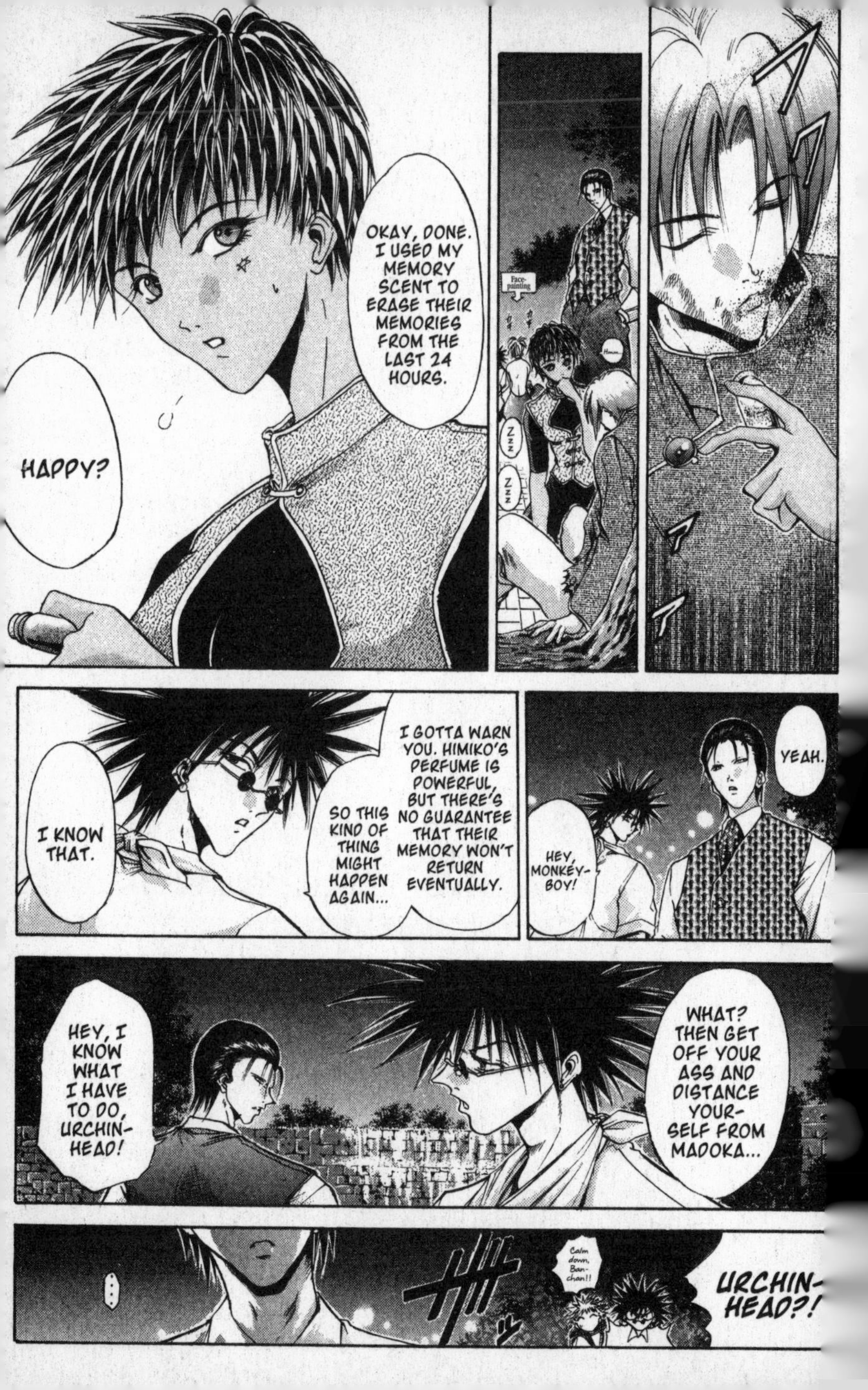
Face-painting
Hmm...
Zzz
Zzz
OKAY, DONE. I USED MY MEMORY SCENT TO ERASE THEIR MEMORIES FROM THE LAST 24 HOURS.
HAPPY?
YEAH.
HEY, MONKEY-BOY!
I GOTTA WARN YOU. HIMIKO'S PERFUME IS POWERFUL, BUT THERE'S NO GUARANTEE THAT THEIR MEMORY WON'T RETURN EVENTUALLY.
SO THIS KIND OF THING MIGHT HAPPEN AGAIN...
I KNOW THAT.
WHAT? THEN GET OFF YOUR ASS AND DISTANCE YOUR-SELF FROM MADOKA...
HEY, I KNOW WHAT I HAVE TO DO, URCHIN-HEAD!
URCHIN-HEAD?!
Calm down, Ban-chan!!
...

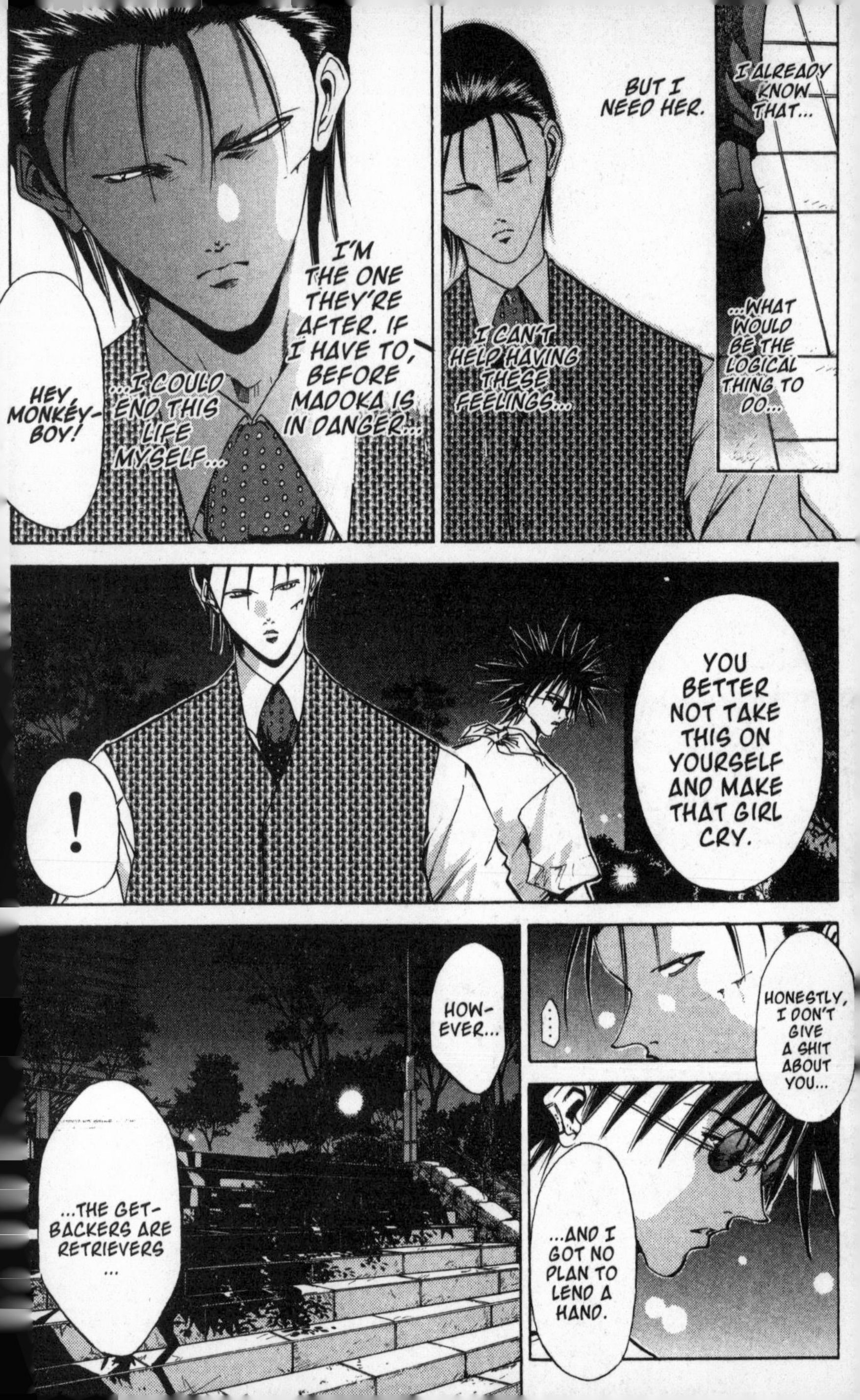
I ALREADY KNOW THAT...
...WHAT WOULD BE THE LOGICAL THING TO DO...
BUT I NEED HER.
I CAN'T HELP HAVING THESE FEELINGS...
I'M THE ONE THEY'RE AFTER. IF I HAVE TO, BEFORE MADOKA IS IN DANGER...
...I COULD END THIS LIFE MYSELF...
HEY, MONKEY-BOY!
YOU BETTER NOT TAKE THIS ON YOURSELF AND MAKE THAT GIRL CRY.
!
HONESTLY, I DON'T GIVE A SHIT ABOUT YOU...
...
...AND I GOT NO PLAN TO LEND A HAND.
HOW-EVER...
...THE GET-BACKERS ARE RETRIEVERS ...

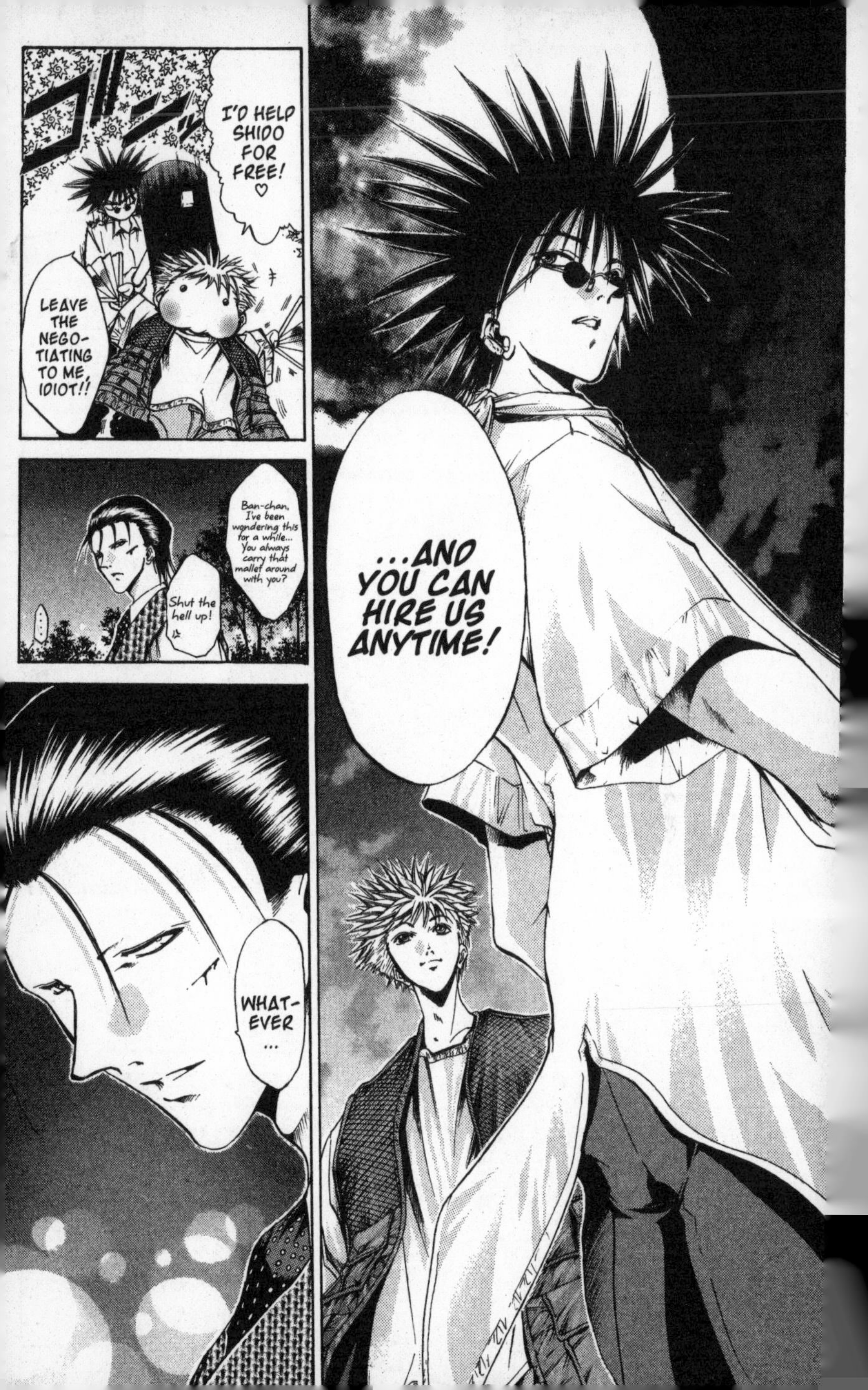
...AND YOU CAN HIRE US ANYTIME!
I'D HELP SHIDO FOR FREE! ♡
LEAVE THE NEGO-TIATING TO ME, IDIOT!!
Ban-chan, I've been wondering this for a while... You always carry that mallet around with you?
Shut the hell up!
...
WHAT-EVER ...

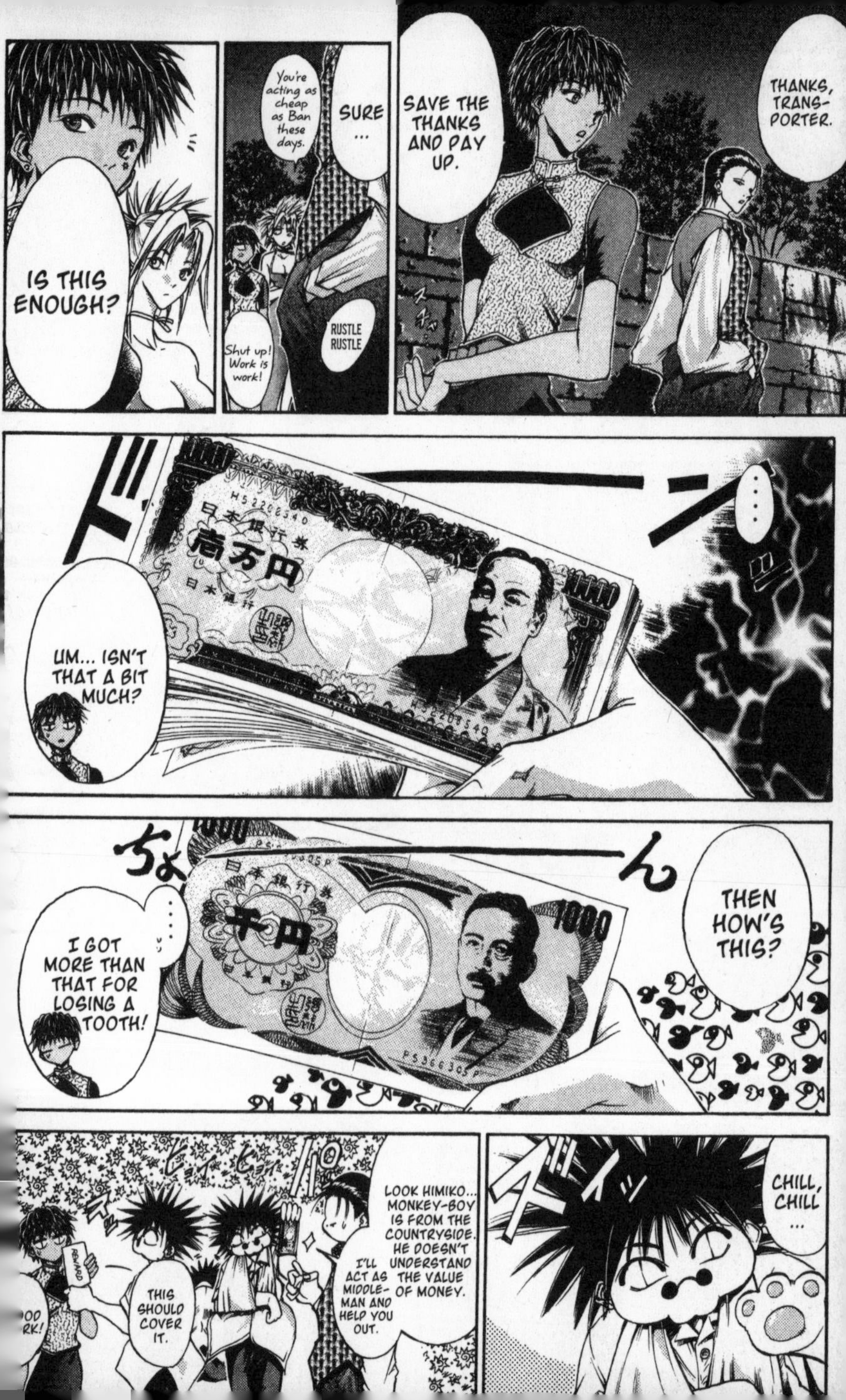
THANKS, TRANSPORTER.
SAVE THE THANKS AND PAY UP.
SURE ...
You're acting as cheap as Ban these days.
RUSTLE RUSTLE
Shut up! Work is work!
IS THIS ENOUGH?
ドーン
...
UM... ISN'T THAT A BIT MUCH?
THEN HOW'S THIS?
ちょーん
......
I GOT MORE THAN THAT FOR LOSING A TOOTH!
CHILL, CHILL ...
LOOK HIMIKO... MONKEY-BOY IS FROM THE COUNTRYSIDE. HE DOESN'T UNDERSTAND THE VALUE OF MONEY.
I'LL ACT AS MIDDLE-MAN AND HELP YOU OUT.
REWARD
THIS SHOULD COVER IT.

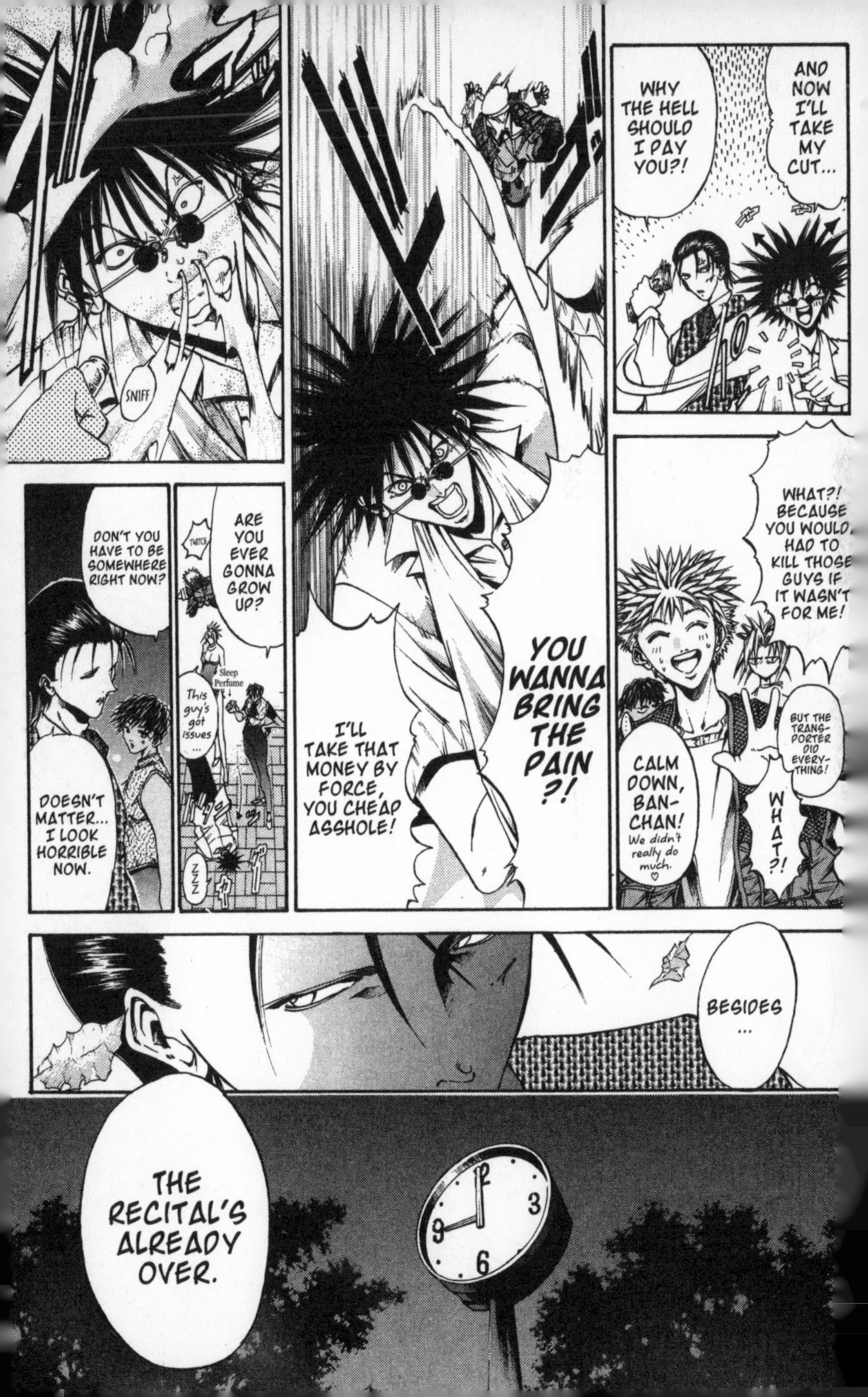
AND NOW I'LL TAKE MY CUT...
WHY THE HELL SHOULD I PAY YOU?!
WHAT?! BECAUSE YOU WOULD, HAD TO KILL THOSE GUYS IF IT WASN'T FOR ME!
BUT THE TRANSPORTER DID EVERYTHING!
WHAT?!
CALM DOWN, BAN-CHAN!
We didn't really do much. ♡
YOU WANNA BRING THE PAIN?!
I'LL TAKE THAT MONEY BY FORCE, YOU CHEAP ASSHOLE!
SNIFF
ARE YOU EVER GONNA GROW UP?
TWITCH
Sleep Perfume
This guy's got issues ...
ZZZ
DON'T YOU HAVE TO BE SOMEWHERE RIGHT NOW?
DOESN'T MATTER... I LOOK HORRIBLE NOW.
BESIDES ...
THE RECITAL'S ALREADY OVER.

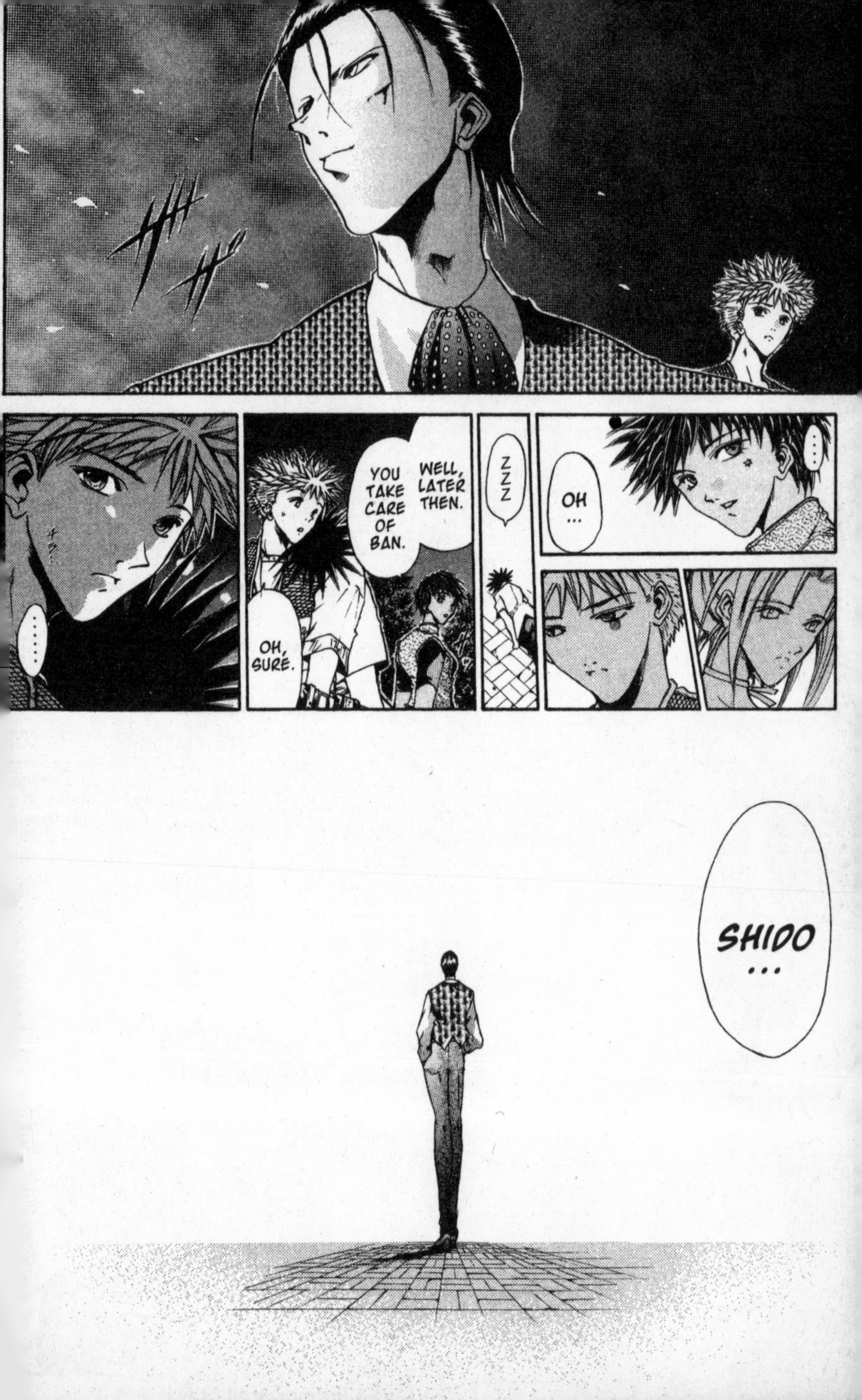
....
OH ...
ZZZ
WELL, LATER THEN.
YOU TAKE CARE OF BAN.
OH, SURE.
......
SHIDO ...

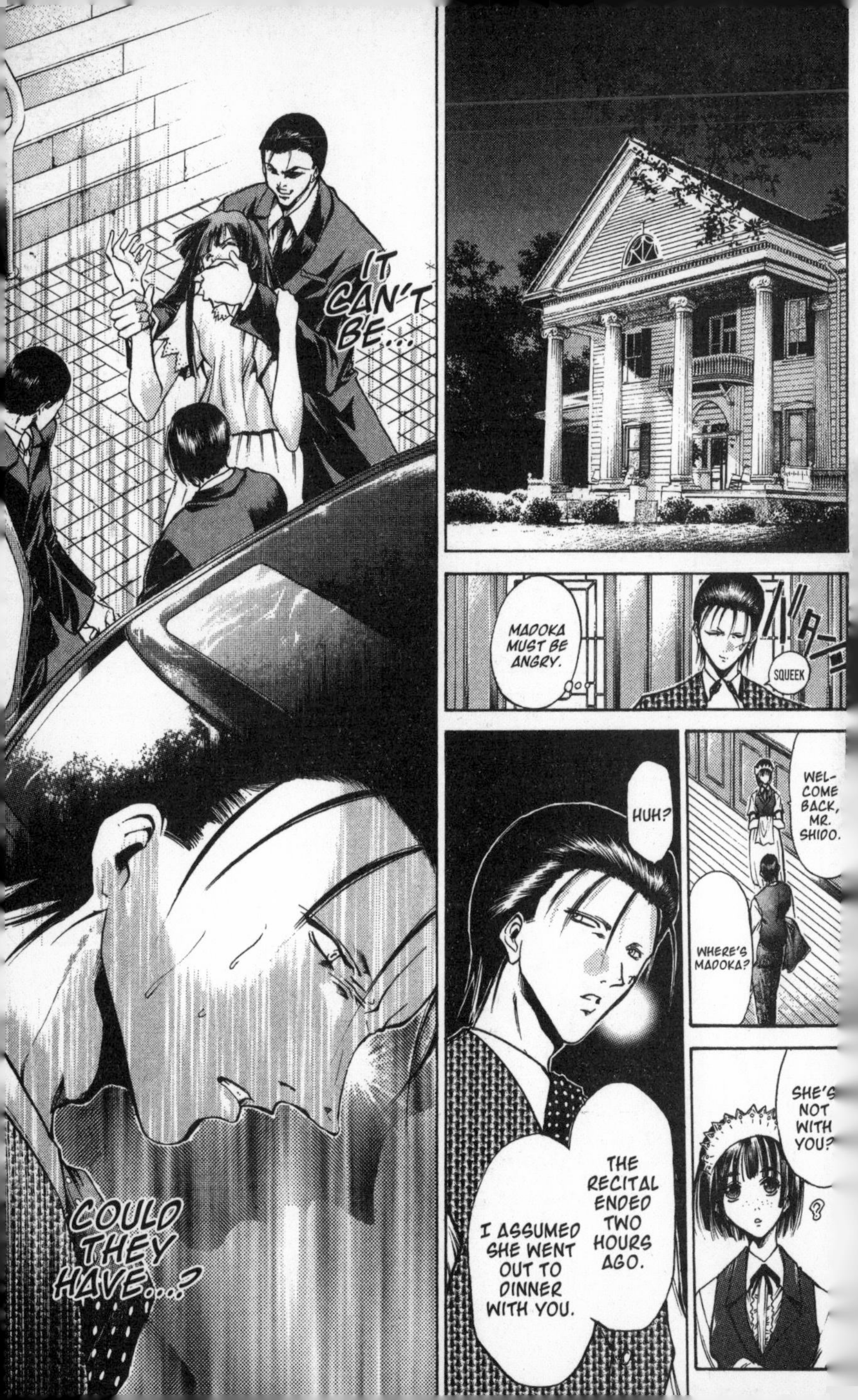
SQUEEK
MADOKA MUST BE ANGRY.
WEL-COME BACK, MR. SHIDO.
WHERE'S MADOKA?
SHE'S NOT WITH YOU?
HUH?
THE RECITAL ENDED TWO HOURS AGO.
I ASSUMED SHE WENT OUT TO DINNER WITH YOU.
IT CAN'T BE...
COULD THEY HAVE...?

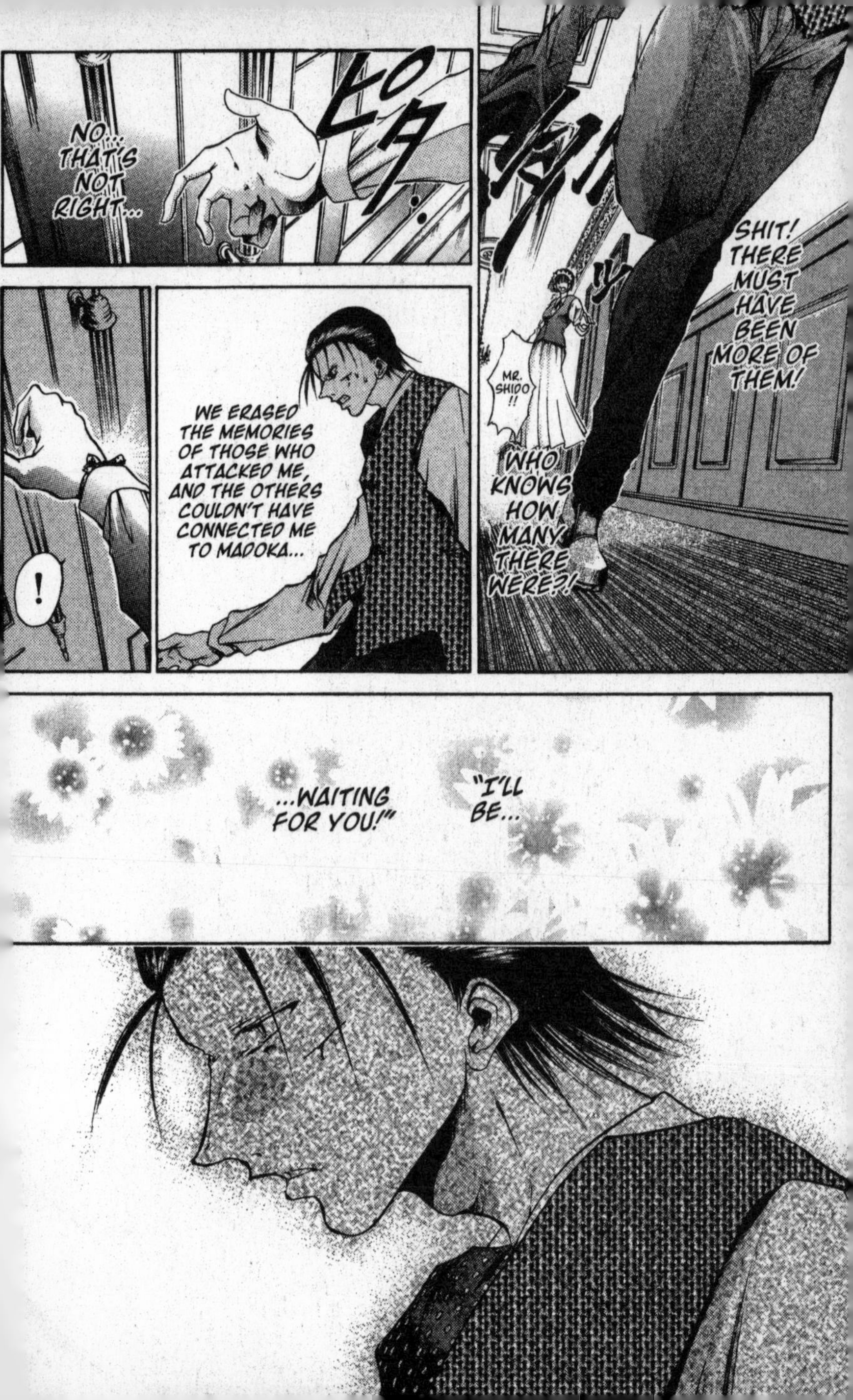
SHIT! THERE MUST HAVE BEEN MORE OF THEM!
MR. SHIDO!!
WHO KNOWS HOW MANY THERE WERE?!
NO... THAT'S NOT RIGHT...
WE ERASED THE MEMORIES OF THOSE WHO ATTACKED ME, AND THE OTHERS COULDN'T HAVE CONNECTED ME TO MADOKA...
!
"I'LL BE...
...WAITING FOR YOU!"

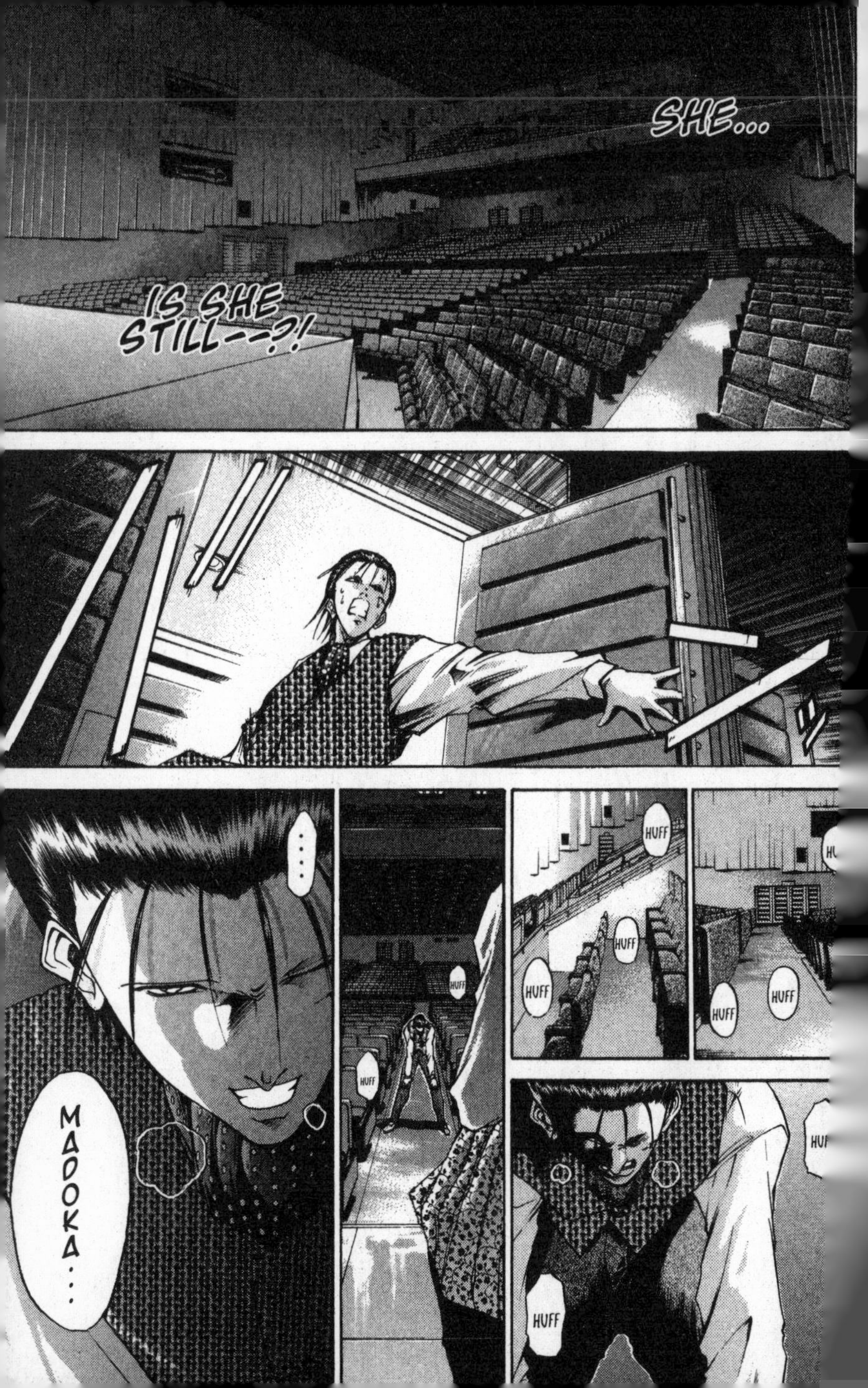
SHE...
IS SHE STILL--?!
HUFF
HUFF
HUFF
HUFF
HUFF
HUFF
HUFF
HUFF
HUFF
....
MADOKA...

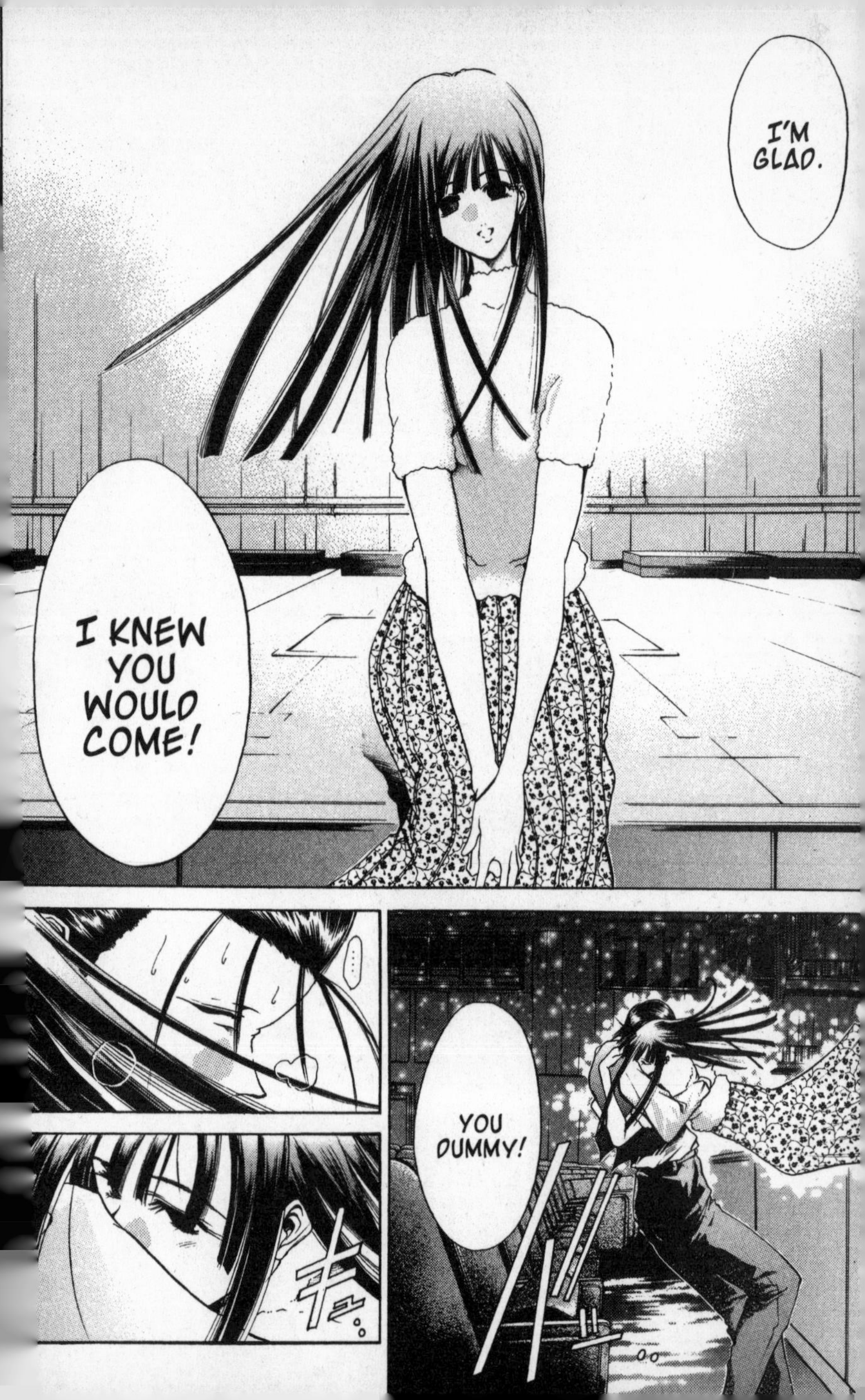
I'M GLAD.
I KNEW YOU WOULD COME!
YOU DUMMY!
...

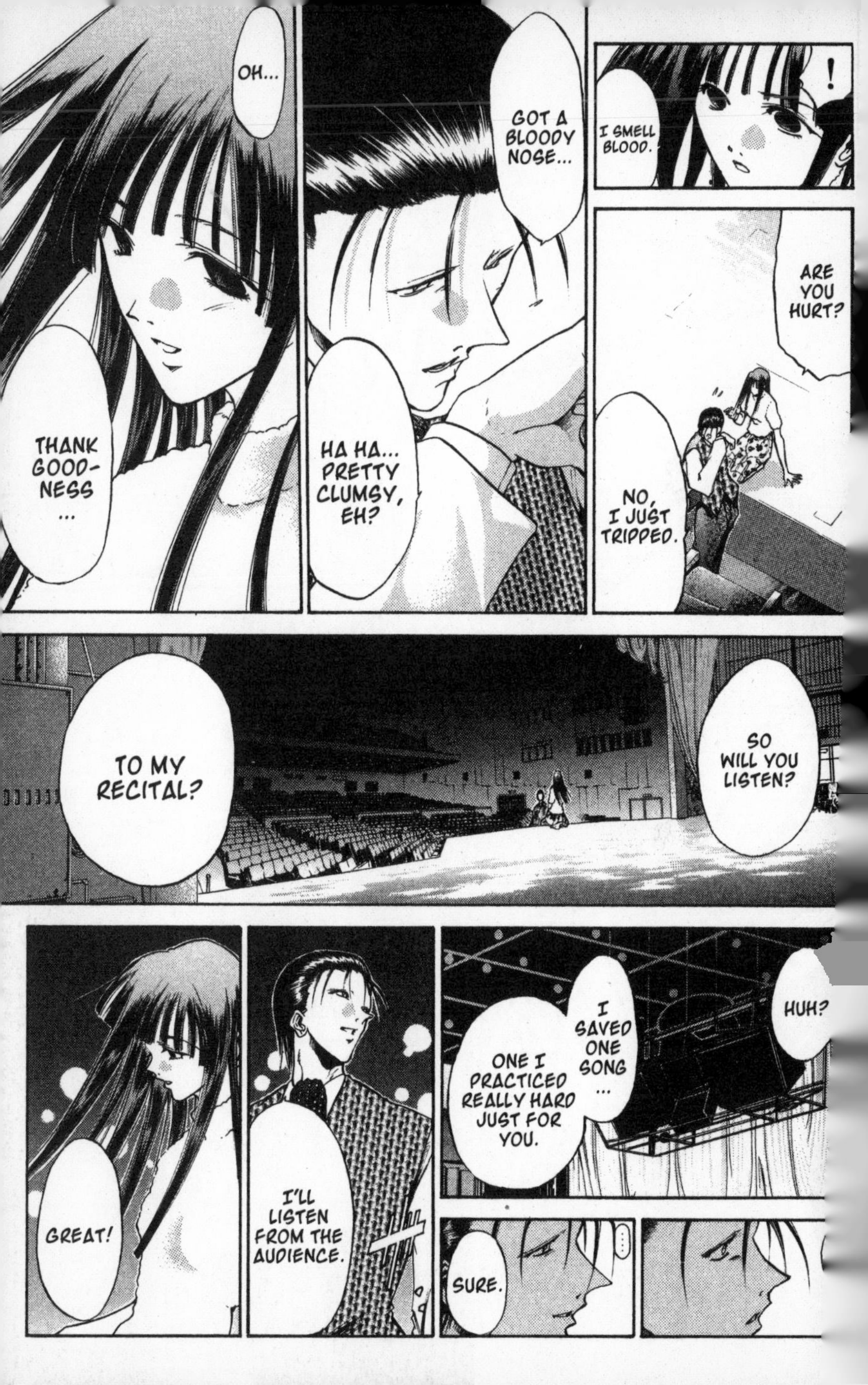
!
I SMELL BLOOD.
ARE YOU HURT?
NO, I JUST TRIPPED.
GOT A BLOODY NOSE...
HA HA... PRETTY CLUMSY, EH?
OH...
THANK GOODNESS ...
SO WILL YOU LISTEN?
TO MY RECITAL?
HUH?
I SAVED ONE SONG ...
ONE I PRACTICED REALLY HARD JUST FOR YOU.
...
SURE.
I'LL LISTEN FROM THE AUDIENCE.
GREAT!

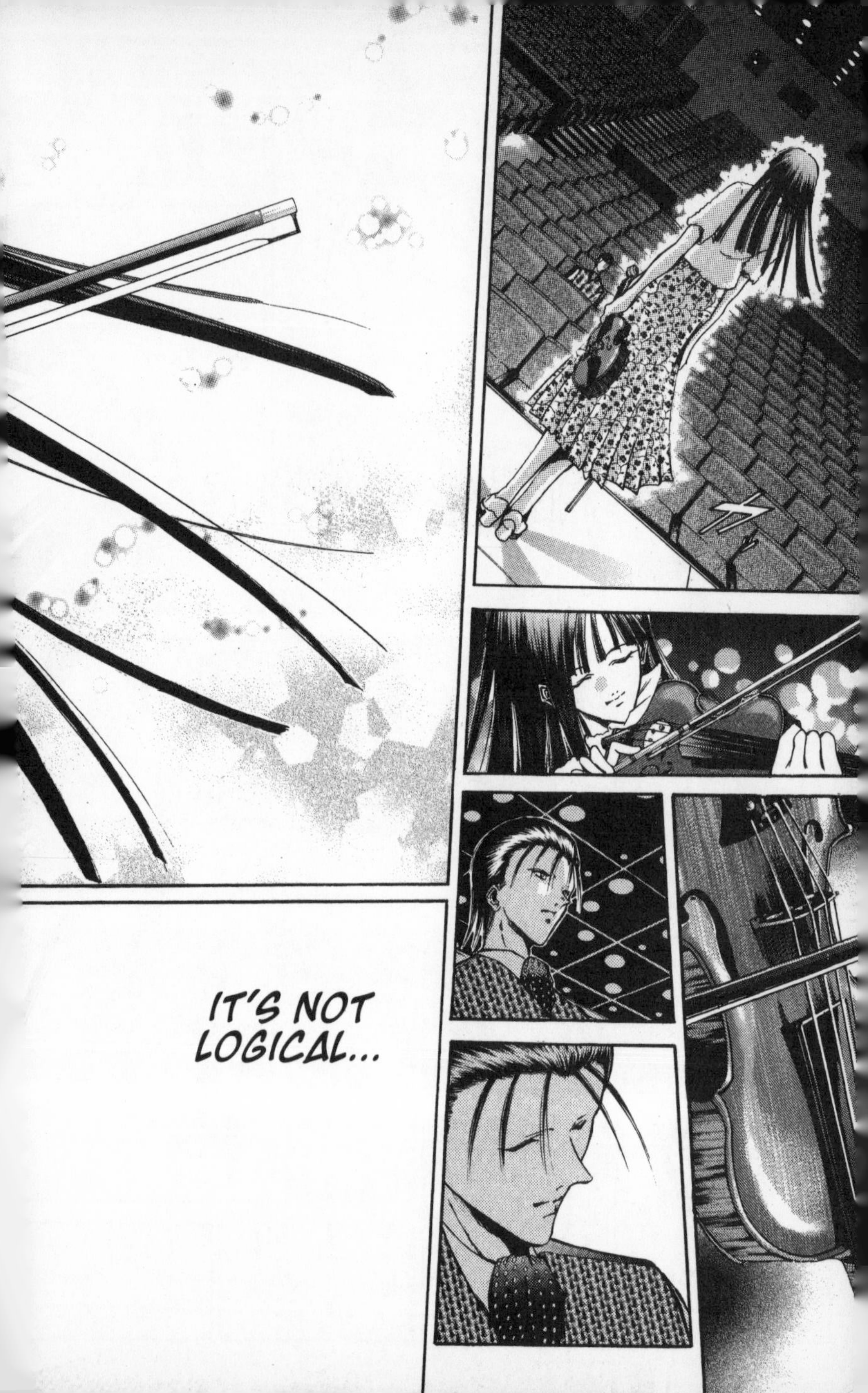
IT'S NOT LOGICAL...

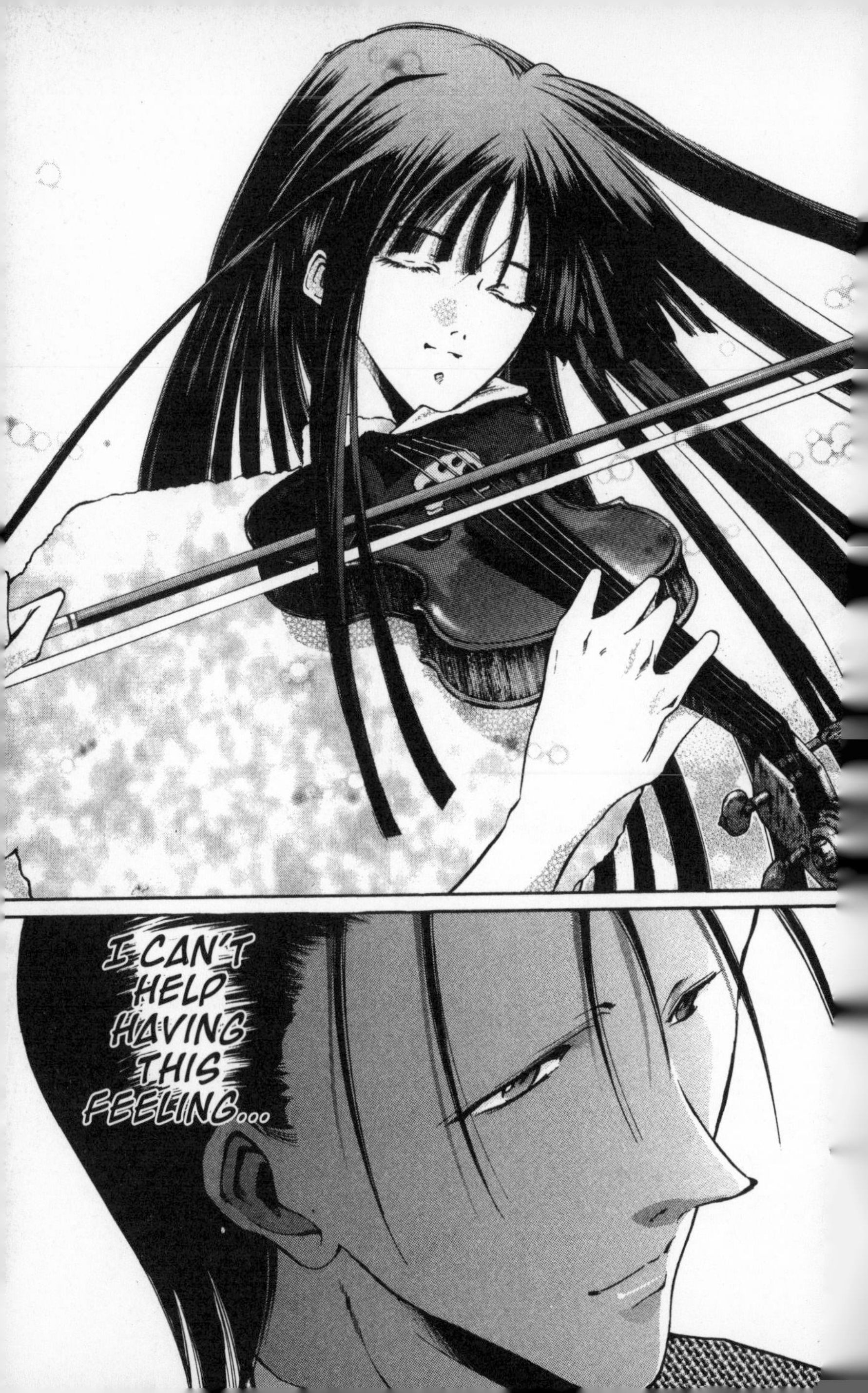
I CAN'T HELP HAVING THIS FEELING...

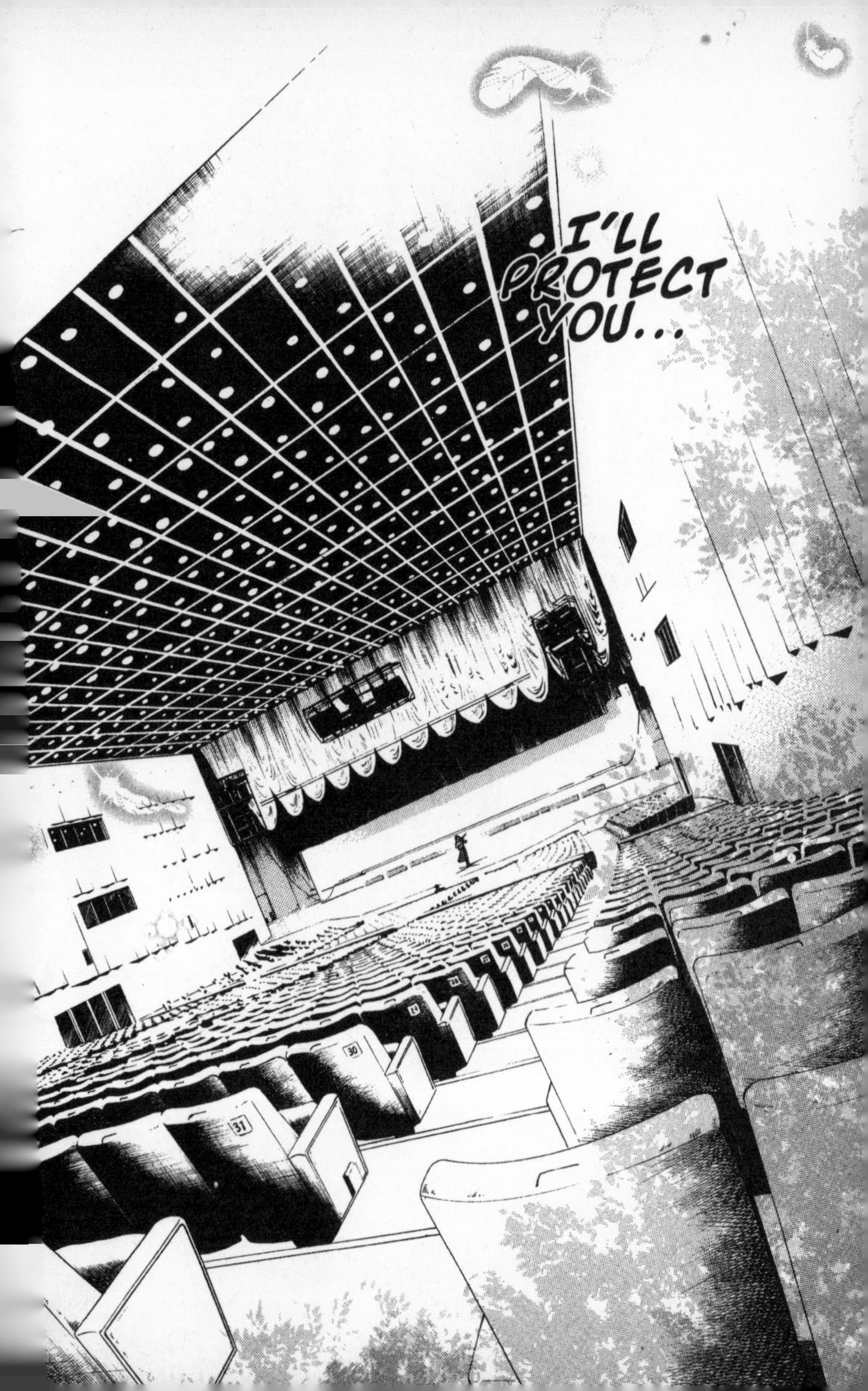
I'LL PROTECT YOU...

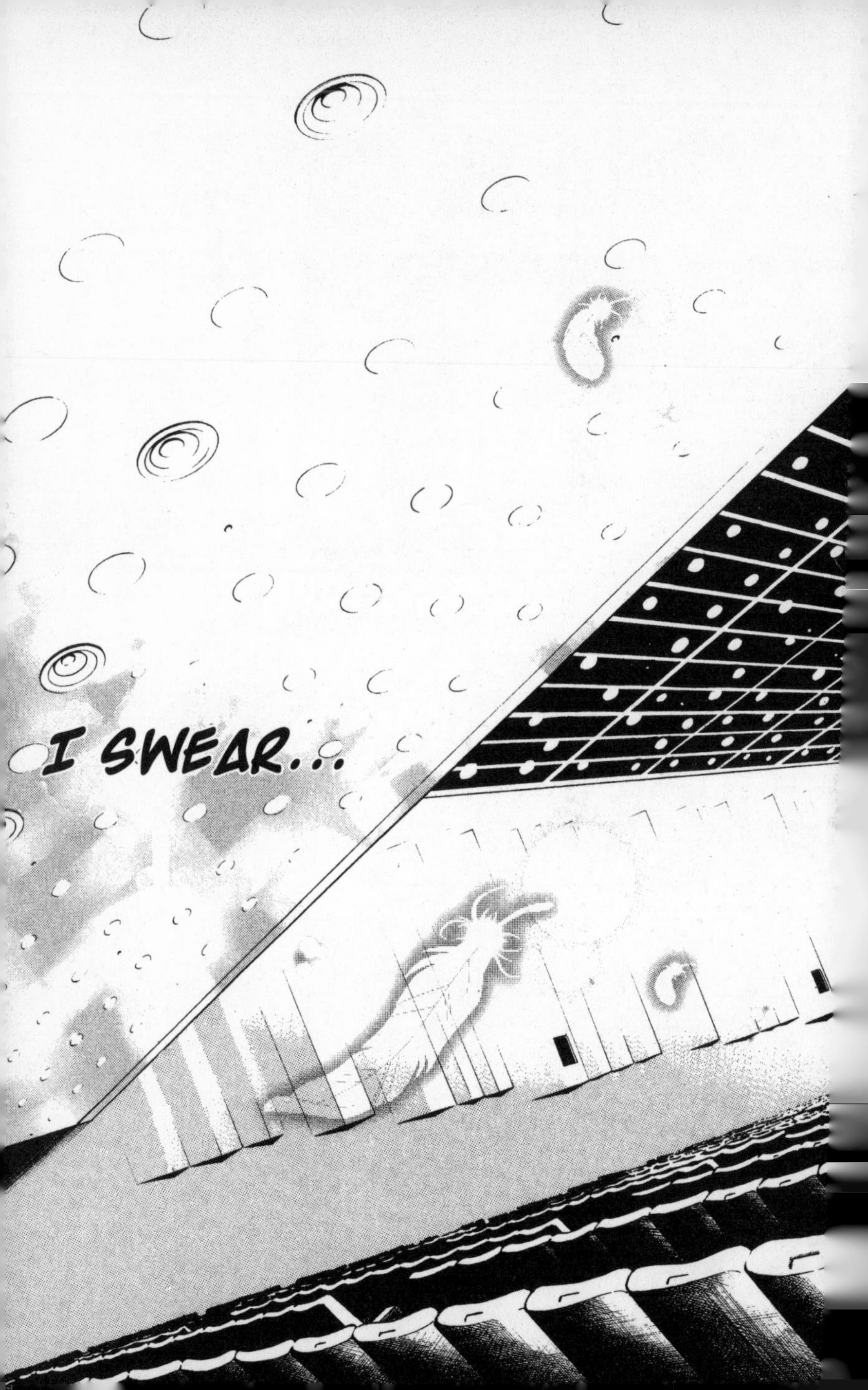
I SWEAR...

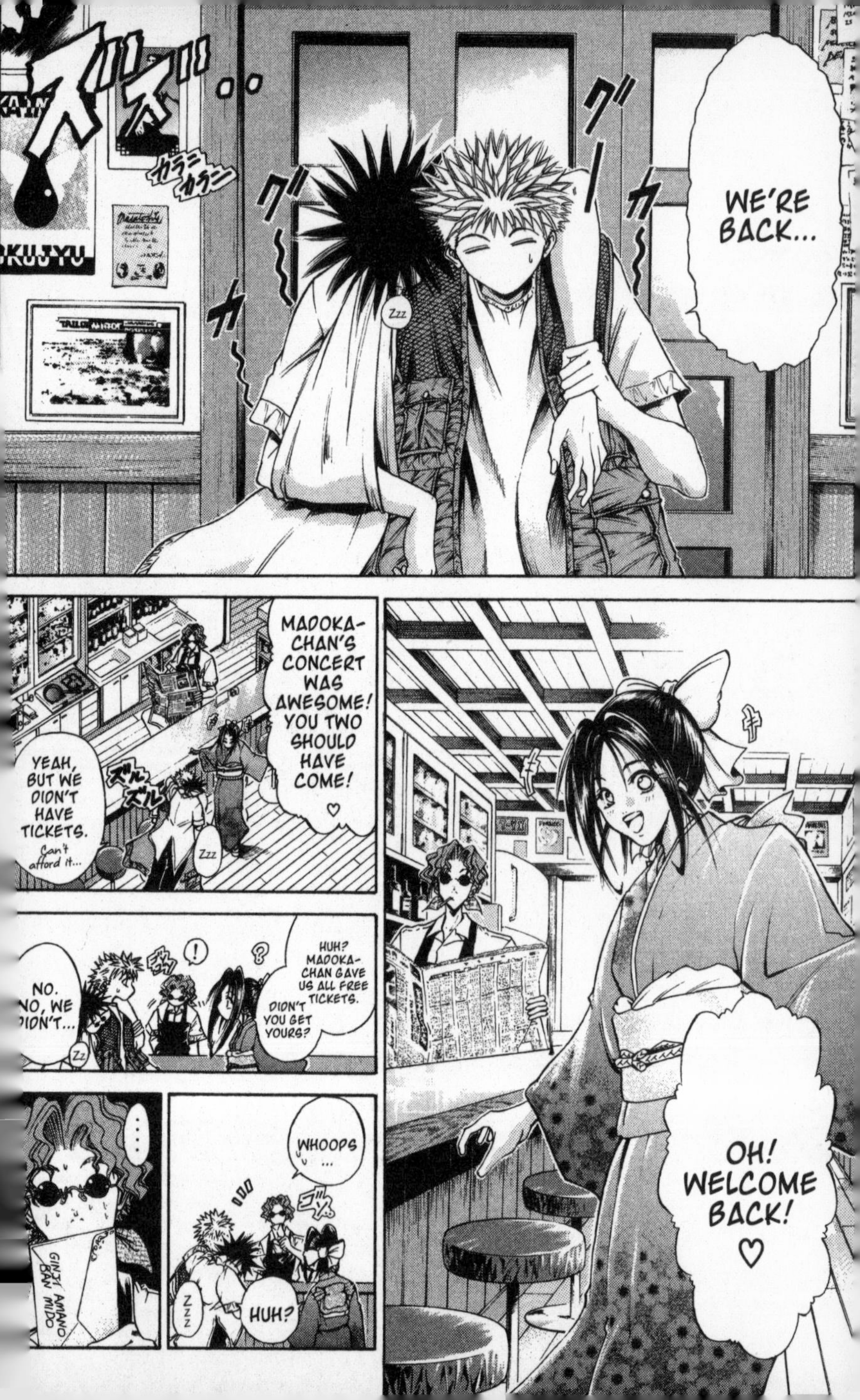
WE'RE BACK...
Zzz
OH! WELCOME BACK! ♡
MADOKA-CHAN'S CONCERT WAS AWESOME! YOU TWO SHOULD HAVE COME! ♡
YEAH, BUT WE DIDN'T HAVE TICKETS.
Can't afford it...
Zzz
HUH? MADOKA-CHAN GAVE US ALL FREE TICKETS.
DIDN'T YOU GET YOURS?
!
?
NO. NO, WE DIDN'T...
Zz
WHOOPS ...
HUH?
ZZZ
....
GINJI, AMANO BAN MIDO

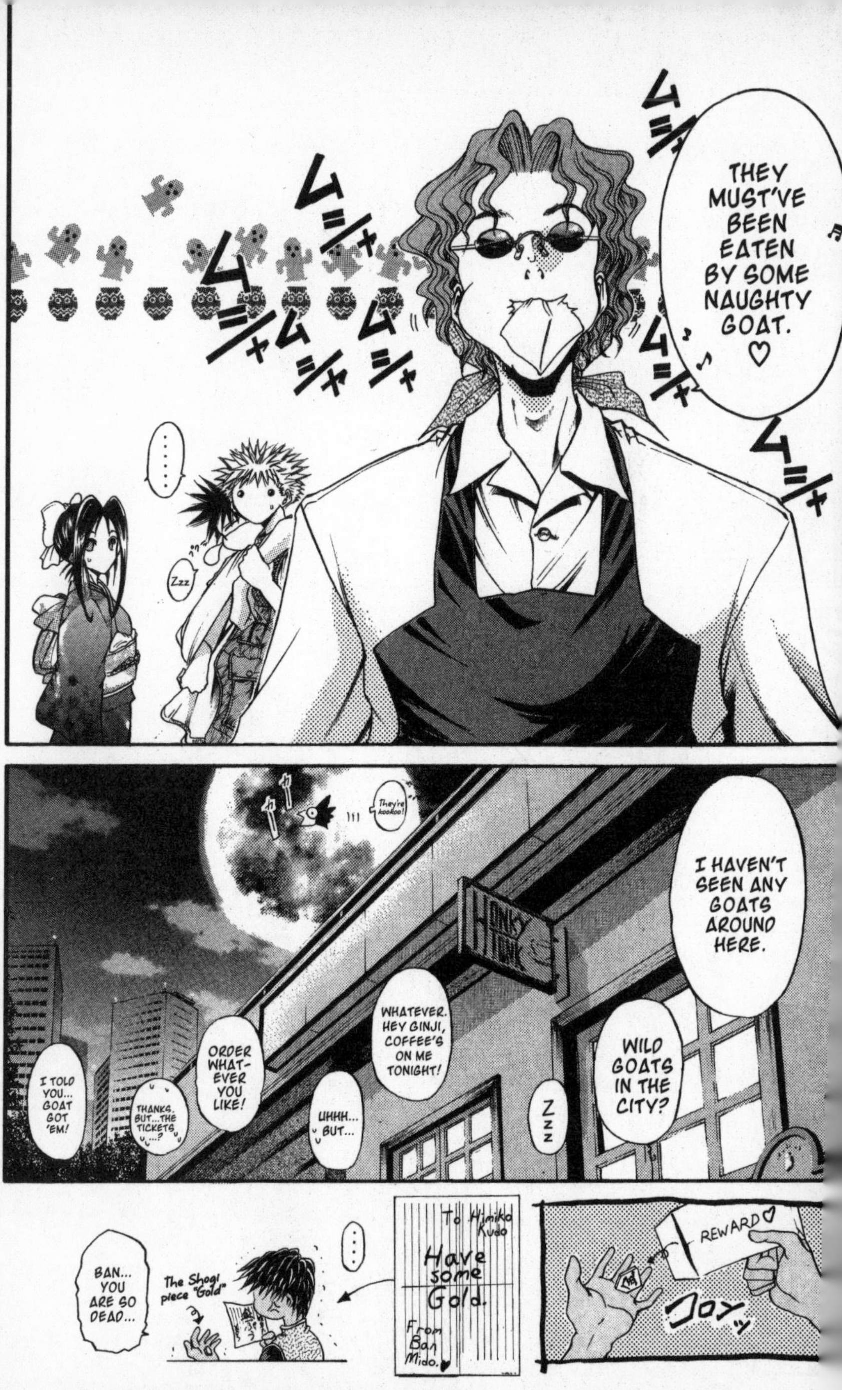
THEY MUST'VE BEEN EATEN BY SOME NAUGHTY GOAT. ♡
ムシャムシャ
......
Zzz
I HAVEN'T SEEN ANY GOATS AROUND HERE.
HONKY TONK
They're kookoo!
WILD GOATS IN THE CITY?
Zzz
WHATEVER. HEY GINJI, COFFEE'S ON ME TONIGHT!
UHHH... BUT...
ORDER WHATEVER YOU LIKE!
THANKS. BUT...THE TICKETS...?
I TOLD YOU... GOAT GOT 'EM!
REWARD♡
To Himiko Kudo
Have some Gold.
From Ban Mido.♥
...
The Shogi piece "Gold"
BAN... YOU ARE SO DEAD...

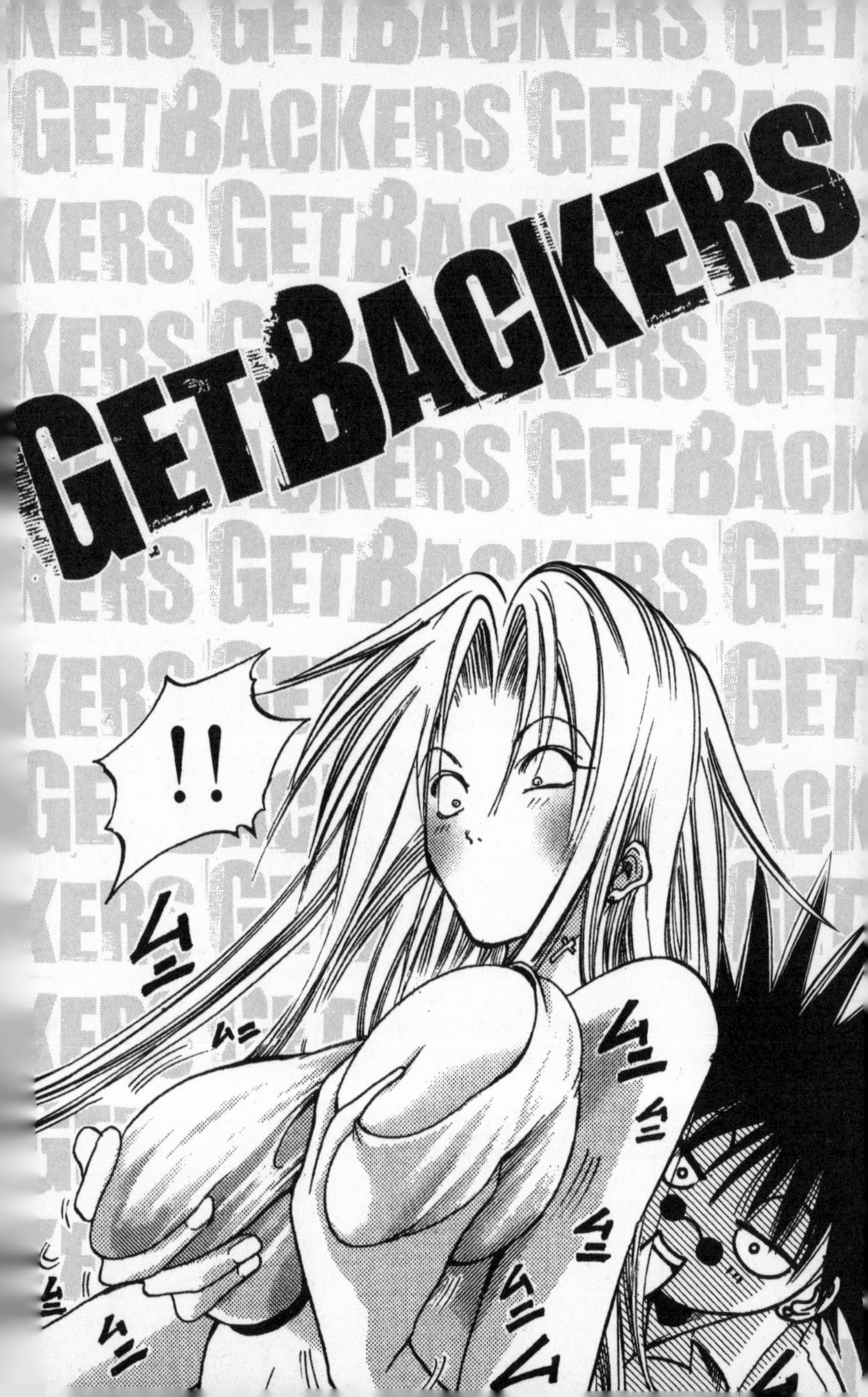
GETBACKERS
!!
ムニ
ムニ
ムニ
ムニ
ムニ
ムニ
ムニ
ムニ

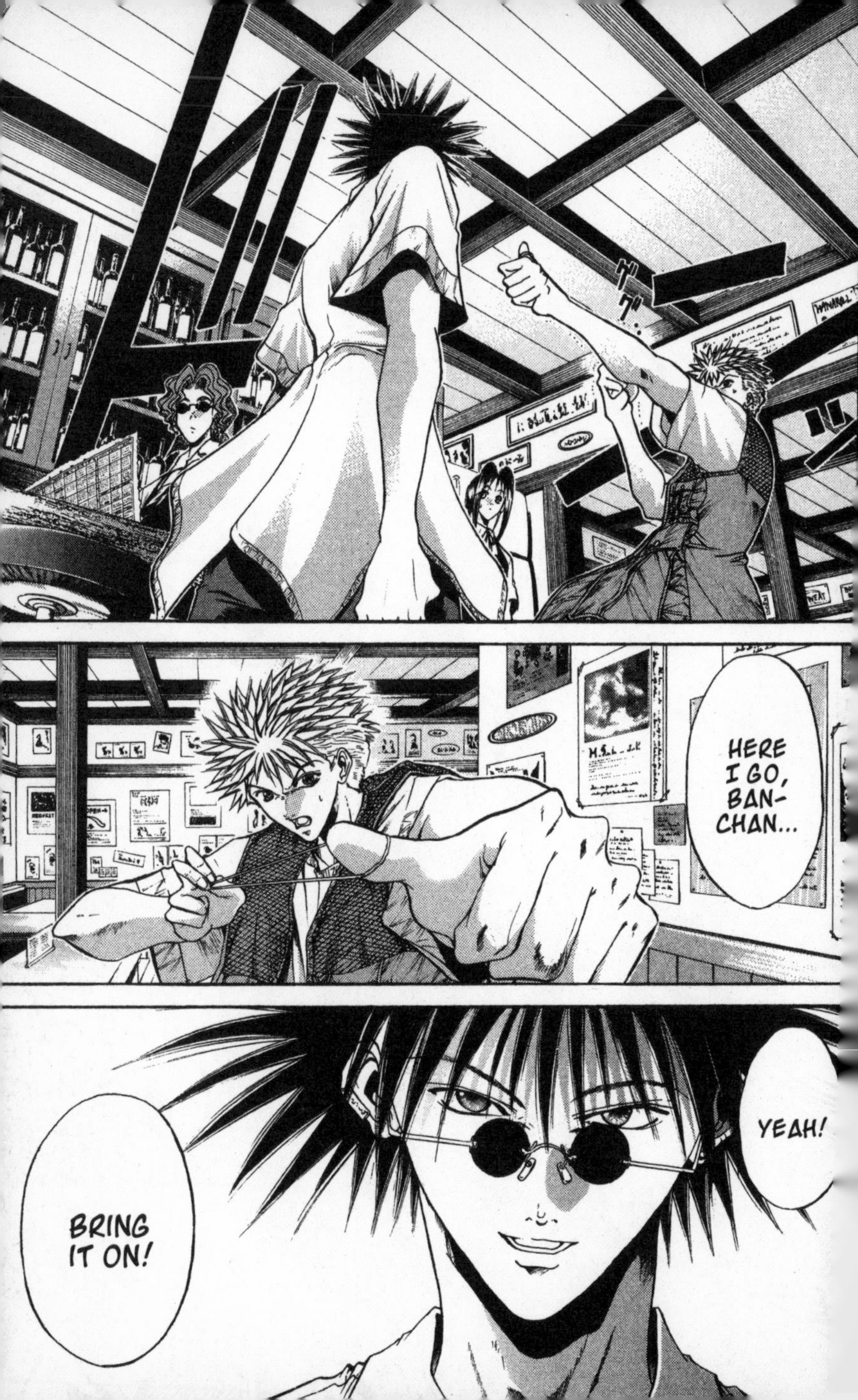
HERE I GO, BAN-CHAN...
YEAH!
BRING IT ON!

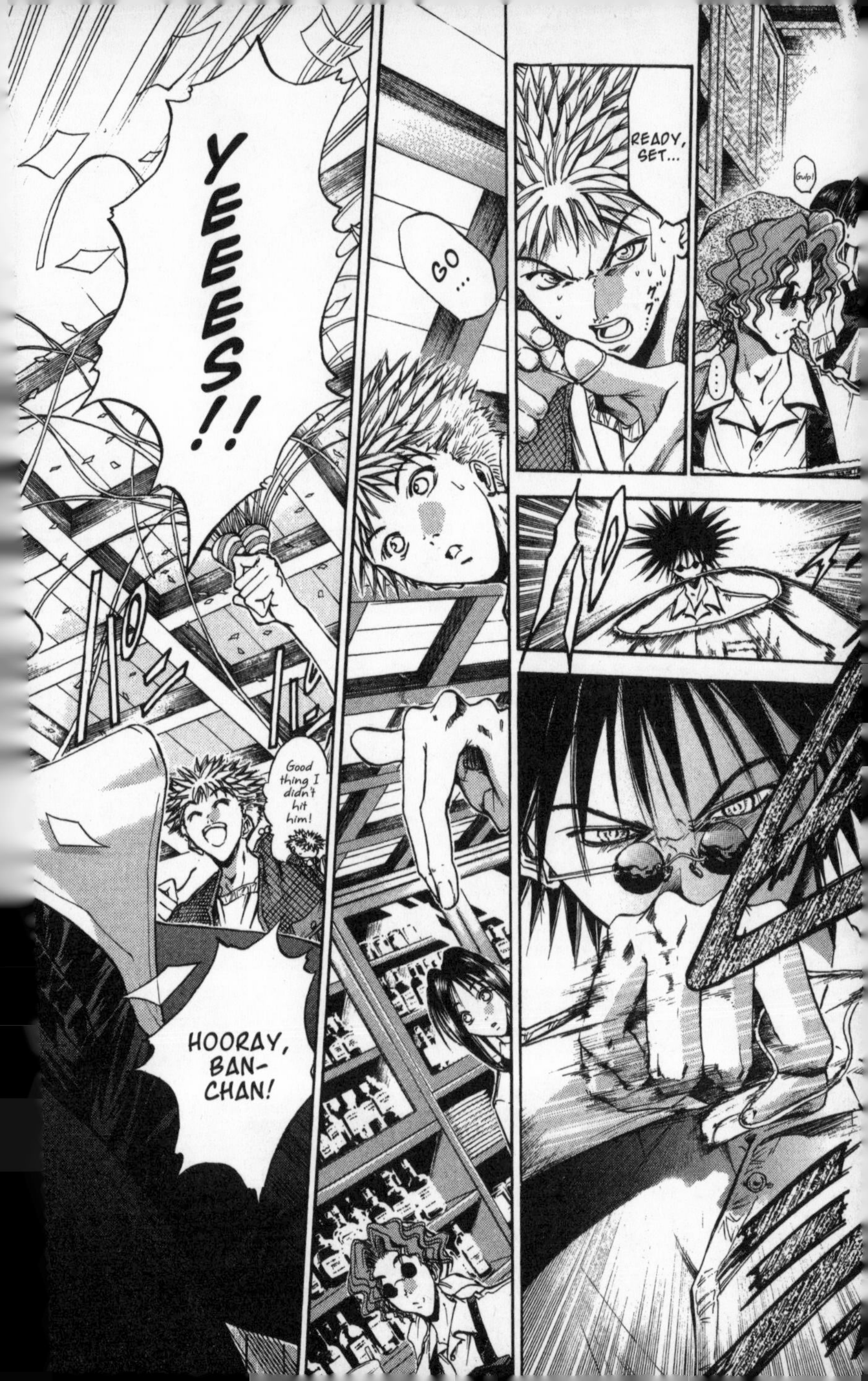
Gulp!
...
READY, SET...
GO...
YEEEES!!
Good thing I didn't hit him!
HOORAY, BAN-CHAN!

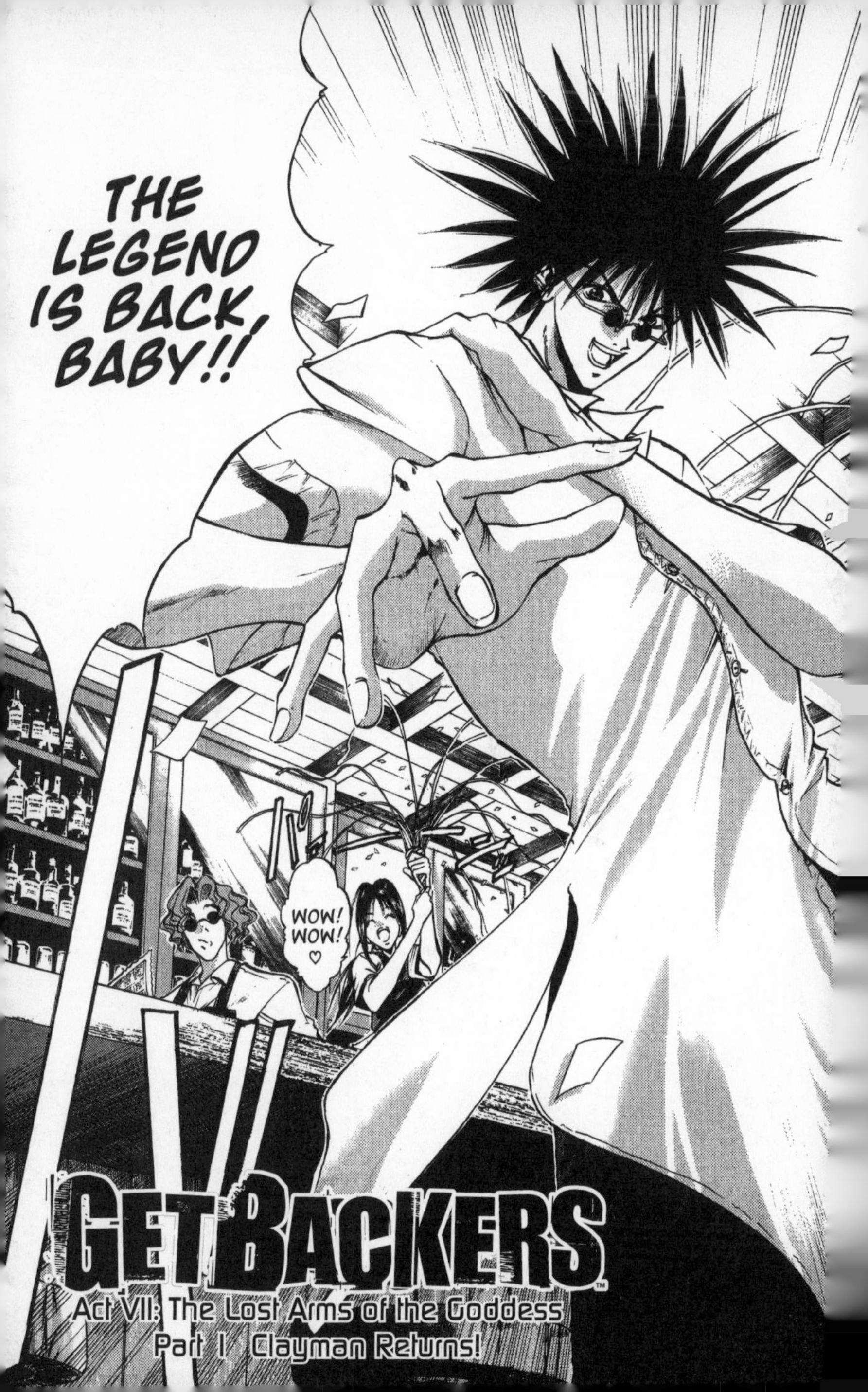
THE LEGEND IS BACK, BABY!!
WOW! WOW! ♡
GETBACKERS™
Act VII: The Lost Arms of the Goddess
Part 1 Clayman Returns!

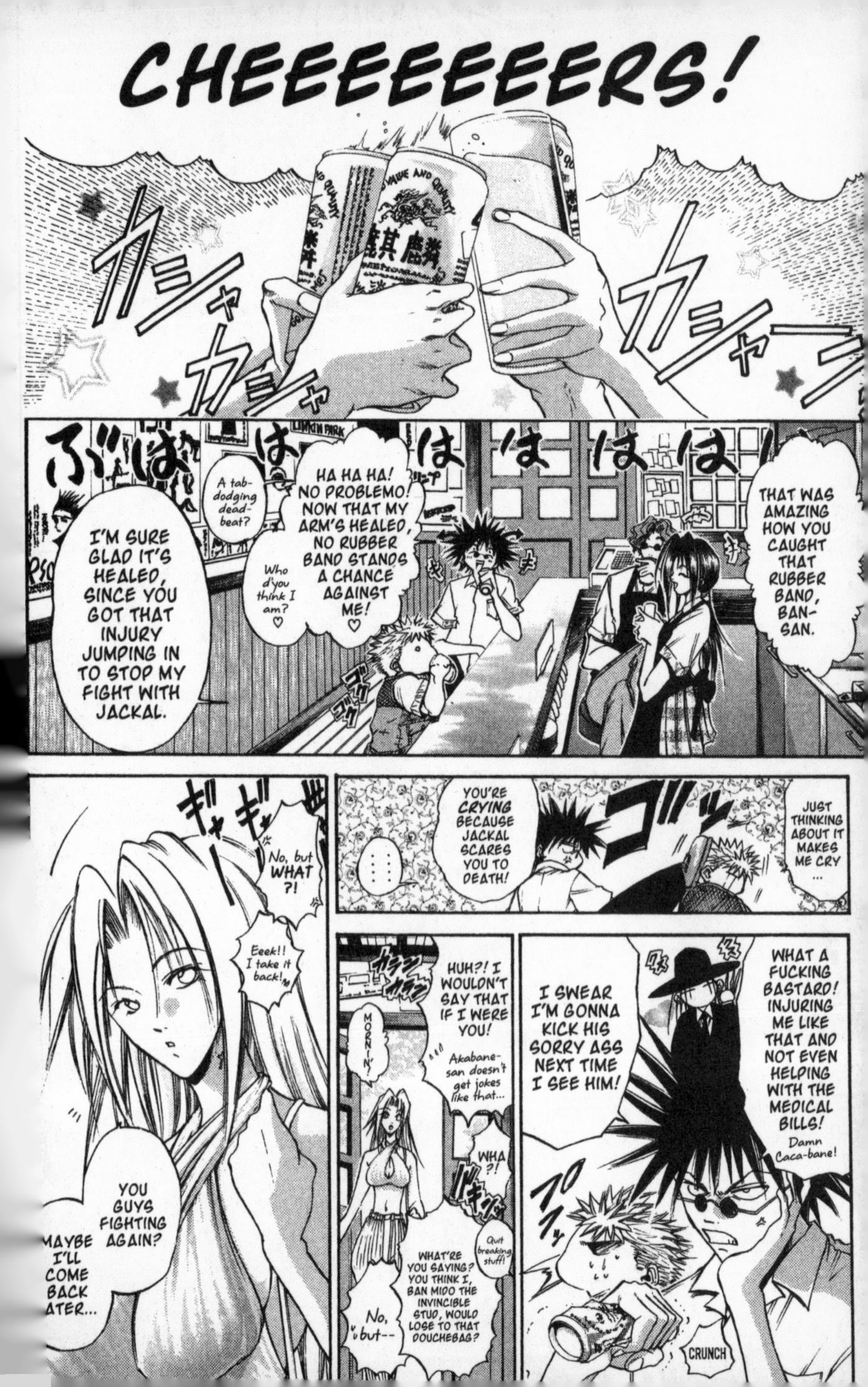
CHEEEEEEERS!
THAT WAS AMAZING HOW YOU CAUGHT THAT RUBBER BAND, BAN-SAN.
HA HA HA! NO PROBLEMO! NOW THAT MY ARM'S HEALED, NO RUBBER BAND STANDS A CHANCE AGAINST ME! ♡
Who d'you think I am? ♡
A tab-dodging dead-beat?
I'M SURE GLAD IT'S HEALED, SINCE YOU GOT THAT INJURY JUMPING IN TO STOP MY FIGHT WITH JACKAL.
JUST THINKING ABOUT IT MAKES ME CRY ...
YOU'RE CRYING BECAUSE JACKAL SCARES YOU TO DEATH!
...
WHAT A FUCKING BASTARD! INJURING ME LIKE THAT AND NOT EVEN HELPING WITH THE MEDICAL BILLS!
Damn Caca-bane!
I SWEAR I'M GONNA KICK HIS SORRY ASS NEXT TIME I SEE HIM!
CRUNCH
HUH?! I WOULDN'T SAY THAT IF I WERE YOU!
Akabane-san doesn't get jokes like that...
MORNIN'!
WHA ?!
Quit breaking stuff!
WHAT'RE YOU SAYING? YOU THINK I, BAN MIDO THE INVINCIBLE STUD, WOULD LOSE TO THAT DOUCHEBAG?
No, but--
No, but WHAT ?!
Eeek!! I take it back!
YOU GUYS FIGHTING AGAIN?
MAYBE I'LL COME BACK LATER...

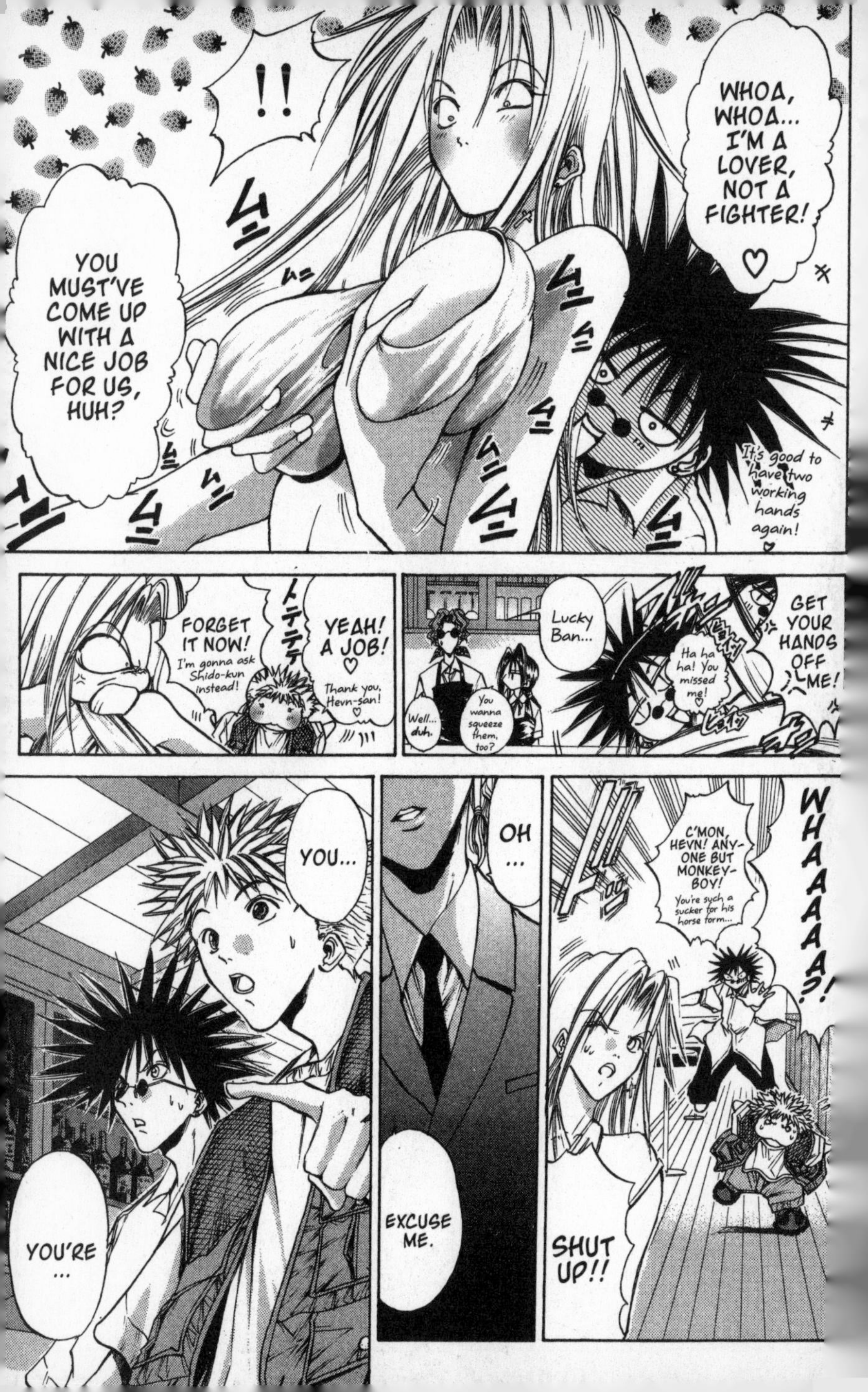
WHOA, WHOA... I'M A LOVER, NOT A FIGHTER! ♡
It's good to have two working hands again! ♡
!!
YOU MUST'VE COME UP WITH A NICE JOB FOR US, HUH?
GET YOUR HANDS OFF ME!
Ha ha ha! You missed me! ♡
Lucky Ban...
You wanna squeeze them, too?
Well... duh.
YEAH! A JOB! ♡
Thank you, Hevn-san! ♡
FORGET IT NOW!
I'm gonna ask Shido-kun instead!
WHAAAAAA?!
C'MON, HEVN! ANY-ONE BUT MONKEY-BOY!
You're such a sucker for his horse form...
SHUT UP!!
OH ...
EXCUSE ME.
YOU...
YOU'RE ...

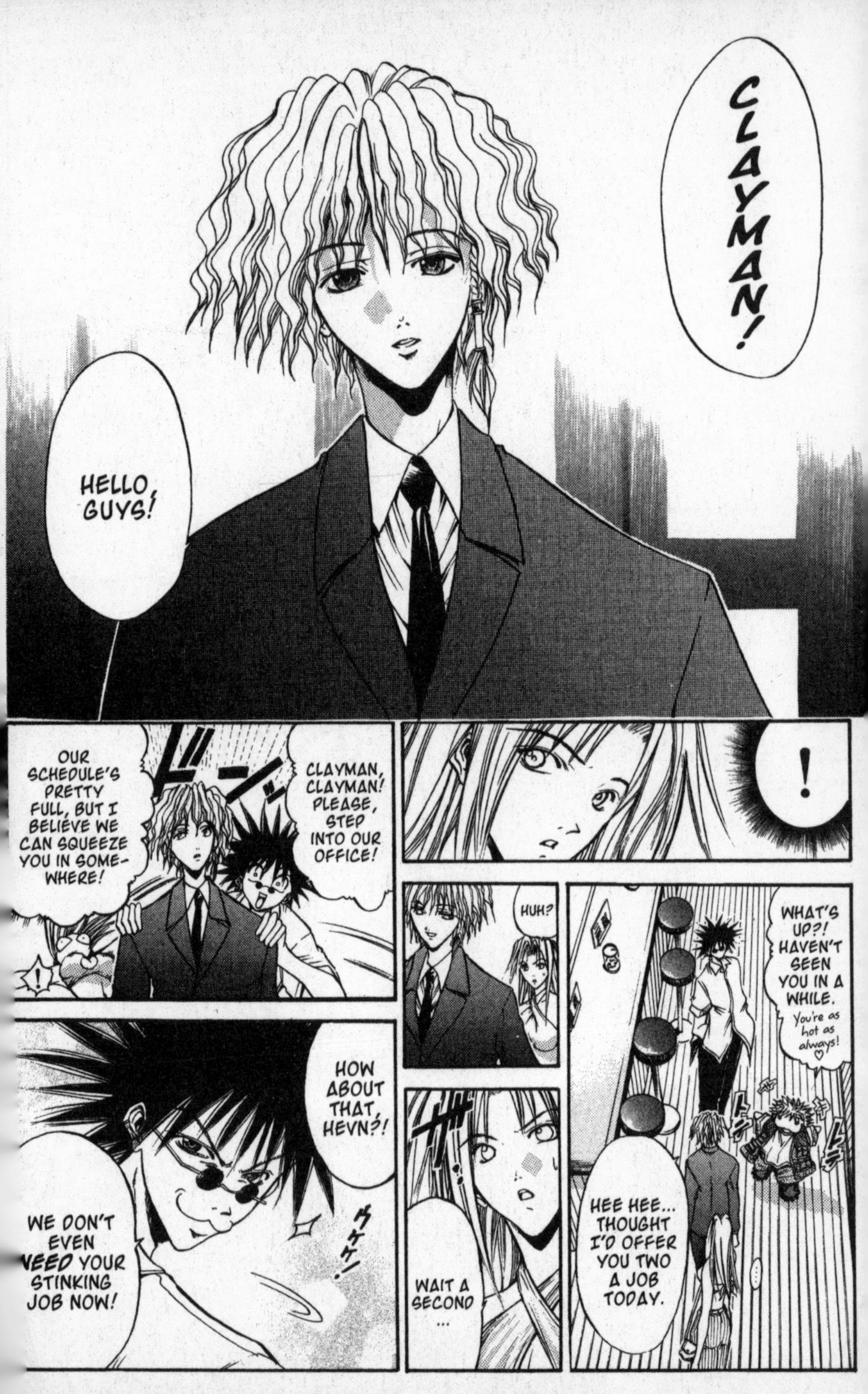
CLAYMAN!
HELLO, GUYS!
!
CLAYMAN, CLAYMAN! PLEASE, STEP INTO OUR OFFICE!
OUR SCHEDULE'S PRETTY FULL, BUT I BELIEVE WE CAN SQUEEZE YOU IN SOME-WHERE!
WHAT'S UP?! HAVEN'T SEEN YOU IN A WHILE.
You're as hot as always! ♡
HEE HEE... THOUGHT I'D OFFER YOU TWO A JOB TODAY.
...
HUH?
WAIT A SECOND ...
HOW ABOUT THAT, HEVN?!
WE DON'T EVEN NEED YOUR STINKING JOB NOW!
ケケケ!

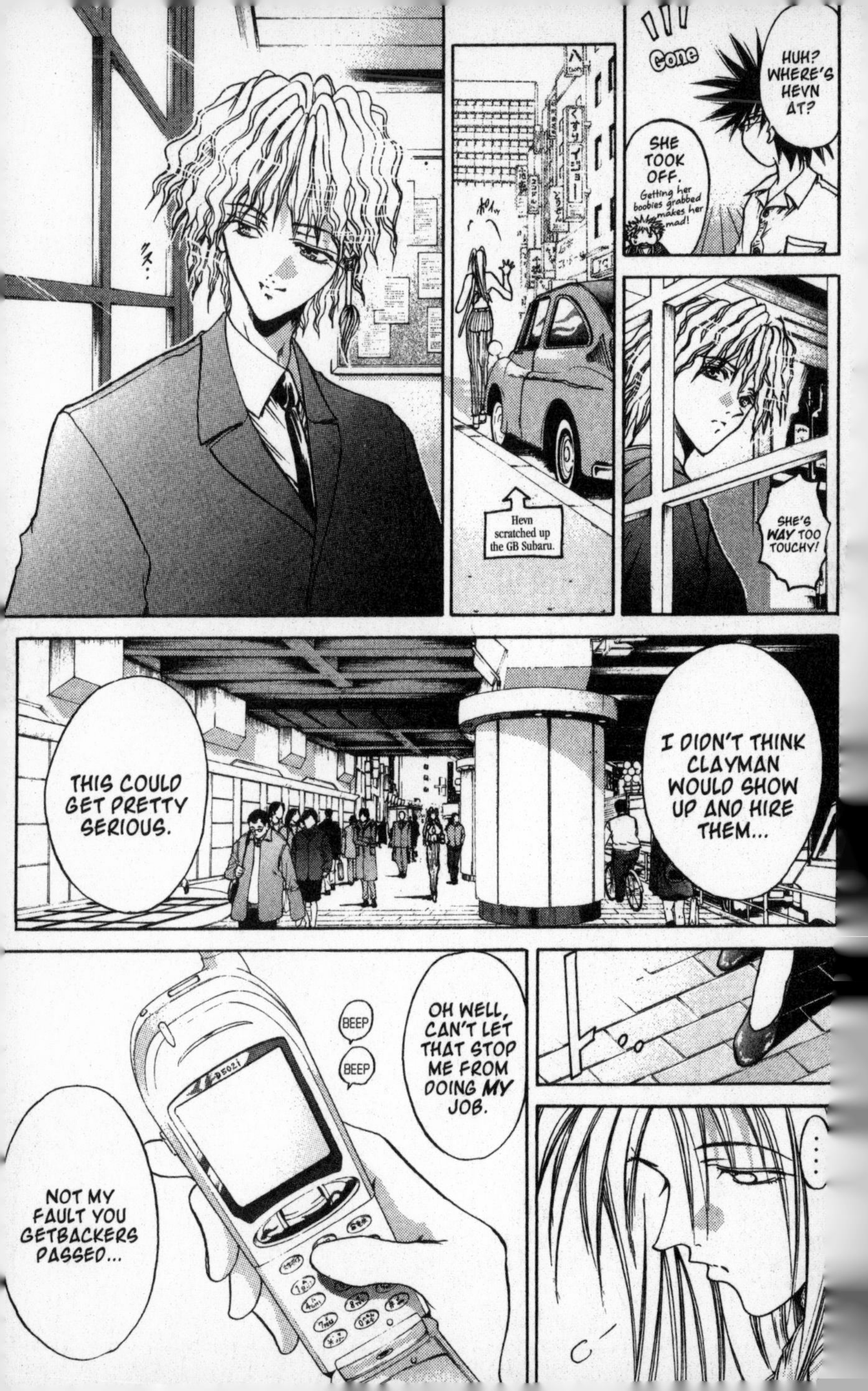
Gone
HUH? WHERE'S HEVN AT?
SHE TOOK OFF.
Getting her boobies grabbed makes her mad!
SHE'S WAY TOO TOUCHY!
Hevn scratched up the GB Subaru.
I DIDN'T THINK CLAYMAN WOULD SHOW UP AND HIRE THEM...
THIS COULD GET PRETTY SERIOUS.
...
OH WELL, CAN'T LET THAT STOP ME FROM DOING MY JOB.
BEEP
BEEP
NOT MY FAULT YOU GETBACKERS PASSED...

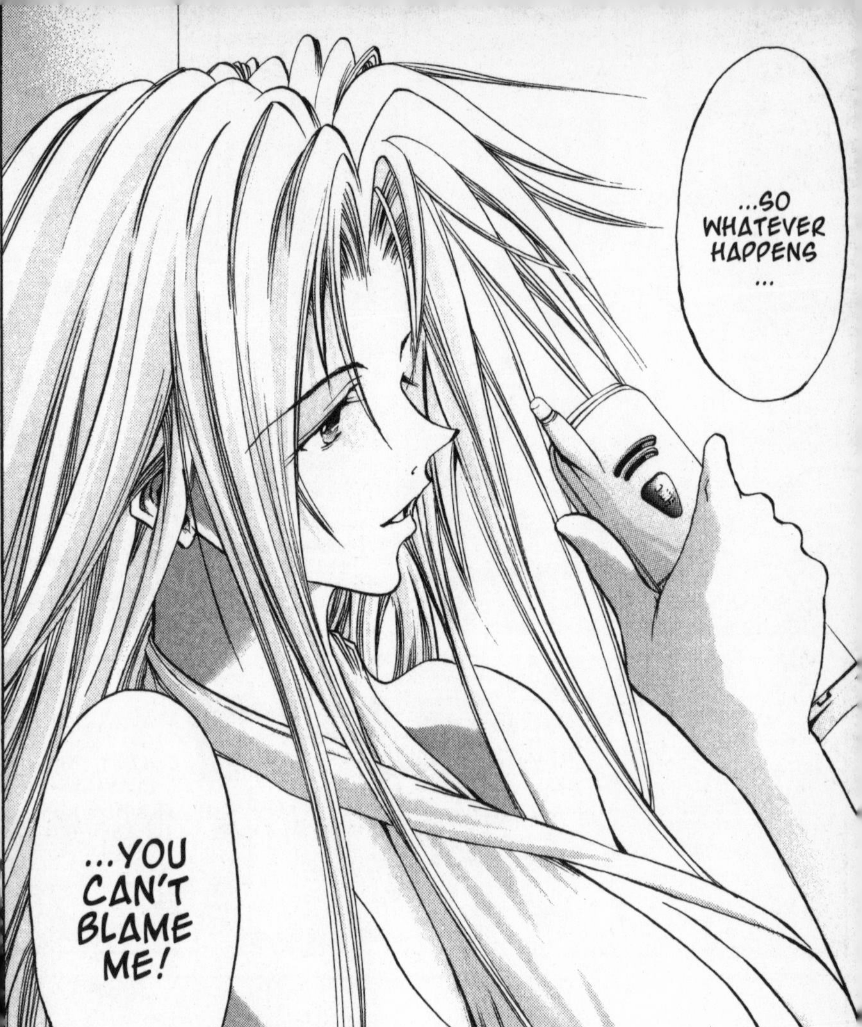
...SO WHATEVER HAPPENS ...
...YOU CAN'T BLAME ME!
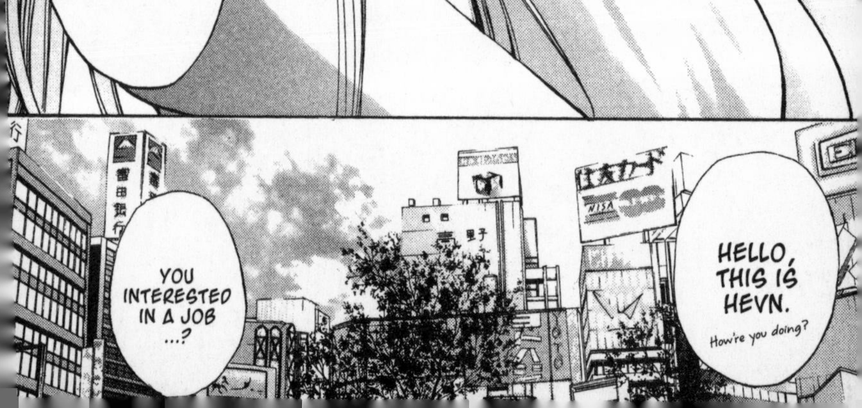
HELLO, THIS IS HEVN.
How're you doing?
YOU INTERESTED IN A JOB ...?

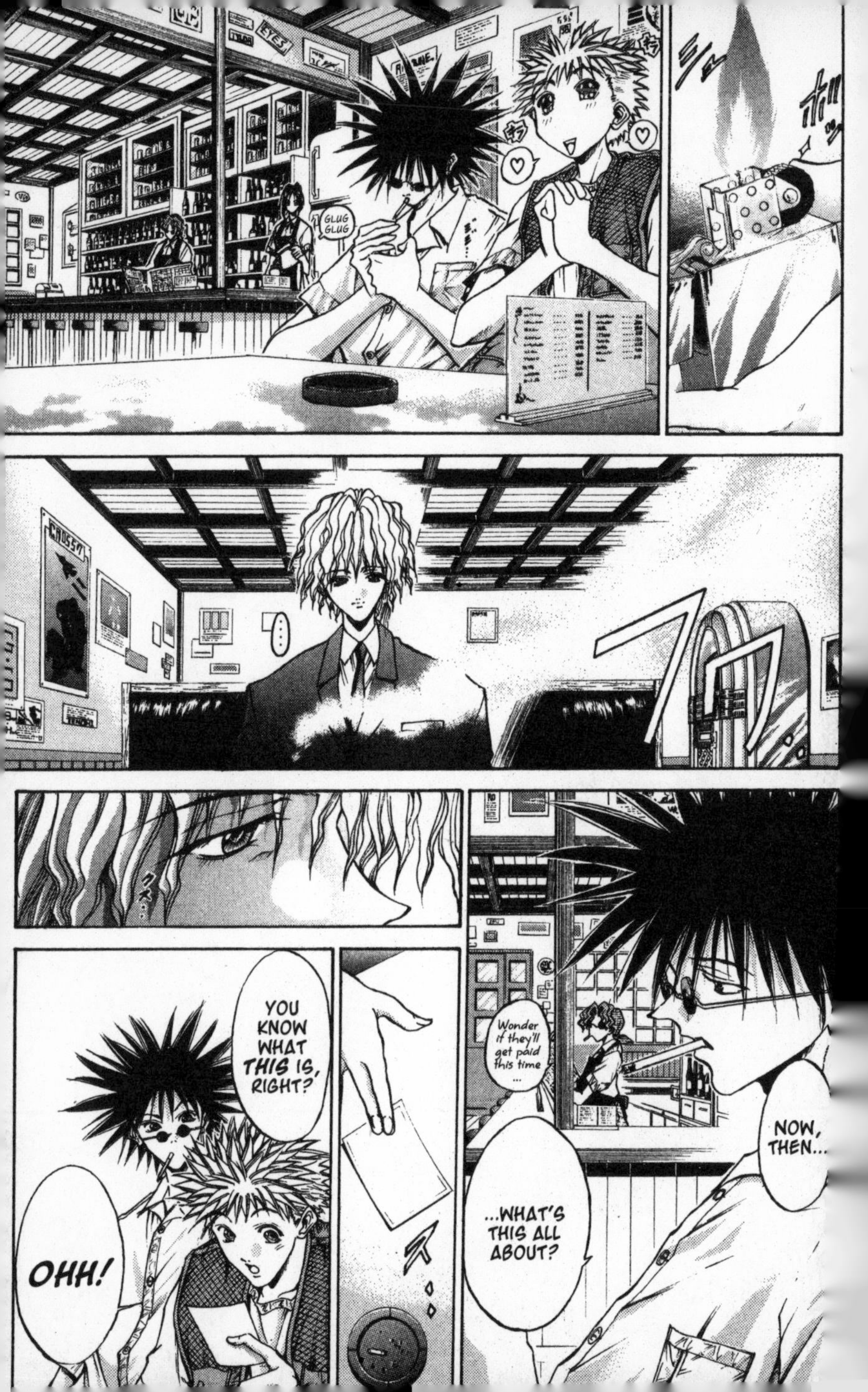
GLUG GLUG
Wonder if they'll get paid this time ...
NOW, THEN...
...WHAT'S THIS ALL ABOUT?
YOU KNOW WHAT THIS IS, RIGHT?
OHH!

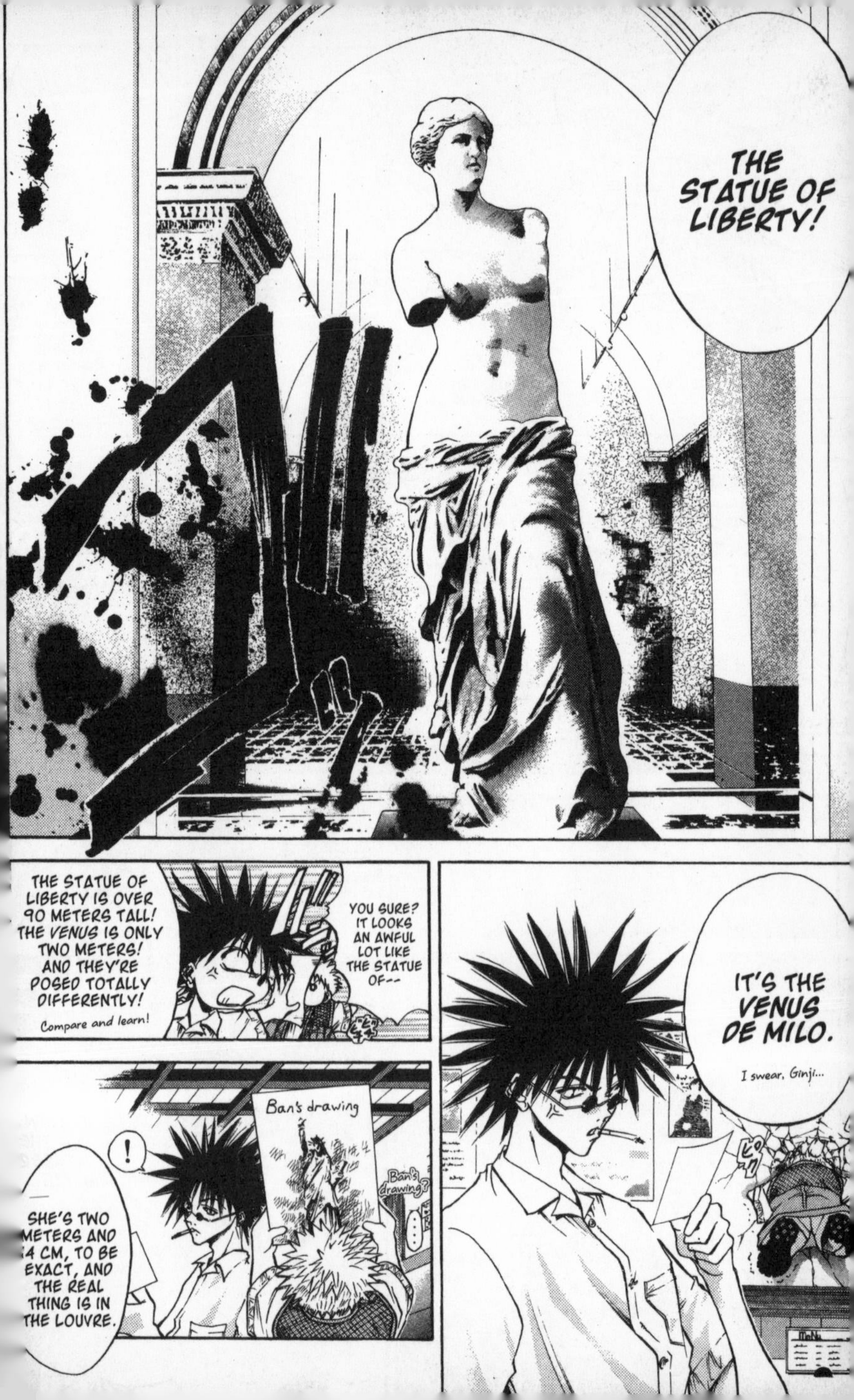
THE STATUE OF LIBERTY!
IT'S THE VENUS DE MILO.
I swear, Ginji...
YOU SURE? IT LOOKS AN AWFUL LOT LIKE THE STATUE OF--
THE STATUE OF LIBERTY IS OVER 90 METERS TALL! THE *VENUS* IS ONLY TWO METERS! AND THEY'RE POSED TOTALLY DIFFERENTLY!
Compare and learn!
Ban's drawing
Ban's drawing?
!
SHE'S TWO METERS AND 4 CM, TO BE EXACT, AND THE REAL THING IS IN THE LOUVRE.

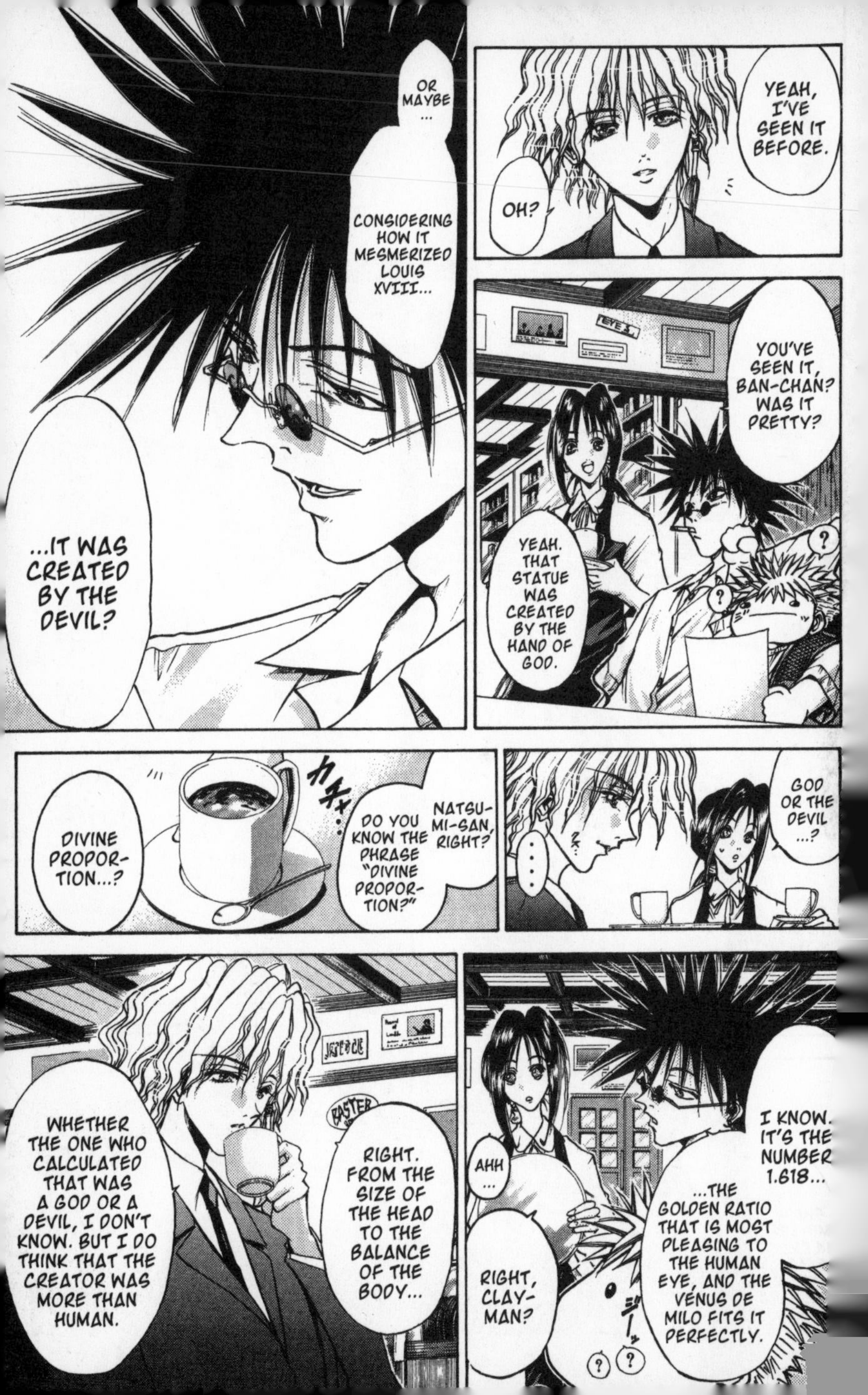
YEAH, I'VE SEEN IT BEFORE.
OH?
YOU'VE SEEN IT, BAN-CHAN? WAS IT PRETTY?
YEAH. THAT STATUE WAS CREATED BY THE HAND OF GOD.
?
?
OR MAYBE...
CONSIDERING HOW IT MESMERIZED LOUIS XVIII...
...IT WAS CREATED BY THE DEVIL?
GOD OR THE DEVIL...?
...
NATSUMI-SAN, RIGHT?
DO YOU KNOW THE PHRASE "DIVINE PROPORTION?"
DIVINE PROPORTION...?
I KNOW. IT'S THE NUMBER 1.618...
...THE GOLDEN RATIO THAT IS MOST PLEASING TO THE HUMAN EYE, AND THE VENUS DE MILO FITS IT PERFECTLY.
AHH...
RIGHT, CLAYMAN?
? ?
RIGHT. FROM THE SIZE OF THE HEAD TO THE BALANCE OF THE BODY...
WHETHER THE ONE WHO CALCULATED THAT WAS A GOD OR A DEVIL, I DON'T KNOW. BUT I DO THINK THAT THE CREATOR WAS MORE THAN HUMAN.

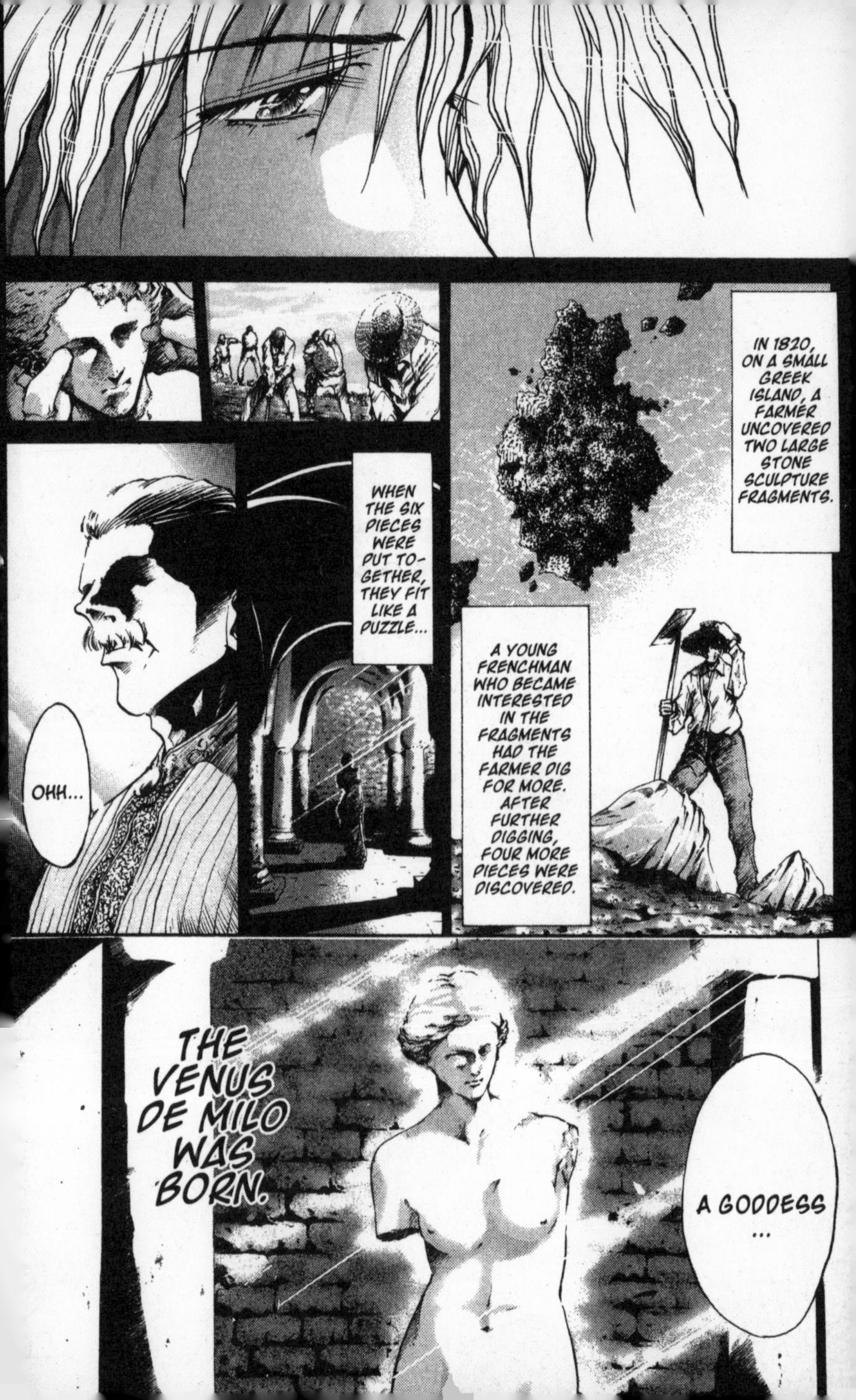
IN 1820, ON A SMALL GREEK ISLAND, A FARMER UNCOVERED TWO LARGE STONE SCULPTURE FRAGMENTS.
A YOUNG FRENCHMAN WHO BECAME INTERESTED IN THE FRAGMENTS HAD THE FARMER DIG FOR MORE. AFTER FURTHER DIGGING, FOUR MORE PIECES WERE DISCOVERED.
WHEN THE SIX PIECES WERE PUT TO-GETHER, THEY FIT LIKE A PUZZLE...
OHH...
A GODDESS ...
THE VENUS DE MILO WAS BORN.

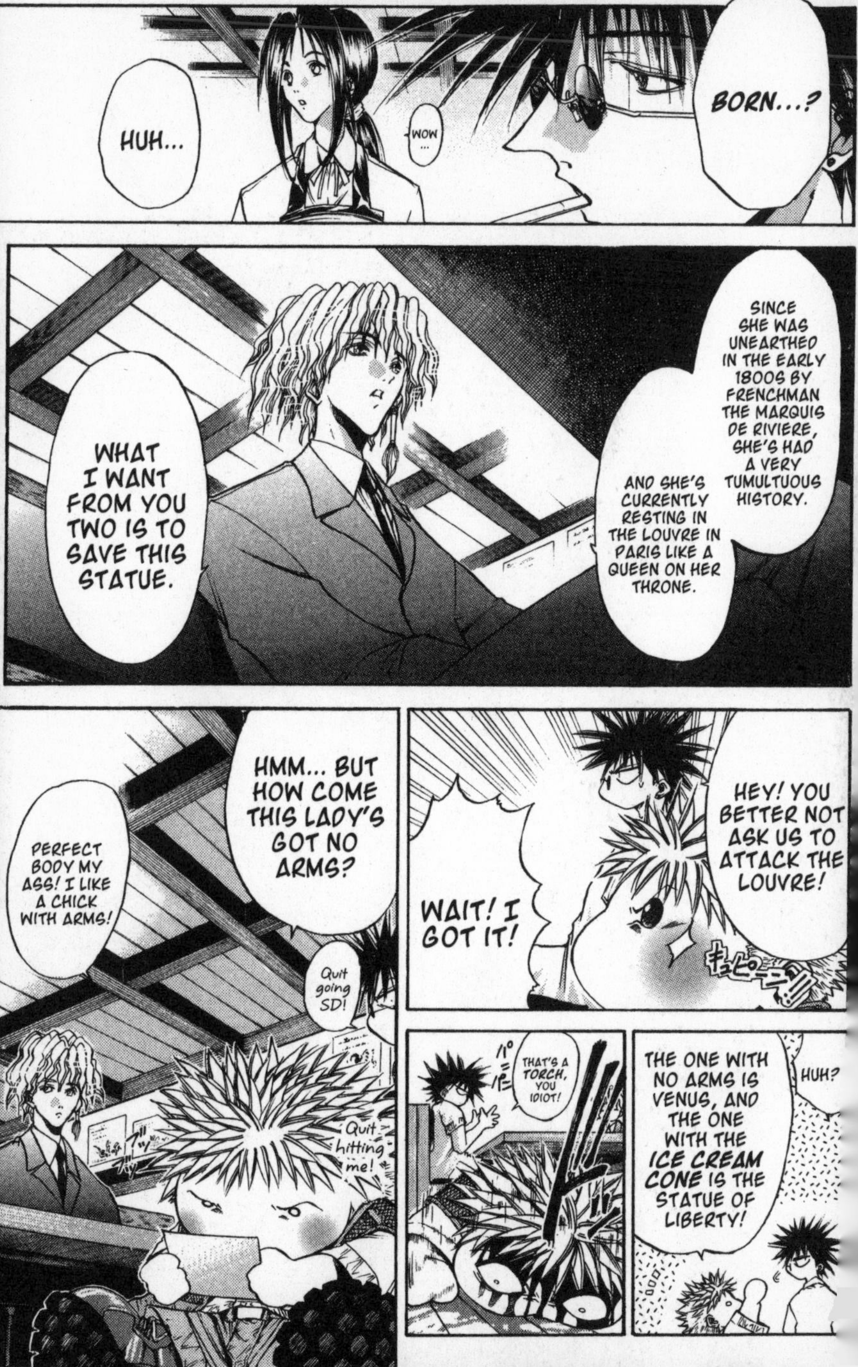
BORN...?
WOW ...
HUH...
SINCE SHE WAS UNEARTHED IN THE EARLY 1800S BY FRENCHMAN THE MARQUIS DE RIVIERE, SHE'S HAD A VERY TUMULTUOUS HISTORY.
AND SHE'S CURRENTLY RESTING IN THE LOUVRE IN PARIS LIKE A QUEEN ON HER THRONE.
WHAT I WANT FROM YOU TWO IS TO SAVE THIS STATUE.
HEY! YOU BETTER NOT ASK US TO ATTACK THE LOUVRE!
WAIT! I GOT IT!
HUH?
THE ONE WITH NO ARMS IS VENUS, AND THE ONE WITH THE ICE CREAM CONE IS THE STATUE OF LIBERTY!
THAT'S A TORCH, YOU IDIOT!
HMM... BUT HOW COME THIS LADY'S GOT NO ARMS?
PERFECT BODY MY ASS! I LIKE A CHICK WITH ARMS!
Quit going SD!
Quit hitting me!

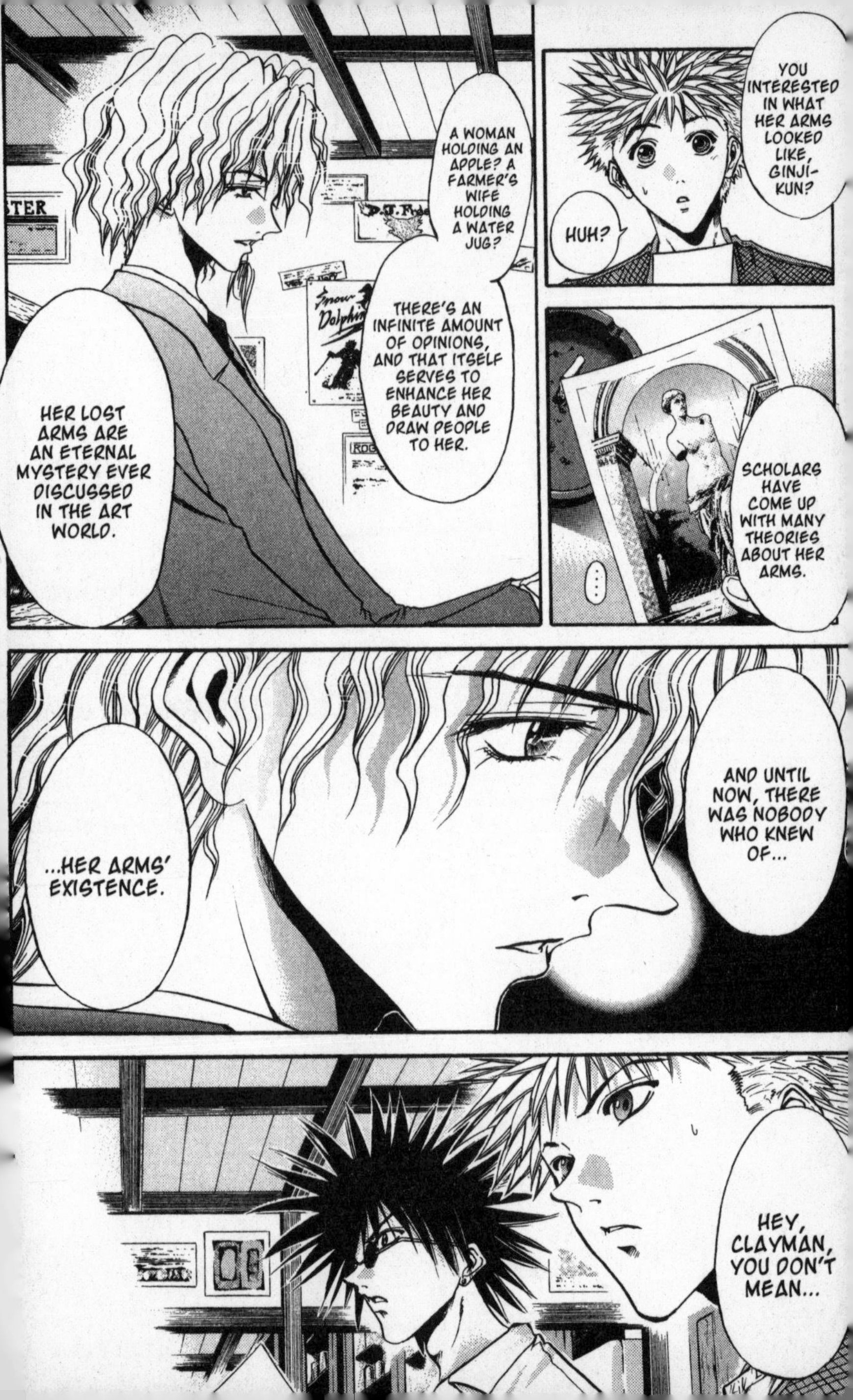
YOU INTERESTED IN WHAT HER ARMS LOOKED LIKE, GINJI-KUN?
HUH?
SCHOLARS HAVE COME UP WITH MANY THEORIES ABOUT HER ARMS.
...
A WOMAN HOLDING AN APPLE? A FARMER'S WIFE HOLDING A WATER JUG?
THERE'S AN INFINITE AMOUNT OF OPINIONS, AND THAT ITSELF SERVES TO ENHANCE HER BEAUTY AND DRAW PEOPLE TO HER.
HER LOST ARMS ARE AN ETERNAL MYSTERY EVER DISCUSSED IN THE ART WORLD.
AND UNTIL NOW, THERE WAS NOBODY WHO KNEW OF...
...HER ARMS' EXISTENCE.
HEY, CLAYMAN, YOU DON'T MEAN...

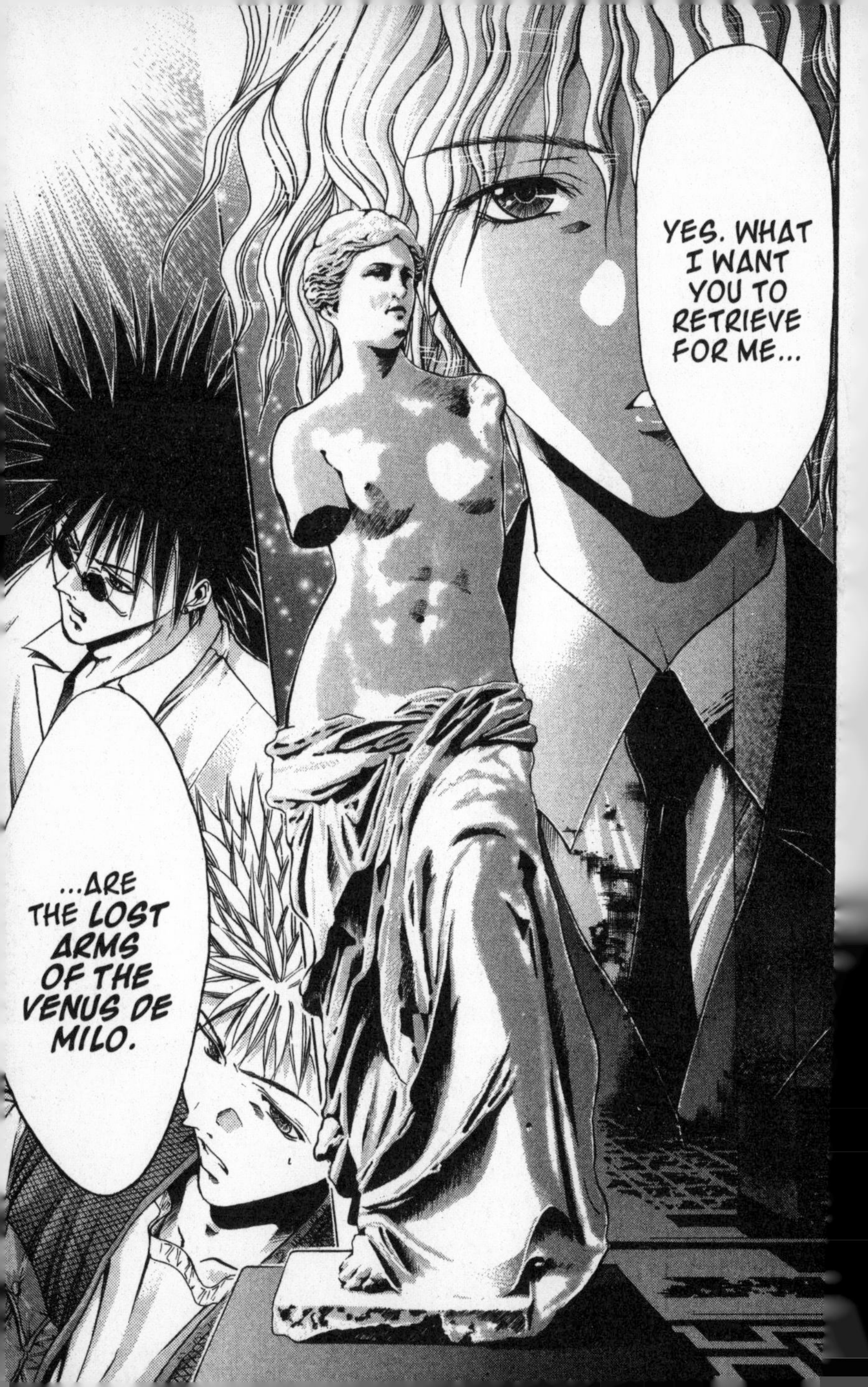
YES. WHAT I WANT YOU TO RETRIEVE FOR ME...
...ARE THE LOST ARMS OF THE VENUS DE MILO.

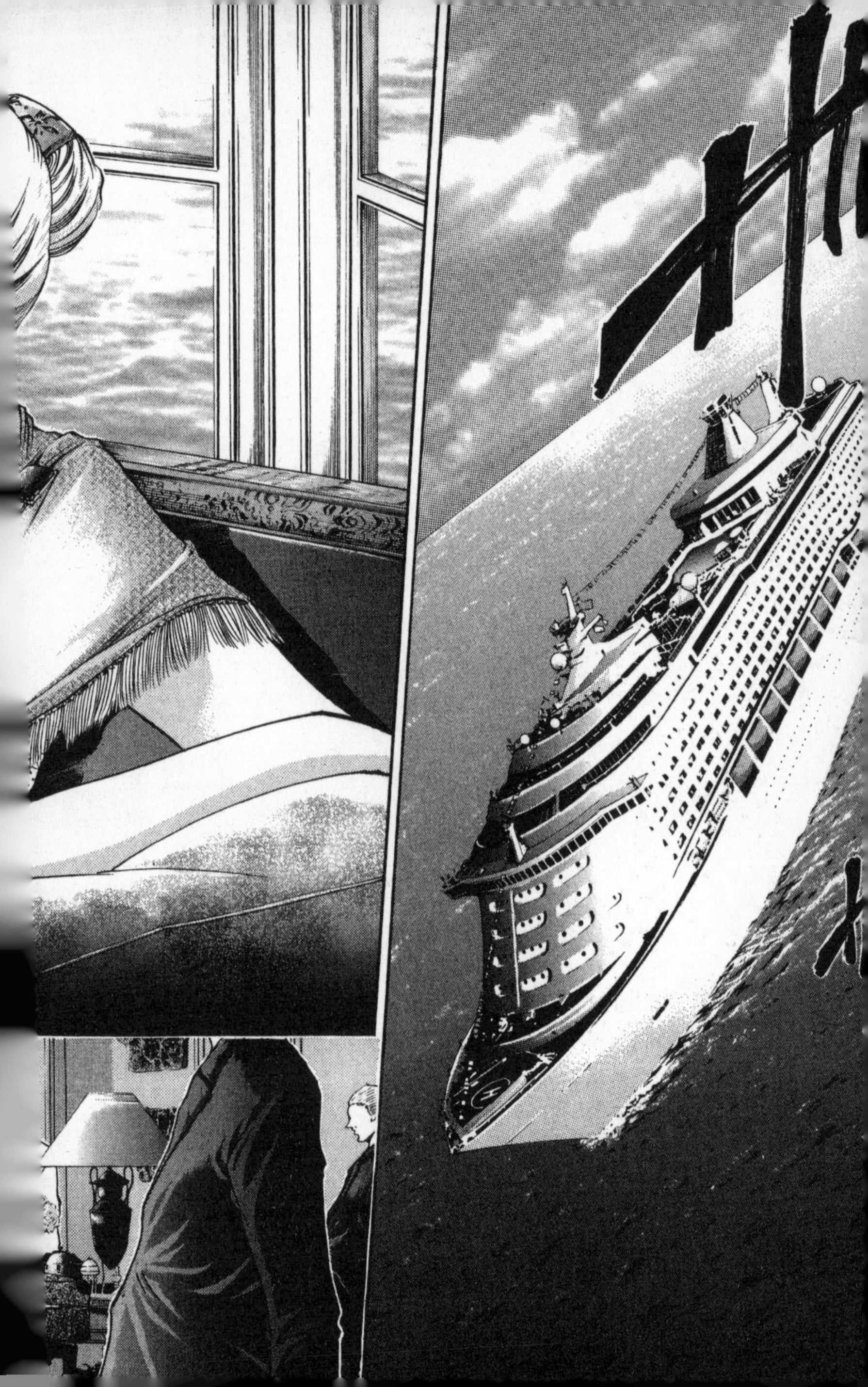

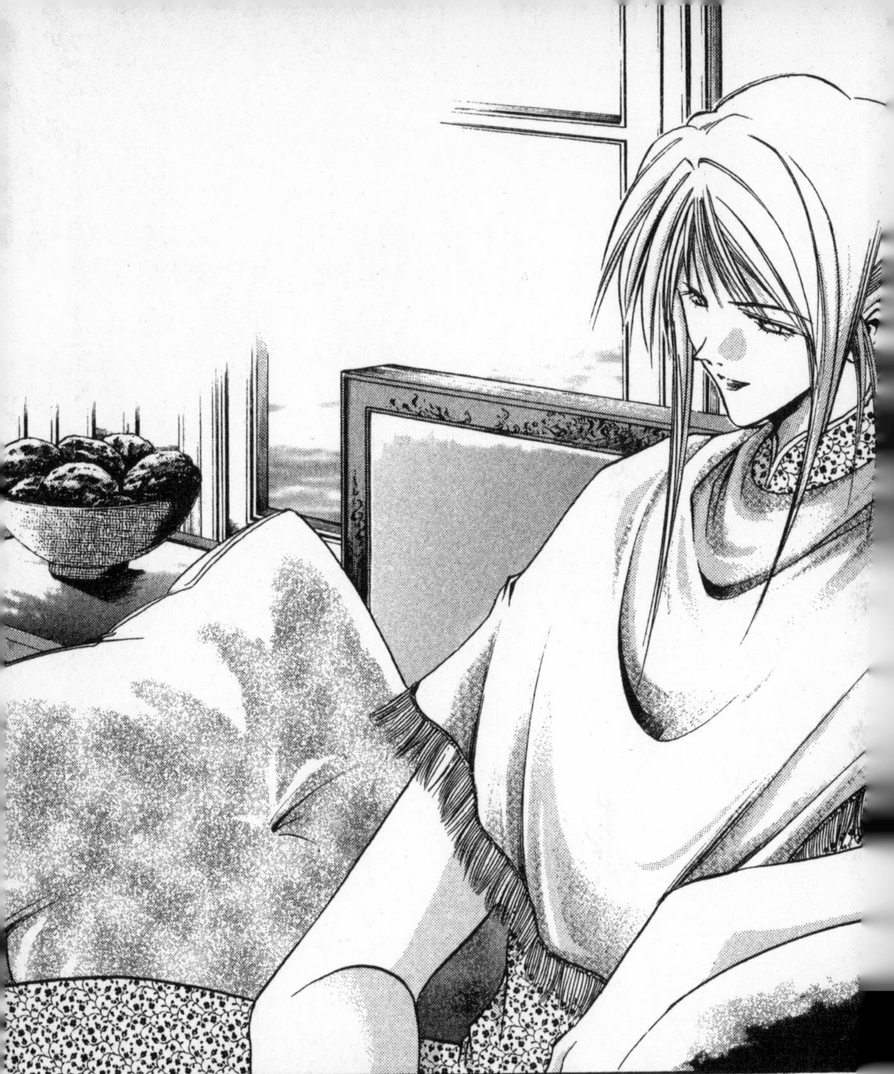
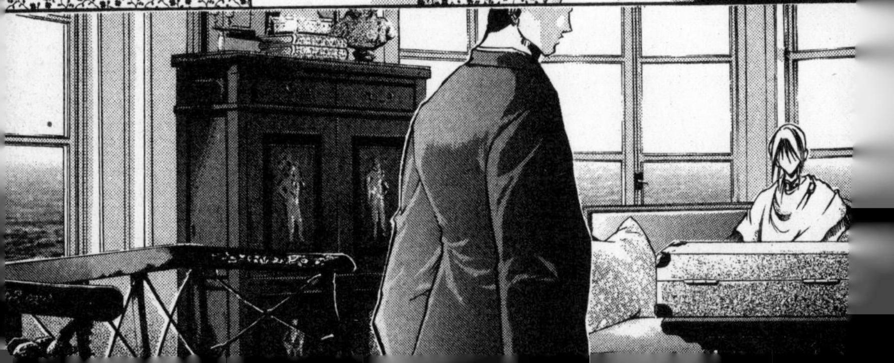

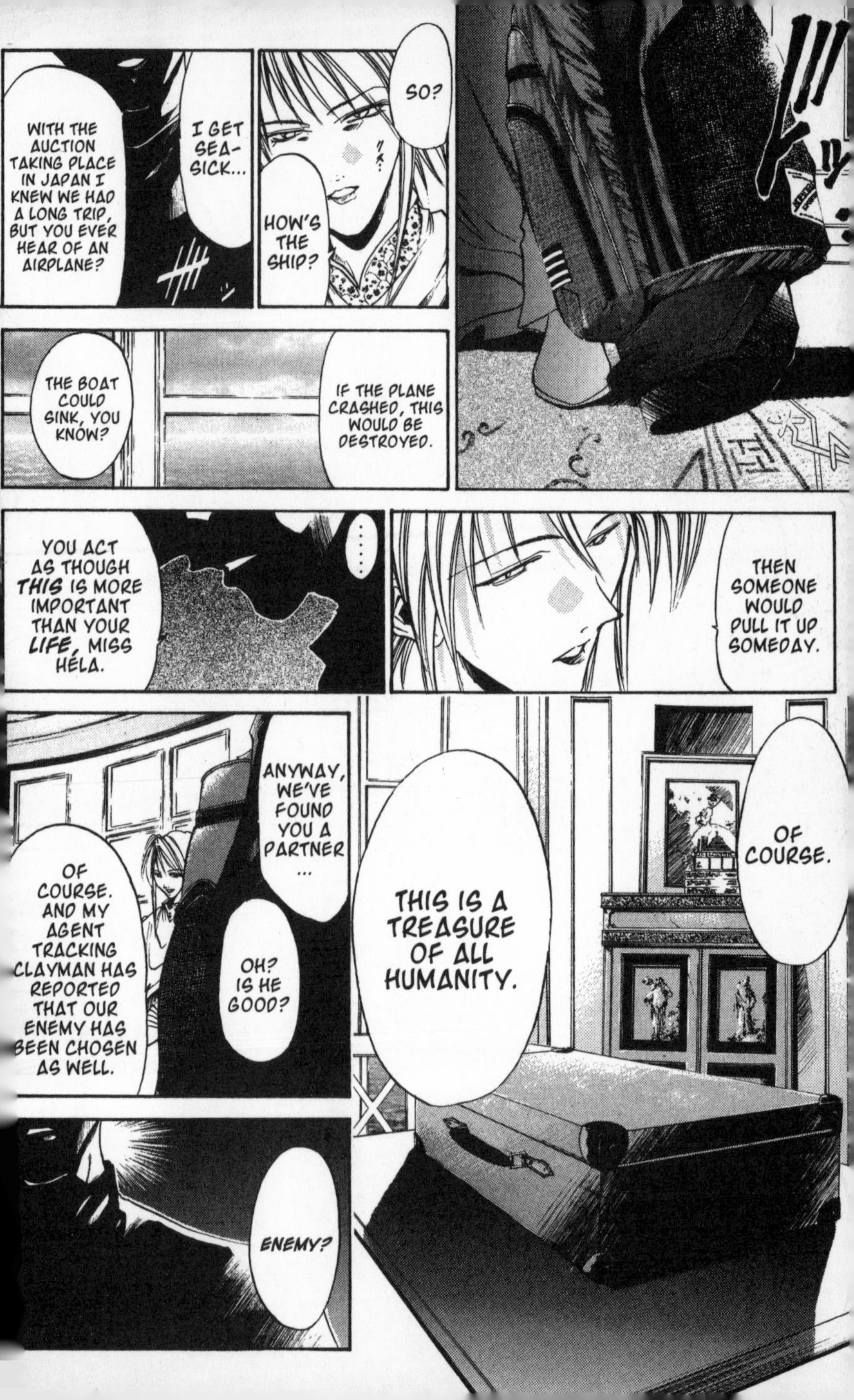

SO?
HOW'S THE SHIP?
I GET SEA-SICK...
WITH THE AUCTION TAKING PLACE IN JAPAN I KNEW WE HAD A LONG TRIP, BUT YOU EVER HEAR OF AN AIRPLANE?
IF THE PLANE CRASHED, THIS WOULD BE DESTROYED.
THE BOAT COULD SINK, YOU KNOW?
THEN SOMEONE WOULD PULL IT UP SOMEDAY.
......
YOU ACT AS THOUGH **THIS** IS MORE IMPORTANT THAN YOUR **LIFE**, MISS HÉLA.
OF COURSE.
THIS IS A TREASURE OF ALL HUMANITY.
ANYWAY, WE'VE FOUND YOU A PARTNER...
OH? IS HE GOOD?
OF COURSE. AND MY AGENT TRACKING CLAYMAN HAS REPORTED THAT OUR ENEMY HAS BEEN CHOSEN AS WELL.
ENEMY?

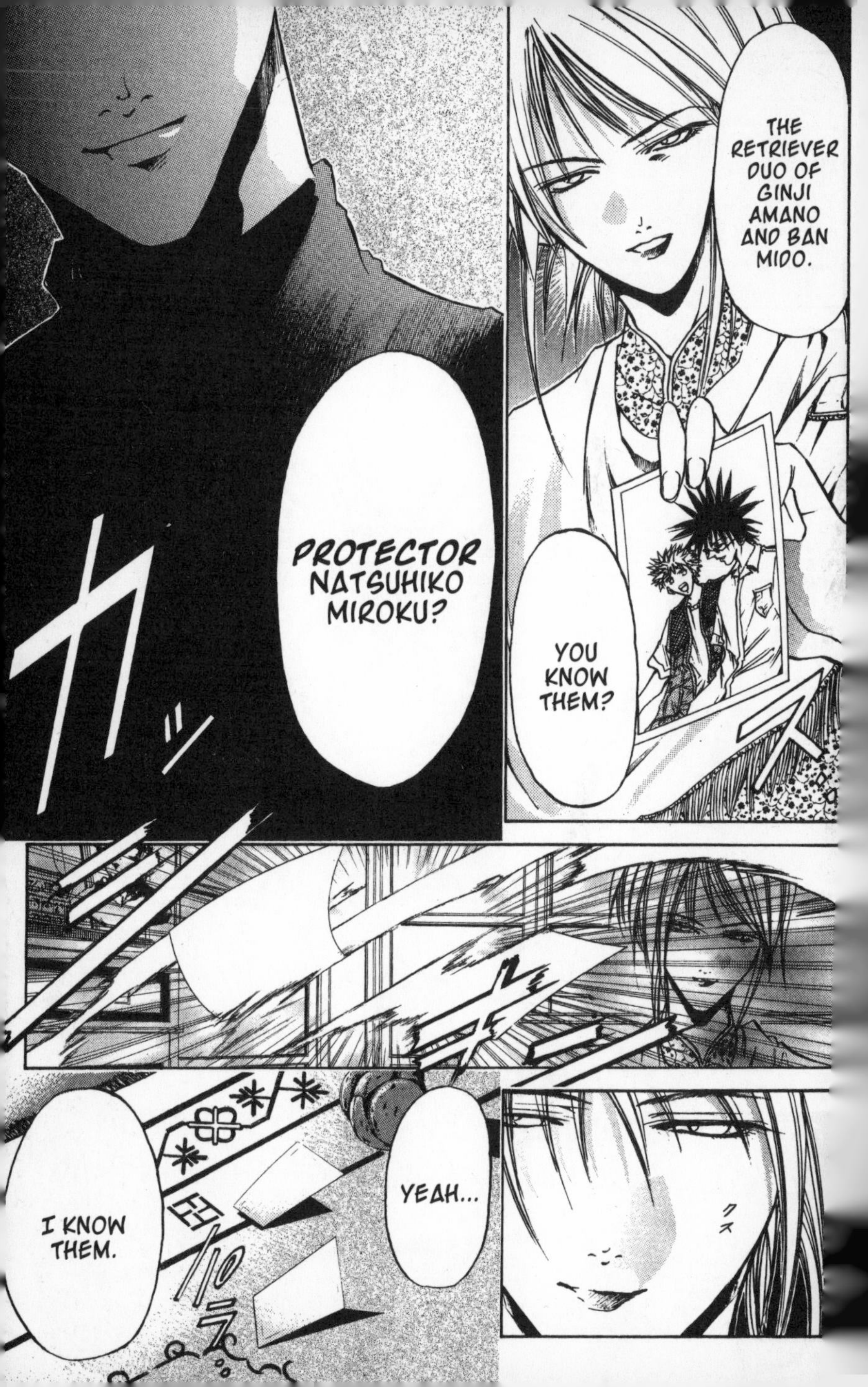
THE RETRIEVER DUO OF GINJI AMANO AND BAN MIDO.
YOU KNOW THEM?
PROTECTOR NATSUHIKO MIROKU?
クス
YEAH...
I KNOW THEM.

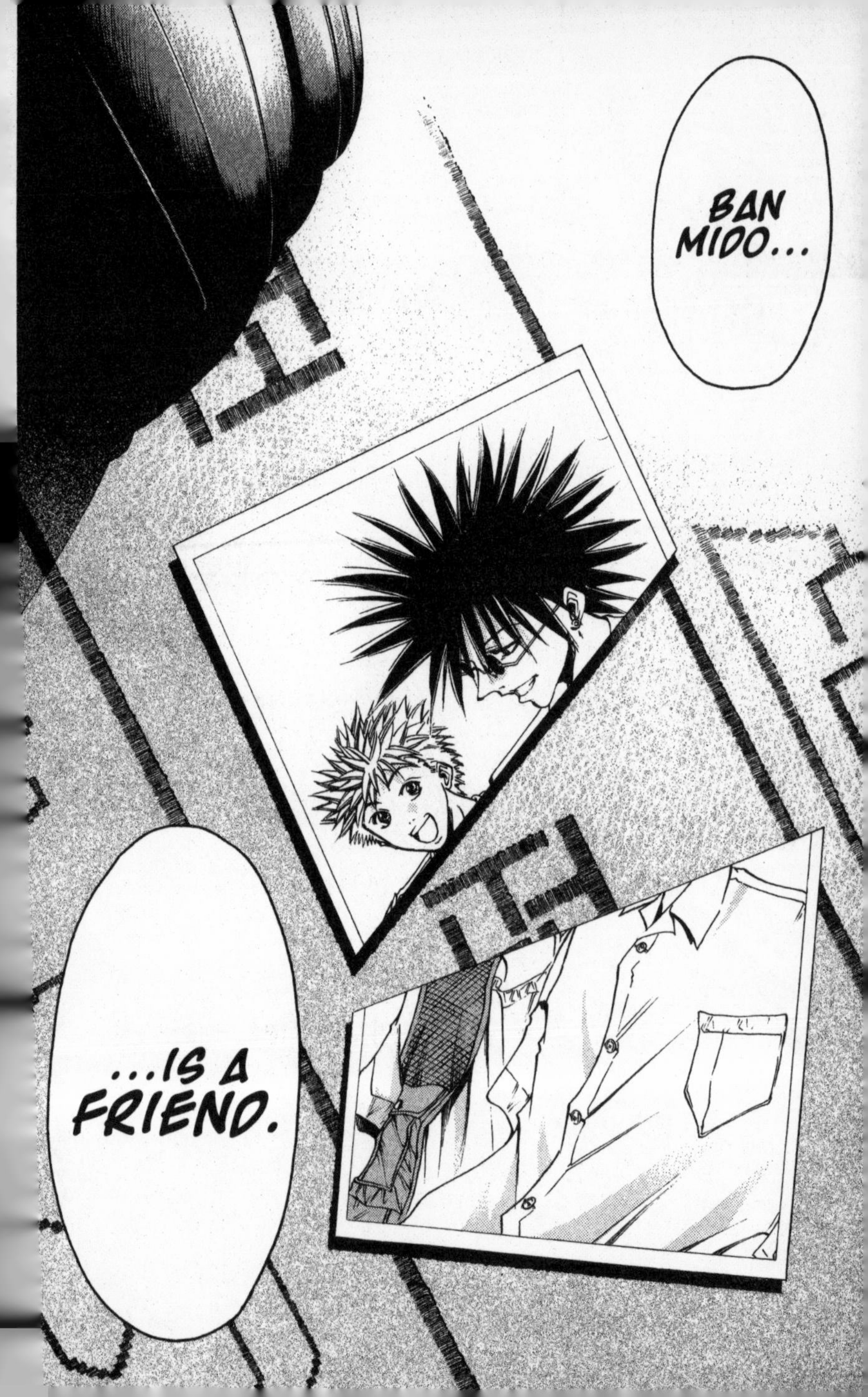
BAN MIDO...
...IS A FRIEND.

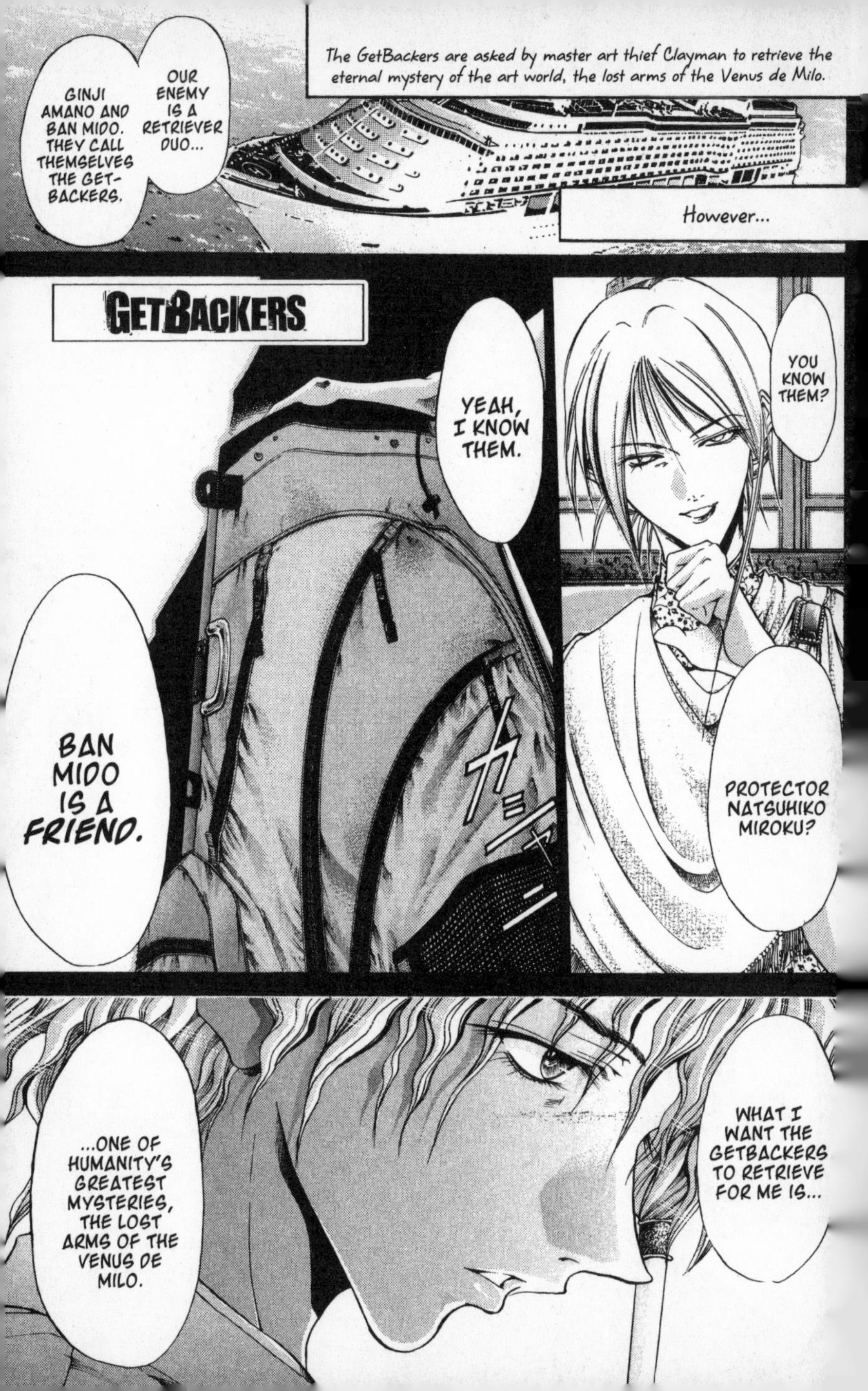
The GetBackers are asked by master art thief Clayman to retrieve the eternal mystery of the art world, the lost arms of the Venus de Milo.
However...
OUR ENEMY IS A RETRIEVER DUO...
GINJI AMANO AND BAN MIDO. THEY CALL THEMSELVES THE GET-BACKERS.
YOU KNOW THEM?
PROTECTOR NATSUHIKO MIROKU?
GETBACKERS
YEAH, I KNOW THEM.
BAN MIDO IS A FRIEND.
WHAT I WANT THE GETBACKERS TO RETRIEVE FOR ME IS...
...ONE OF HUMANITY'S GREATEST MYSTERIES, THE LOST ARMS OF THE VENUS DE MILO.

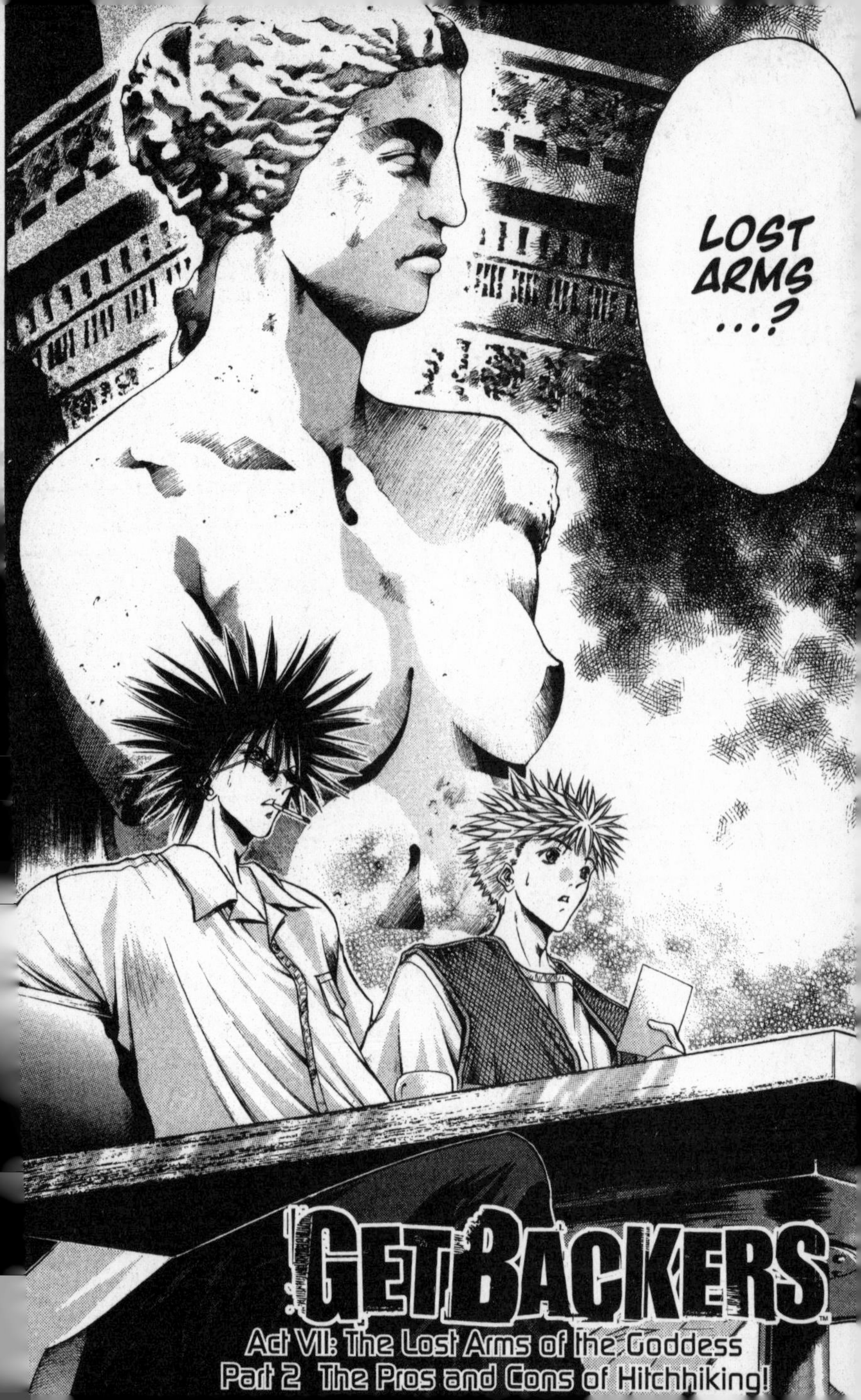
LOST ARMS ...?
GETBACKERS
Act VII: The Lost Arms of the Goddess
Part 2 The Pros and Cons of Hitchhiking!

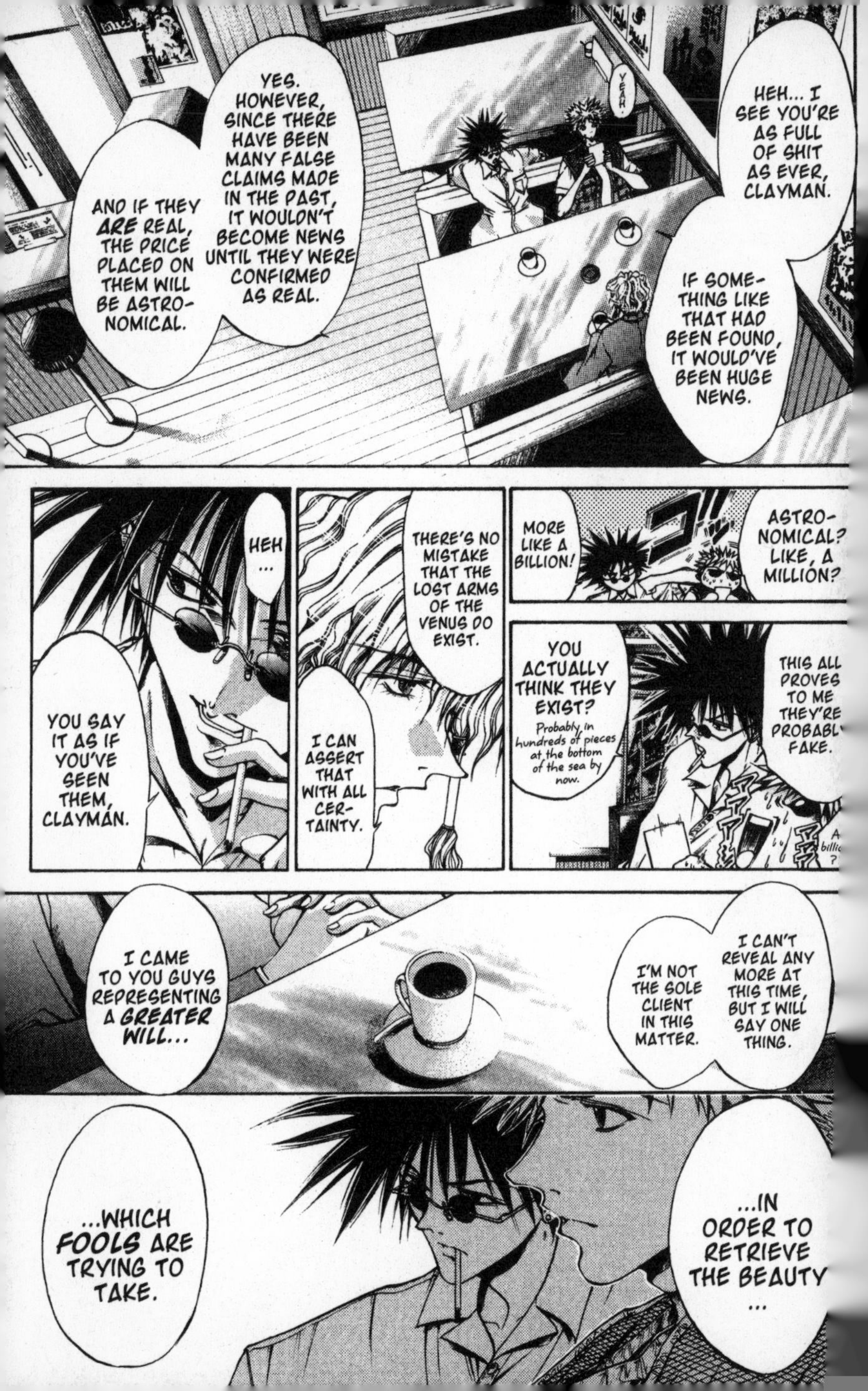
HEH... I SEE YOU'RE AS FULL OF SHIT AS EVER, CLAYMAN.
IF SOME-THING LIKE THAT HAD BEEN FOUND, IT WOULD'VE BEEN HUGE NEWS.
YEAH.
YES. HOWEVER, SINCE THERE HAVE BEEN MANY FALSE CLAIMS MADE IN THE PAST, IT WOULDN'T BECOME NEWS UNTIL THEY WERE CONFIRMED AS REAL.
AND IF THEY ARE REAL, THE PRICE PLACED ON THEM WILL BE ASTRO-NOMICAL.
ASTRO-NOMICAL? LIKE, A MILLION?
MORE LIKE A BILLION!
THIS ALL PROVES TO ME THEY'RE PROBABL FAKE.
YOU ACTUALLY THINK THEY EXIST?
Probably in hundreds of pieces at the bottom of the sea by now.
THERE'S NO MISTAKE THAT THE LOST ARMS OF THE VENUS DO EXIST.
I CAN ASSERT THAT WITH ALL CER-TAINTY.
HEH...
YOU SAY IT AS IF YOU'VE SEEN THEM, CLAYMAN.
I CAN'T REVEAL ANY MORE AT THIS TIME, BUT I WILL SAY ONE THING.
I'M NOT THE SOLE CLIENT IN THIS MATTER.
I CAME TO YOU GUYS REPRESENTING A GREATER WILL...
...IN ORDER TO RETRIEVE THE BEAUTY...
...WHICH FOOLS ARE TRYING TO TAKE.

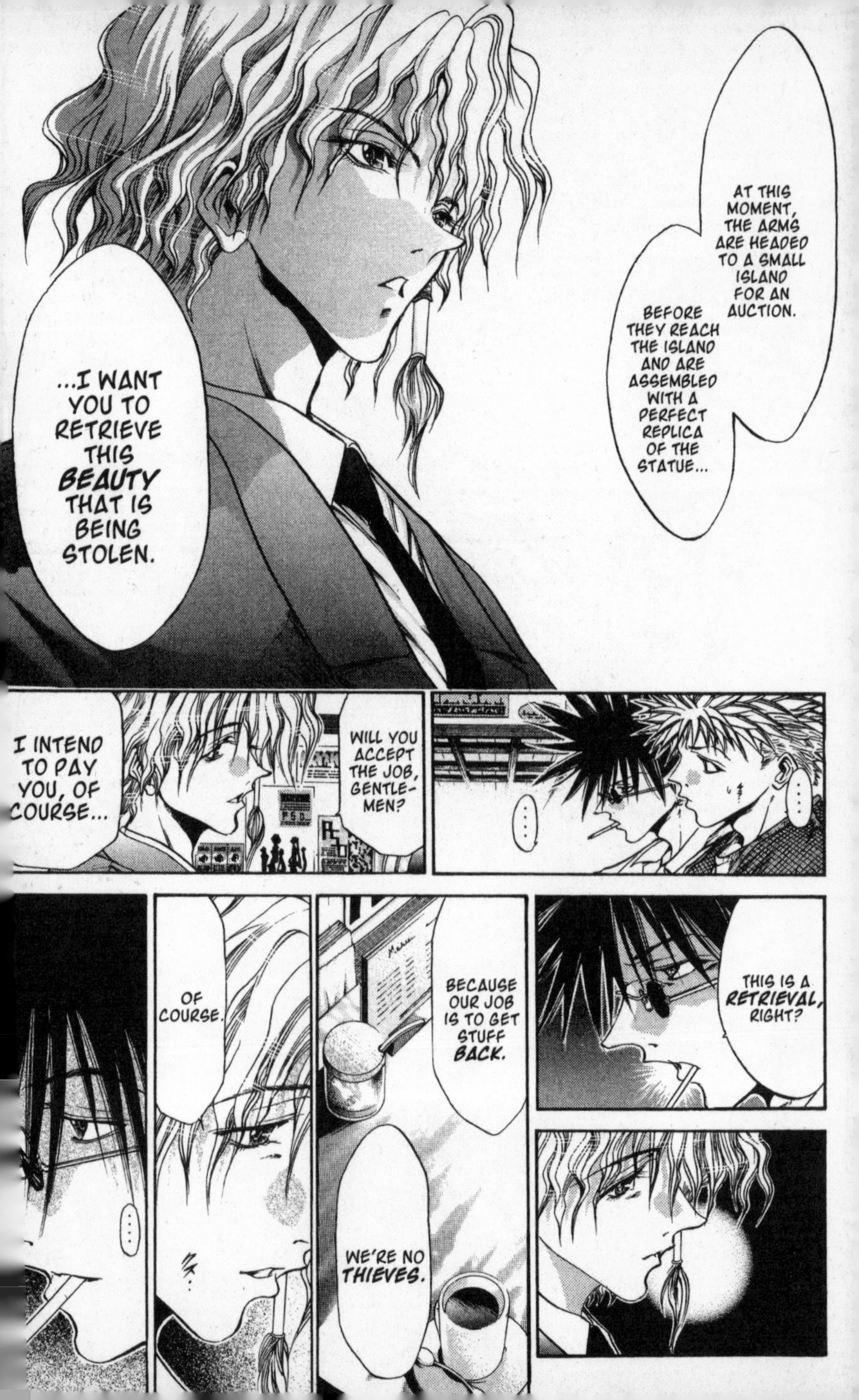
AT THIS MOMENT, THE ARMS ARE HEADED TO A SMALL ISLAND FOR AN AUCTION.
BEFORE THEY REACH THE ISLAND AND ARE ASSEMBLED WITH A PERFECT REPLICA OF THE STATUE...
...I WANT YOU TO RETRIEVE THIS ***BEAUTY*** THAT IS BEING STOLEN.
....
....
WILL YOU ACCEPT THE JOB, GENTLE-MEN?
I INTEND TO PAY YOU, OF COURSE...
THIS IS A ***RETRIEVAL***, RIGHT?
BECAUSE OUR JOB IS TO GET STUFF ***BACK.***
WE'RE NO ***THIEVES.***
OF COURSE.
....

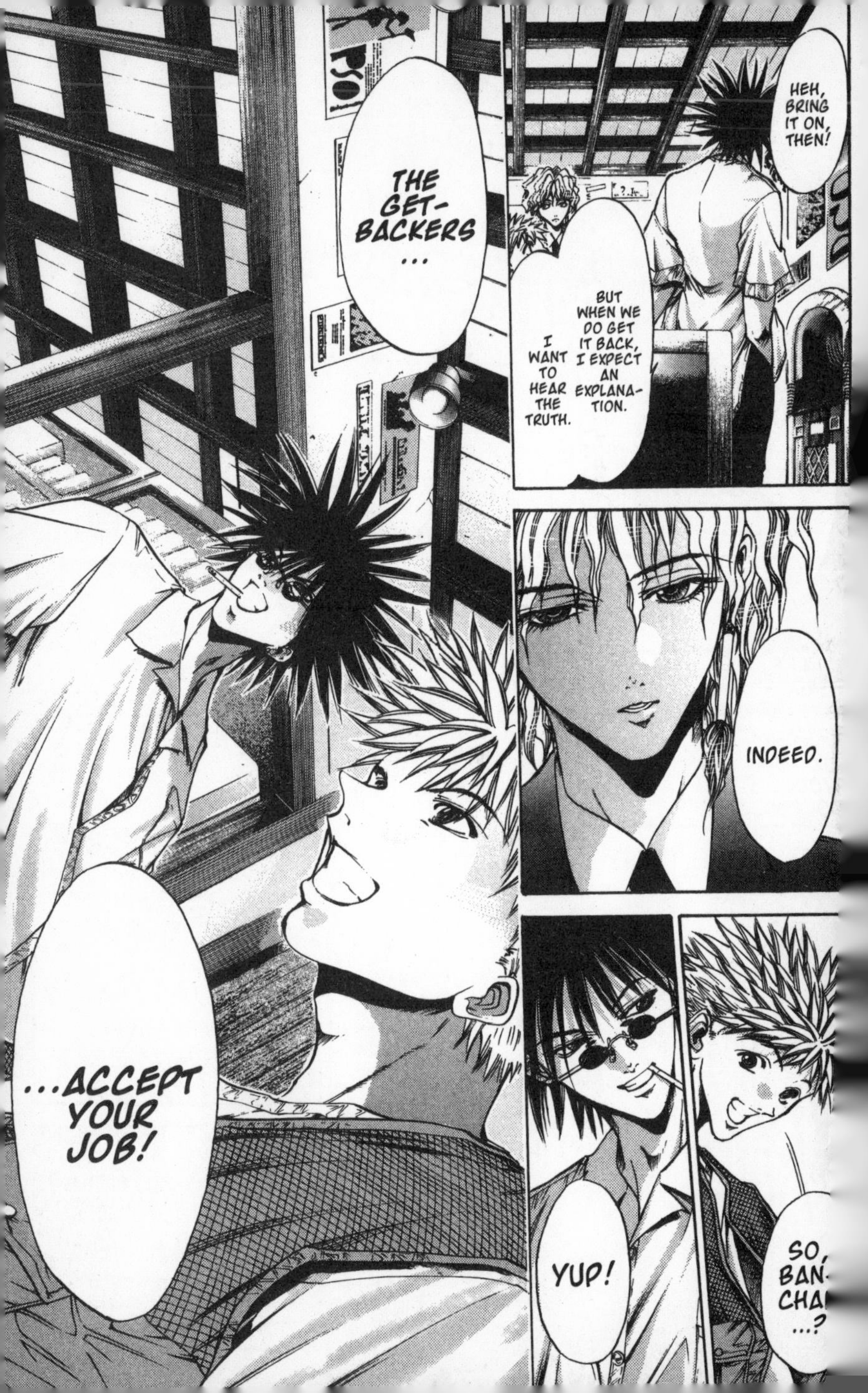
HEH, BRING IT ON, THEN!
BUT WHEN WE DO GET IT BACK, I EXPECT AN EXPLANATION.
I WANT TO HEAR THE TRUTH.
INDEED.
SO, BAN-CHA...?
YUP!
THE GET-BACKERS...
...ACCEPT YOUR JOB!

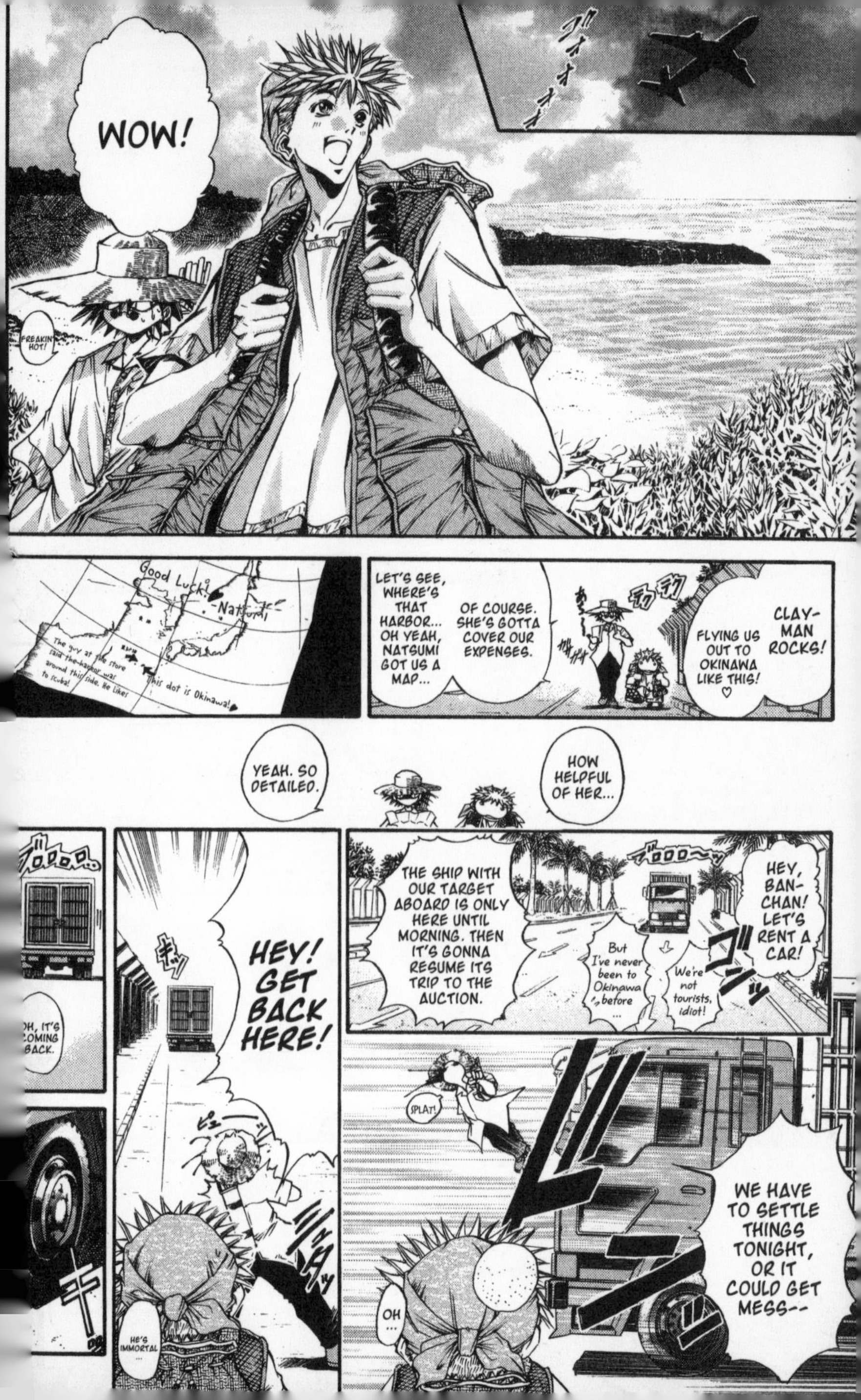
WOW!
FREAKIN' HOT!
CLAY-MAN ROCKS!
FLYING US OUT TO OKINAWA LIKE THIS! ♡
LET'S SEE, WHERE'S THAT HARBOR... OH YEAH, NATSUMI GOT US A MAP...
OF COURSE. SHE'S GOTTA COVER OUR EXPENSES.
Good Luck! -Natsumi
The guy at the store said the harbor was around this side. He likes to scuba!
This dot is Okinawa!♥
HOW HELPFUL OF HER...
YEAH. SO DETAILED.
HEY, BAN-CHAN! LET'S RENT A CAR!
THE SHIP WITH OUR TARGET ABOARD IS ONLY HERE UNTIL MORNING. THEN IT'S GONNA RESUME ITS TRIP TO THE AUCTION.
But I've never been to Okinawa before...
We're not tourists, idiot!
WE HAVE TO SETTLE THINGS TONIGHT, OR IT COULD GET MESS--
SPLAT!
OH...
HEY! GET BACK HERE!
HE'S IMMORTAL...
H, IT'S OMING BACK.

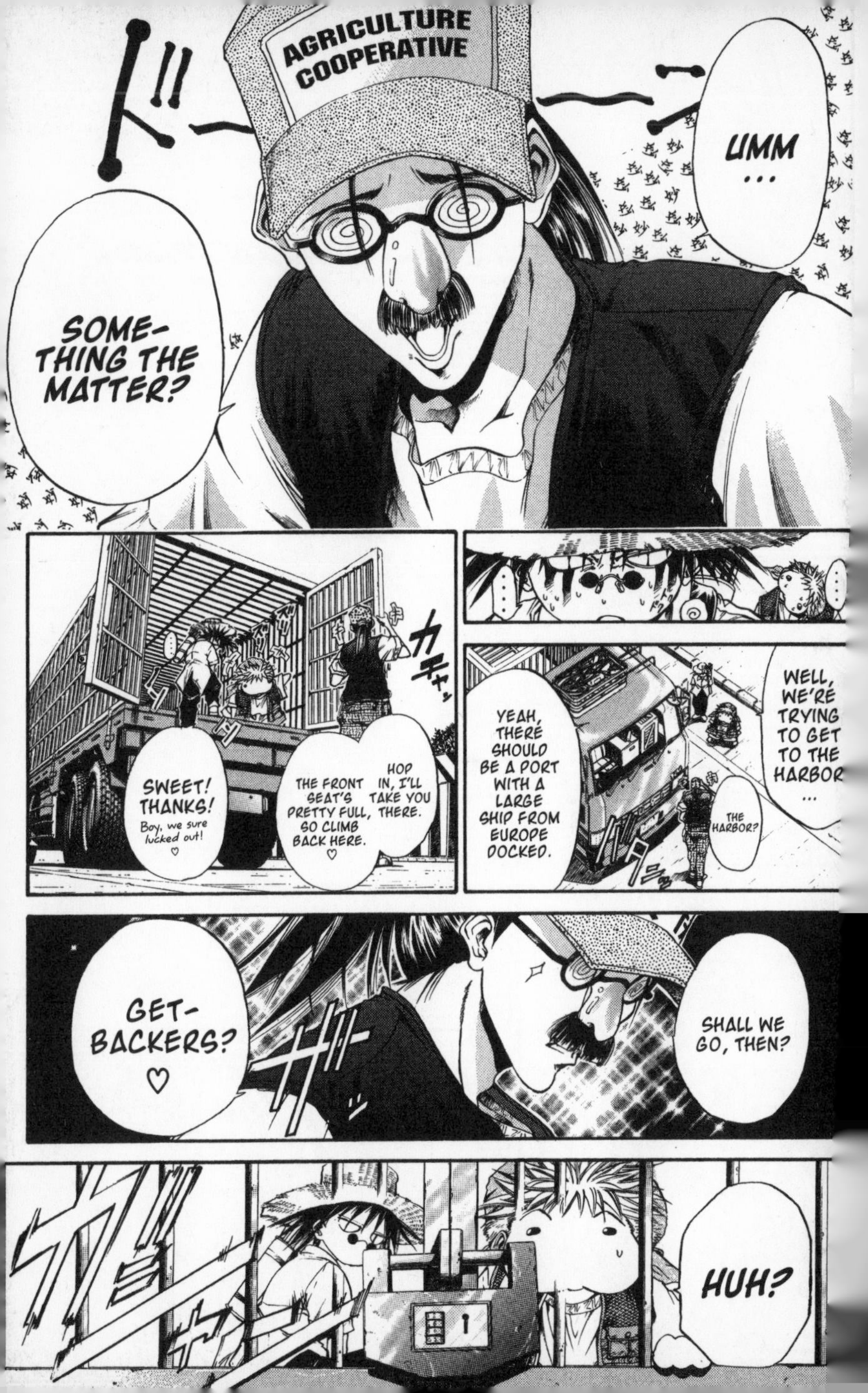
AGRICULTURE COOPERATIVE
UMM ...
SOMETHING THE MATTER?
WELL, WE'RE TRYING TO GET TO THE HARBOR ...
THE HARBOR?
YEAH, THERE SHOULD BE A PORT WITH A LARGE SHIP FROM EUROPE DOCKED.
HOP IN, I'LL TAKE YOU THERE.
THE FRONT SEAT'S PRETTY FULL, SO CLIMB BACK HERE. ♡
SWEET! THANKS!
Boy, we sure lucked out! ♡
SHALL WE GO, THEN?
GET-BACKERS? ♡
HUH?

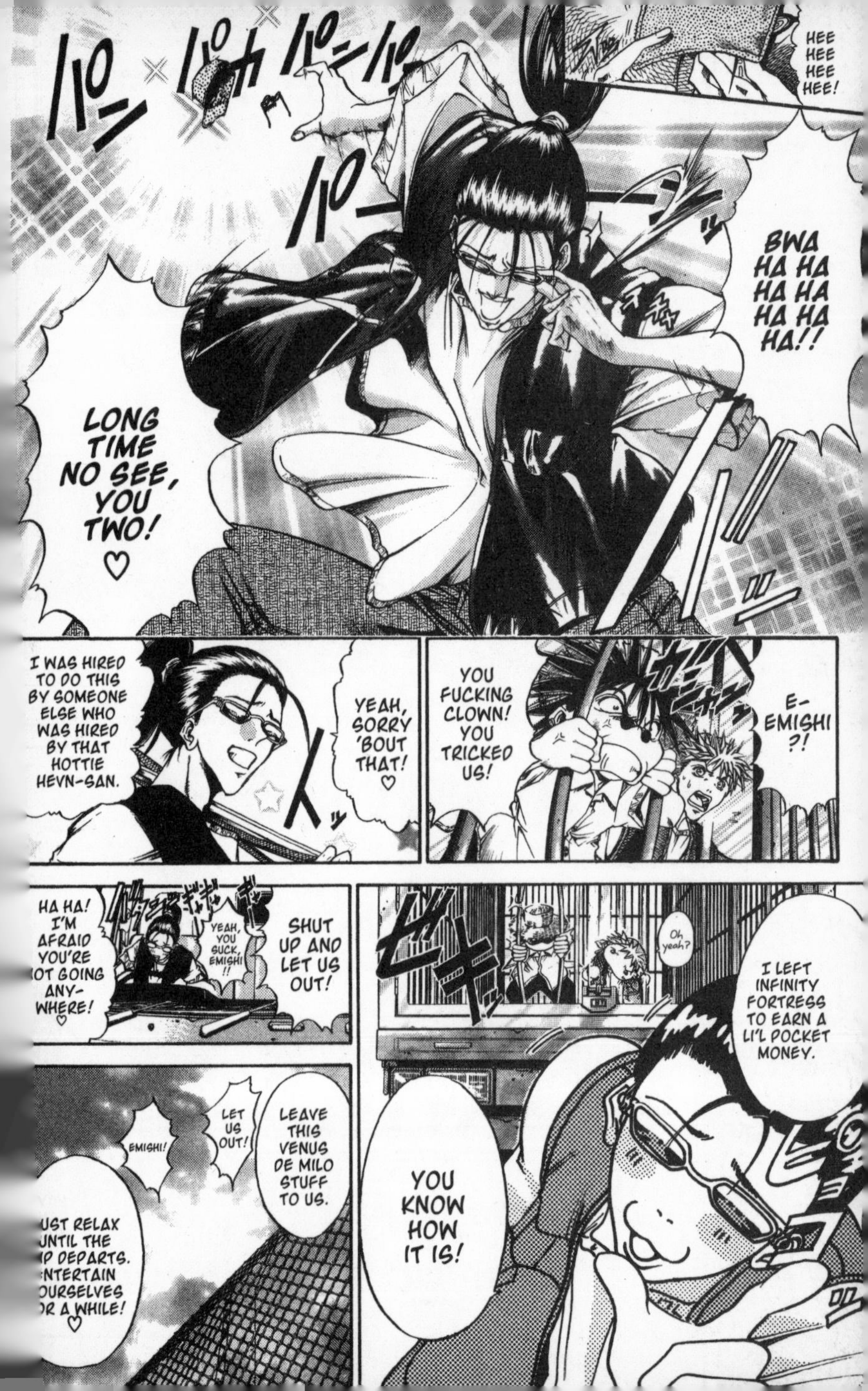
HEE HEE HEE HEE!
BWA HA HA HA HA HA HA HA!!
LONG TIME NO SEE, YOU TWO! ♡
E-EMISHI?!
YOU FUCKING CLOWN! YOU TRICKED US!
YEAH, SORRY 'BOUT THAT! ♡
I WAS HIRED TO DO THIS BY SOMEONE ELSE WHO WAS HIRED BY THAT HOTTIE HEVN-SAN.
I LEFT INFINITY FORTRESS TO EARN A LI'L POCKET MONEY.
Oh yeah?
YOU KNOW HOW IT IS!
SHUT UP AND LET US OUT!
YEAH, YOU SUCK, EMISHI!!
HA HA! I'M AFRAID YOU'RE OT GOING ANY-WHERE! ♡
LEAVE THIS VENUS DE MILO STUFF TO US.
LET US OUT!
EMISHI!
UST RELAX UNTIL THE IP DEPARTS. NTERTAIN OURSELVES OR A WHILE! ♡

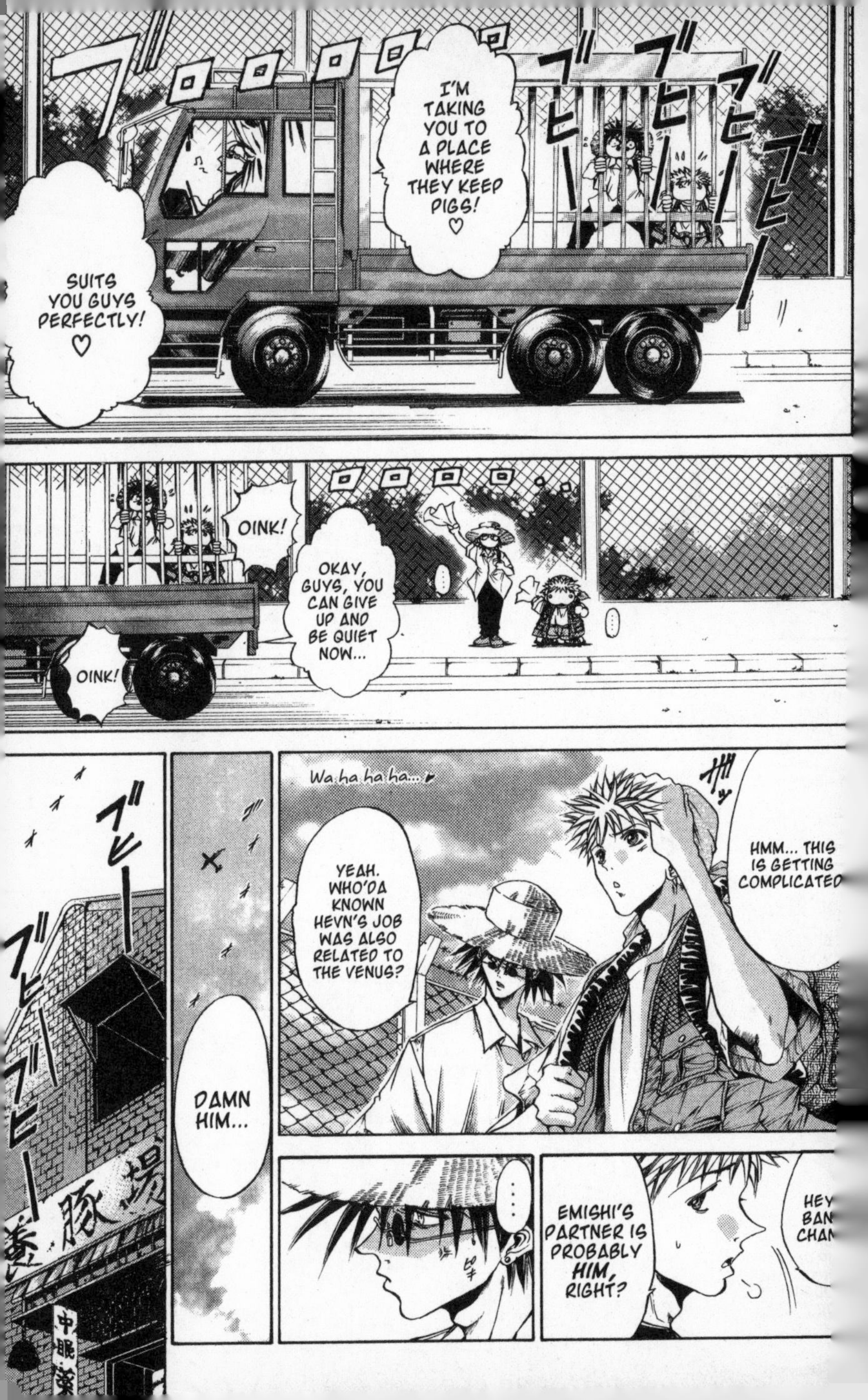
I'M TAKING YOU TO A PLACE WHERE THEY KEEP PIGS! ♡
SUITS YOU GUYS PERFECTLY! ♡
...
OKAY, GUYS, YOU CAN GIVE UP AND BE QUIET NOW...
...
OINK!
OINK!
HMM... THIS IS GETTING COMPLICATED
Wa ha ha ha...
YEAH. WHO'DA KNOWN HEVN'S JOB WAS ALSO RELATED TO THE VENUS?
DAMN HIM...
HEY BAN CHAN
EMISHI'S PARTNER IS PROBABLY HIM, RIGHT?
....

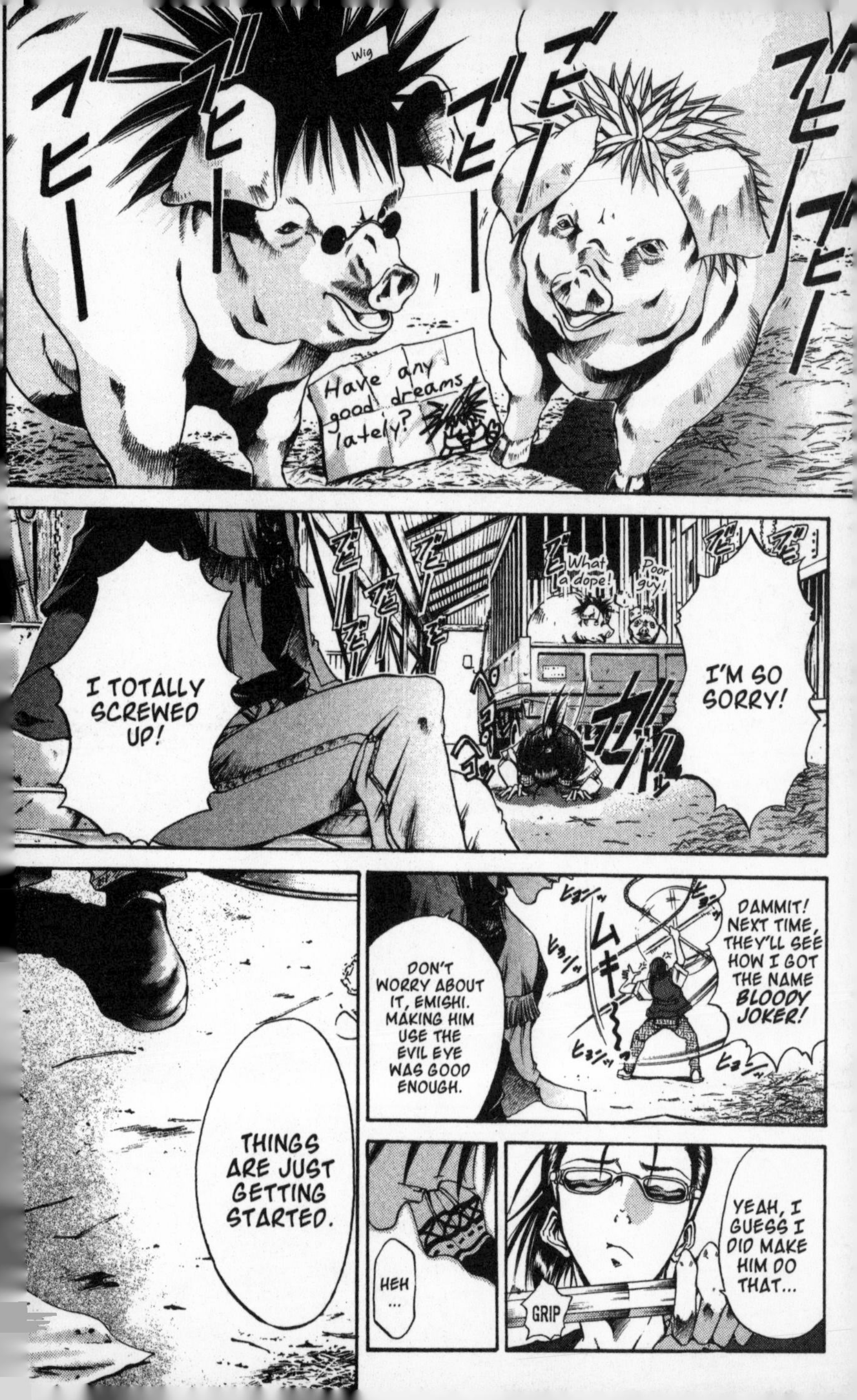
Wig
Have any good dreams lately?
Poor guy!
What a dope!
I'M SO SORRY!
I TOTALLY SCREWED UP!
DAMMIT! NEXT TIME, THEY'LL SEE HOW I GOT THE NAME BLOODY JOKER!
DON'T WORRY ABOUT IT, EMISHI. MAKING HIM USE THE EVIL EYE WAS GOOD ENOUGH.
YEAH, I GUESS I DID MAKE HIM DO THAT...
GRIP
HEH ...
THINGS ARE JUST GETTING STARTED.

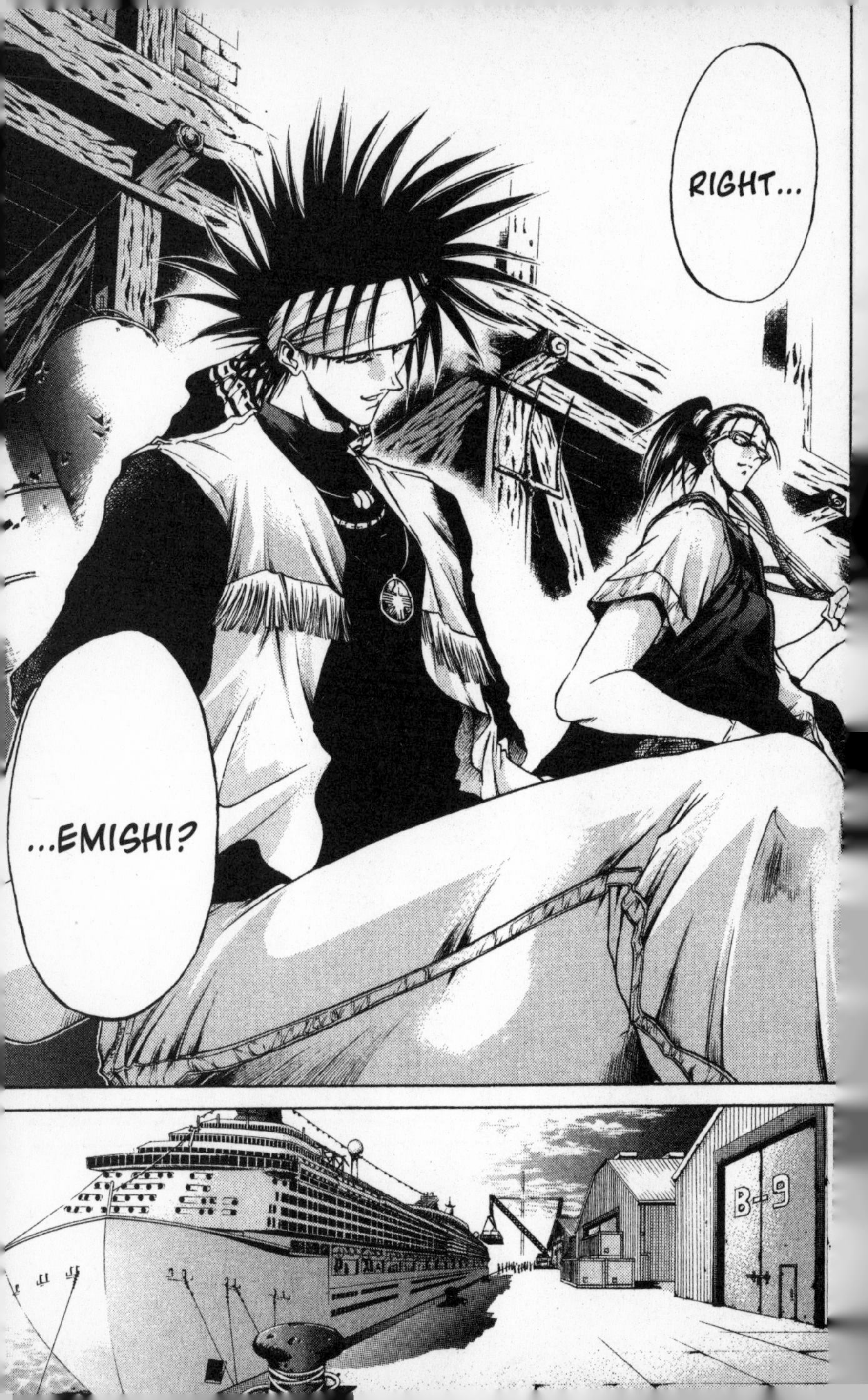
RIGHT...
...EMISHI?
B-9

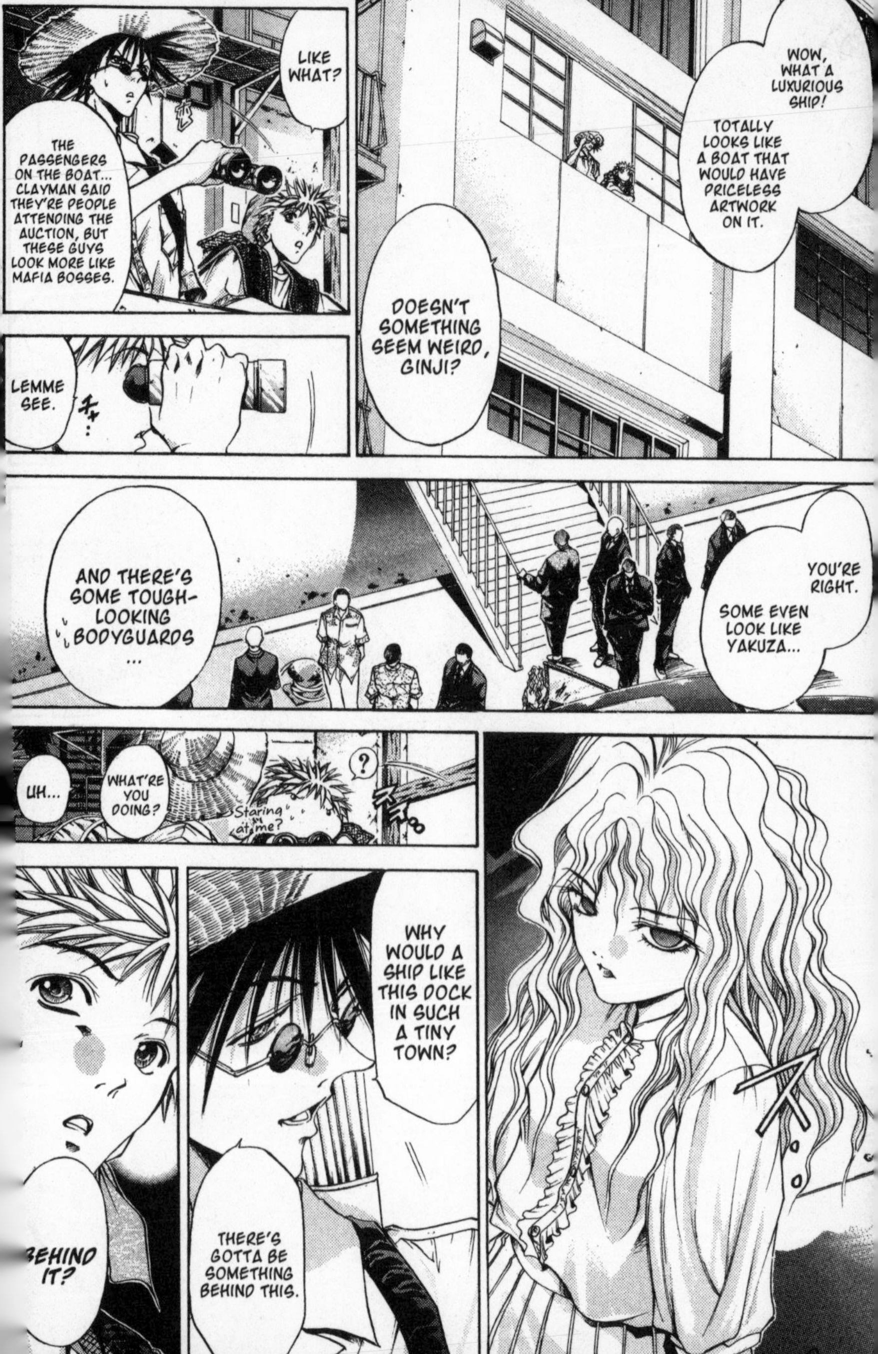
WOW, WHAT A LUXURIOUS SHIP!
TOTALLY LOOKS LIKE A BOAT THAT WOULD HAVE PRICELESS ARTWORK ON IT.
DOESN'T SOMETHING SEEM WEIRD, GINJI?
LIKE WHAT?
THE PASSENGERS ON THE BOAT... CLAYMAN SAID THEY'RE PEOPLE ATTENDING THE AUCTION, BUT THESE GUYS LOOK MORE LIKE MAFIA BOSSES.
LEMME SEE.
YOU'RE RIGHT.
SOME EVEN LOOK LIKE YAKUZA...
AND THERE'S SOME TOUGH-LOOKING BODYGUARDS ...
?
WHAT'RE YOU DOING?
Staring at me?
UH...
WHY WOULD A SHIP LIKE THIS DOCK IN SUCH A TINY TOWN?
THERE'S GOTTA BE SOMETHING BEHIND THIS.
BEHIND IT?

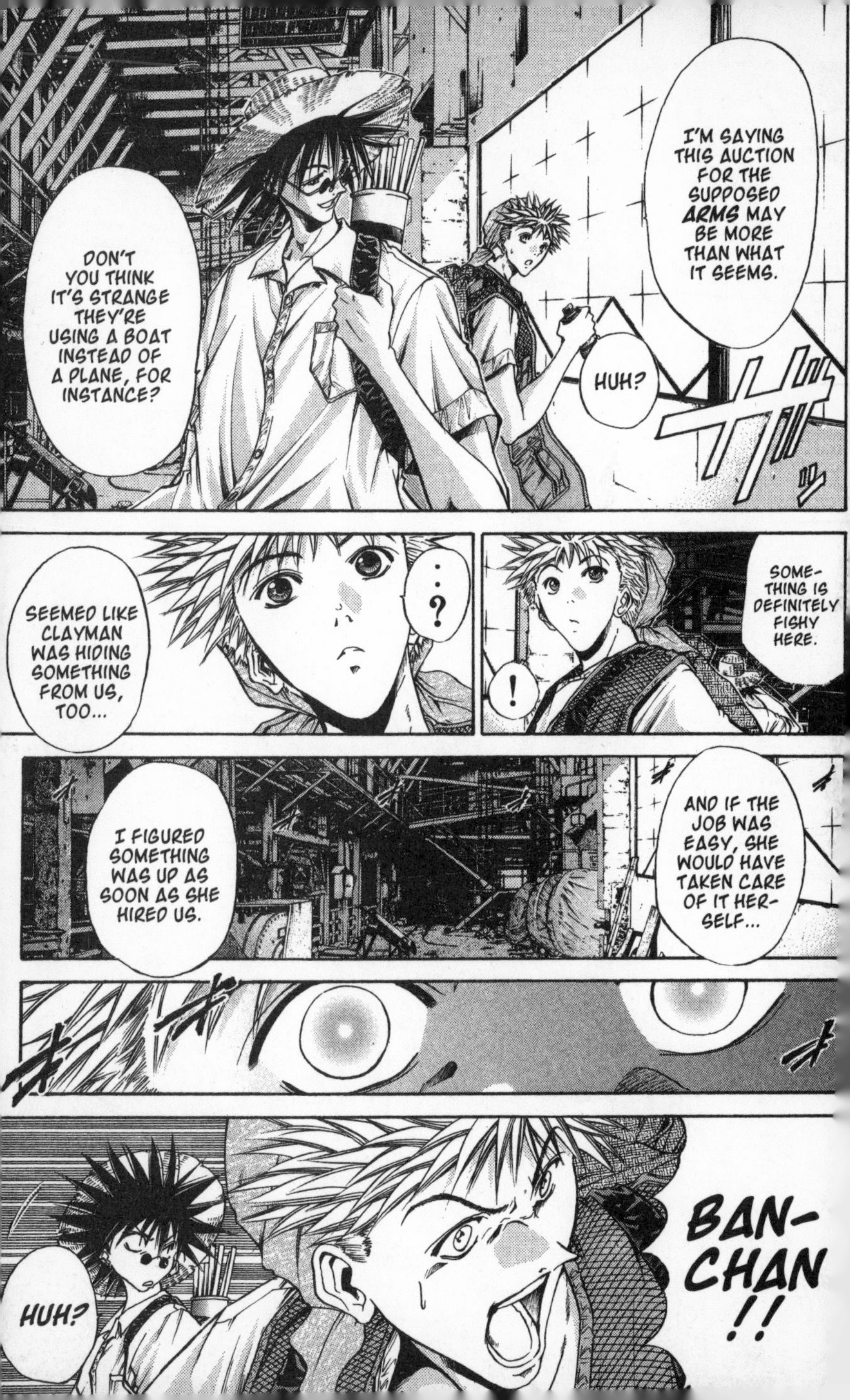
I'M SAYING THIS AUCTION FOR THE SUPPOSED **ARMS** MAY BE MORE THAN WHAT IT SEEMS.
HUH?
DON'T YOU THINK IT'S STRANGE THEY'RE USING A BOAT INSTEAD OF A PLANE, FOR INSTANCE?
SOME-THING IS DEFINITELY FISHY HERE.
!
?
SEEMED LIKE CLAYMAN WAS HIDING SOMETHING FROM US, TOO...
AND IF THE JOB WAS EASY, SHE WOULD HAVE TAKEN CARE OF IT HER-SELF...
I FIGURED SOMETHING WAS UP AS SOON AS SHE HIRED US.
BAN-CHAN!!
HUH?

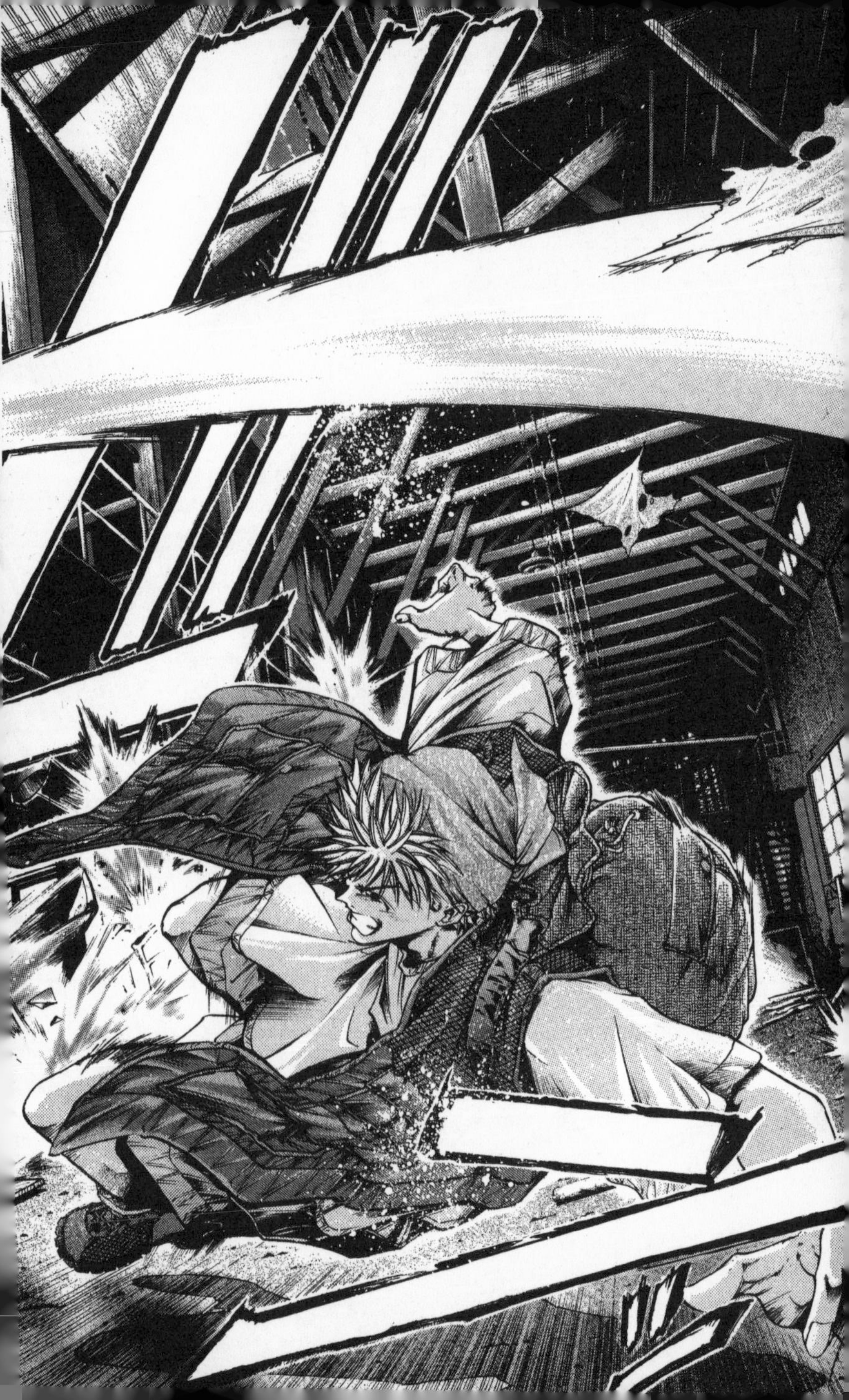

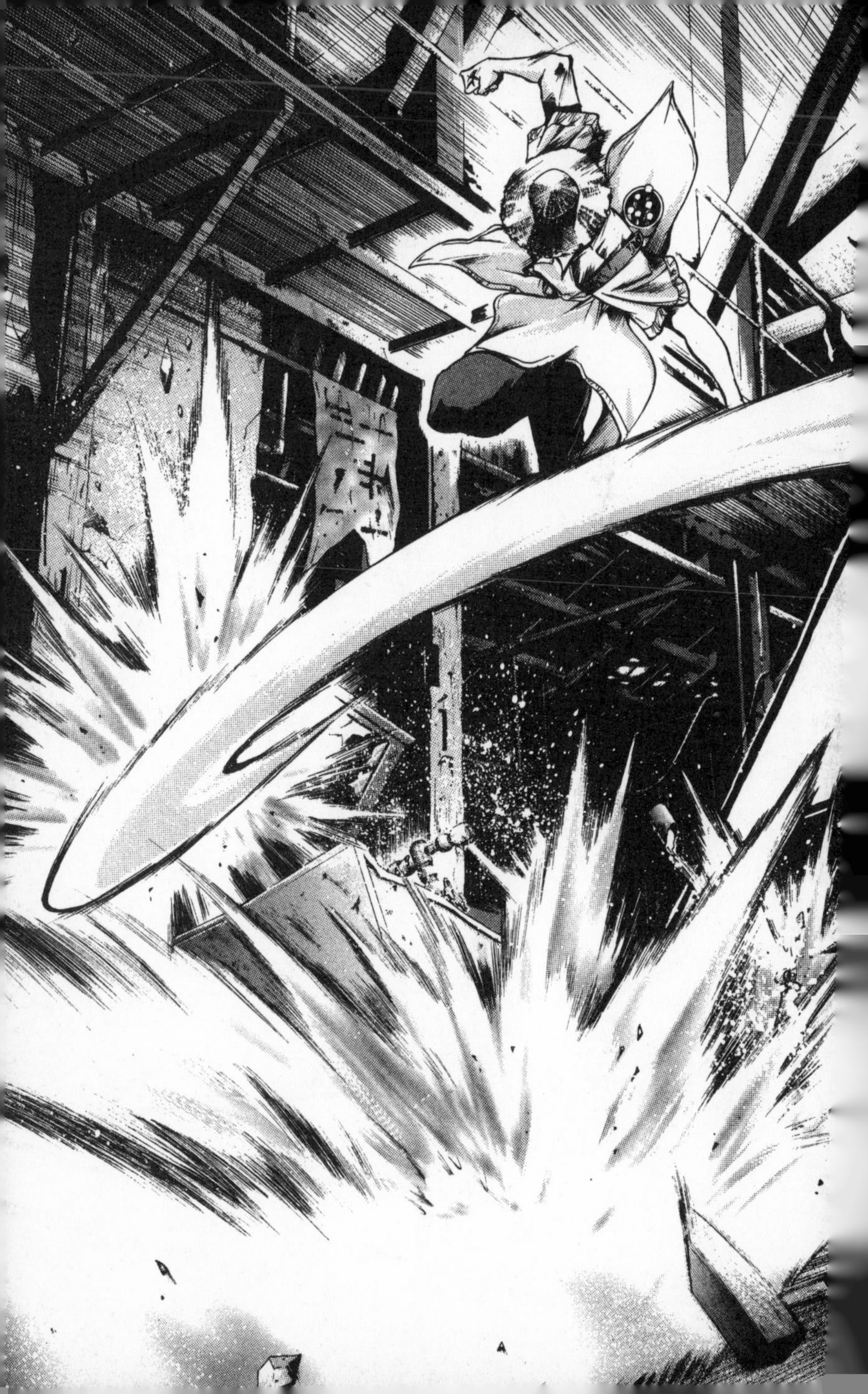

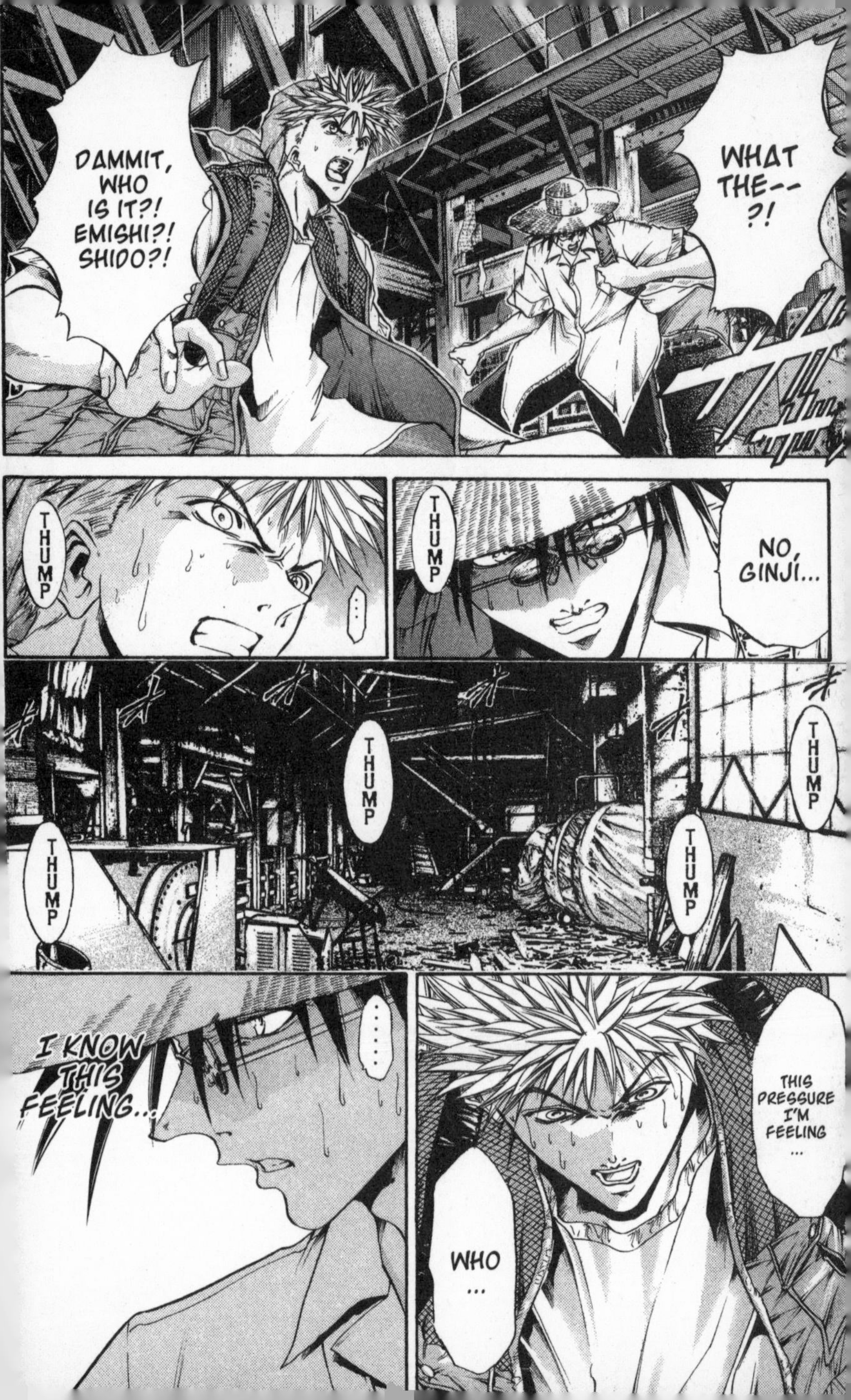
WHAT THE--?!
DAMMIT, WHO IS IT?! EMISHI?! SHIDO?!
NO, GINJI...
THUMP
...
THUMP
THUMP
THUMP
THUMP
THUMP
THUMP
THIS PRESSURE I'M FEELING ...
WHO ...
......
I KNOW THIS FEELING...

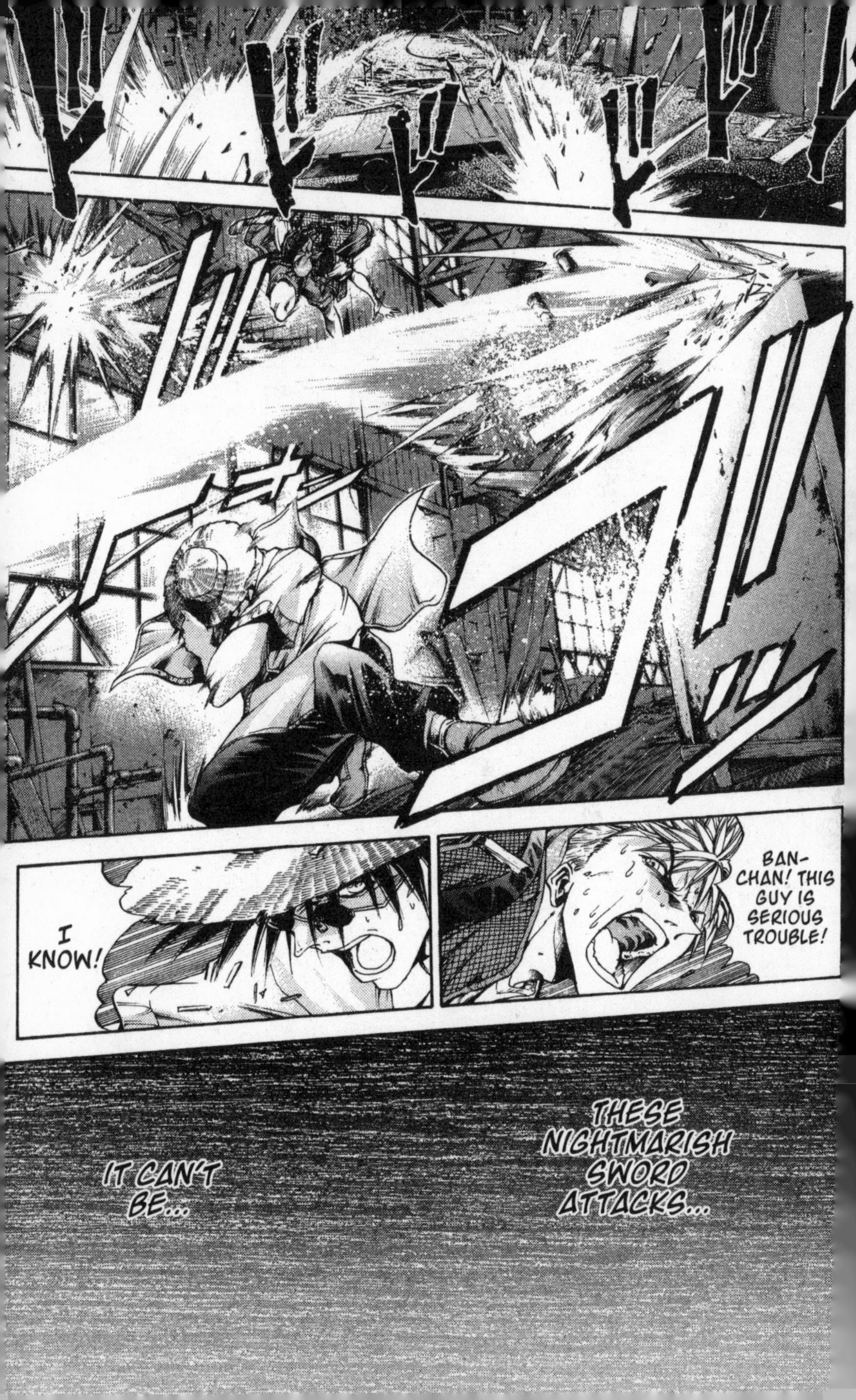
BAN-CHAN! THIS GUY IS SERIOUS TROUBLE!
I KNOW!
THESE NIGHTMARISH SWORD ATTACKS...
IT CAN'T BE...

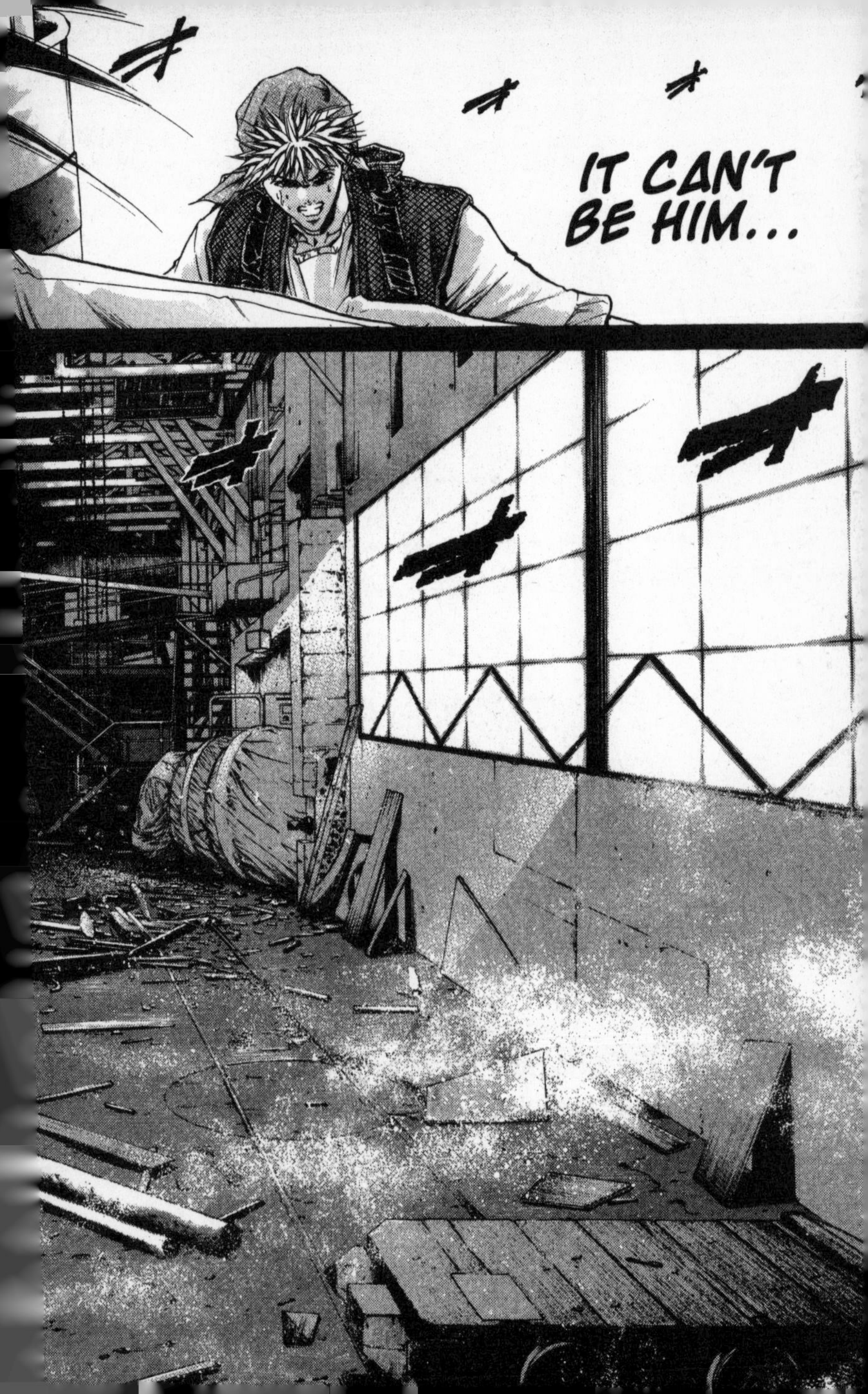
IT CAN'T BE HIM...

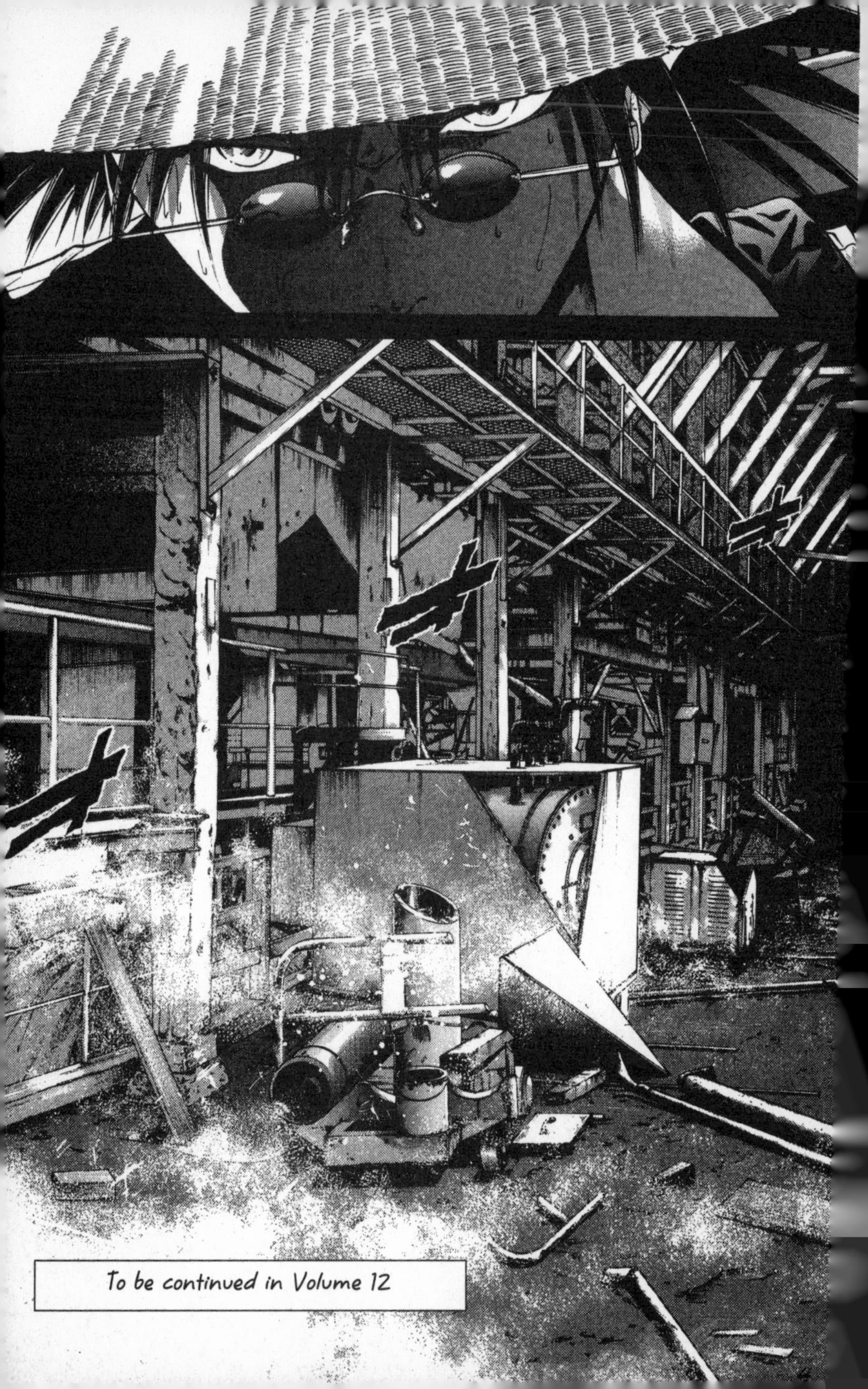
To be continued in Volume 12

In the next electrifying volume of

GETBACKERS™

Who is this mysterious attacker who's got even Ban Mido worried? Protector Natsuhiko Miroku and his family won't reveal themselves quite yet, but their partner is someone Ginji is certainly none too happy to see. Getting onto the ship that's the only transportation to the remote island where the Venus de Milo's lost arms will be auctioned off won't be at all easy with them plus some dangerous Chinese assassins guarding the gangway! The duo gets separated as Ginji predictably takes candy from a stranger and Ban is left trying to make friends with sharks, squids, and octopuses.

The underworld auction organizer and the owner of the Venus' arms both have their own reasons for staging the art auction of the century, and what's this? Both are connected to Infinity Fortress somehow? It seems like the past just won't leave our heroes alone! With Ban and Ginji competing against Beastmaster Shido Fuyuki and Bloody Joker Haruki Emishi for the right to break up the auction before it begins, it's no song and dance routine for the *GetBackers* in the next exciting volume!

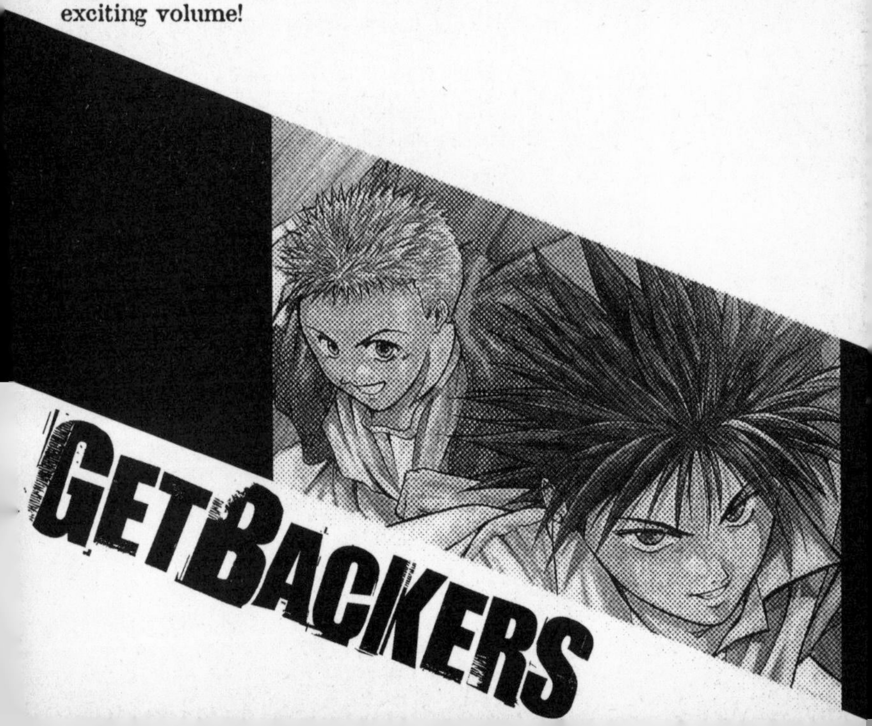
GETBACKERS

スタッフ紹介

土屋 奈朋	NAHO TSUCHIYA
榎並 博昭	HIROAKI ENAMI
岡田 明典	AKINORI OKADA
寺嶋 裕二	YŪJI TERAJIMA
伊川 良樹	YOSHIKI IKAWA

SPECIAL THANKS

大石 知哉	TOMOYA ŌISHI
寺谷 一三	KAZUMI TERATANI
新村圭一郎	KEIICHIRŌ NIIMURA
板羽 美奈	MINA ITABA

EDITOR

TETSUYA NOZAKI

KIICHIRŌ SUGAWARA

CHYONGHYON PAKU

GETBACKERS

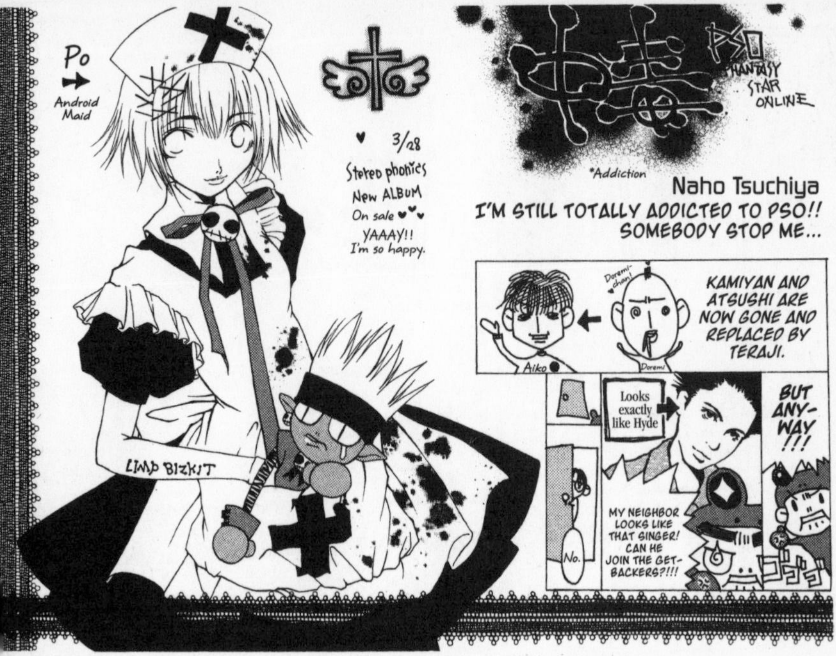
PSO
PHANTASY STAR ONLINE
*Addiction
Naho Tsuchiya
I'M STILL TOTALLY ADDICTED TO PSO!! SOMEBODY STOP ME...
KAMIYAN AND ATSUSHI ARE NOW GONE AND REPLACED BY TERAJI.
Doremi-chan!
Aiko
Doremi
BUT ANY-WAY!!!
Looks exactly like Hyde
MY NEIGHBOR LOOKS LIKE THAT SINGER! CAN HE JOIN THE GET-BACKERS?!!!
No.
3/28
Stereo phonics New ALBUM On sale
YAAAY!! I'm so happy.
Po
Android Maid
LIMP BIZKIT

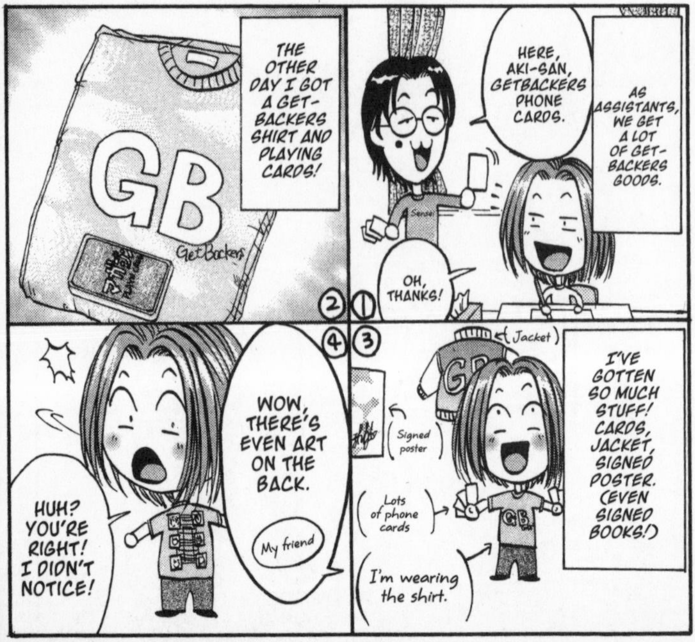
1
AS ASSISTANTS, WE GET A LOT OF GET-BACKERS GOODS.
HERE, AKI-SAN, GETBACKERS PHONE CARDS.
Sensei
OH, THANKS!
2
THE OTHER DAY I GOT A GET-BACKERS SHIRT AND PLAYING CARDS!
GB
GetBackers
3
I'VE GOTTEN SO MUCH STUFF! CARDS, JACKET, SIGNED POSTER. (EVEN SIGNED BOOKS!)
(Jacket)
Signed poster
Lots of phone cards
I'm wearing the shirt.
GB
4
WOW, THERE'S EVEN ART ON THE BACK.
My friend
HUH? YOU'RE RIGHT! I DIDN'T NOTICE!

Hiroaki Enami

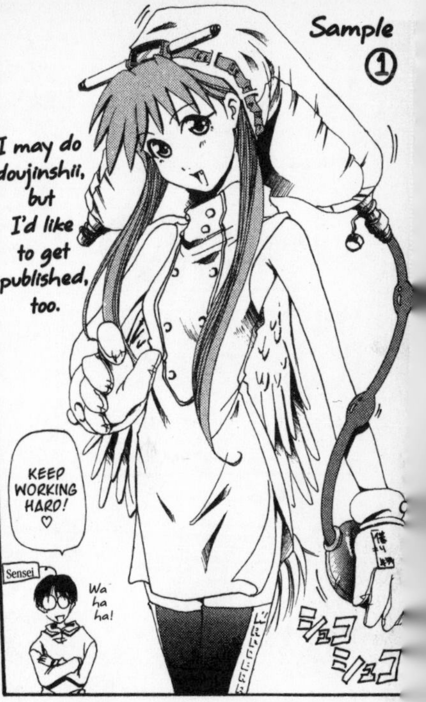
Sample 1
I may do doujinshii, but I'd like to get published, too.
KEEP WORKING HARD! ♡
Sensei
Wa ha ha!
シュコシュコ

How Did I Ever Graduate School? –Akinori Okada

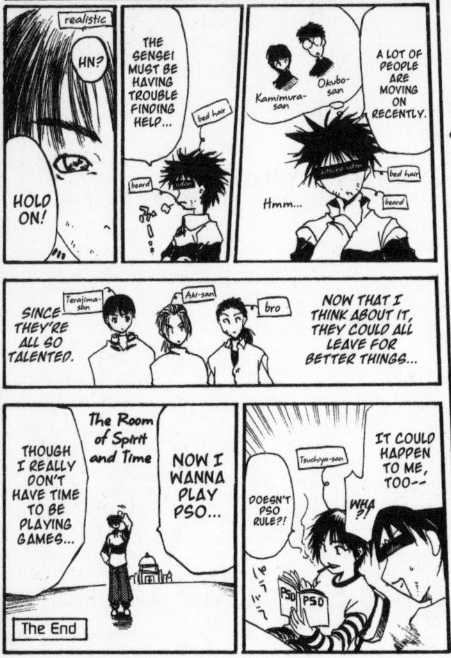
A LOT OF PEOPLE ARE MOVING ON RECENTLY.
Okubo-san
Kamimura-san
bed hair
beard
Hmm...
THE SENSEI MUST BE HAVING TROUBLE FINDING HELP...
bed hair
beard
realistic
HN?
HOLD ON!
NOW THAT I THINK ABOUT IT, THEY COULD ALL LEAVE FOR BETTER THINGS...
bro
Aki-san
Terajima-san
SINCE THEY'RE ALL SO TALENTED.
IT COULD HAPPEN TO ME, TOO--
Tsuchiya-san
WHA?!
DOESN'T PSO RULE?!
PSO
PSO
NOW I WANNA PLAY PSO...
The Room of Spirit and Time
THOUGH I REALLY DON'T HAVE TIME TO BE PLAYING GAMES...
The End

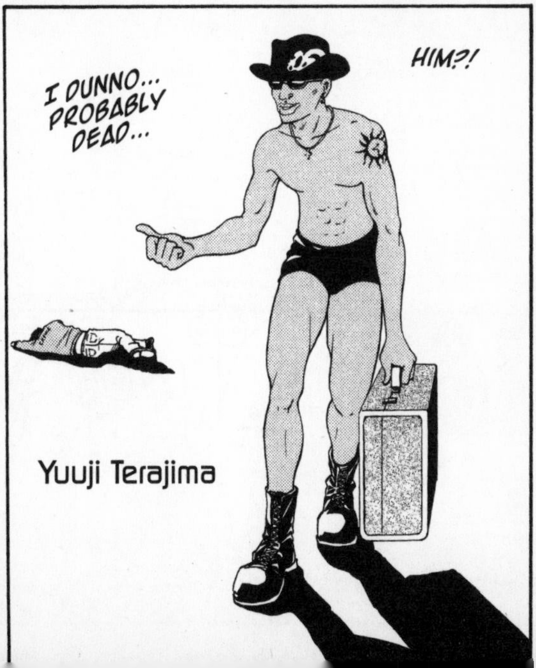
HIM?!
I DUNNO... PROBABLY DEAD...
Yuuji Terajima

Ranking Time!

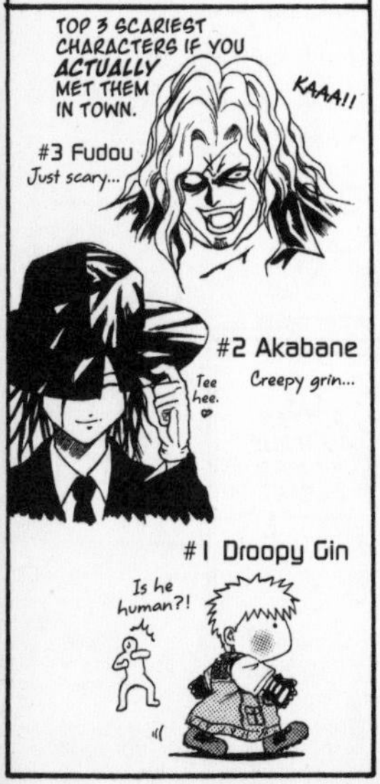
TOP 3 SCARIEST CHARACTERS IF YOU ACTUALLY MET THEM IN TOWN.
KAAA!!
#3 Fudou
Just scary...
#2 Akabane
Tee hee.
Creepy grin...
#1 Droopy Gin
Is he human?!

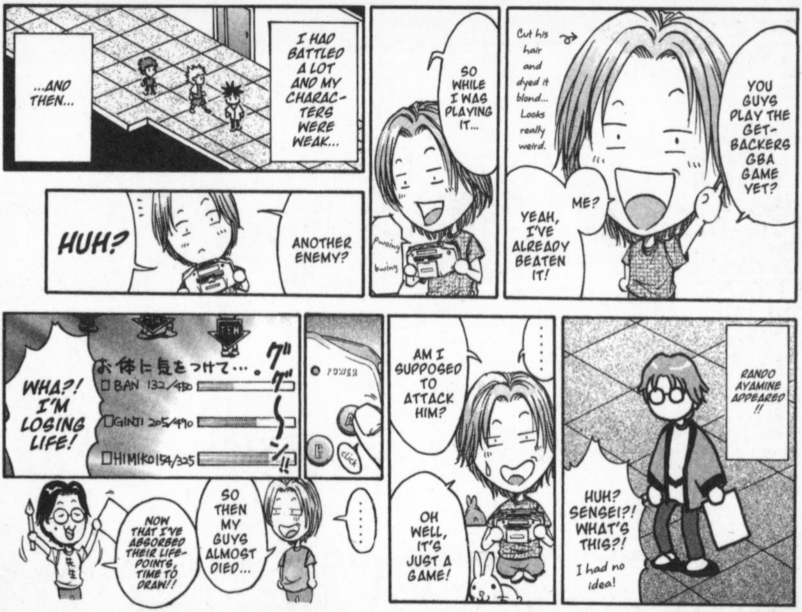
Cut his hair and dyed it blond... Looks really weird.
YOU GUYS PLAY THE GET-BACKERS GBA GAME YET?
ME?
YEAH, I'VE ALREADY BEATEN IT!
SO WHILE I WAS PLAYING IT...
Pwoing
bwing
I HAD BATTLED A LOT AND MY CHARACTERS WERE WEAK...
...AND THEN...
ANOTHER ENEMY?
HUH?
RANDO AYAMINE APPEARED!!
HUH? SENSEI?! WHAT'S THIS?!
I had no idea!
......
AM I SUPPOSED TO ATTACK HIM?
OH WELL, IT'S JUST A GAME!
POWER
click
お体に気をつけて…。
グゲ〜ン!!
BAN 132/480
GINJI 205/490
HIMIKO 154/325
WHA?! I'M LOSING LIFE!
......
SO THEN MY GUYS ALMOST DIED...
NOW THAT I'VE ABSORBED THEIR LIFE-POINTS, TIME TO DRAW!!
先生

I NOW OWN SEVEN RABBITS.

HIROAKI ENAMI

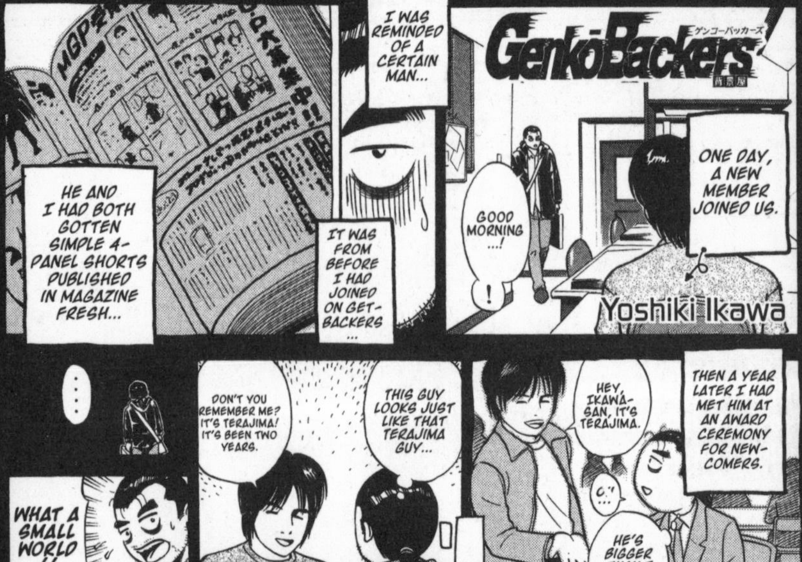
GenkoBackers
ゲンコーバッカーズ
ONE DAY, A NEW MEMBER JOINED US.
GOOD MORNING...!
!
Yoshiki Ikawa
I WAS REMINDED OF A CERTAIN MAN...
IT WAS FROM BEFORE I HAD JOINED ON GET-BACKERS...
HE AND I HAD BOTH GOTTEN SIMPLE 4-PANEL SHORTS PUBLISHED IN MAGAZINE FRESH...
THEN A YEAR LATER I HAD MET HIM AT AN AWARD CEREMONY FOR NEW-COMERS.
HEY, IKAWA-SAN, IT'S TERAJIMA.
?!
HE'S BIGGER THAN I IMAGINED...
THIS GUY LOOKS JUST LIKE THAT TERAJIMA GUY...
DON'T YOU REMEMBER ME? IT'S TERAJIMA! IT'S BEEN TWO YEARS.
HUH?!
....
WHAT A SMALL WORLD!!

SEE YOU NEXT TIME!

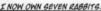

TOKYOPOP SHOP

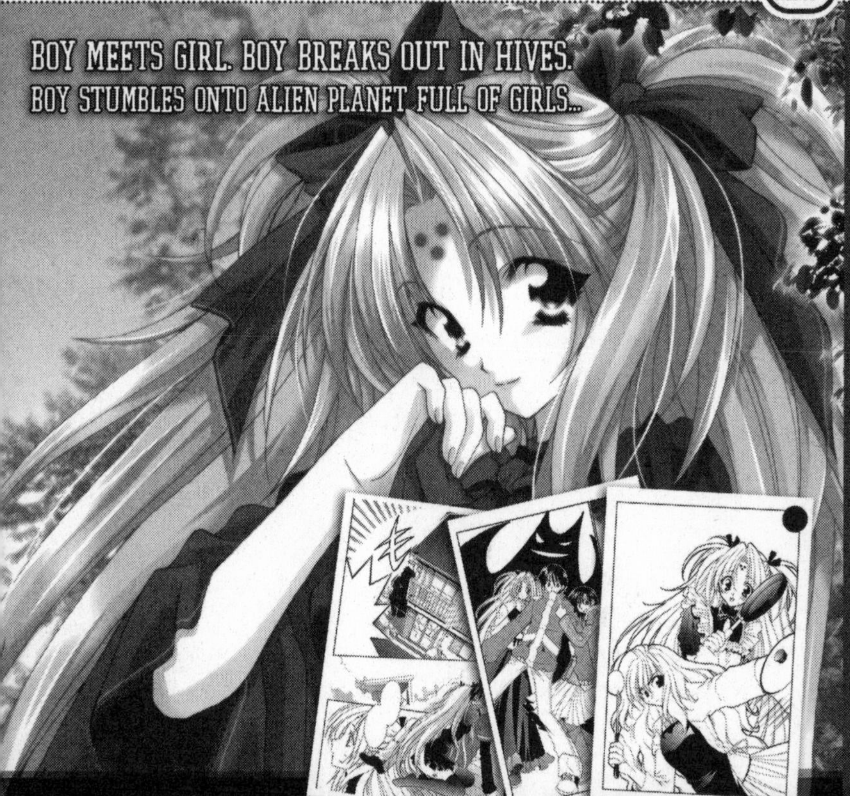

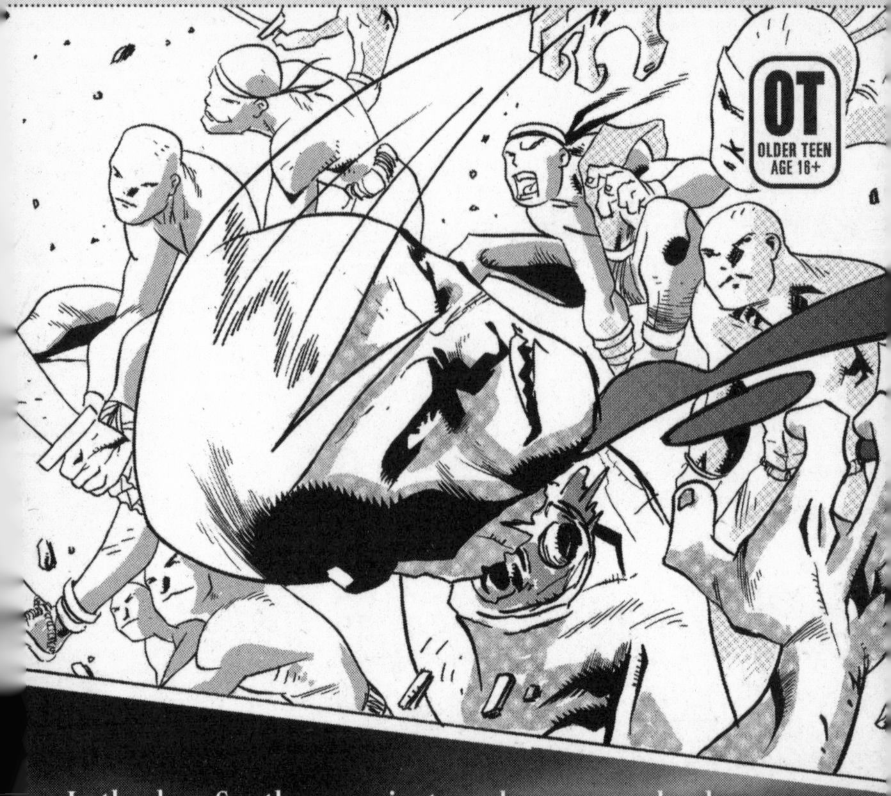
OT
OLDER TEEN
AGE 16+

In the deep South, an ancient voodoo curse unleashes the War on Flesh—a hellish plague of voracious Ew Chott hornets that raises an army of the walking dead. This undead army spreads the plague by ripping the hearts out of living creatures to make room for a Black Heart hive, all in preparation for the most awesome incarnation of evil ever imagined… An unlikely group of five mis-matched individuals have to put their differences aside to try to destroy the onslaught of evil before it's too late.

VOODOO MAKES A MAN NASTY!

Preview the manga at:
www.TOKYOPOP.com/waronflesh

WAR ON FLESH

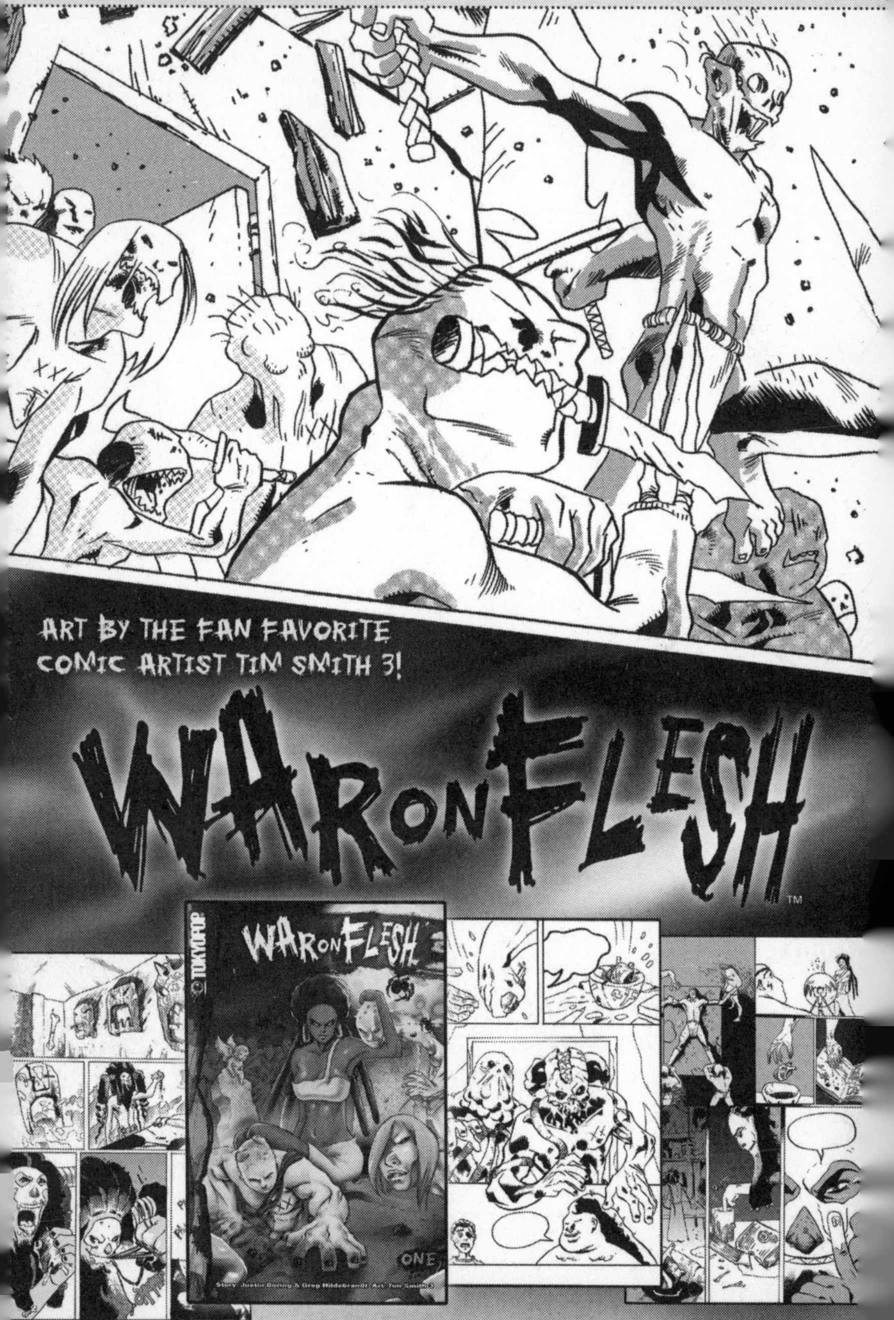
ART BY THE FAN FAVORITE
COMIC ARTIST TIM SMITH 3!
WAR ON FLESH™
WAR ON FLESH
TOKYOPOP
ONE

PhD: PHANTASY DEGREE

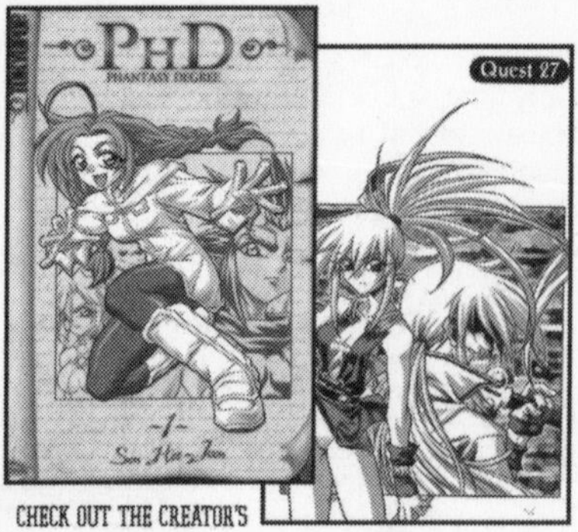
PhD
PHANTASY DEGREE
Quest 27

CHECK OUT THE CREATOR'S *iD_eNTITY*

BY SON HEE-JOON

So you think you've got it rough at *your* school? Try attending classes at Demon School Hades! When sassy, young Sang makes her monster matriculation to this arcane academy, all hell breaks loose—literally! But what would you expect when the graduating class consists of a werewolf, a mummy and demons by the score? Son Hee-Joon's underworld adventure is pure escapist fun. Always packed with action and often silly in the best sense, *PhD* never takes itself too seriously or lets the reader stop to catch his breath.

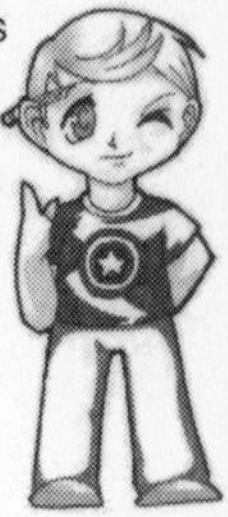

~Bryce P. Coleman, Editor

BOYS BE...

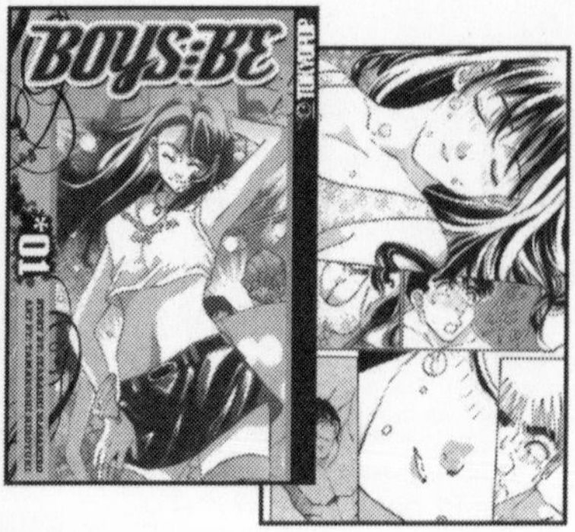
BOYS BE

BY MASAHIRO ITABASHI & HIROYUKI TAMAKOSHI

Boys Be... is a series of short stories. But although the hero's name changes from tale to tale, he remains Everyboy—that dorky high school guy who'll do anything to score with the girl of his dreams. You know him. Perhaps you *are* him. He is a dirty mind with the soul of a poet, a stumblebum with a heart of sterling. We follow this guy on quest after quest to woo his lady loves. We savor his victory; we reel with his defeat...and the experience is touching, funny and above all human.

Still not convinced? I have two words for you: fan service.

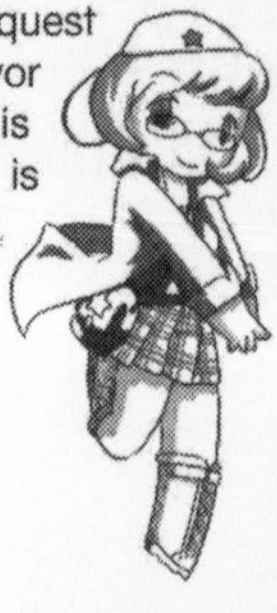

~Carol Fox, Editor

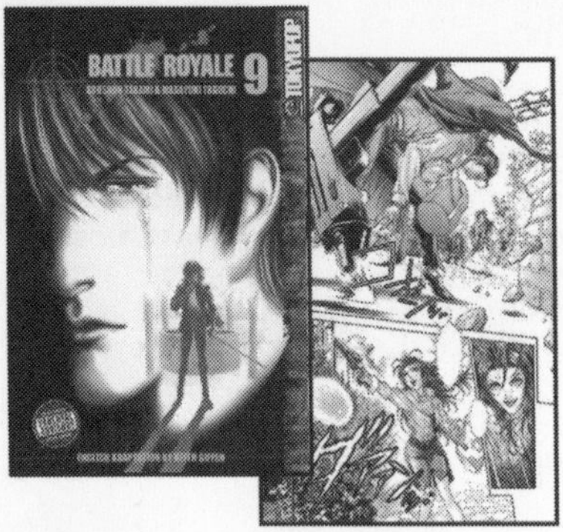
BATTLE ROYALE 9
TOKYOPOP

BATTLE ROYALE

As far as cautionary tales go, you couldn't get any timelier than *Battle Royale*. Telling the bleak story of a class of middle school students who are forced to fight one another to the death on national television, Koushun Takami and Masayuki Taguchi have created a dark satire that's sickening, yet undeniably exciting as well. And if we have that reaction reading it, it becomes alarmingly clear how the students could be so easily swayed into *doing* it.

~Tim Beedle, Editor

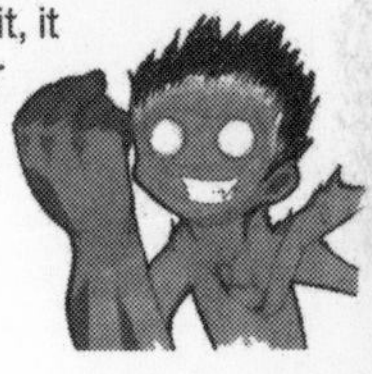

BY KOUSHUN TAKAMI & MASAYUKI TAGUCHI

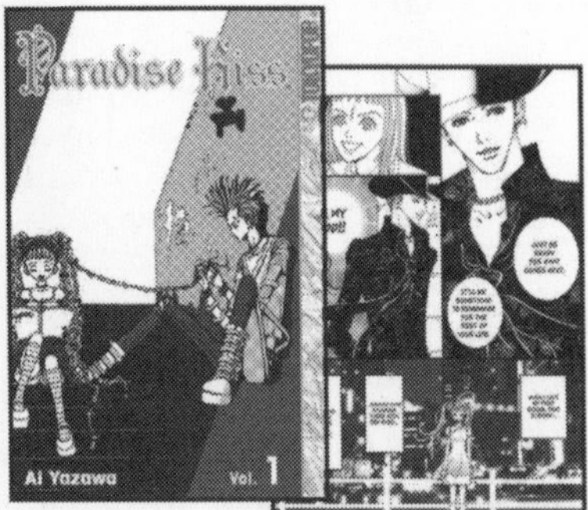
Paradise Kiss
Ai Yazawa
Vol. 1

PARADISE KISS

The clothes! The romance! The clothes! The intrigue! And did I mention the clothes?! *Paradise Kiss* is the best fashion manga ever written, from one of the hottest shojo artists in Japan. Ai Yazawa is the coolest. Not only did she create the character designs for *Princess Ai*, which were amazing, but she also produced five fab volumes of *Paradise Kiss*, a manga series bursting with fashion and passion. Read it and be inspired.

~Julie Taylor, Sr. Editor

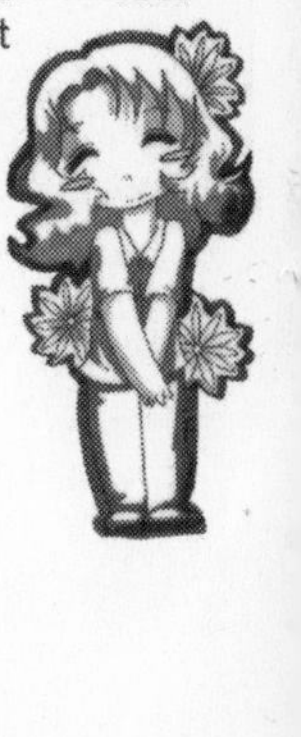

BY AI YAZAWA

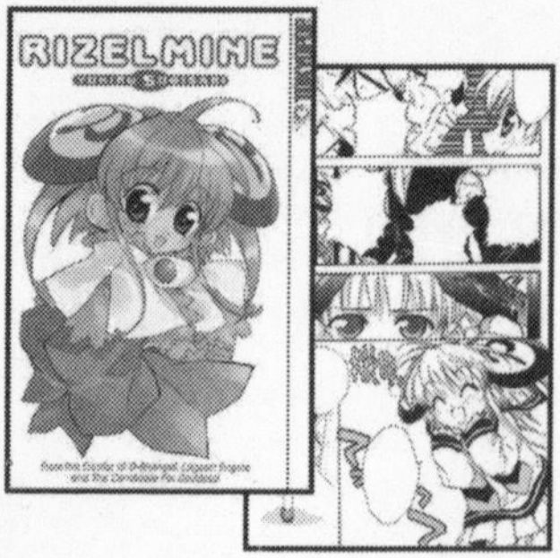
RIZELMINE

RIZELMINE

BY YUKIRU SUGISAKI

Tomonori Iwaki is a hapless fifteen-year-old whose life is turned upside down when the government announces that he's a married man! His blushing bride is Rizel, apparently the adorable product of an experiment. She does her best to win her new man's heart in this wacky romantic comedy from the creator of *D•N•Angel*!

Inspiration for the hit anime!

T TEEN AGE 13+

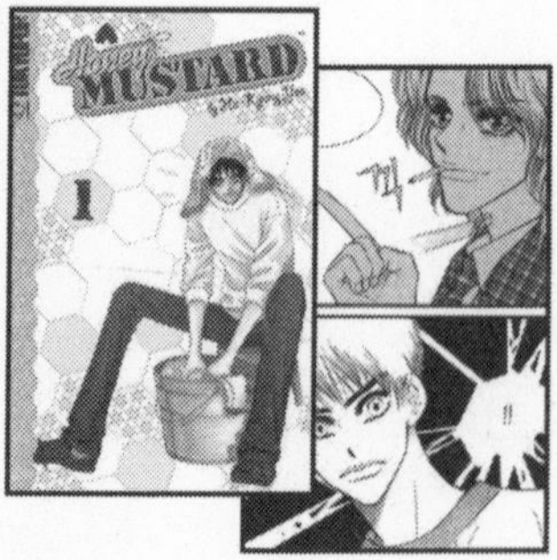
Honey MUSTARD
1

HONEY MUSTARD

BY HO-KYUNG YEO

When Ara works up the nerve to ask out the guy she has a crush on, she ends up kissing the wrong boy! The juicy smooch is witnessed by the school's puritanical chaperone, who tells their strict families. With everyone in an uproar, the only way everyone will be appeased is if the two get married—and have kids!

T TEEN AGE 13+

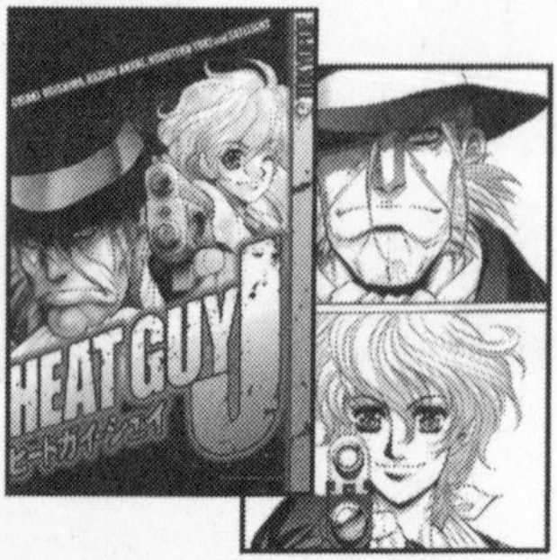
HEAT GUY J
ヒートガイ・ジェイ

HEAT GUY J

BY CHIAKI OGISHIMA, KAZUKI AKANE, NOBUTERU YUKI & SATELIGHT

Daisuke Aurora and his android partner, Heat Guy J, work with a special division of peacekeepers to keep anything illegal off the streets. However, that doesn't sit too well with the new ruthless and well-armed mob leader. In the city that never sleeps, will Daisuke and Heat Guy J end up sleeping with the fishes?

The anime favorite as seen on MTV is now an action-packed manga!

T TEEN AGE 13+

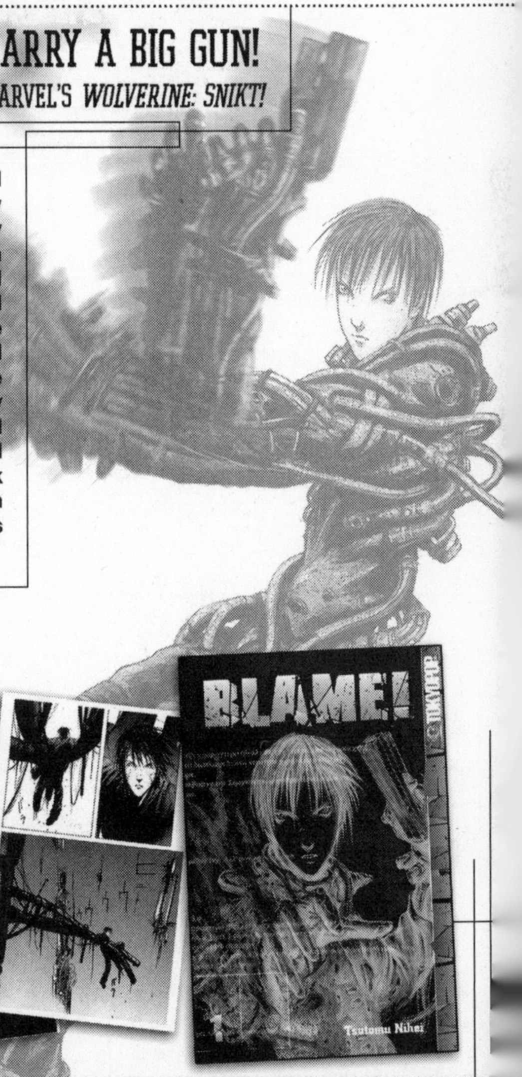
BLAME!
TOKYOPOP
1
Tsutomu Nihei

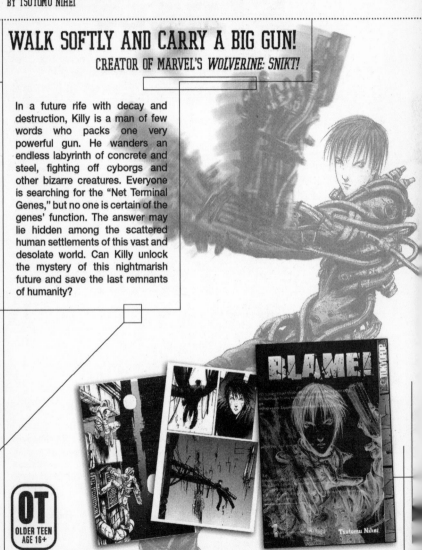

STOP!

This is the back of the book.
You wouldn't want to spoil a great ending!

This book is printed "manga-style," in the authentic Japanese right-to-left format. Since none of the artwork has been flipped or altered, readers get to experience the story just as the creator intended. You've been asking for it, so TOKYOPOP® delivered: authentic, hot-off-the-press, and far more fun!

DIRECTIONS

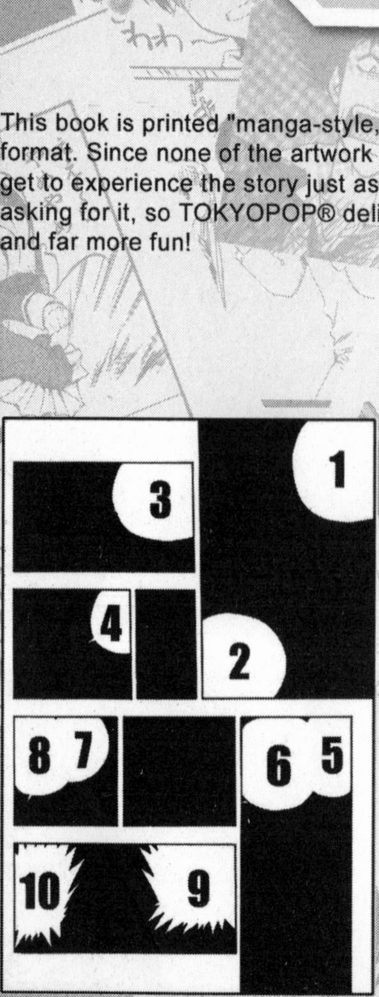

If this is your first time reading manga-style, here's a quick guide to help you understand how it works.

It's easy... just start in the top right panel and follow the numbers. Have fun, and look for more 100% authentic manga from TOKYOPOP®!